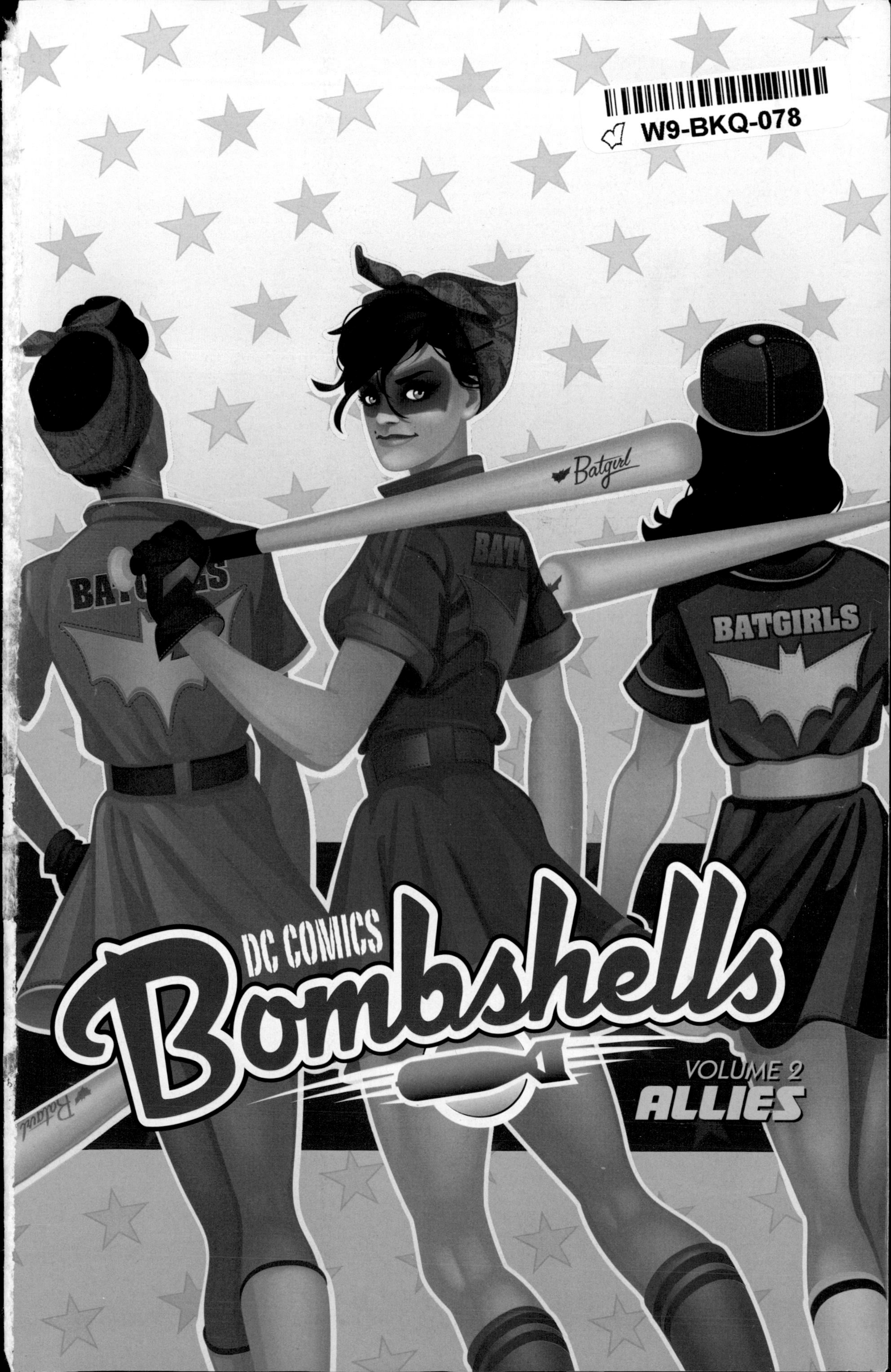
Batgirl
BATGIRLS
BATGIRLS
DC COMICS
Bombshells
VOLUME 2
ALLIES

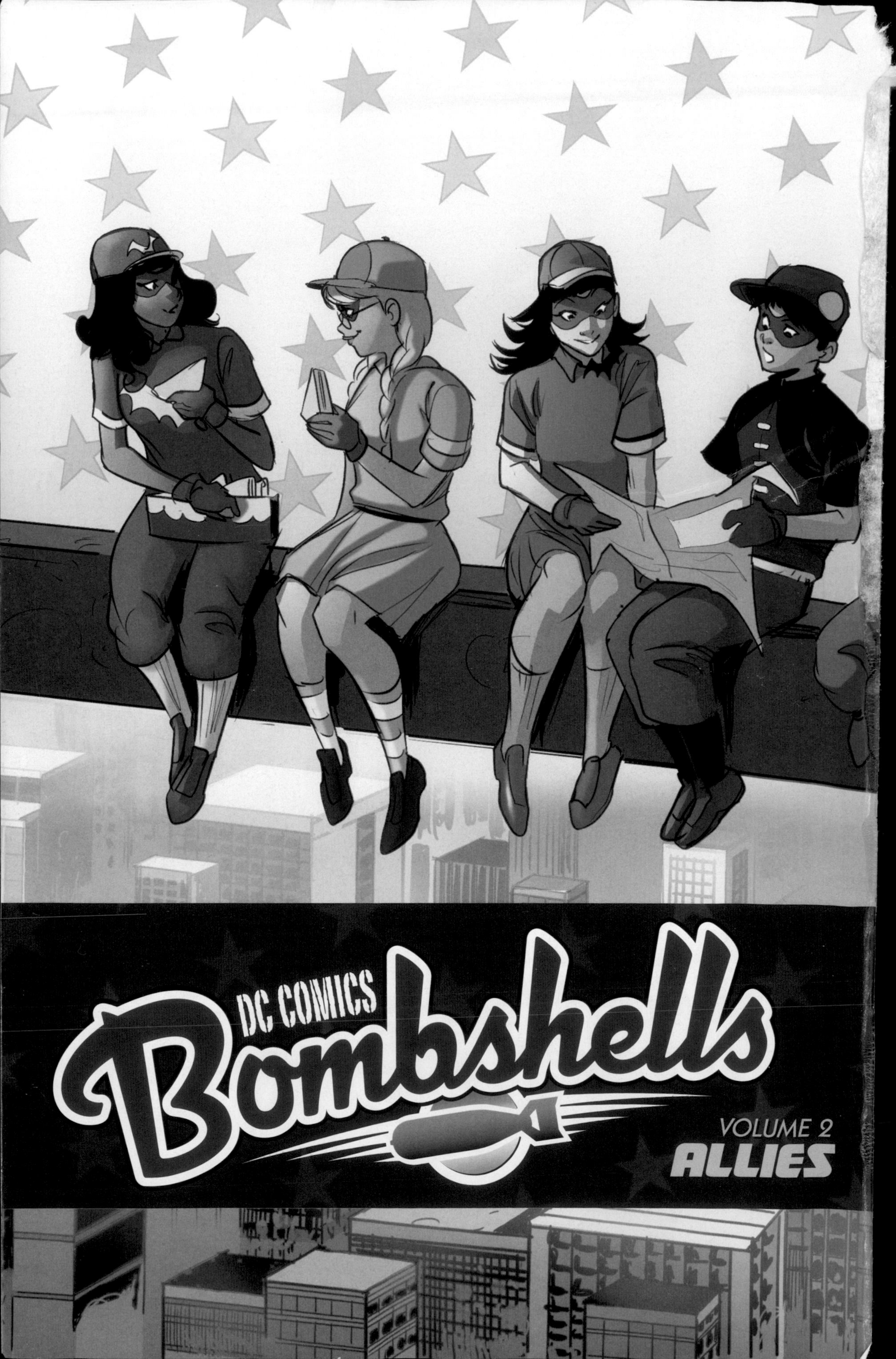
DC COMICS
Bombshells
VOLUME 2
ALLIES

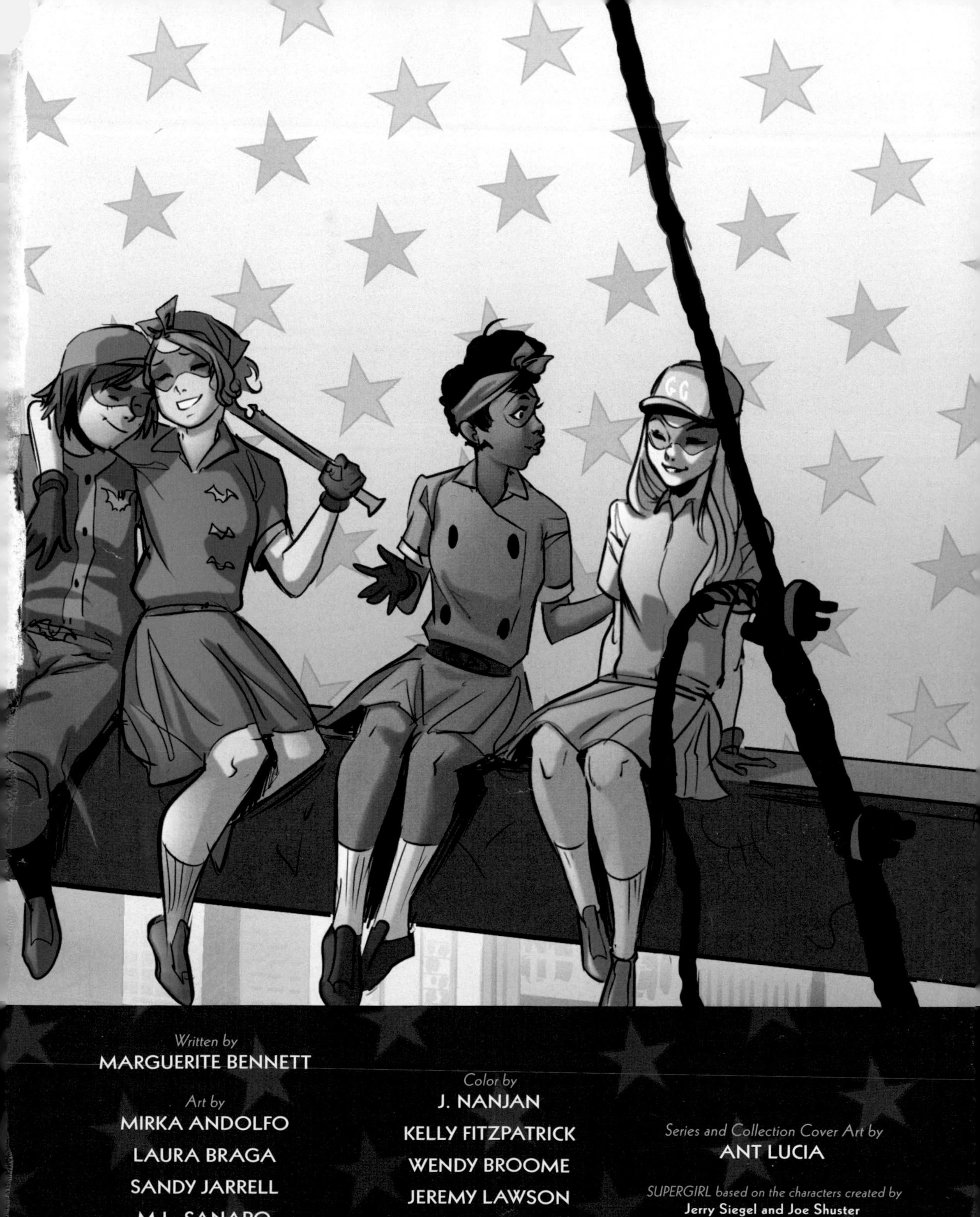

G G

Written by
MARGUERITE BENNETT

Art by
MIRKA ANDOLFO
LAURA BRAGA
SANDY JARRELL
M.L. SANAPO
JUAN ALBARRAN
MARGUERITE SAUVAGE

Color by
J. NANJAN
KELLY FITZPATRICK
WENDY BROOME
JEREMY LAWSON

Letters by
WES ABBOTT

Series and Collection Cover Art by
ANT LUCIA

SUPERGIRL based on the characters created by
Jerry Siegel and Joe Shuster
By special arrangement with the Jerry Siegel family

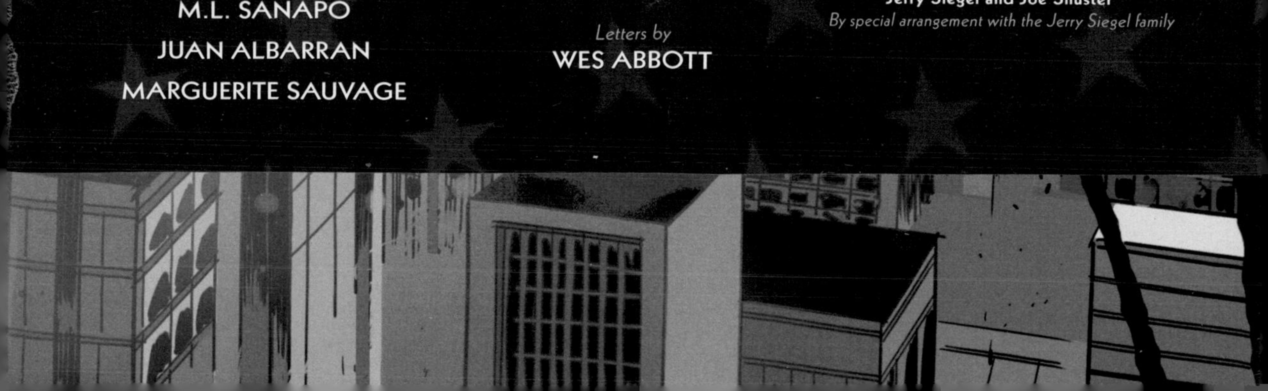

JIM CHADWICK Editor – Original Series
JESSICA CHEN Associate Editor – Original Series
JEB WOODARD Group Editor – Collected Editions
LIZ ERICKSON Editor – Collected Edition
STEVE COOK Design Director – Books
CURTIS KING JR. Publication Design

BOB HARRAS Senior VP – Editor-in-Chief, DC Comics

DIANE NELSON President
DAN DIDIO and JIM LEE Co-Publishers
GEOFF JOHNS Chief Creative Officer
AMIT DESAI Senior VP – Marketing & Global Franchise Management
NAIRI GARDINER Senior VP – Finance
SAM ADES VP – Digital Marketing
BOBBIE CHASE VP – Talent Development
MARK CHIARELLO Senior VP – Art, Design & Collected Editions
JOHN CUNNINGHAM VP – Content Strategy
ANNE DEPIES VP – Strategy Planning & Reporting
DON FALLETTI VP – Manufacturing Operations
LAWRENCE GANEM VP – Editorial Administration & Talent Relations
ALISON GILL Senior VP – Manufacturing & Operations
HANK KANALZ Senior VP – Editorial Strategy & Administration
JAY KOGAN VP – Legal Affairs
DEREK MADDALENA Senior VP – Sales & Business Development
JACK MAHAN VP – Business Affairs
DAN MIRON VP – Sales Planning & Trade Development
NICK NAPOLITANO VP – Manufacturing Administration
CAROL ROEDER VP – Marketing
EDDIE SCANNELL VP – Mass Account & Digital Sales
COURTNEY SIMMONS Senior VP – Publicity & Communications
JIM (SKI) SOKOLOWSKI VP – Comic Book Specialty & Newsstand Sales
SANDY YI Senior VP – Global Franchise Management

DC COMICS: BOMBSHELLS VOLUME 2: ALLIES

Published by DC Comics. Compilation and
all new material Copyright © 2016 DC Comics.
All Rights Reserved.

Originally published in single magazine form
in DC COMICS: BOMBSHELLS 7-12 and online
as DC COMICS: BOMBSHELLS Digital Chapters
19-36 Copyright © 2015, 2016 DC Comics. All Rights
Reserved. All characters, their distinctive likenesses
and related elements featured in this publication are
trademarks of DC Comics. The stories, characters and
incidents featured in this publication are entirely
fictional. DC Comics does not read or accept
unsolicited ideas, stories or artwork.

DC Comics
2900 West Alameda Ave., Burbank, CA 91505
Printed by RR Donnelley, Owensville, MO, USA.
6/10/16. First Printing.
ISBN: 978-1-4012-6448-2

PEFC Certified

Printed on paper from
sustainably managed
forests and controlled
sources

PEFC/29-31-75   www.pefc.org

Library of Congress Cataloging-in-Publication
Data is available.

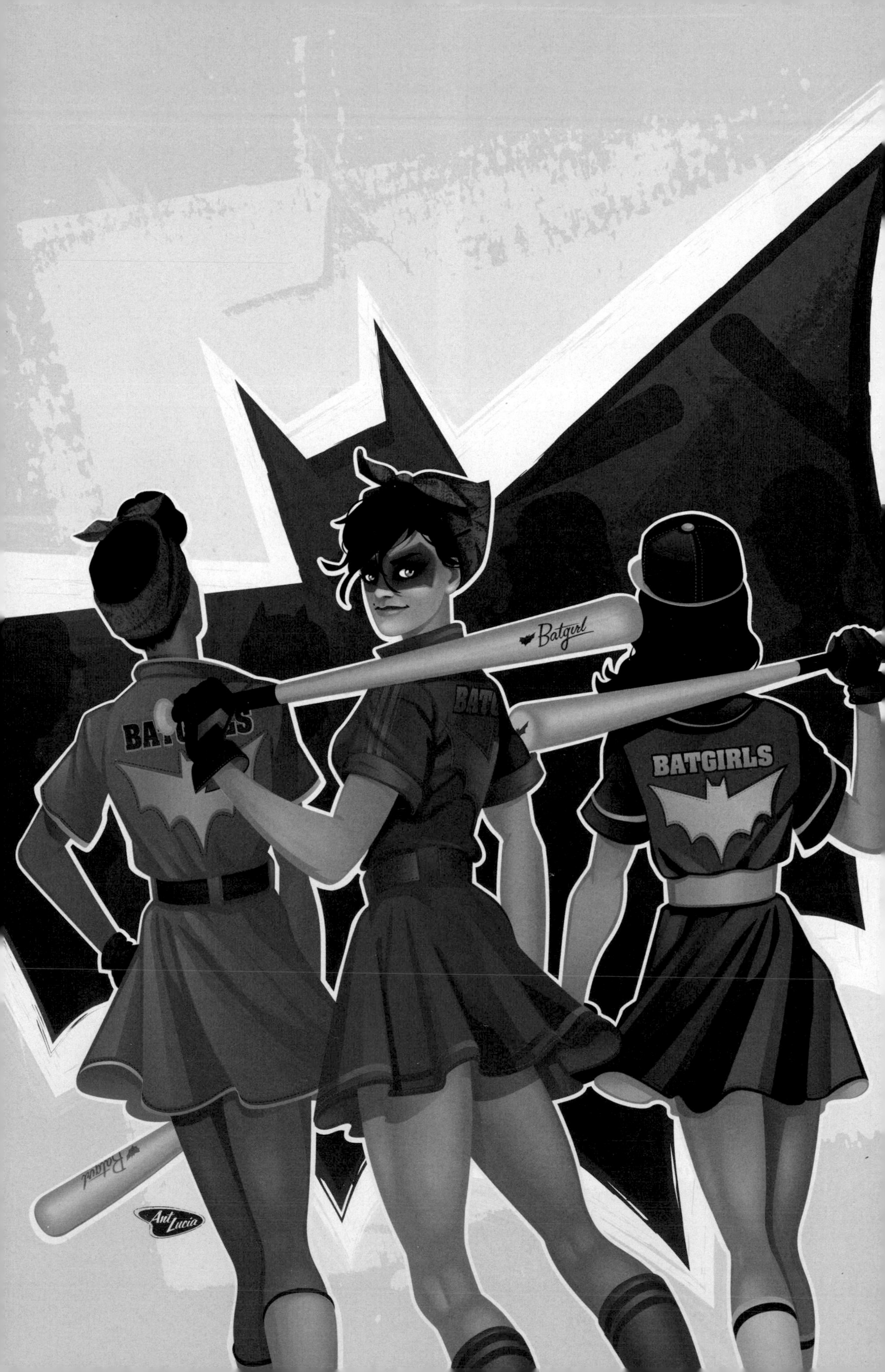
Batgirl
BATGIRLS
BATGIRLS
Ant Lucia

ALLIES
PART ONE

MARGUERITE BENNETT
Writer

MIRKA ANDOLFO
Artist

WENDY BROOME
Colorist

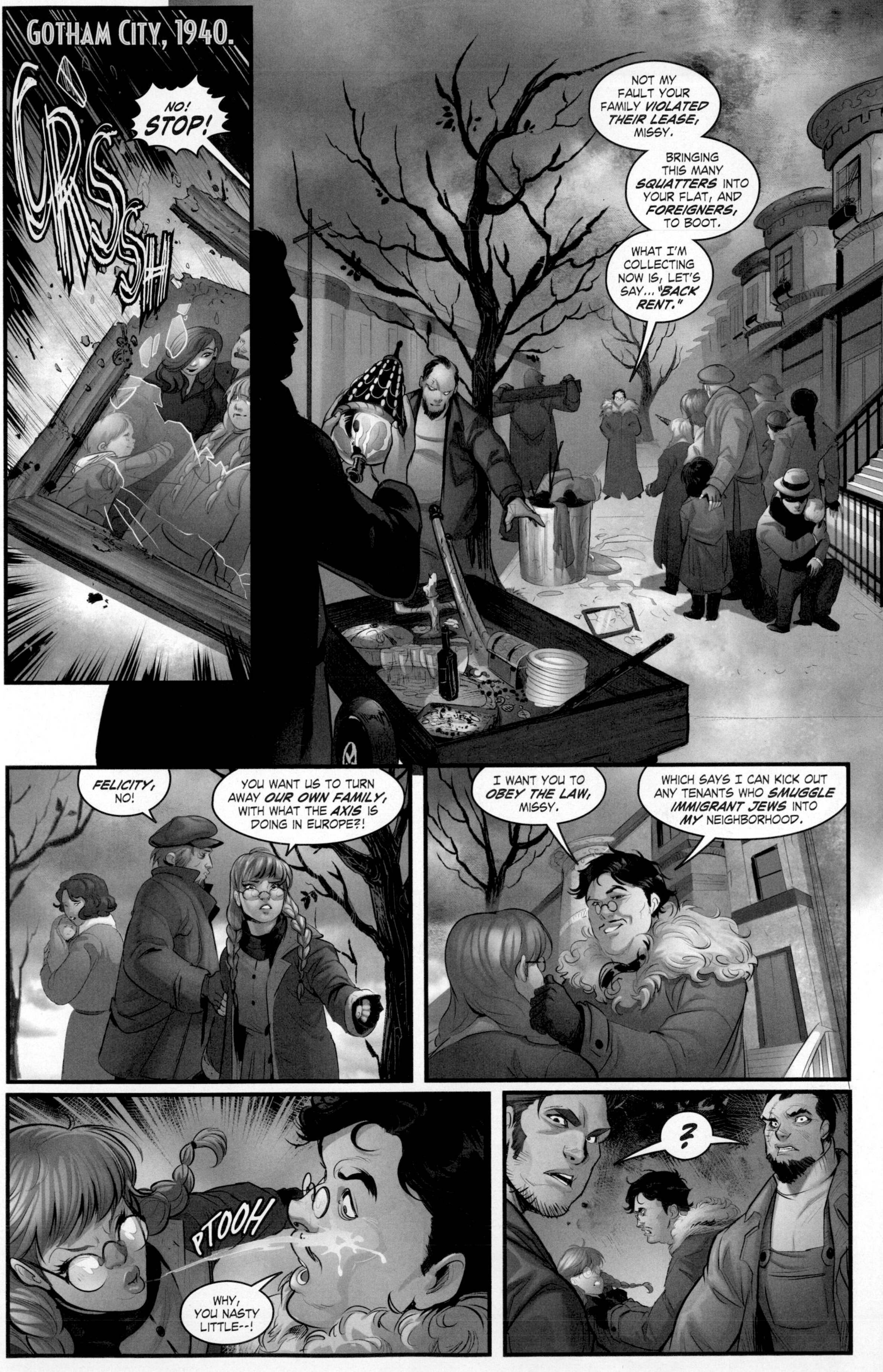
GOTHAM CITY, 1940.
CRSSSH
NO! STOP!
NOT MY FAULT YOUR FAMILY VIOLATED THEIR LEASE, MISSY.
BRINGING THIS MANY SQUATTERS INTO YOUR FLAT, AND FOREIGNERS, TO BOOT.
WHAT I'M COLLECTING NOW IS, LET'S SAY... "BACK RENT."
FELICITY, NO!
YOU WANT US TO TURN AWAY OUR OWN FAMILY, WITH WHAT THE AXIS IS DOING IN EUROPE?!
I WANT YOU TO OBEY THE LAW, MISSY.
WHICH SAYS I CAN KICK OUT ANY TENANTS WHO SMUGGLE IMMIGRANT JEWS INTO MY NEIGHBORHOOD.
PTOOH
WHY, YOU NASTY LITTLE--!
?

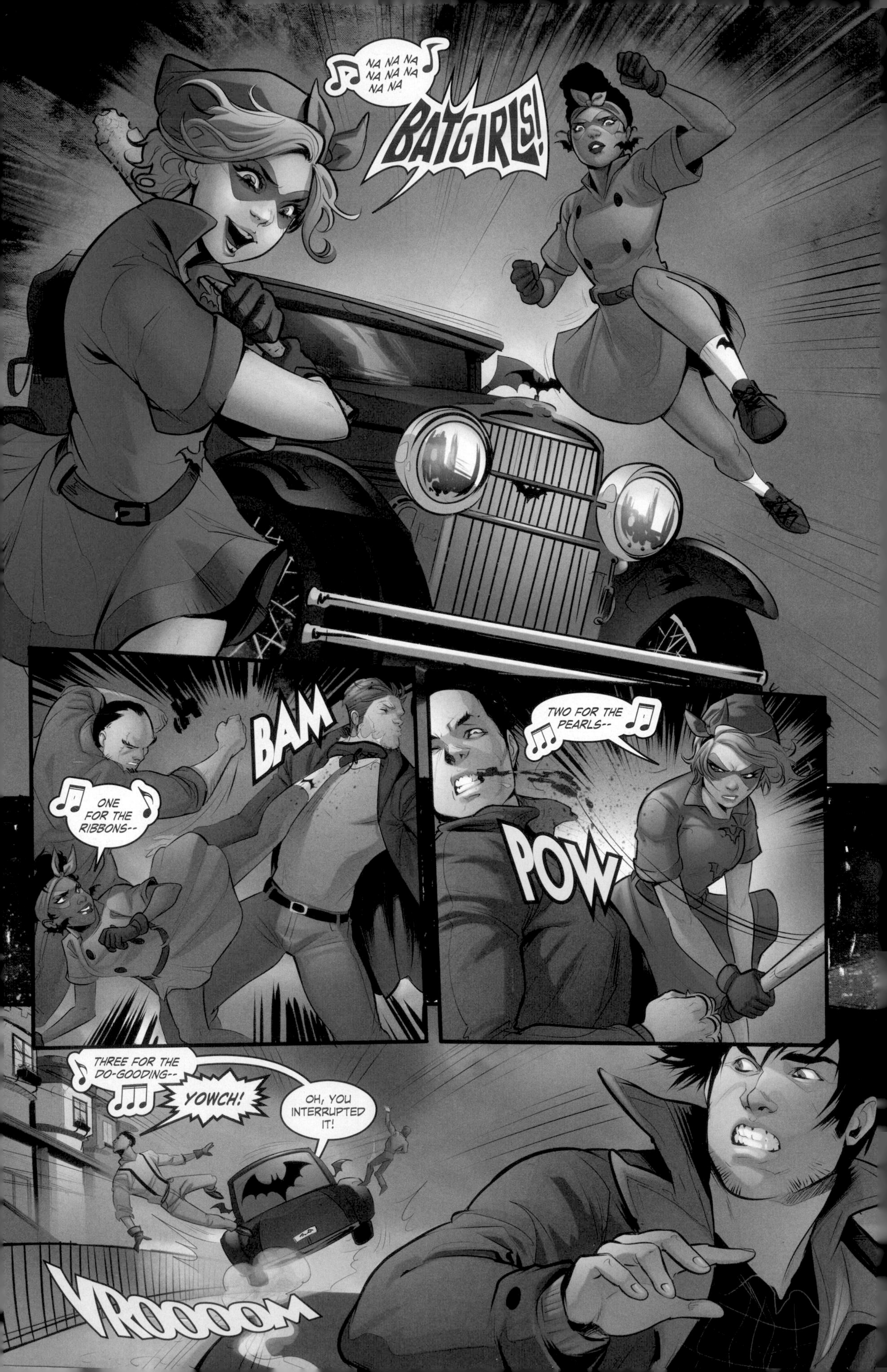
NA NA NA NA NA NA NA NA
BATGIRLS!
BAM
ONE FOR THE RIBBONS--
TWO FOR THE PEARLS--
POW
THREE FOR THE DO-GOODING--
YOWCH!
OH, YOU INTERRUPTED IT!
VROOOOOM

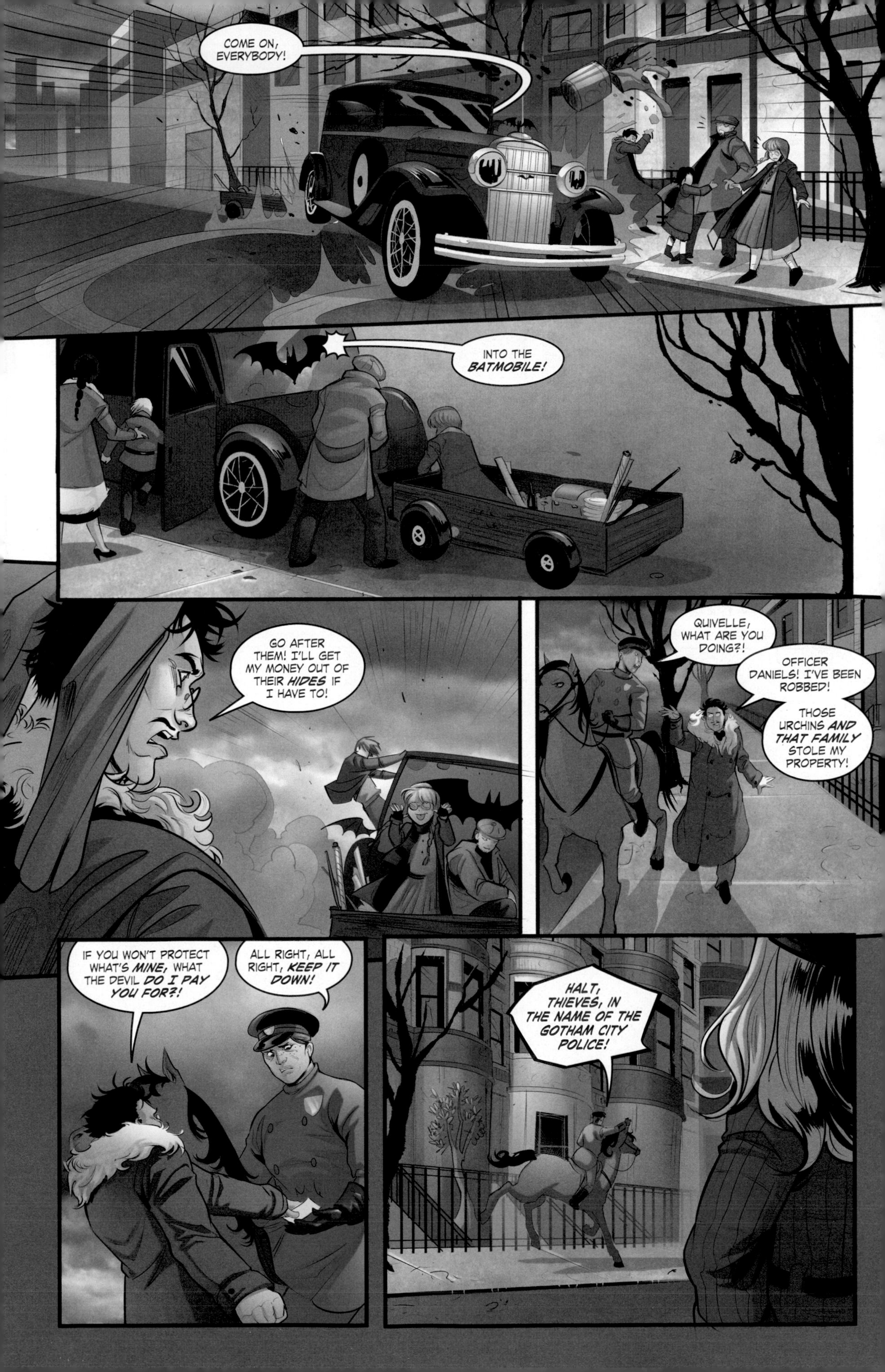

COME ON, EVERYBODY!
INTO THE BATMOBILE!
GO AFTER THEM! I'LL GET MY MONEY OUT OF THEIR HIDES IF I HAVE TO!
QUIVELLE, WHAT ARE YOU DOING?!
OFFICER DANIELS! I'VE BEEN ROBBED!
THOSE URCHINS AND THAT FAMILY STOLE MY PROPERTY!
IF YOU WON'T PROTECT WHAT'S MINE, WHAT THE DEVIL DO I PAY YOU FOR?!
ALL RIGHT, ALL RIGHT, KEEP IT DOWN!
HALT, THIEVES, IN THE NAME OF THE GOTHAM CITY POLICE!

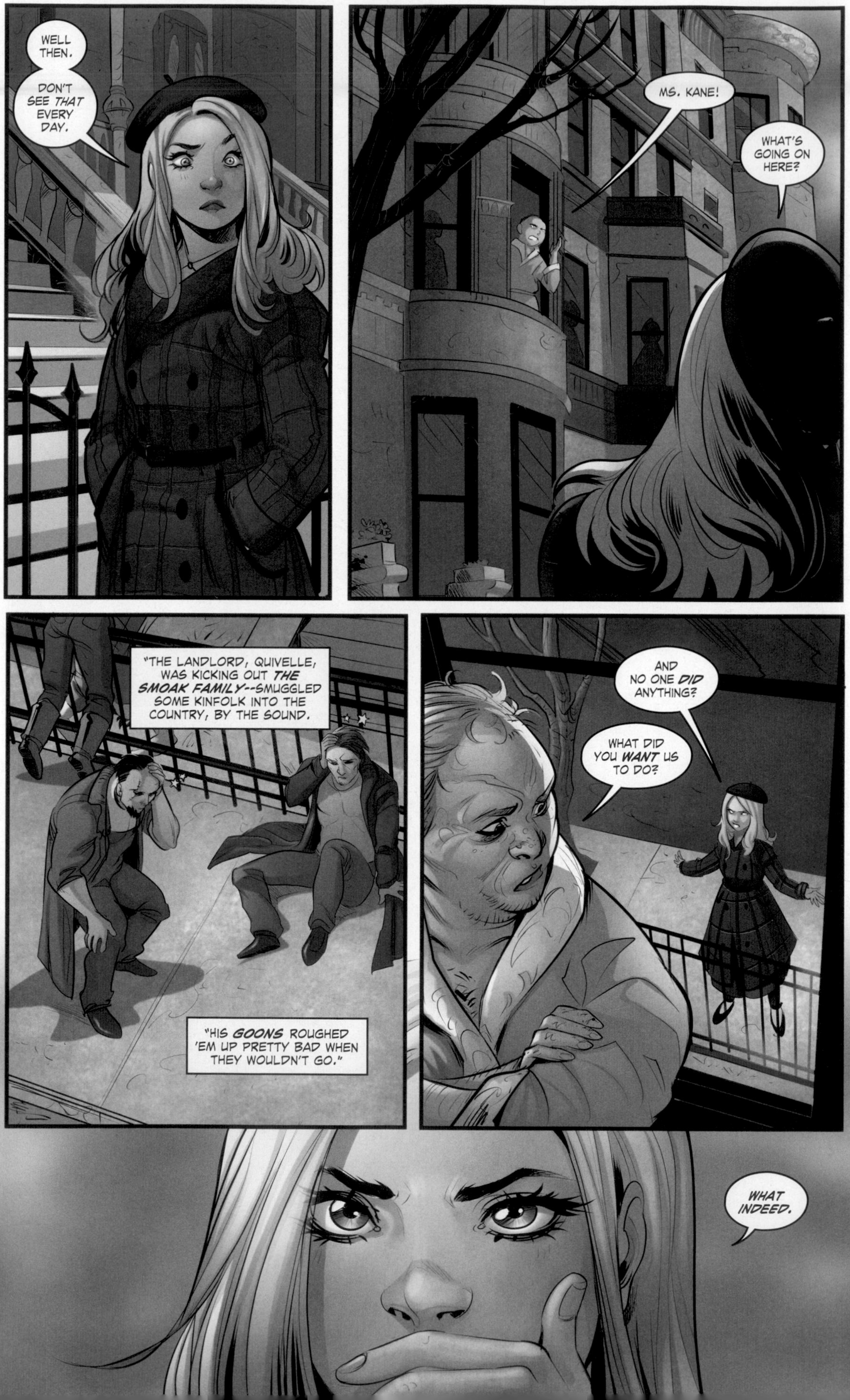
WELL THEN.
DON'T SEE *THAT* EVERY DAY.
MS. KANE!
WHAT'S GOING ON HERE?
"THE LANDLORD, QUIVELLE, WAS KICKING OUT ***THE SMOAK FAMILY***--SMUGGLED SOME KINFOLK INTO THE COUNTRY, BY THE SOUND.
"HIS ***GOONS*** ROUGHED 'EM UP PRETTY BAD WHEN THEY WOULDN'T GO."
AND NO ONE ***DID*** ANYTHING?
WHAT DID YOU ***WANT*** US TO DO?
WHAT INDEED.

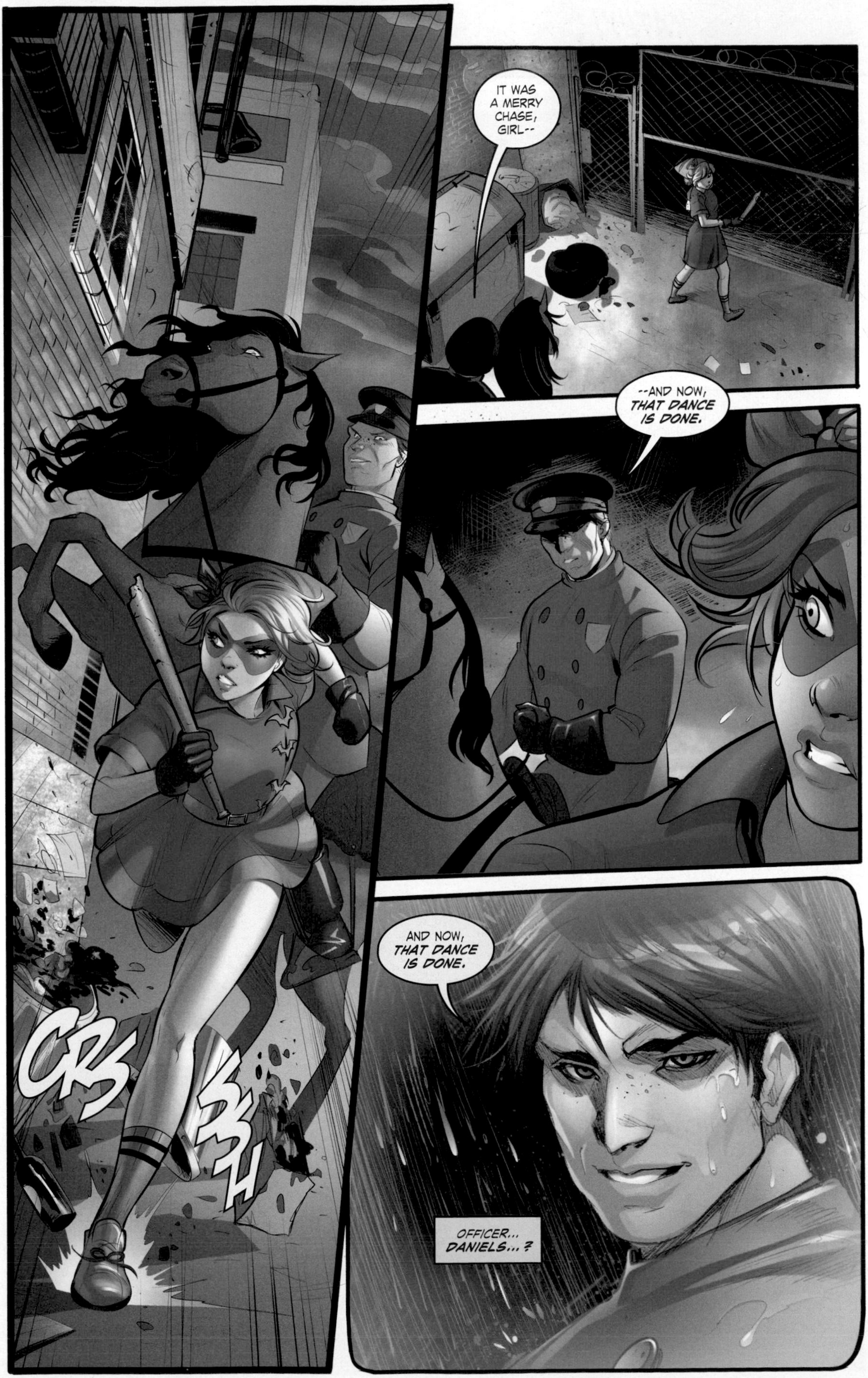
CRSSSH
IT WAS A MERRY CHASE, GIRL--
--AND NOW, THAT DANCE IS DONE.
AND NOW, THAT DANCE IS DONE.
OFFICER... DANIELS...?

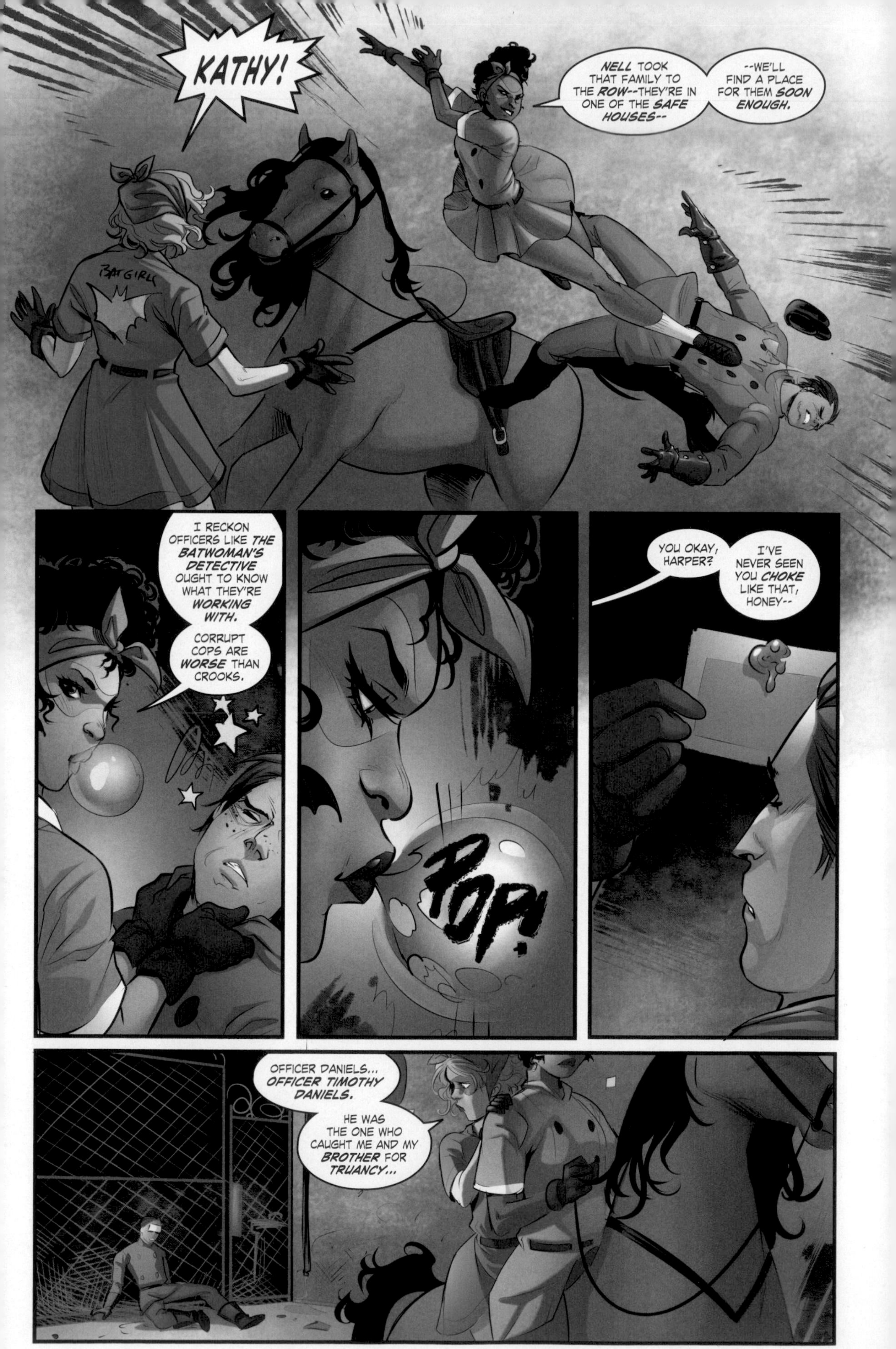
KATHY!
NELL TOOK THAT FAMILY TO THE ROW--THEY'RE IN ONE OF THE SAFE HOUSES--
--WE'LL FIND A PLACE FOR THEM SOON ENOUGH.
BATGIRLS
I RECKON OFFICERS LIKE THE BATWOMAN'S DETECTIVE OUGHT TO KNOW WHAT THEY'RE WORKING WITH.
CORRUPT COPS ARE WORSE THAN CROOKS.
POP!
YOU OKAY, HARPER?
I'VE NEVER SEEN YOU CHOKE LIKE THAT, HONEY--
OFFICER DANIELS... OFFICER TIMOTHY DANIELS.
HE WAS THE ONE WHO CAUGHT ME AND MY BROTHER FOR TRUANCY...

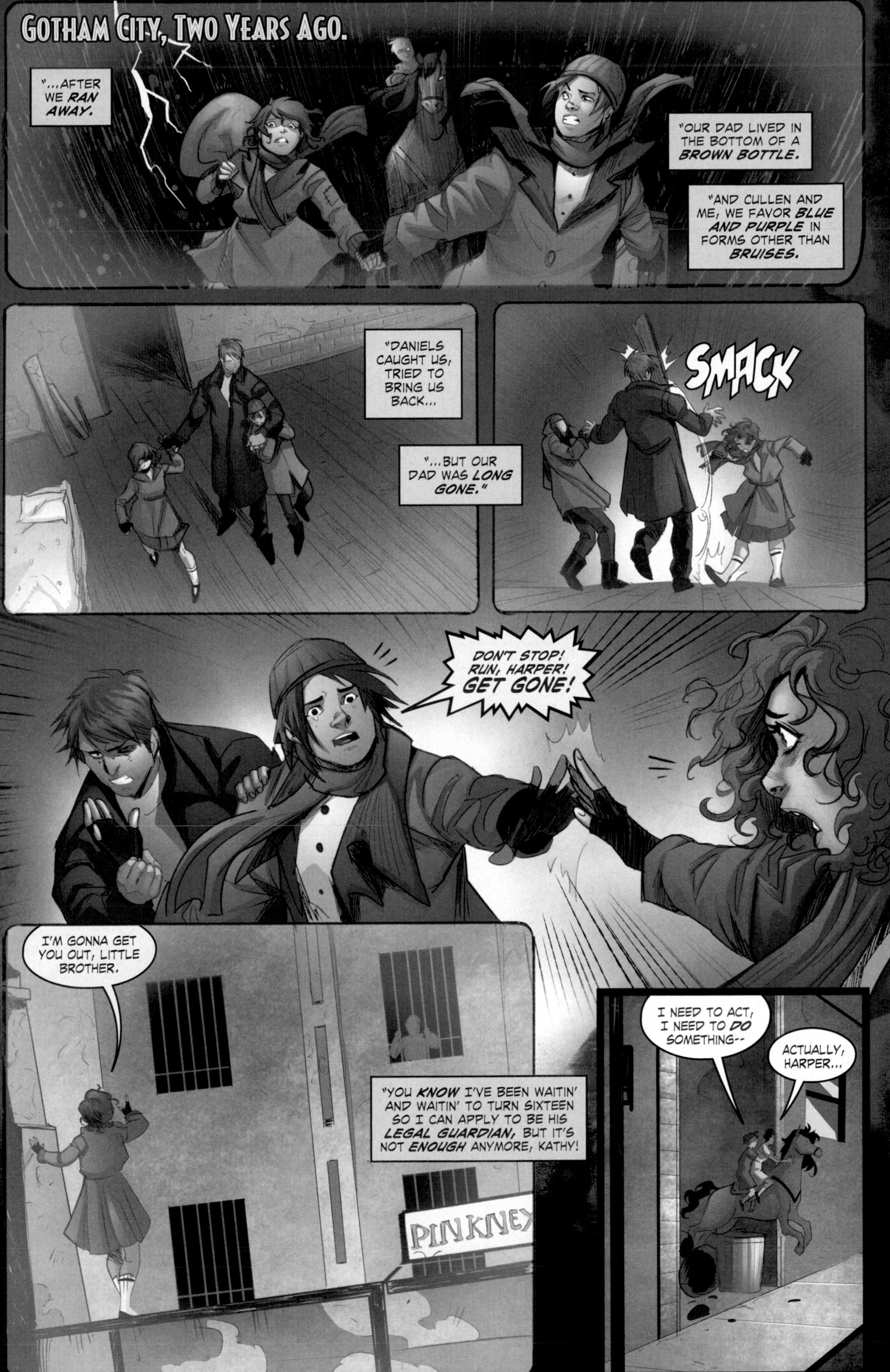
GOTHAM CITY, TWO YEARS AGO.
"...AFTER WE RAN AWAY.
"OUR DAD LIVED IN THE BOTTOM OF A BROWN BOTTLE.
"AND CULLEN AND ME, WE FAVOR BLUE AND PURPLE IN FORMS OTHER THAN BRUISES.
"DANIELS CAUGHT US, TRIED TO BRING US BACK...
"...BUT OUR DAD WAS LONG GONE."
SMACK
DON'T STOP! RUN, HARPER! GET GONE!
I'M GONNA GET YOU OUT, LITTLE BROTHER.
"YOU KNOW I'VE BEEN WAITIN' AND WAITIN' TO TURN SIXTEEN SO I CAN APPLY TO BE HIS LEGAL GUARDIAN, BUT IT'S NOT ENOUGH ANYMORE, KATHY!
PINKNEY
I NEED TO ACT, I NEED TO DO SOMETHING--
ACTUALLY, HARPER...

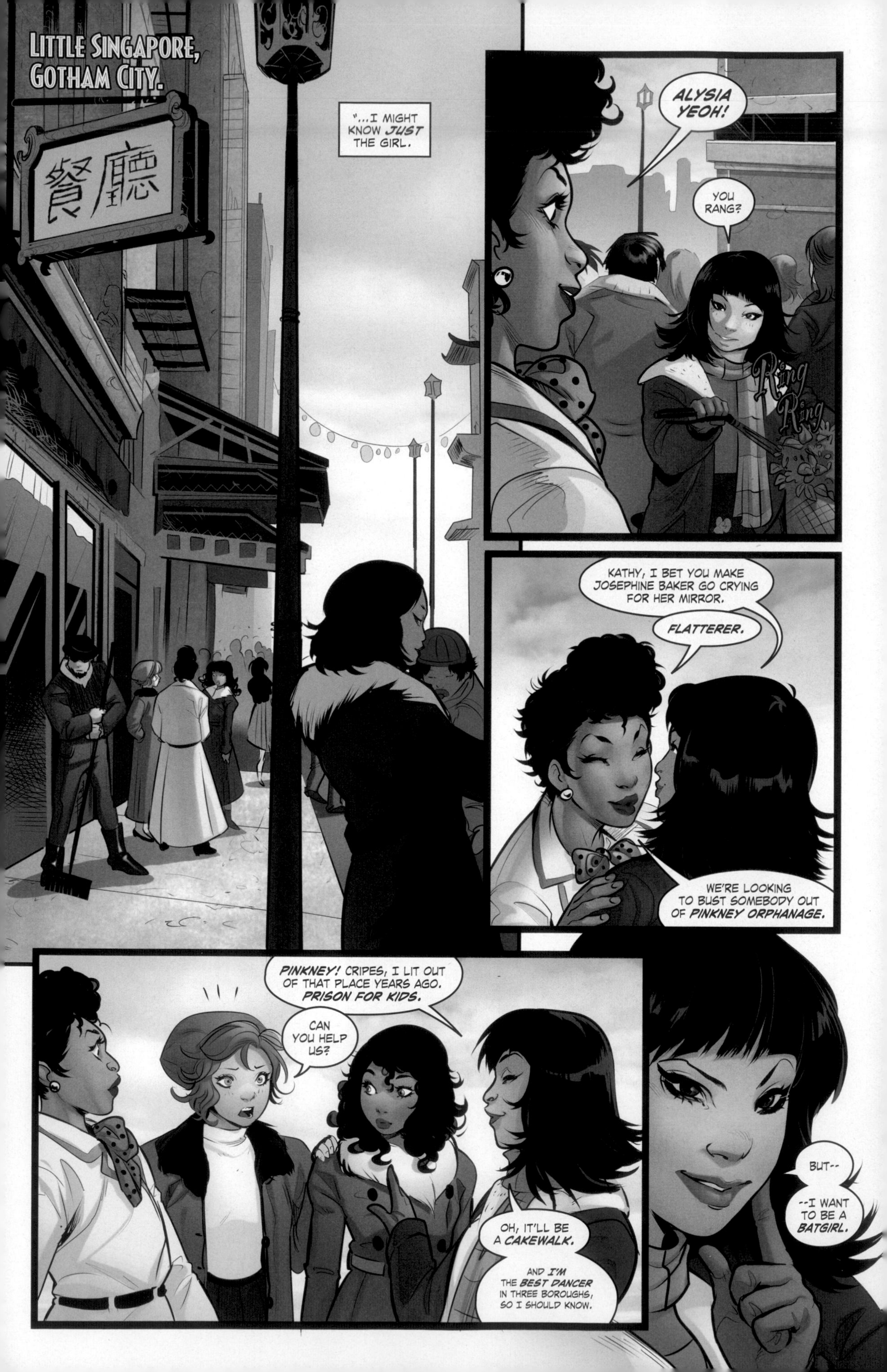

LITTLE SINGAPORE, GOTHAM CITY.
餐廳
"...I MIGHT KNOW JUST THE GIRL.
ALYSIA YEOH!
YOU RANG?
RING RING
KATHY, I BET YOU MAKE JOSEPHINE BAKER GO CRYING FOR HER MIRROR.
FLATTERER.
WE'RE LOOKING TO BUST SOMEBODY OUT OF PINKNEY ORPHANAGE.
PINKNEY! CRIPES, I LIT OUT OF THAT PLACE YEARS AGO. PRISON FOR KIDS.
CAN YOU HELP US?
OH, IT'LL BE A CAKEWALK.
AND I'M THE BEST DANCER IN THREE BOROUGHS, SO I SHOULD KNOW.
BUT--
--I WANT TO BE A BATGIRL.

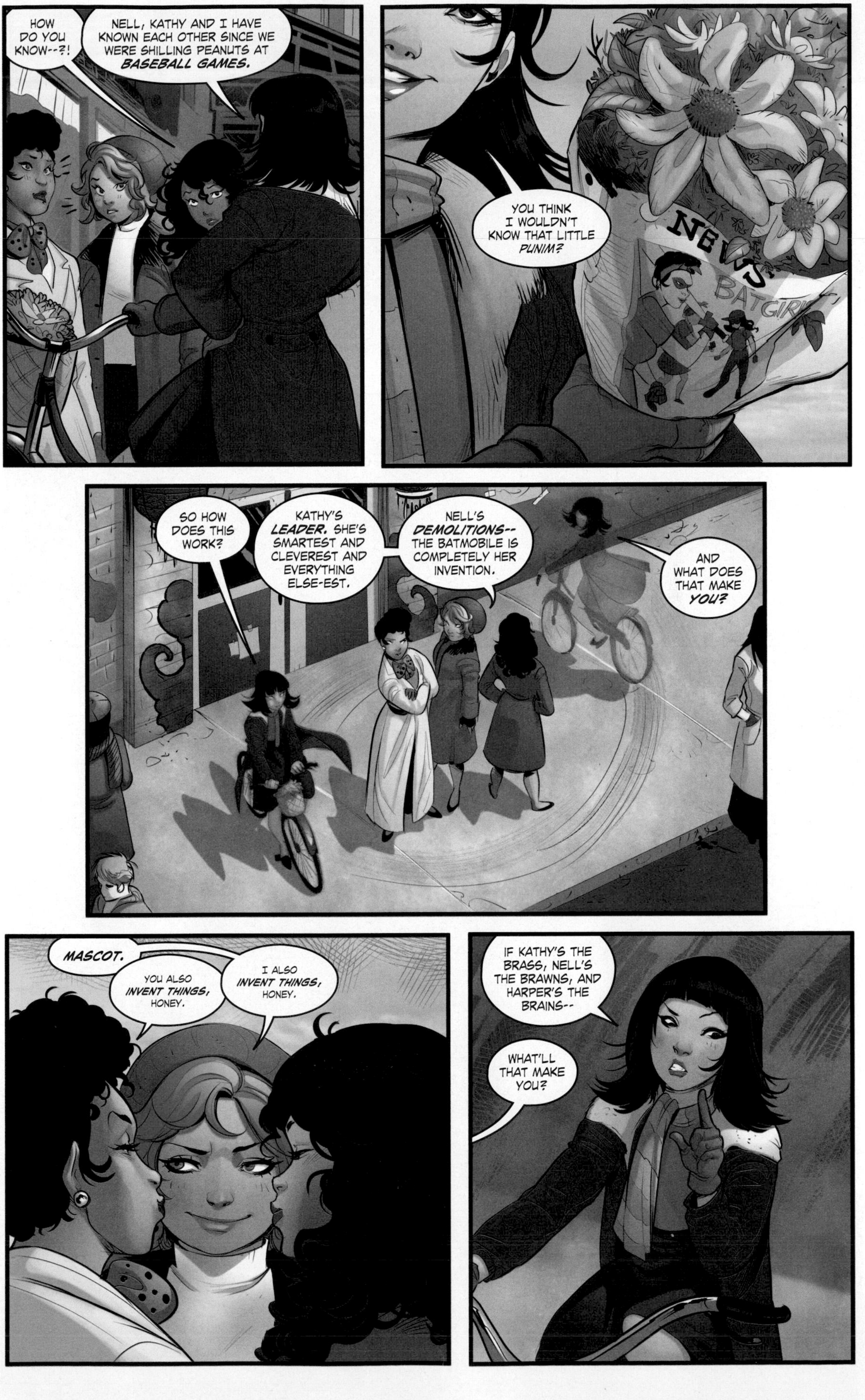

HOW DO YOU KNOW--?!
NELL, KATHY AND I HAVE KNOWN EACH OTHER SINCE WE WERE SHILLING PEANUTS AT BASEBALL GAMES.
YOU THINK I WOULDN'T KNOW THAT LITTLE PUNIM?
NEWS
BATGIRL
SO HOW DOES THIS WORK?
KATHY'S LEADER. SHE'S SMARTEST AND CLEVEREST AND EVERYTHING ELSE-EST.
NELL'S DEMOLITIONS-- THE BATMOBILE IS COMPLETELY HER INVENTION.
AND WHAT DOES THAT MAKE YOU?
MASCOT.
YOU ALSO INVENT THINGS, HONEY.
I ALSO INVENT THINGS, HONEY.
IF KATHY'S THE BRASS, NELL'S THE BRAWNS, AND HARPER'S THE BRAINS--
WHAT'LL THAT MAKE YOU?

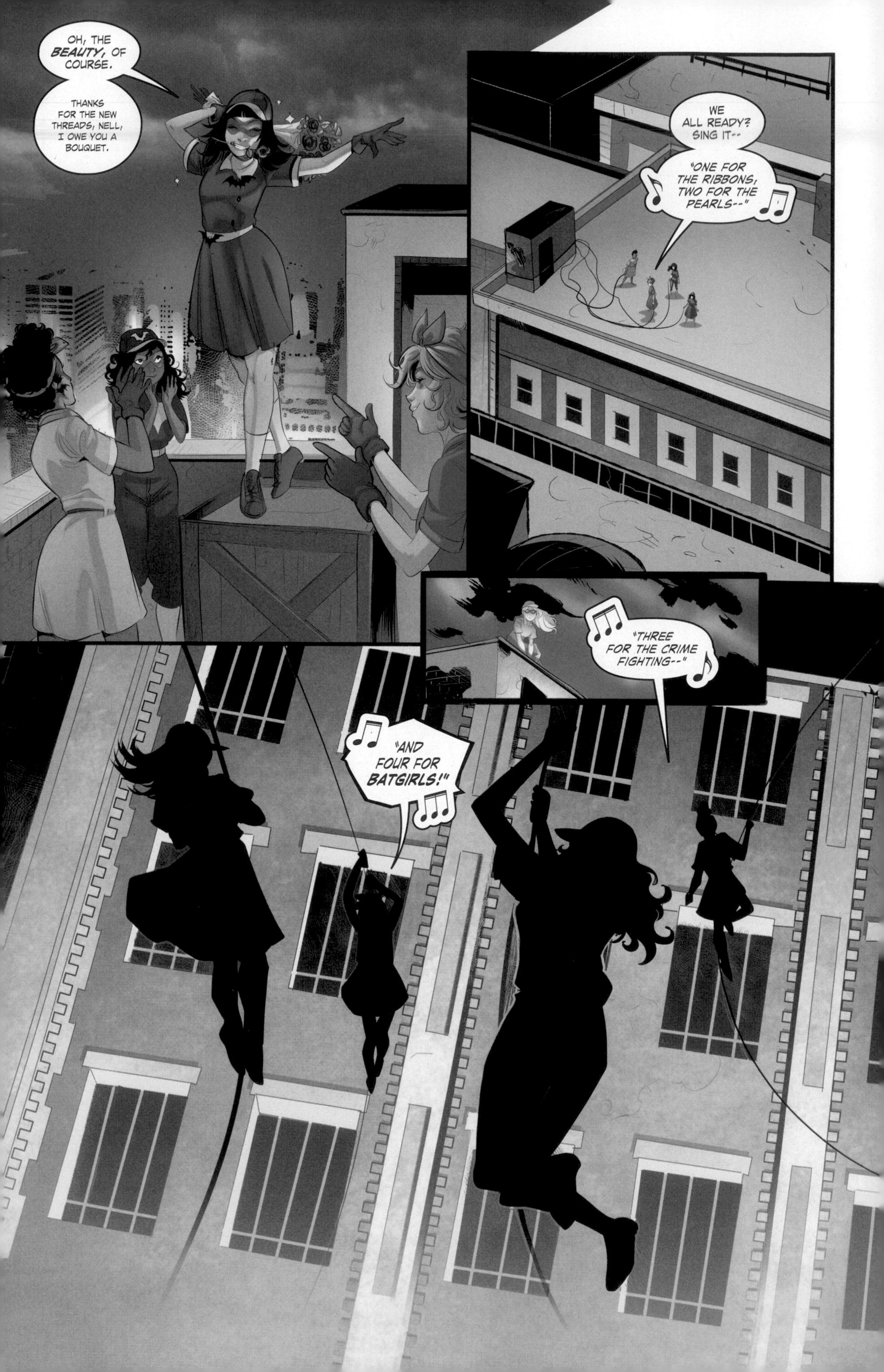
OH, THE BEAUTY, OF COURSE.
THANKS FOR THE NEW THREADS, NELL, I OWE YOU A BOUQUET.
WE ALL READY? SING IT--
"ONE FOR THE RIBBONS, TWO FOR THE PEARLS--"
"THREE FOR THE CRIME FIGHTING--"
"AND FOUR FOR BATGIRLS!"

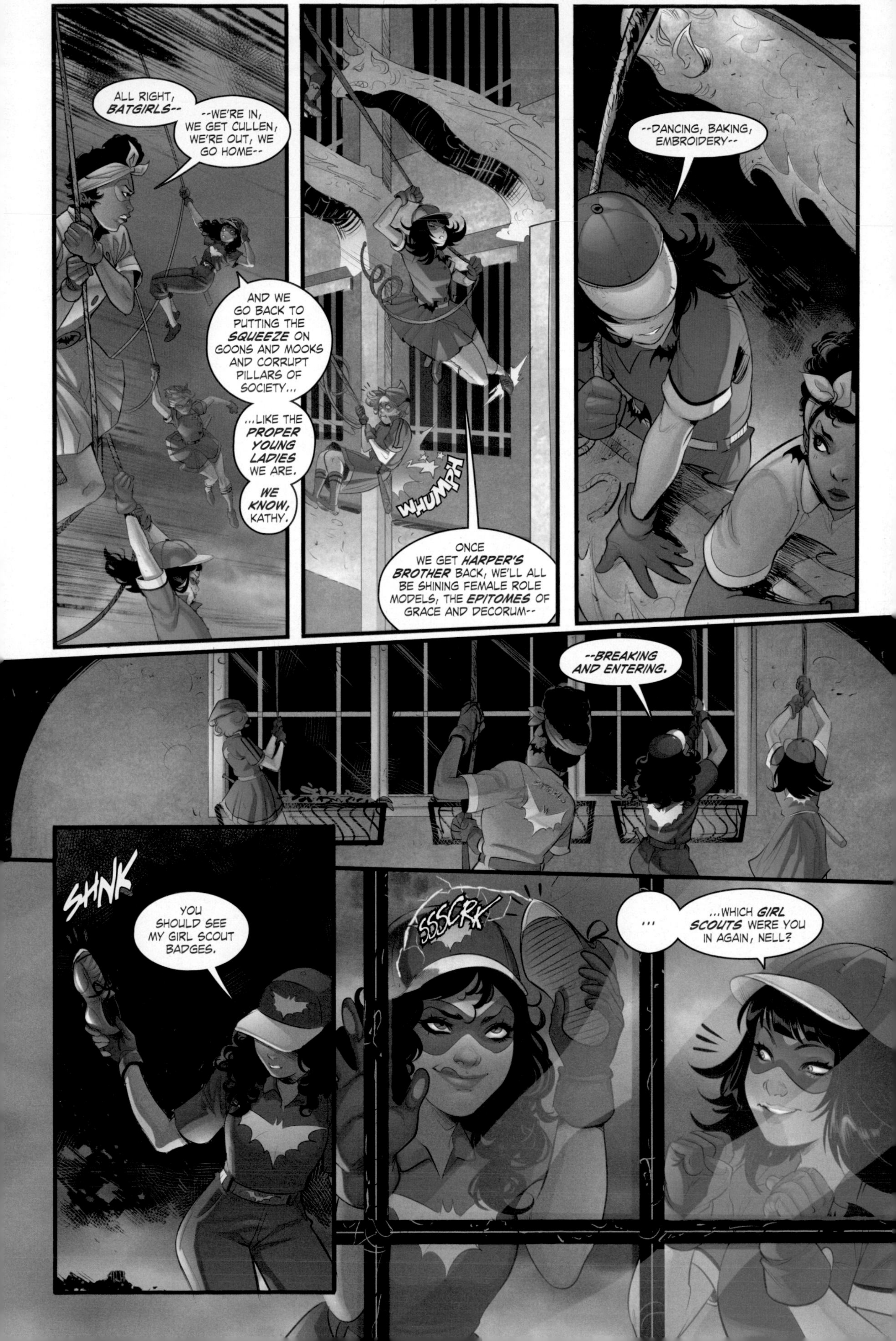
ALL RIGHT, BATGIRLS--
--WE'RE IN, WE GET CULLEN, WE'RE OUT, WE GO HOME--
AND WE GO BACK TO PUTTING THE SQUEEZE ON GOONS AND MOOKS AND CORRUPT PILLARS OF SOCIETY...
...LIKE THE PROPER YOUNG LADIES WE ARE.
WE KNOW, KATHY.
WHUMPH
ONCE WE GET HARPER'S BROTHER BACK, WE'LL ALL BE SHINING FEMALE ROLE MODELS, THE EPITOMES OF GRACE AND DECORUM--
--DANCING, BAKING, EMBROIDERY--
--BREAKING AND ENTERING.
SHNK
YOU SHOULD SEE MY GIRL SCOUT BADGES.
SSSCRK
...
...WHICH GIRL SCOUTS WERE YOU IN AGAIN, NELL?

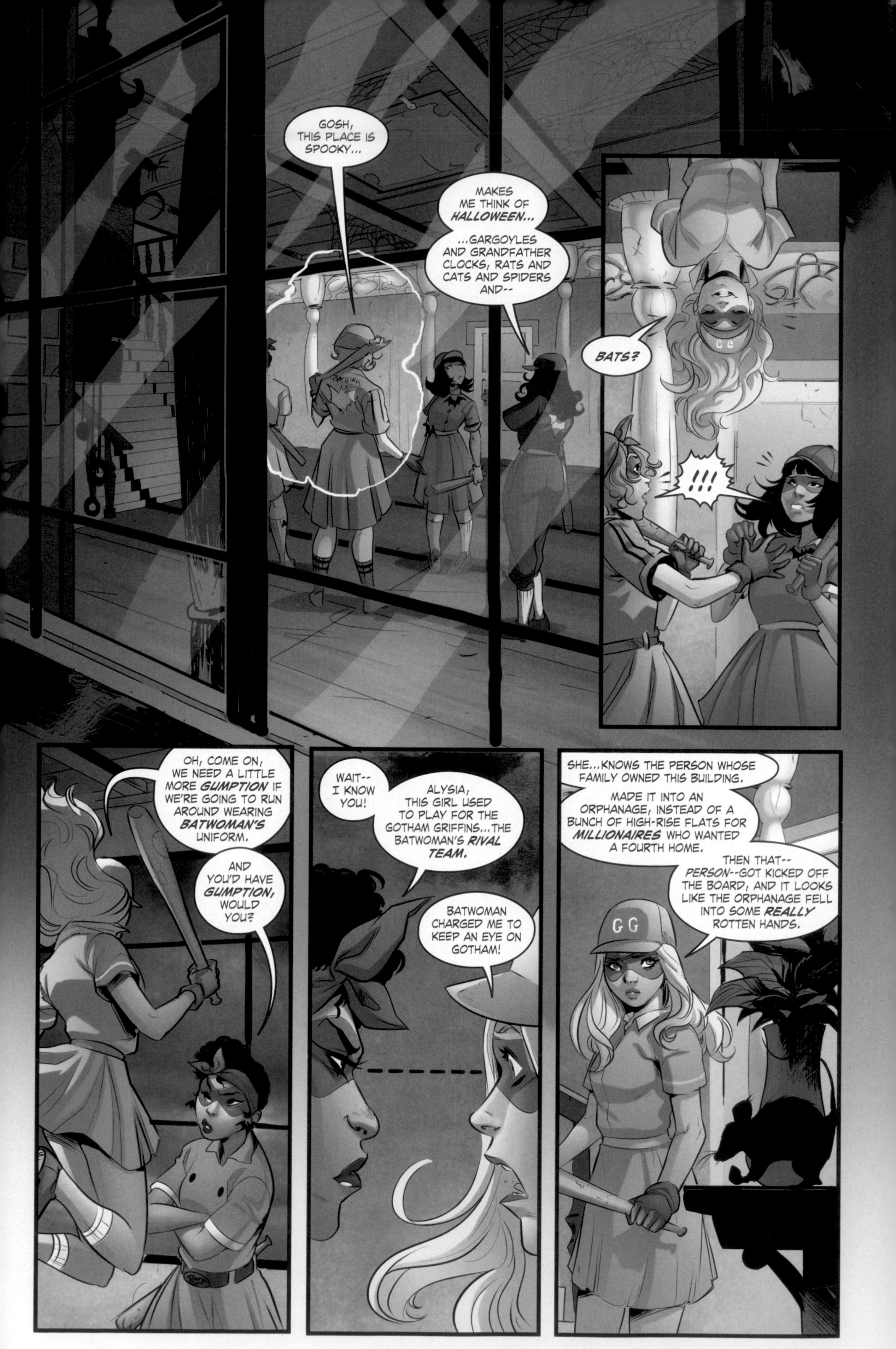
GOSH, THIS PLACE IS SPOOKY...
MAKES ME THINK OF HALLOWEEN...
...GARGOYLES AND GRANDFATHER CLOCKS, RATS AND CATS AND SPIDERS AND--
BATS?
!!!
OH, COME ON, WE NEED A LITTLE MORE GUMPTION IF WE'RE GOING TO RUN AROUND WEARING BATWOMAN'S UNIFORM.
AND YOU'D HAVE GUMPTION, WOULD YOU?
WAIT-- I KNOW YOU!
ALYSIA, THIS GIRL USED TO PLAY FOR THE GOTHAM GRIFFINS...THE BATWOMAN'S RIVAL TEAM.
BATWOMAN CHARGED ME TO KEEP AN EYE ON GOTHAM!
SHE...KNOWS THE PERSON WHOSE FAMILY OWNED THIS BUILDING.
MADE IT INTO AN ORPHANAGE, INSTEAD OF A BUNCH OF HIGH-RISE FLATS FOR MILLIONAIRES WHO WANTED A FOURTH HOME.
THEN THAT-- PERSON--GOT KICKED OFF THE BOARD, AND IT LOOKS LIKE THE ORPHANAGE FELL INTO SOME REALLY ROTTEN HANDS.

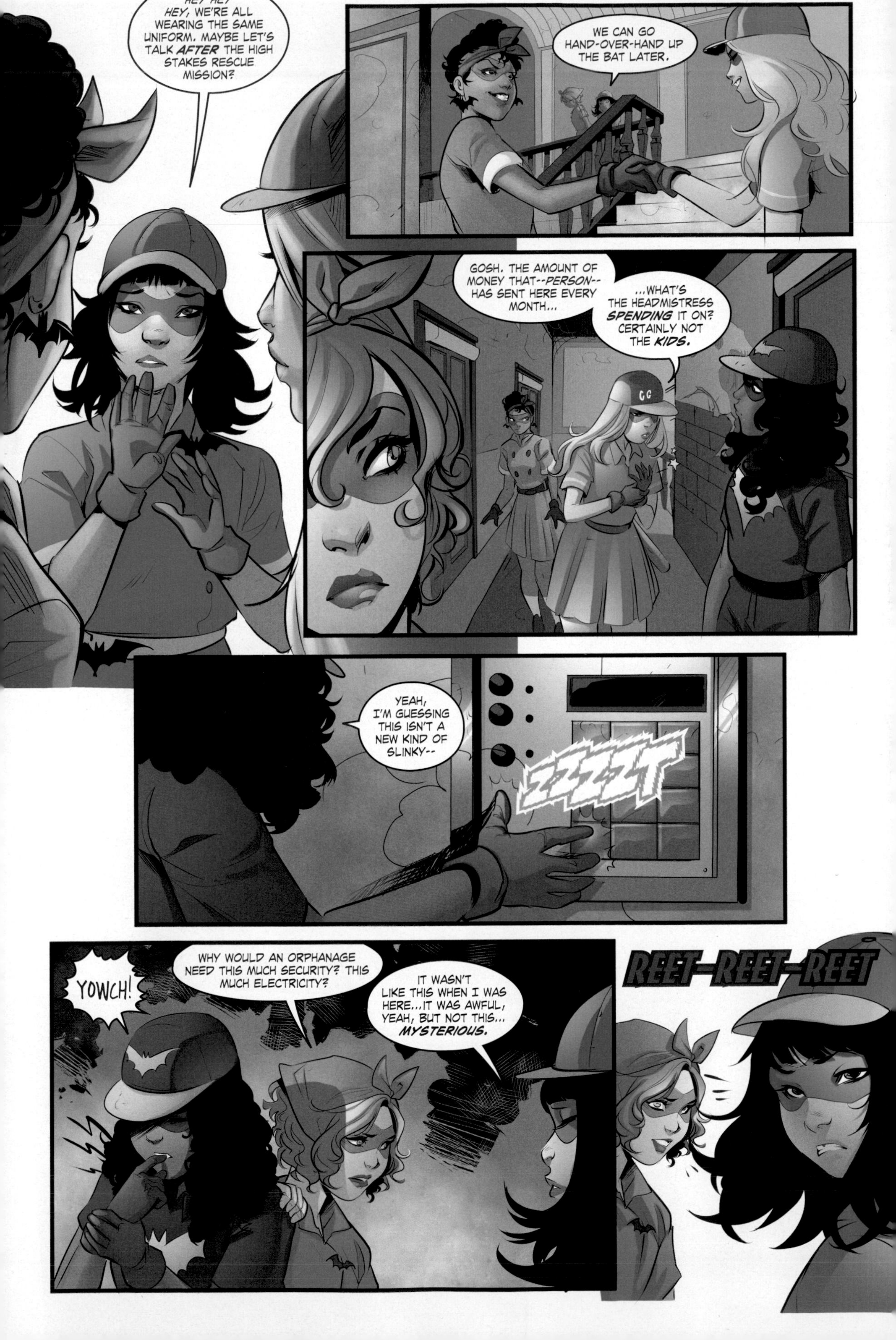
HEY HEY HEY, WE'RE ALL WEARING THE SAME UNIFORM. MAYBE LET'S TALK AFTER THE HIGH STAKES RESCUE MISSION?
WE CAN GO HAND-OVER-HAND UP THE BAT LATER.
GOSH. THE AMOUNT OF MONEY THAT--PERSON--HAS SENT HERE EVERY MONTH...
...WHAT'S THE HEADMISTRESS SPENDING IT ON? CERTAINLY NOT THE KIDS.
YEAH, I'M GUESSING THIS ISN'T A NEW KIND OF SLINKY--
ZZZZT
YOWCH!
WHY WOULD AN ORPHANAGE NEED THIS MUCH SECURITY? THIS MUCH ELECTRICITY?
IT WASN'T LIKE THIS WHEN I WAS HERE...IT WAS AWFUL, YEAH, BUT NOT THIS... MYSTERIOUS.
REET-REET-REET

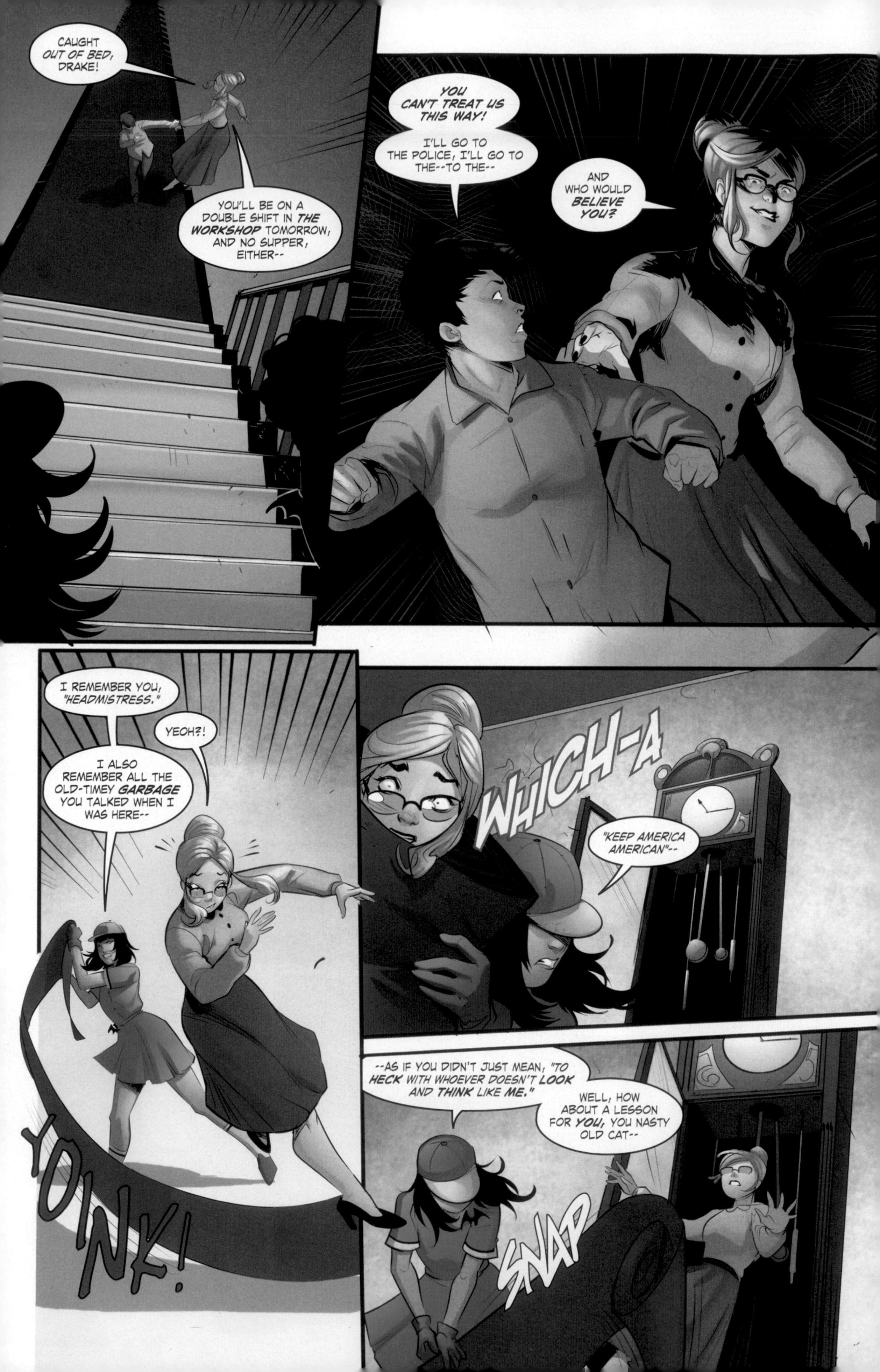
CAUGHT OUT OF BED, DRAKE!
YOU'LL BE ON A DOUBLE SHIFT IN THE WORKSHOP TOMORROW, AND NO SUPPER, EITHER--
YOU CAN'T TREAT US THIS WAY!
I'LL GO TO THE POLICE, I'LL GO TO THE--TO THE--
AND WHO WOULD BELIEVE YOU?
I REMEMBER YOU, "HEADMISTRESS."
YEOH?!
I ALSO REMEMBER ALL THE OLD-TIMEY GARBAGE YOU TALKED WHEN I WAS HERE--
YOINK!
WHICH-A
"KEEP AMERICA AMERICAN"--
--AS IF YOU DIDN'T JUST MEAN, "TO HECK WITH WHOEVER DOESN'T LOOK AND THINK LIKE ME."
WELL, HOW ABOUT A LESSON FOR YOU, YOU NASTY OLD CAT--
SNAP

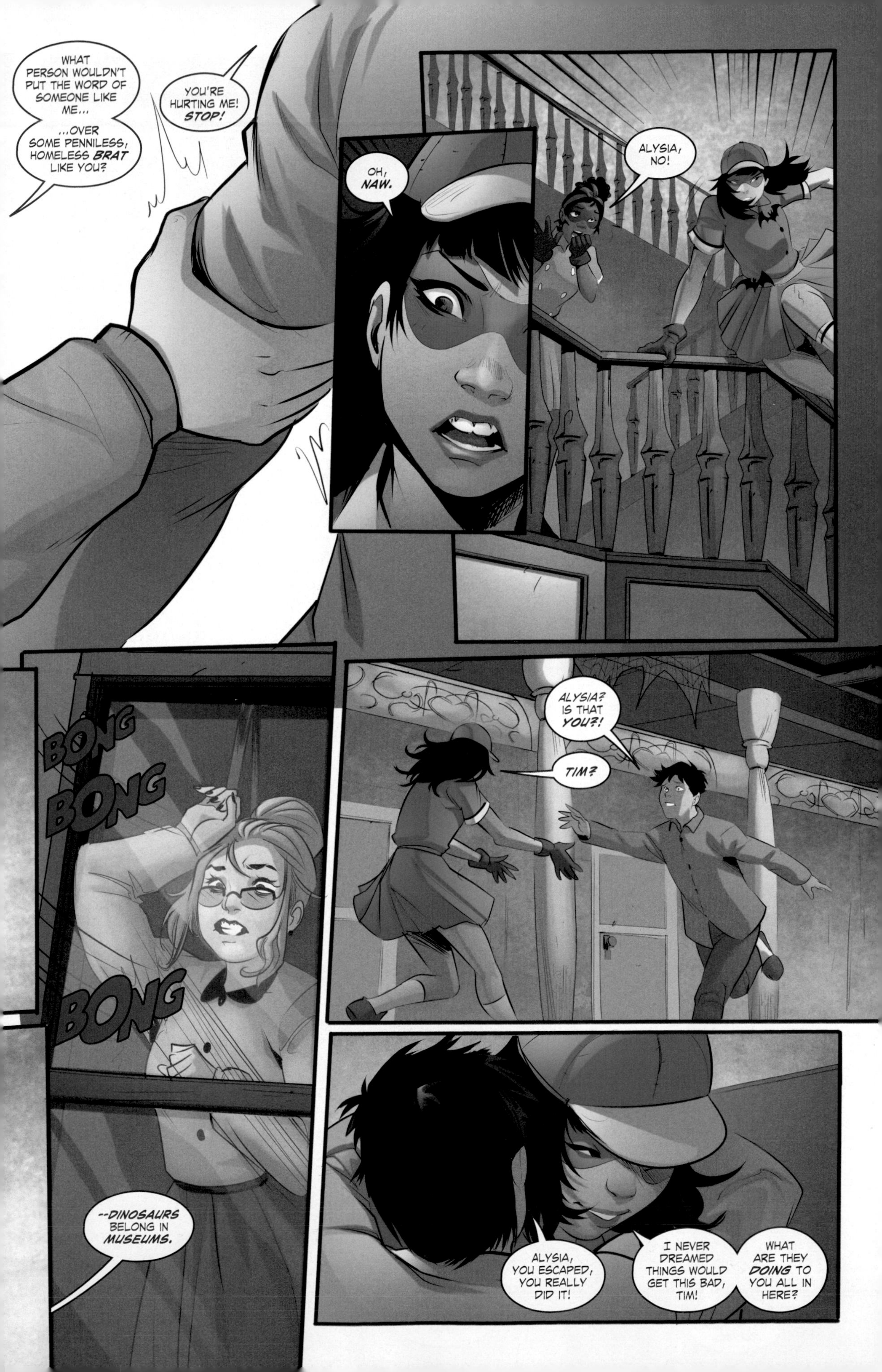
WHAT PERSON WOULDN'T PUT THE WORD OF SOMEONE LIKE ME...
...OVER SOME PENNILESS, HOMELESS BRAT LIKE YOU?
YOU'RE HURTING ME! STOP!
OH, NAW.
ALYSIA, NO!
BONG
BONG
BONG
--DINOSAURS BELONG IN MUSEUMS.
ALYSIA? IS THAT YOU?!
TIM?
ALYSIA, YOU ESCAPED, YOU REALLY DID IT!
I NEVER DREAMED THINGS WOULD GET THIS BAD, TIM!
WHAT ARE THEY DOING TO YOU ALL IN HERE?

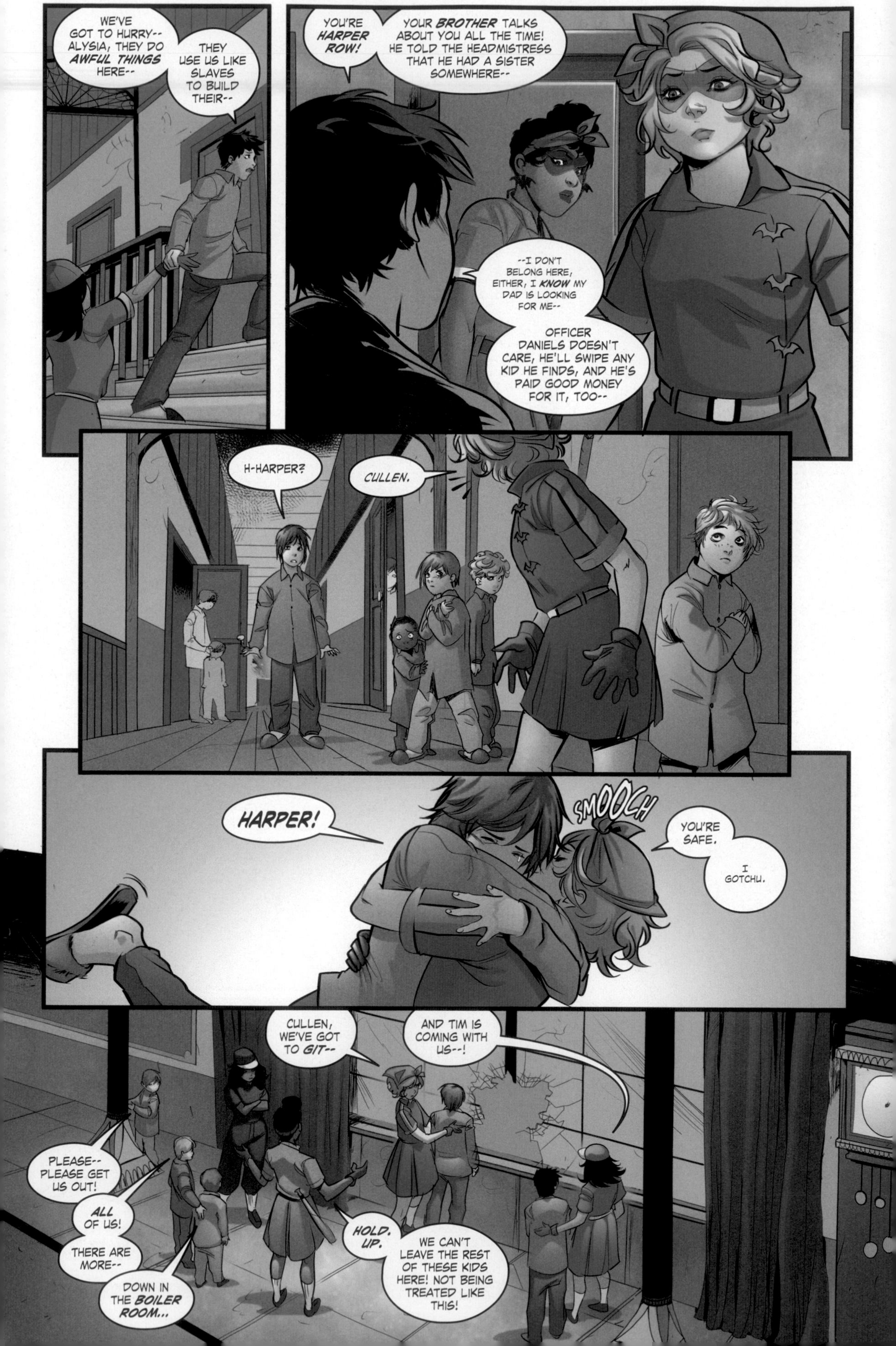

WE'VE GOT TO HURRY-- ALYSIA, THEY DO AWFUL THINGS HERE--
THEY USE US LIKE SLAVES TO BUILD THEIR--
YOU'RE HARPER ROW!
YOUR BROTHER TALKS ABOUT YOU ALL THE TIME! HE TOLD THE HEADMISTRESS THAT HE HAD A SISTER SOMEWHERE--
--I DON'T BELONG HERE, EITHER, I KNOW MY DAD IS LOOKING FOR ME--
OFFICER DANIELS DOESN'T CARE, HE'LL SWIPE ANY KID HE FINDS, AND HE'S PAID GOOD MONEY FOR IT, TOO--
H-HARPER?
CULLEN.
HARPER!
SMOOCH
YOU'RE SAFE.
I GOTCHU.
CULLEN, WE'VE GOT TO GIT--
AND TIM IS COMING WITH US--!
PLEASE-- PLEASE GET US OUT!
ALL OF US!
THERE ARE MORE--
DOWN IN THE BOILER ROOM...
HOLD. UP.
WE CAN'T LEAVE THE REST OF THESE KIDS HERE! NOT BEING TREATED LIKE THIS!

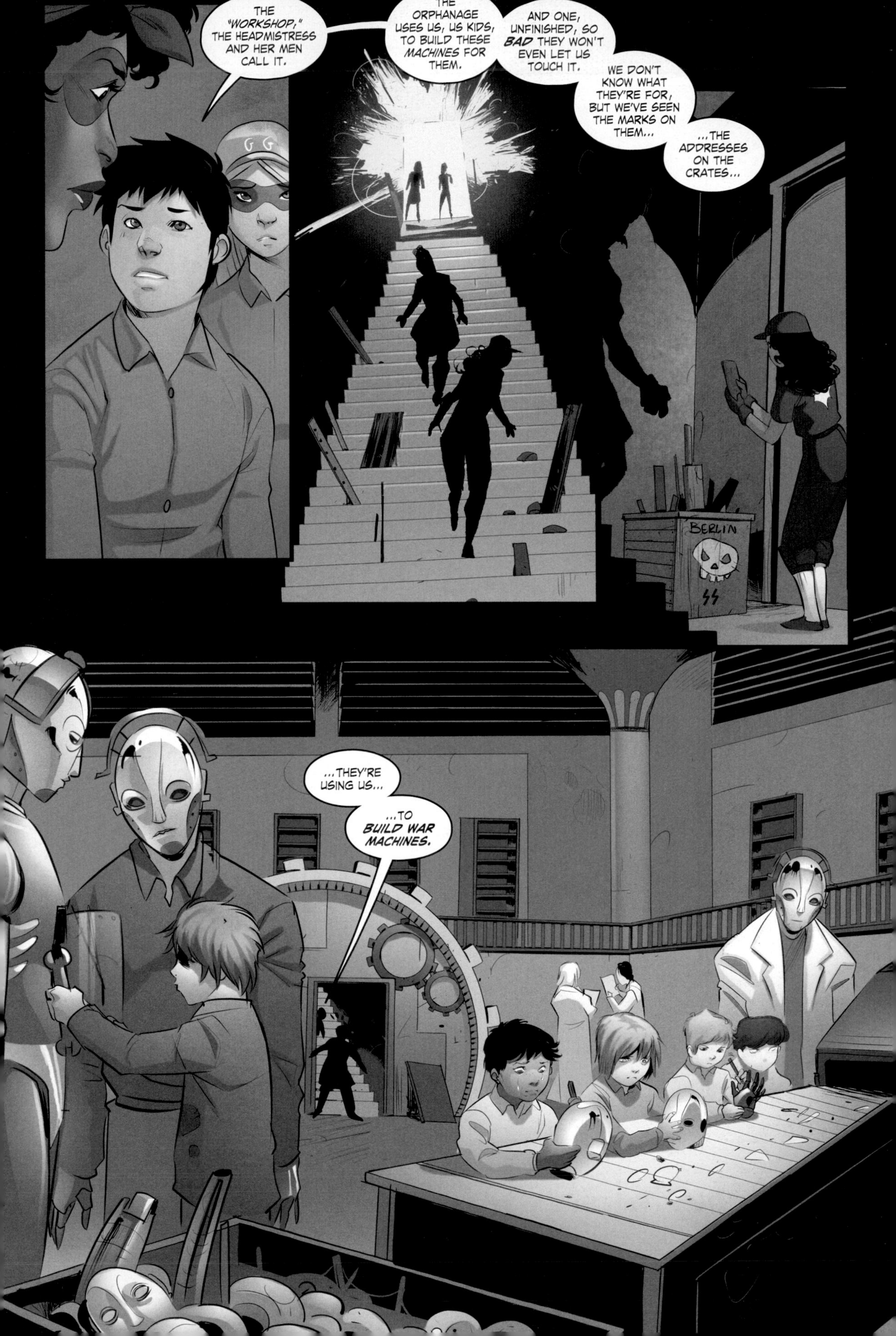
THE "WORKSHOP," THE HEADMISTRESS AND HER MEN CALL IT.
THE ORPHANAGE USES US, US KIDS, TO BUILD THESE MACHINES FOR THEM.
AND ONE, UNFINISHED, SO BAD THEY WON'T EVEN LET US TOUCH IT.
WE DON'T KNOW WHAT THEY'RE FOR, BUT WE'VE SEEN THE MARKS ON THEM...
...THE ADDRESSES ON THE CRATES...
BERLIN
SS
...THEY'RE USING US...
...TO BUILD WAR MACHINES.

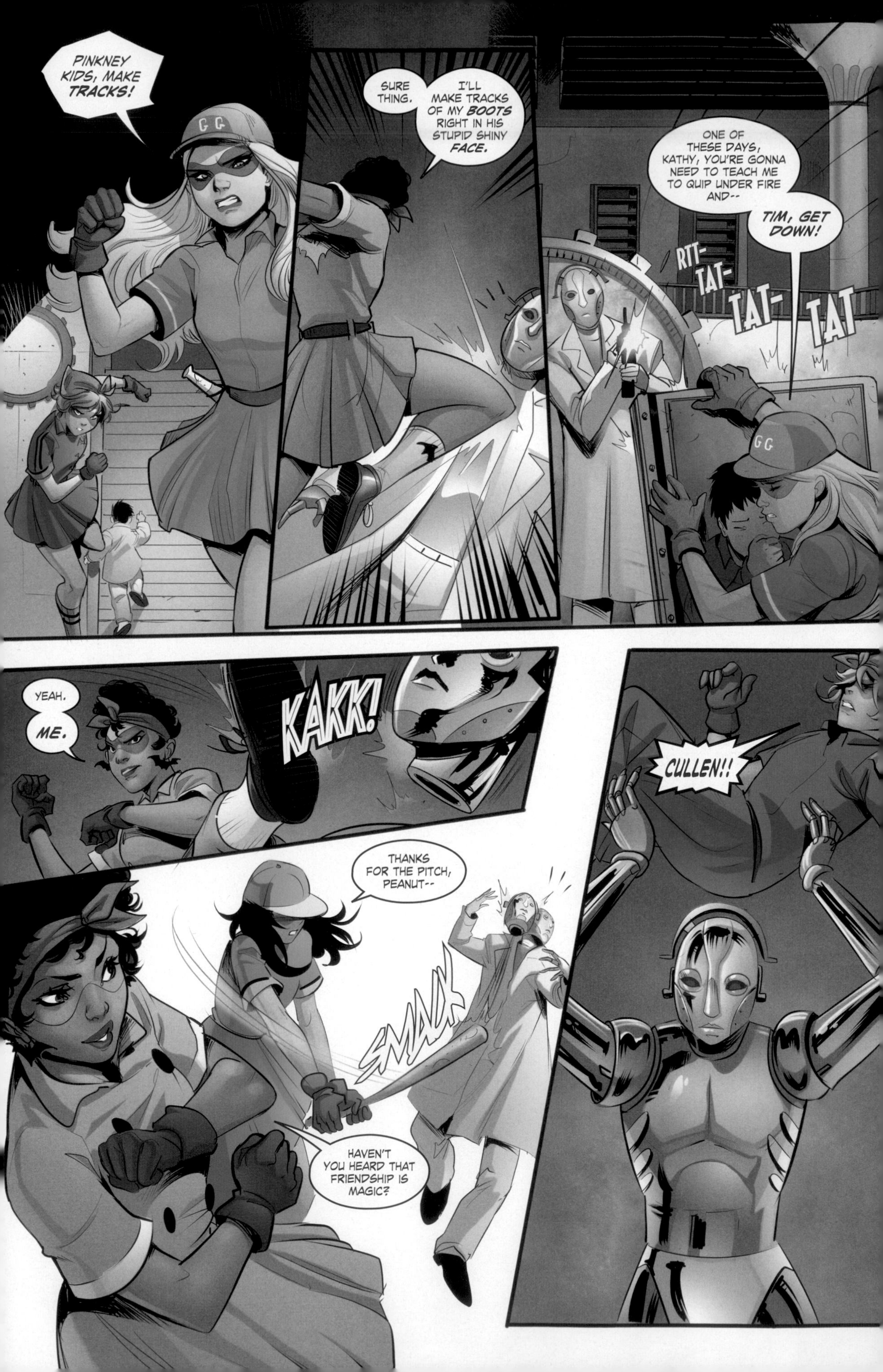
PINKNEY KIDS, MAKE TRACKS!
SURE THING.
I'LL MAKE TRACKS OF MY BOOTS RIGHT IN HIS STUPID SHINY FACE.
ONE OF THESE DAYS, KATHY, YOU'RE GONNA NEED TO TEACH ME TO QUIP UNDER FIRE AND--
TIM, GET DOWN!
RTT-TAT-TAT-TAT
YEAH.
ME.
KAKK!
CULLEN!!
THANKS FOR THE PITCH, PEANUT--
SMAK
HAVEN'T YOU HEARD THAT FRIENDSHIP IS MAGIC?

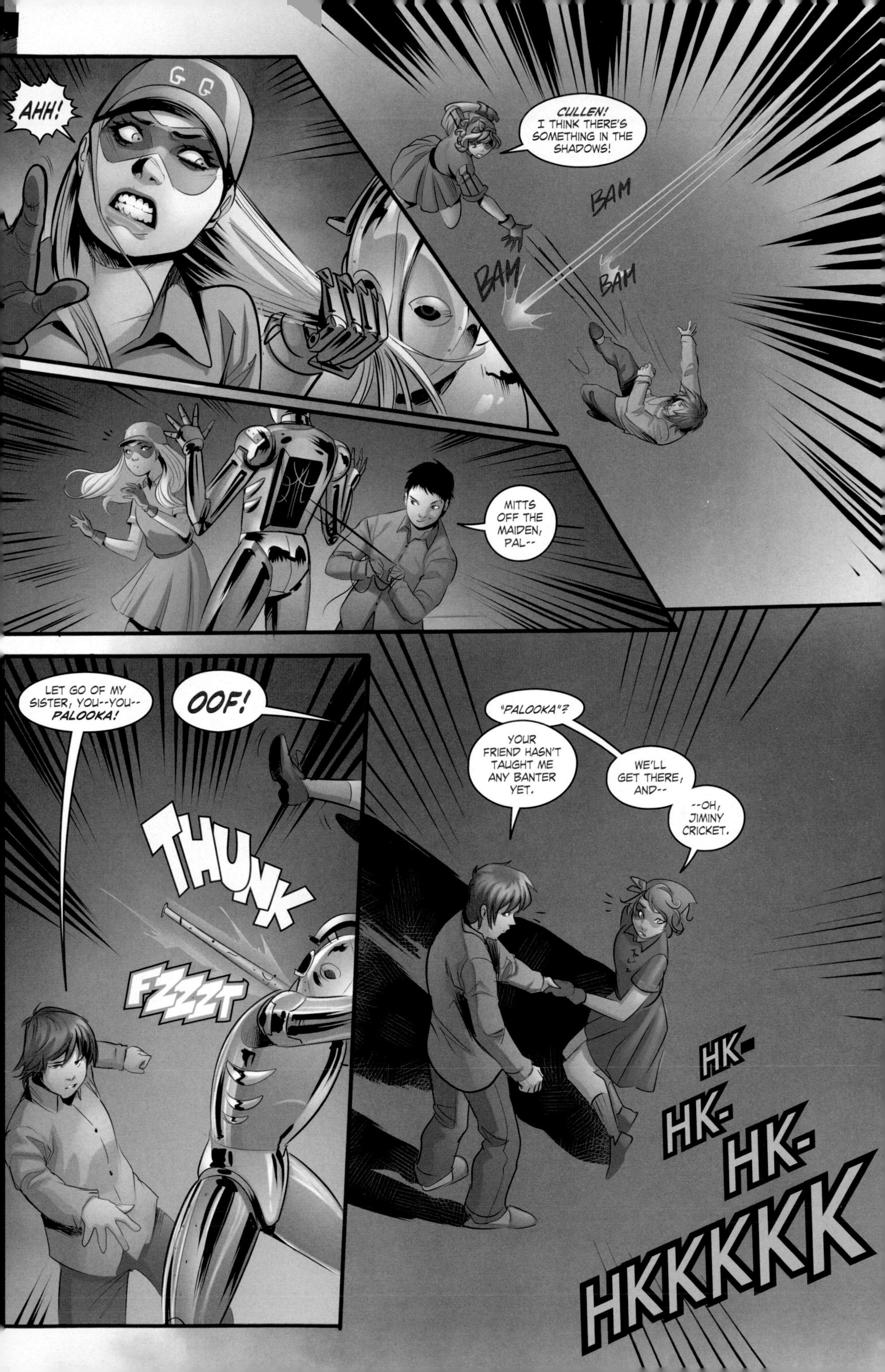
AHH!
CULLEN! I THINK THERE'S SOMETHING IN THE SHADOWS!
BAM
BAM
BAM
MITTS OFF THE MAIDEN, PAL--
LET GO OF MY SISTER, YOU--YOU--PALOOKA!
OOF!
THUNK
FZZZT
"PALOOKA"?
YOUR FRIEND HASN'T TAUGHT ME ANY BANTER YET.
WE'LL GET THERE, AND--
--OH, JIMINY CRICKET.
HK-
HK-
HK-
HKKKKK

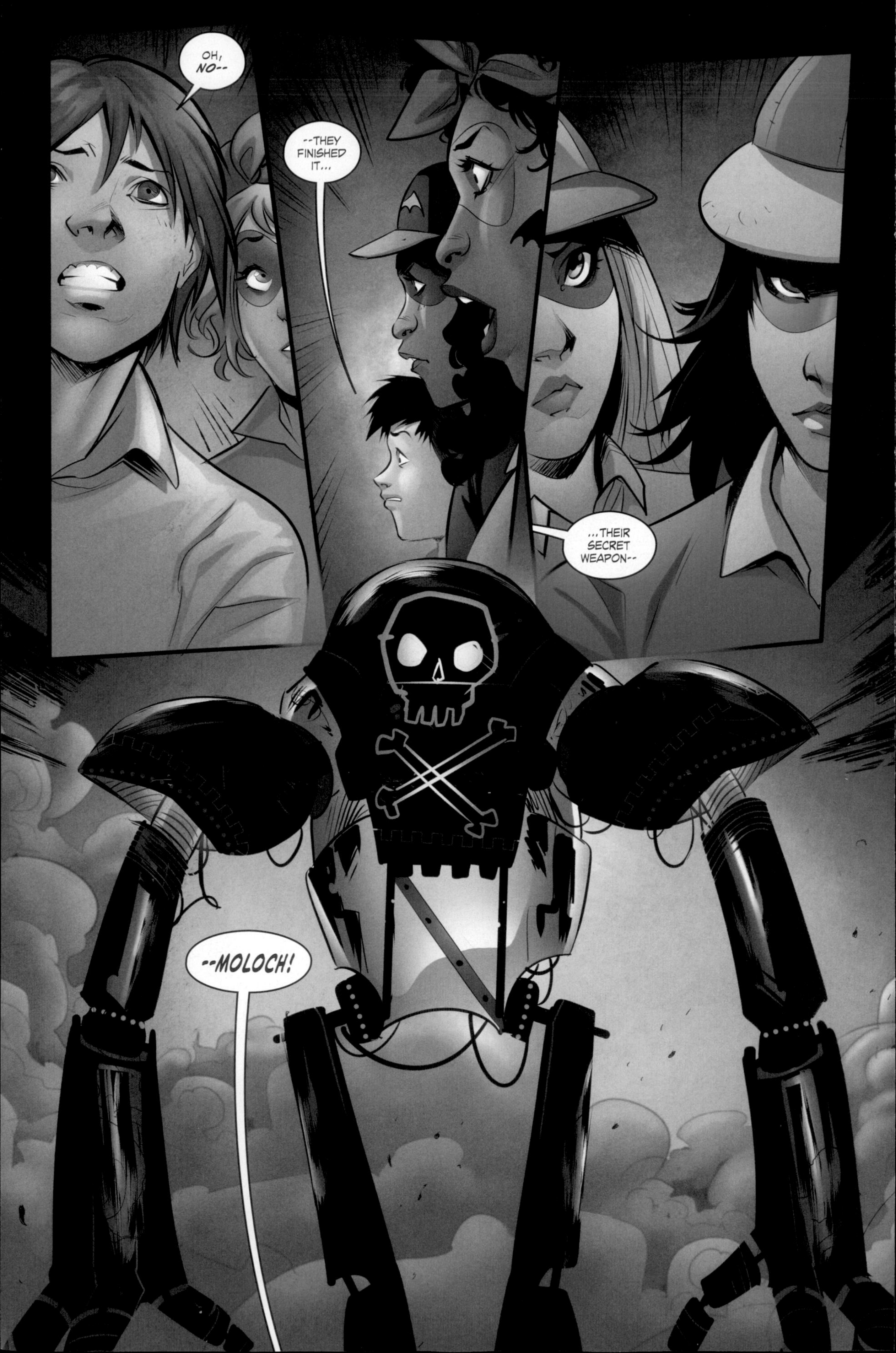
OH, NO--
--THEY FINISHED IT...
...THEIR SECRET WEAPON--
--MOLOCH!

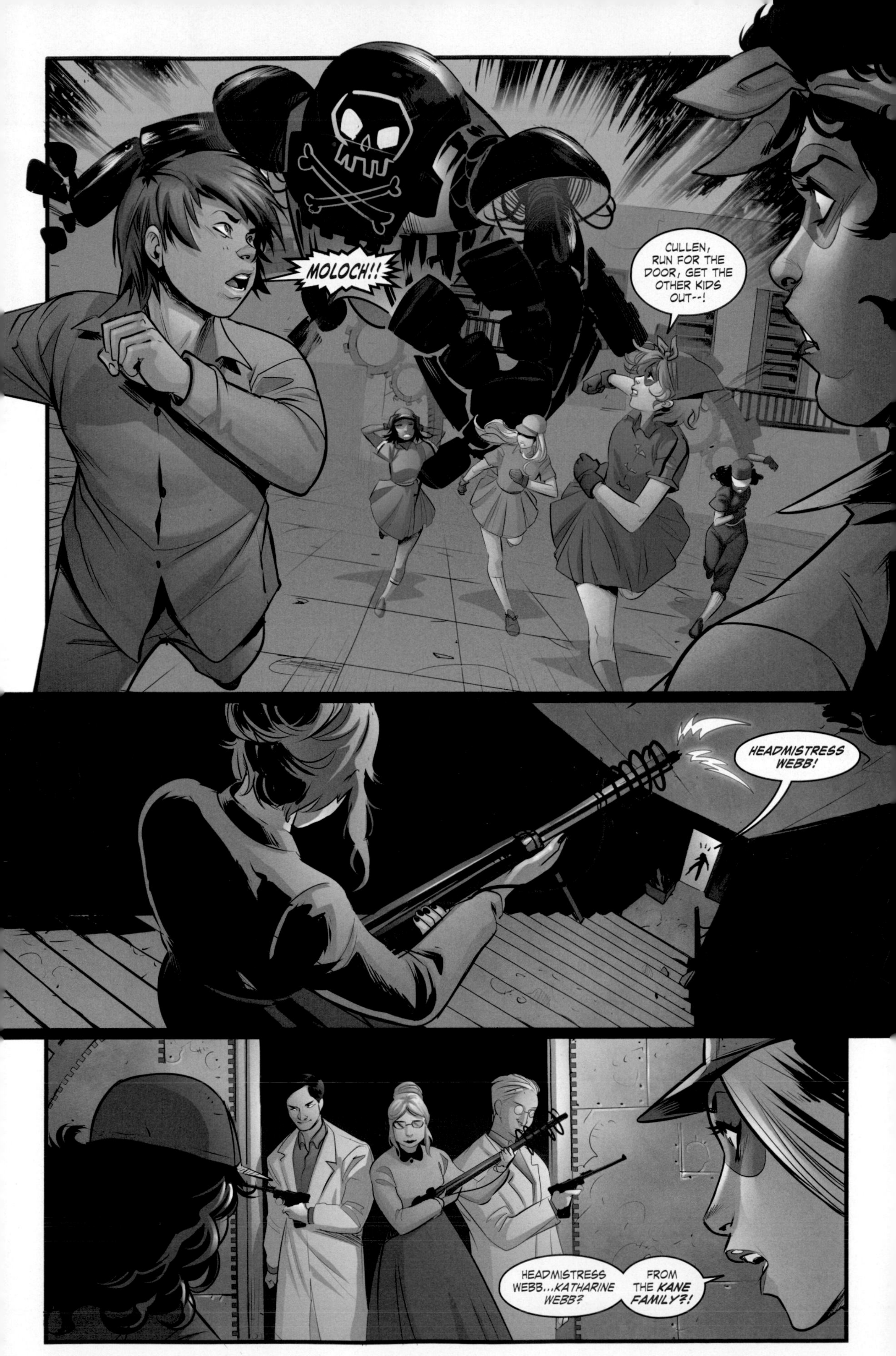
MOLOCH!!
CULLEN, RUN FOR THE DOOR, GET THE OTHER KIDS OUT--!
HEADMISTRESS WEBB!
HEADMISTRESS WEBB...KATHARINE WEBB?
FROM THE KANE FAMILY?!

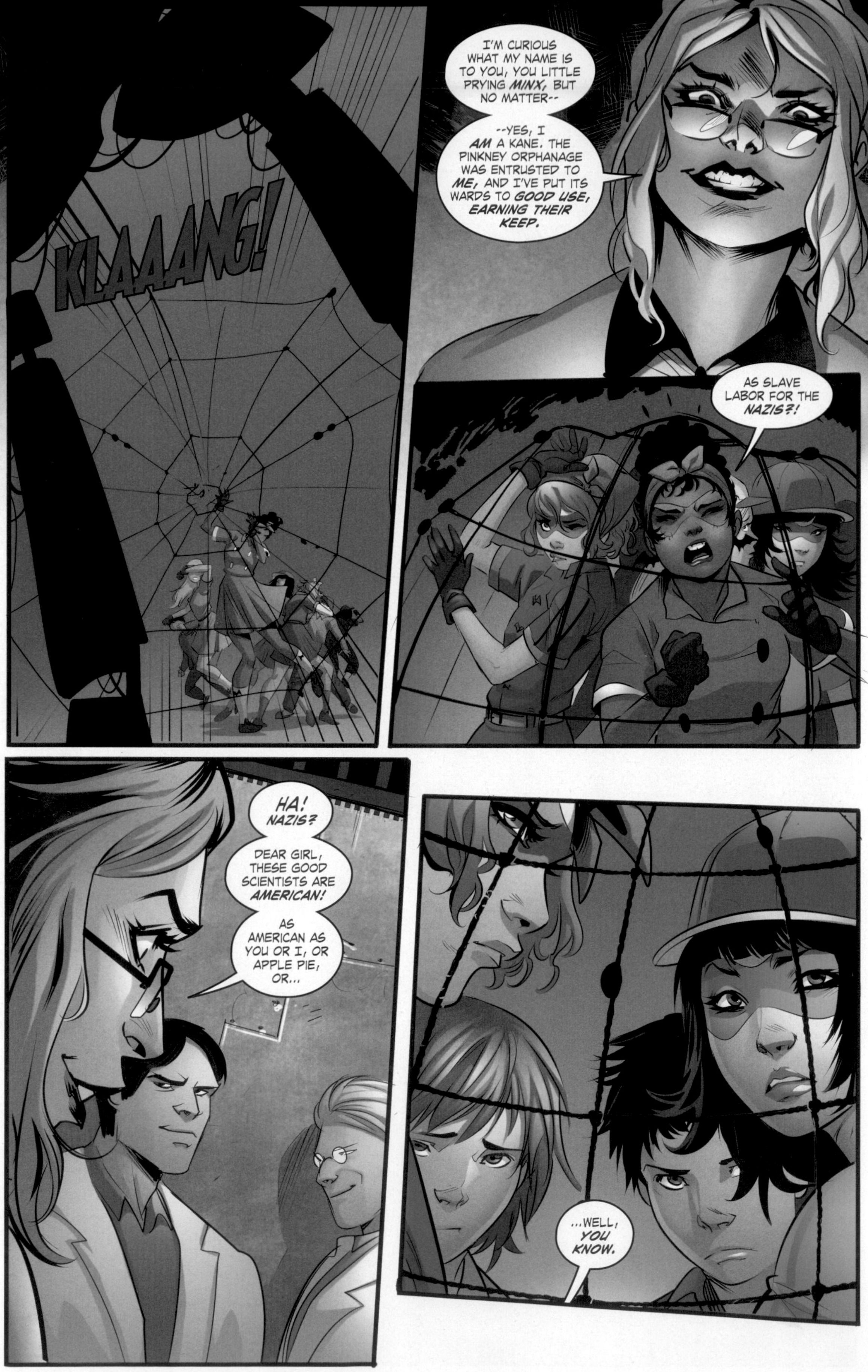
KLAAANG!
I'M CURIOUS WHAT MY NAME IS TO YOU, YOU LITTLE PRYING MINX, BUT NO MATTER--
--YES, I AM A KANE. THE PINKNEY ORPHANAGE WAS ENTRUSTED TO ME, AND I'VE PUT ITS WARDS TO GOOD USE, EARNING THEIR KEEP.
AS SLAVE LABOR FOR THE NAZIS?!
HA! NAZIS?
DEAR GIRL, THESE GOOD SCIENTISTS ARE AMERICAN!
AS AMERICAN AS YOU OR I, OR APPLE PIE, OR...
...WELL, YOU KNOW.

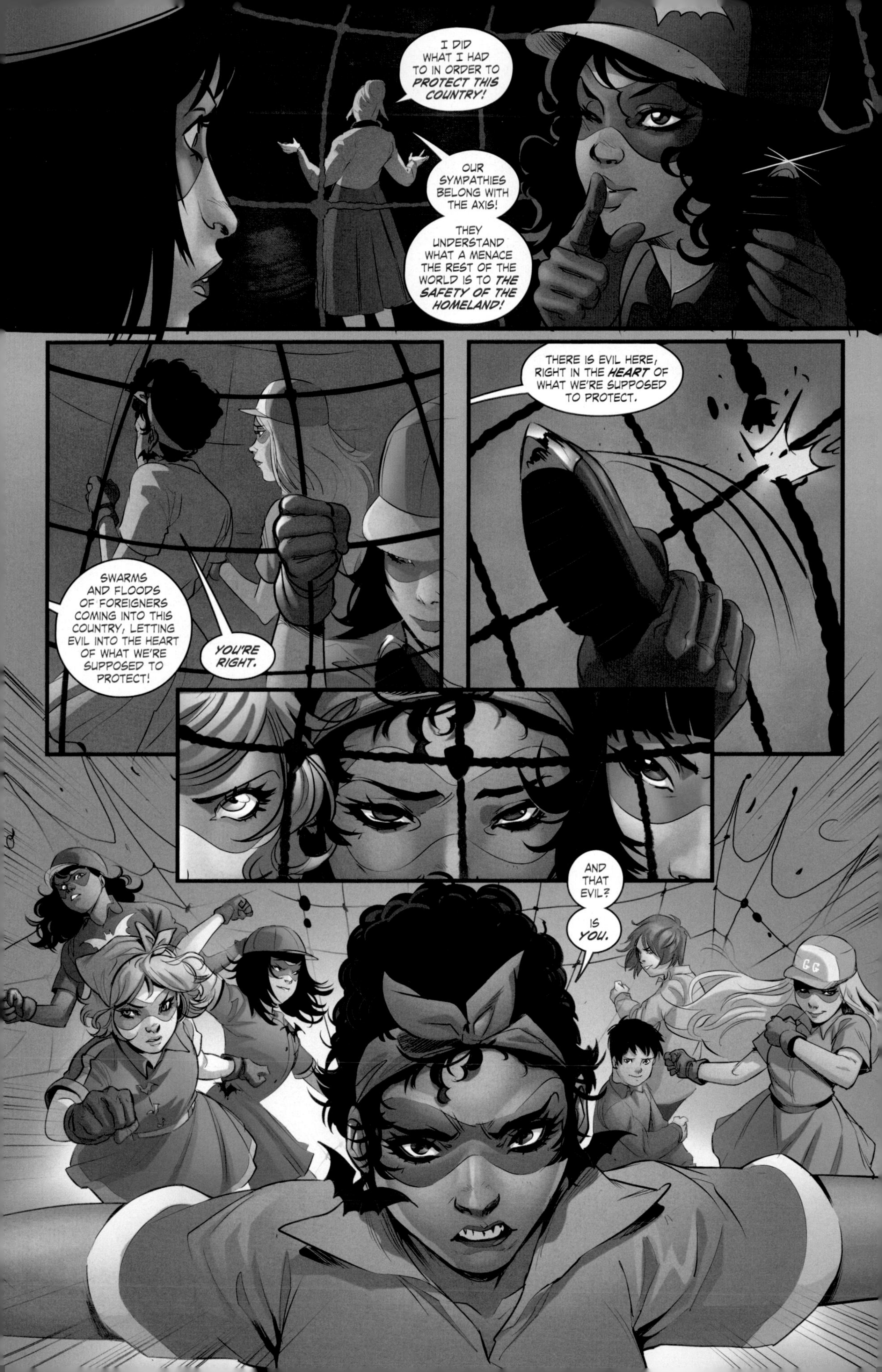
I DID WHAT I HAD TO IN ORDER TO PROTECT THIS COUNTRY!
OUR SYMPATHIES BELONG WITH THE AXIS!
THEY UNDERSTAND WHAT A MENACE THE REST OF THE WORLD IS TO THE SAFETY OF THE HOMELAND!
SWARMS AND FLOODS OF FOREIGNERS COMING INTO THIS COUNTRY, LETTING EVIL INTO THE HEART OF WHAT WE'RE SUPPOSED TO PROTECT!
YOU'RE RIGHT.
THERE IS EVIL HERE, RIGHT IN THE HEART OF WHAT WE'RE SUPPOSED TO PROTECT.
AND THAT EVIL?
IS YOU.

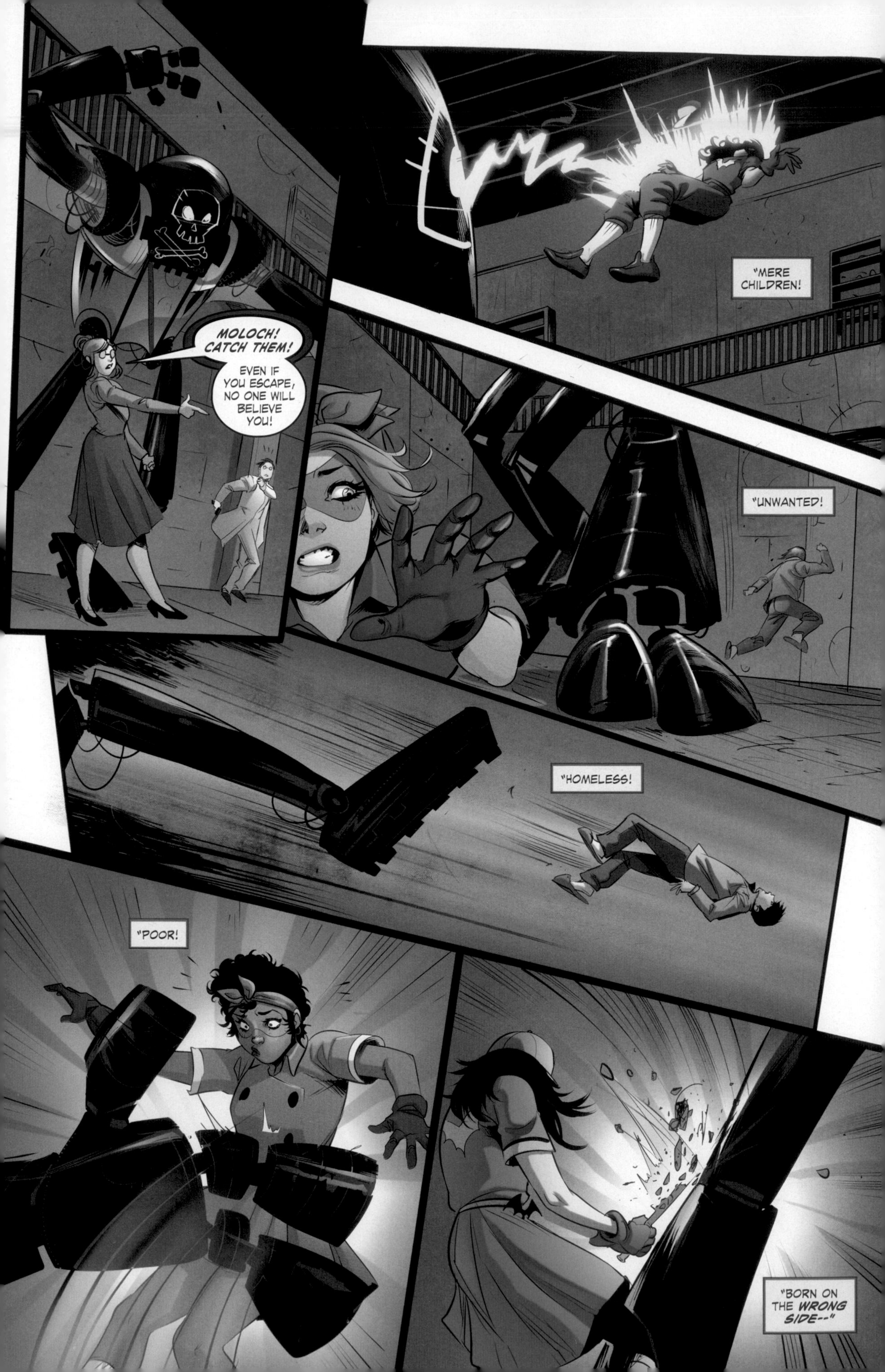
MOLOCH! CATCH THEM!
EVEN IF YOU ESCAPE, NO ONE WILL BELIEVE YOU!
"MERE CHILDREN!
"UNWANTED!
"HOMELESS!
"POOR!
"BORN ON THE WRONG SIDE--"

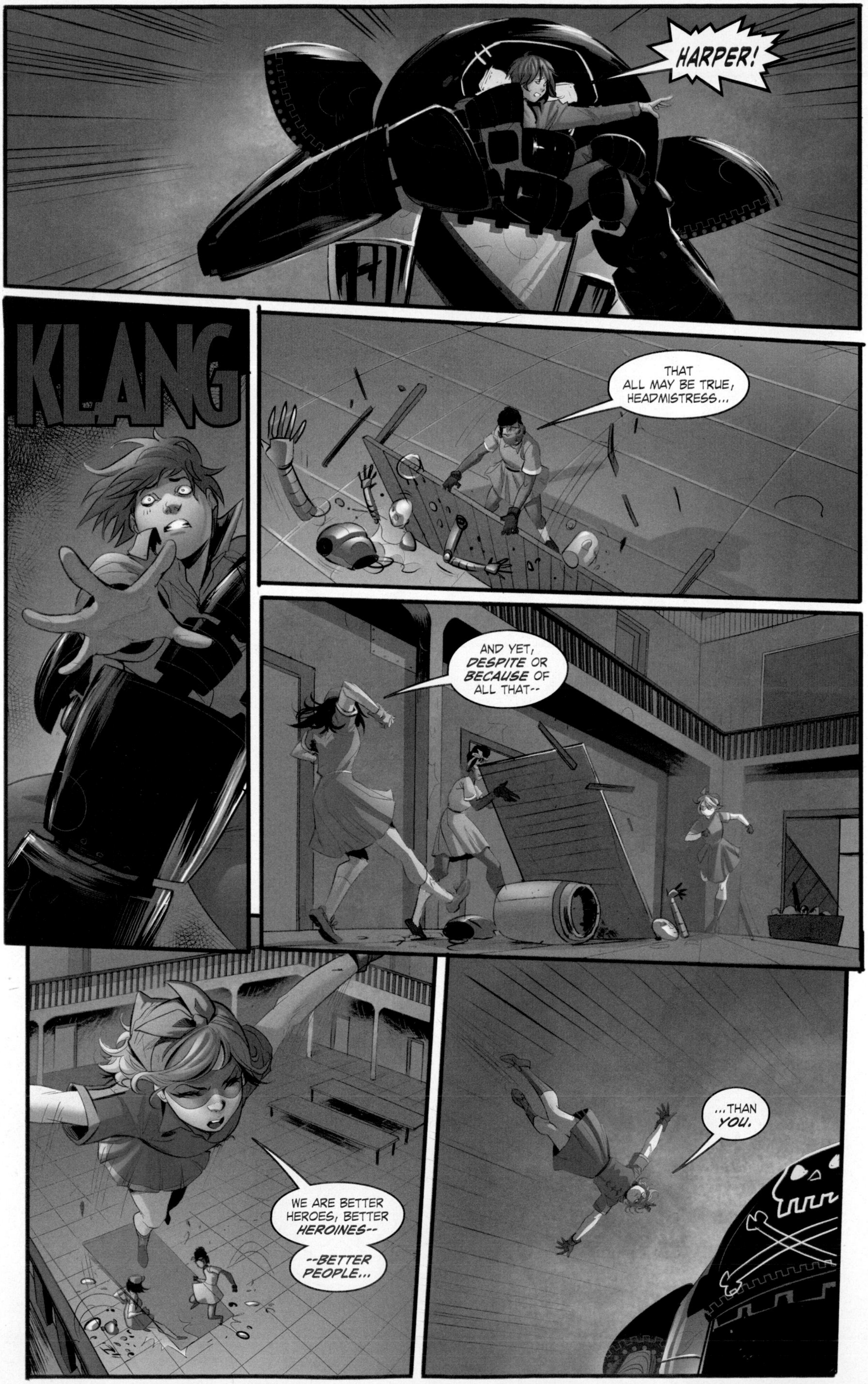
HARPER!
KLANG
THAT ALL MAY BE TRUE, HEADMISTRESS...
AND YET, DESPITE OR BECAUSE OF ALL THAT--
WE ARE BETTER HEROES, BETTER HEROINES--
--BETTER PEOPLE...
...THAN YOU.

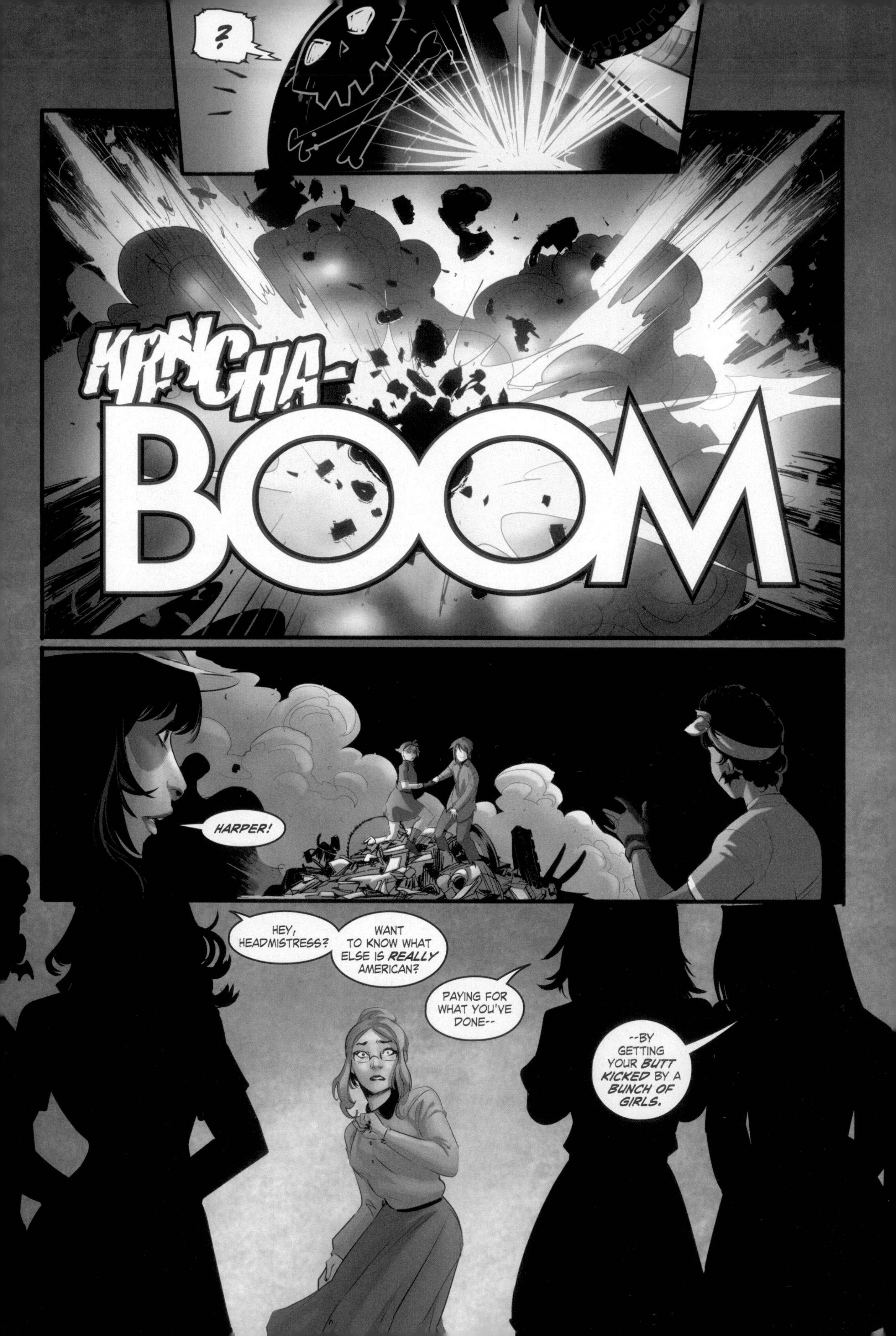
?
KRRCHA-
BOOM
HARPER!
HEY, HEADMISTRESS?
WANT TO KNOW WHAT ELSE IS *REALLY* AMERICAN?
PAYING FOR WHAT YOU'VE DONE--
--BY GETTING YOUR *BUTT KICKED* BY A *BUNCH OF GIRLS.*

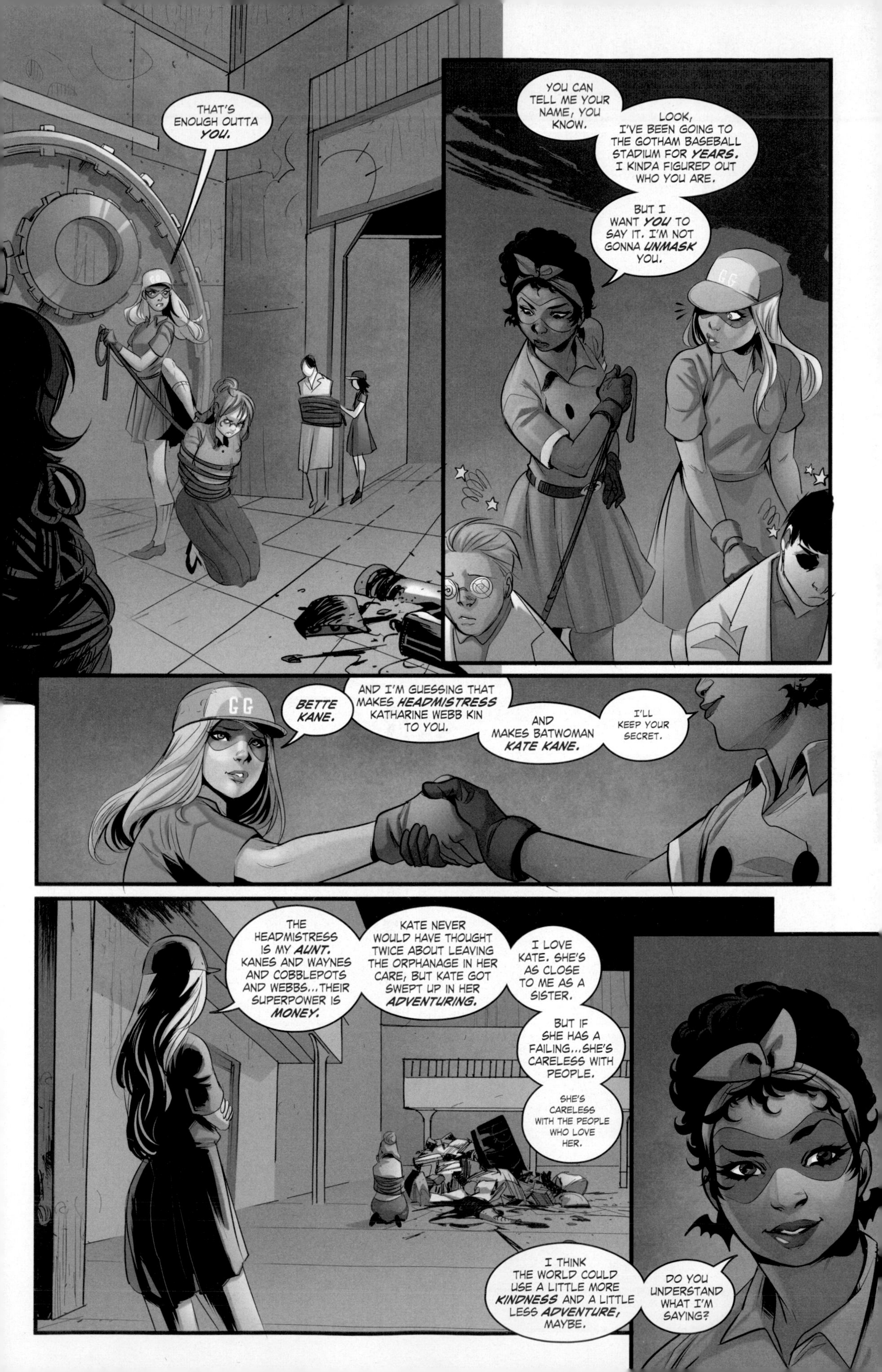
THAT'S ENOUGH OUTTA *YOU.*
YOU CAN TELL ME YOUR NAME, YOU KNOW.
LOOK, I'VE BEEN GOING TO THE GOTHAM BASEBALL STADIUM FOR *YEARS.* I KINDA FIGURED OUT WHO YOU ARE.
BUT I WANT *YOU* TO SAY IT. I'M NOT GONNA *UNMASK* YOU.
BETTE KANE.
AND I'M GUESSING THAT MAKES *HEADMISTRESS* KATHARINE WEBB KIN TO YOU.
AND MAKES BATWOMAN *KATE KANE.*
I'LL KEEP YOUR SECRET.
THE HEADMISTRESS IS MY *AUNT.* KANES AND WAYNES AND COBBLEPOTS AND WEBBS...THEIR SUPERPOWER IS *MONEY.*
KATE NEVER WOULD HAVE THOUGHT TWICE ABOUT LEAVING THE ORPHANAGE IN HER CARE, BUT KATE GOT SWEPT UP IN HER *ADVENTURING.*
I LOVE KATE. SHE'S AS CLOSE TO ME AS A SISTER.
BUT IF SHE HAS A FAILING...SHE'S CARELESS WITH PEOPLE.
SHE'S CARELESS WITH THE PEOPLE WHO LOVE HER.
I THINK THE WORLD COULD USE A LITTLE MORE *KINDNESS* AND A LITTLE LESS *ADVENTURE,* MAYBE.
DO YOU UNDERSTAND WHAT I'M SAYING?

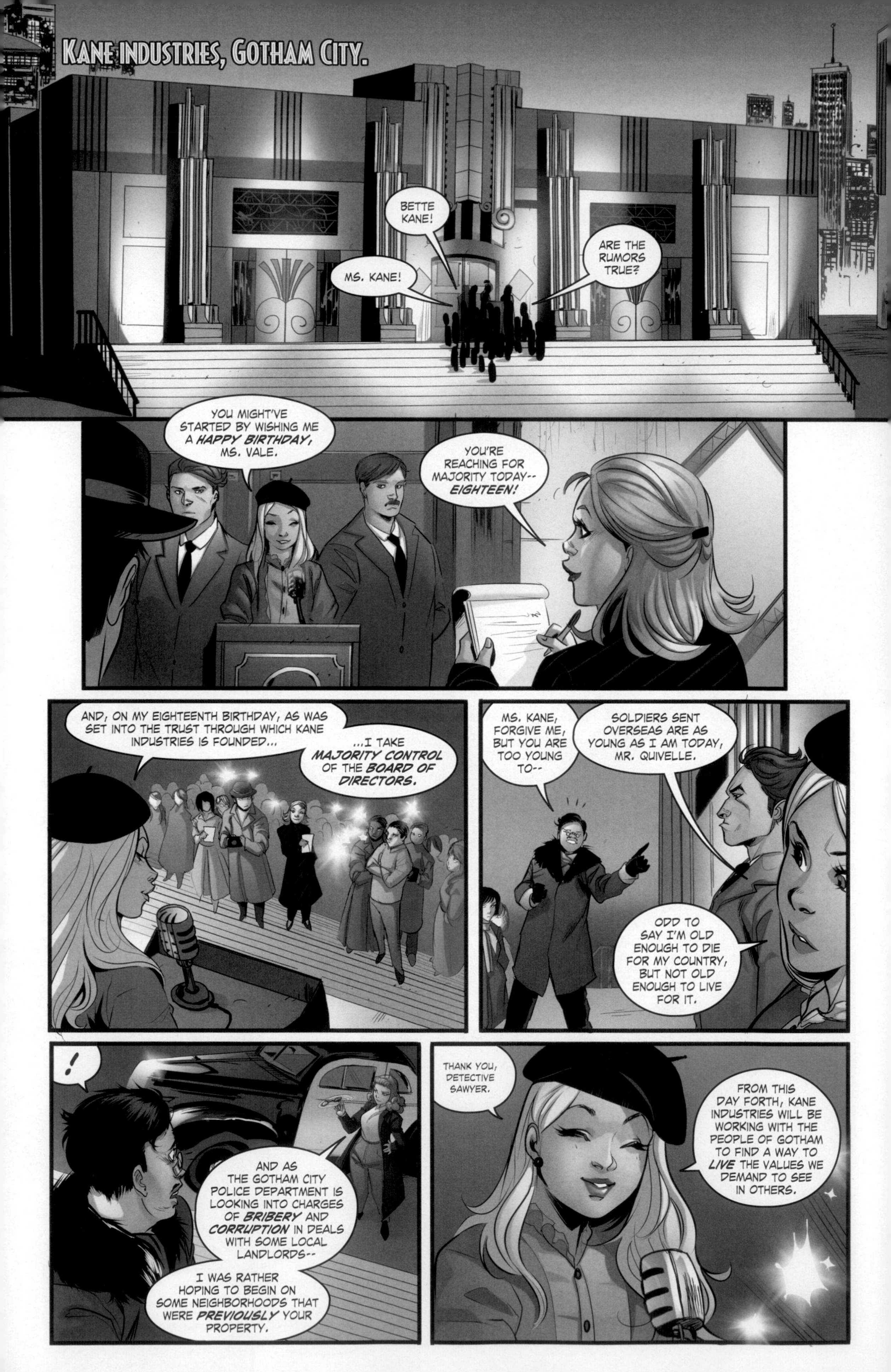
KANE INDUSTRIES, GOTHAM CITY.
BETTE KANE!
MS. KANE!
ARE THE RUMORS TRUE?
YOU MIGHT'VE STARTED BY WISHING ME A HAPPY BIRTHDAY, MS. VALE.
YOU'RE REACHING FOR MAJORITY TODAY-- EIGHTEEN!
AND, ON MY EIGHTEENTH BIRTHDAY, AS WAS SET INTO THE TRUST THROUGH WHICH KANE INDUSTRIES IS FOUNDED...
...I TAKE MAJORITY CONTROL OF THE BOARD OF DIRECTORS.
MS. KANE, FORGIVE ME, BUT YOU ARE TOO YOUNG TO--
SOLDIERS SENT OVERSEAS ARE AS YOUNG AS I AM TODAY, MR. QUIVELLE.
ODD TO SAY I'M OLD ENOUGH TO DIE FOR MY COUNTRY, BUT NOT OLD ENOUGH TO LIVE FOR IT.
!
AND AS THE GOTHAM CITY POLICE DEPARTMENT IS LOOKING INTO CHARGES OF BRIBERY AND CORRUPTION IN DEALS WITH SOME LOCAL LANDLORDS--
I WAS RATHER HOPING TO BEGIN ON SOME NEIGHBORHOODS THAT WERE PREVIOUSLY YOUR PROPERTY.
THANK YOU, DETECTIVE SAWYER.
FROM THIS DAY FORTH, KANE INDUSTRIES WILL BE WORKING WITH THE PEOPLE OF GOTHAM TO FIND A WAY TO LIVE THE VALUES WE DEMAND TO SEE IN OTHERS.

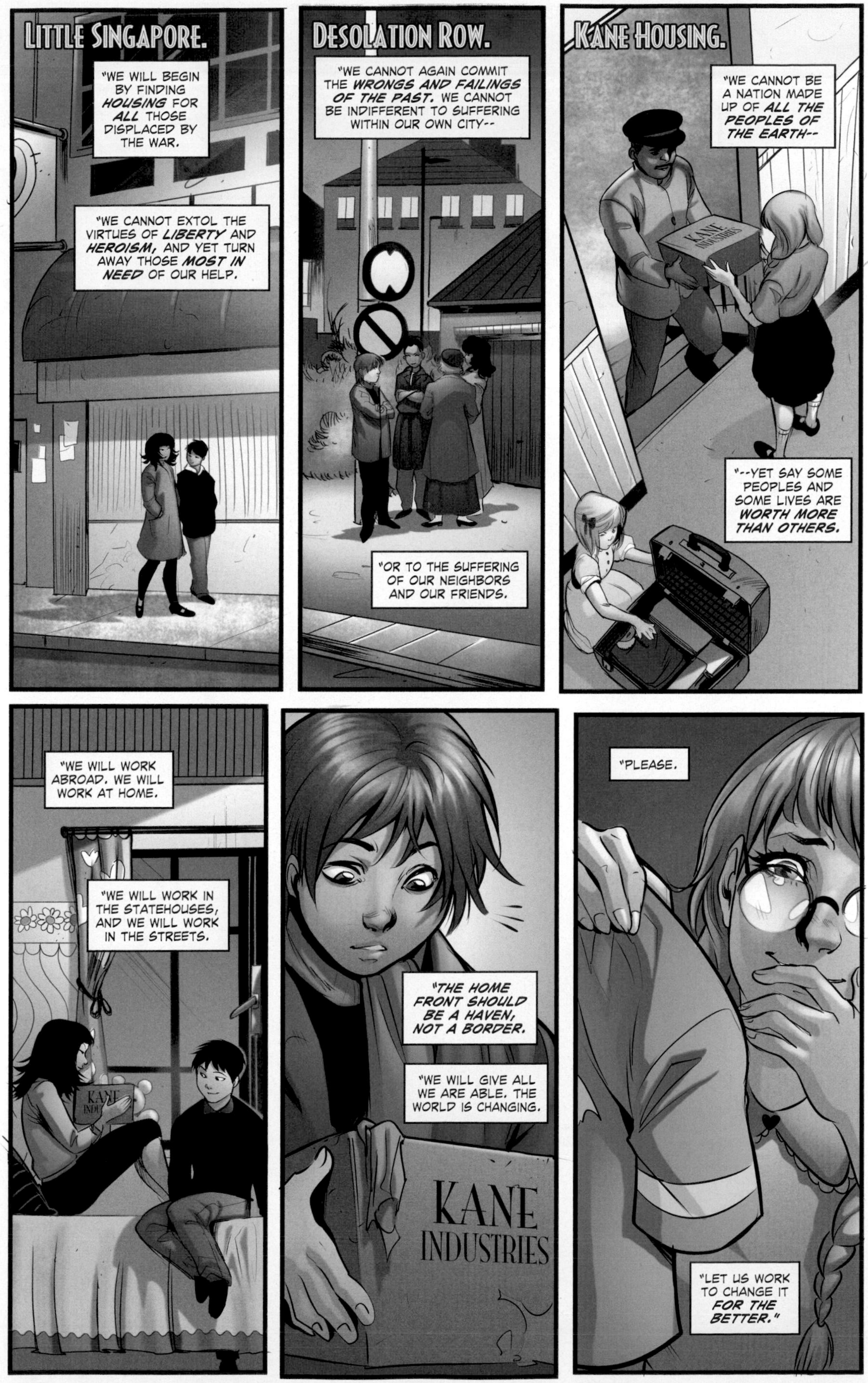
LITTLE SINGAPORE.
"WE WILL BEGIN BY FINDING *HOUSING* FOR *ALL* THOSE DISPLACED BY THE WAR.
"WE CANNOT EXTOL THE VIRTUES OF *LIBERTY* AND *HEROISM,* AND YET TURN AWAY THOSE *MOST IN NEED* OF OUR HELP.
DESOLATION ROW.
"WE CANNOT AGAIN COMMIT THE *WRONGS AND FAILINGS OF THE PAST.* WE CANNOT BE INDIFFERENT TO SUFFERING WITHIN OUR OWN CITY--
"OR TO THE SUFFERING OF OUR NEIGHBORS AND OUR FRIENDS.
KANE HOUSING.
"WE CANNOT BE A NATION MADE UP OF *ALL THE PEOPLES OF THE EARTH--*
KANE INDUSTRIES
"--YET SAY SOME PEOPLES AND SOME LIVES ARE *WORTH MORE THAN OTHERS.*
"WE WILL WORK ABROAD. WE WILL WORK AT HOME.
"WE WILL WORK IN THE STATEHOUSES, AND WE WILL WORK IN THE STREETS.
"THE HOME FRONT SHOULD BE A HAVEN, NOT A BORDER.
"WE WILL GIVE ALL WE ARE ABLE. THE WORLD IS CHANGING.
KANE INDUSTRIES
"PLEASE.
"LET US WORK TO CHANGE IT *FOR THE BETTER."*

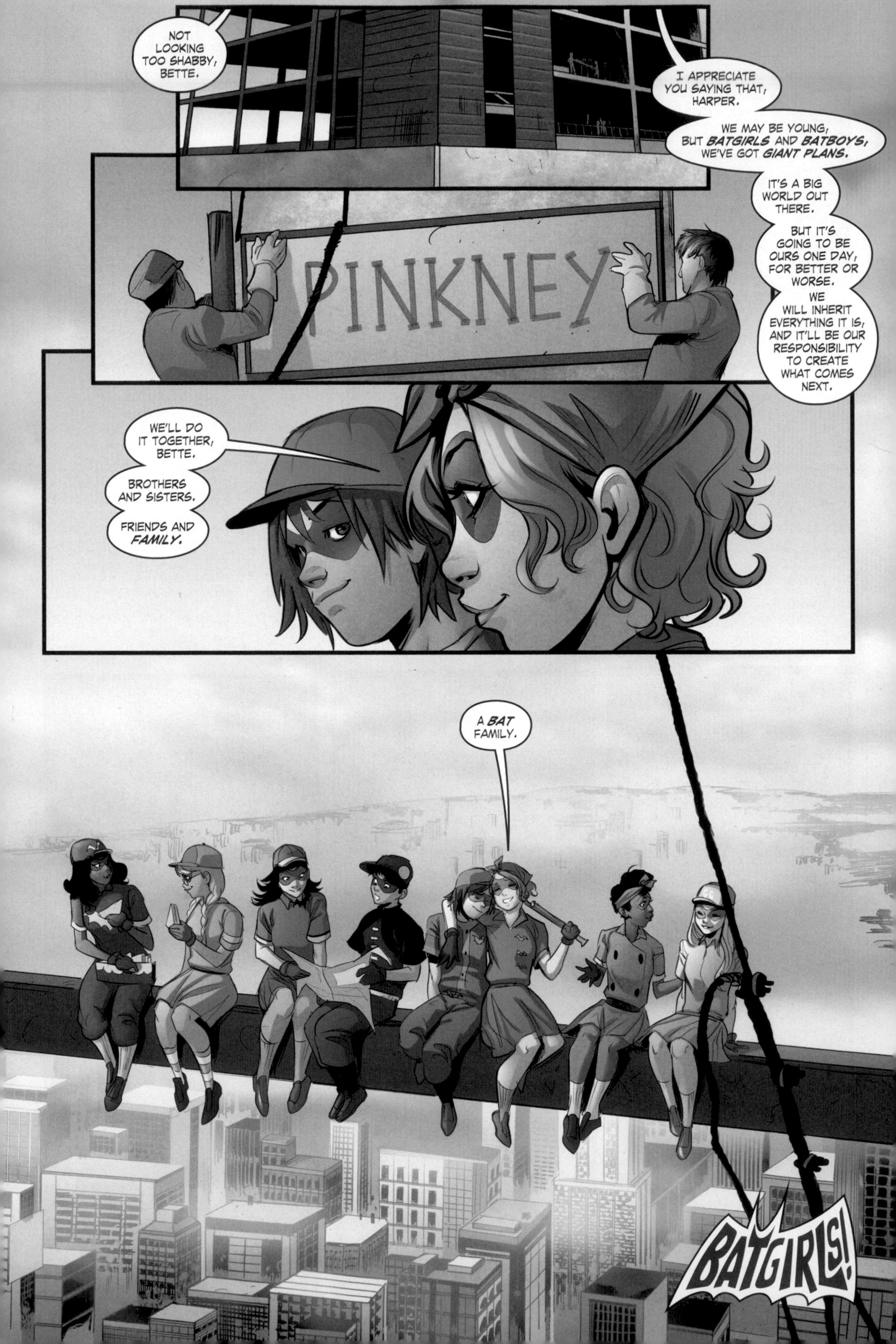
NOT LOOKING TOO SHABBY, BETTE.
I APPRECIATE YOU SAYING THAT, HARPER.
WE MAY BE YOUNG, BUT BATGIRLS AND BATBOYS, WE'VE GOT GIANT PLANS.
IT'S A BIG WORLD OUT THERE.
BUT IT'S GOING TO BE OURS ONE DAY, FOR BETTER OR WORSE.
WE WILL INHERIT EVERYTHING IT IS, AND IT'LL BE OUR RESPONSIBILITY TO CREATE WHAT COMES NEXT.
PINKNEY
WE'LL DO IT TOGETHER, BETTE.
BROTHERS AND SISTERS.
FRIENDS AND FAMILY.
A BAT FAMILY.
BATGIRLS!

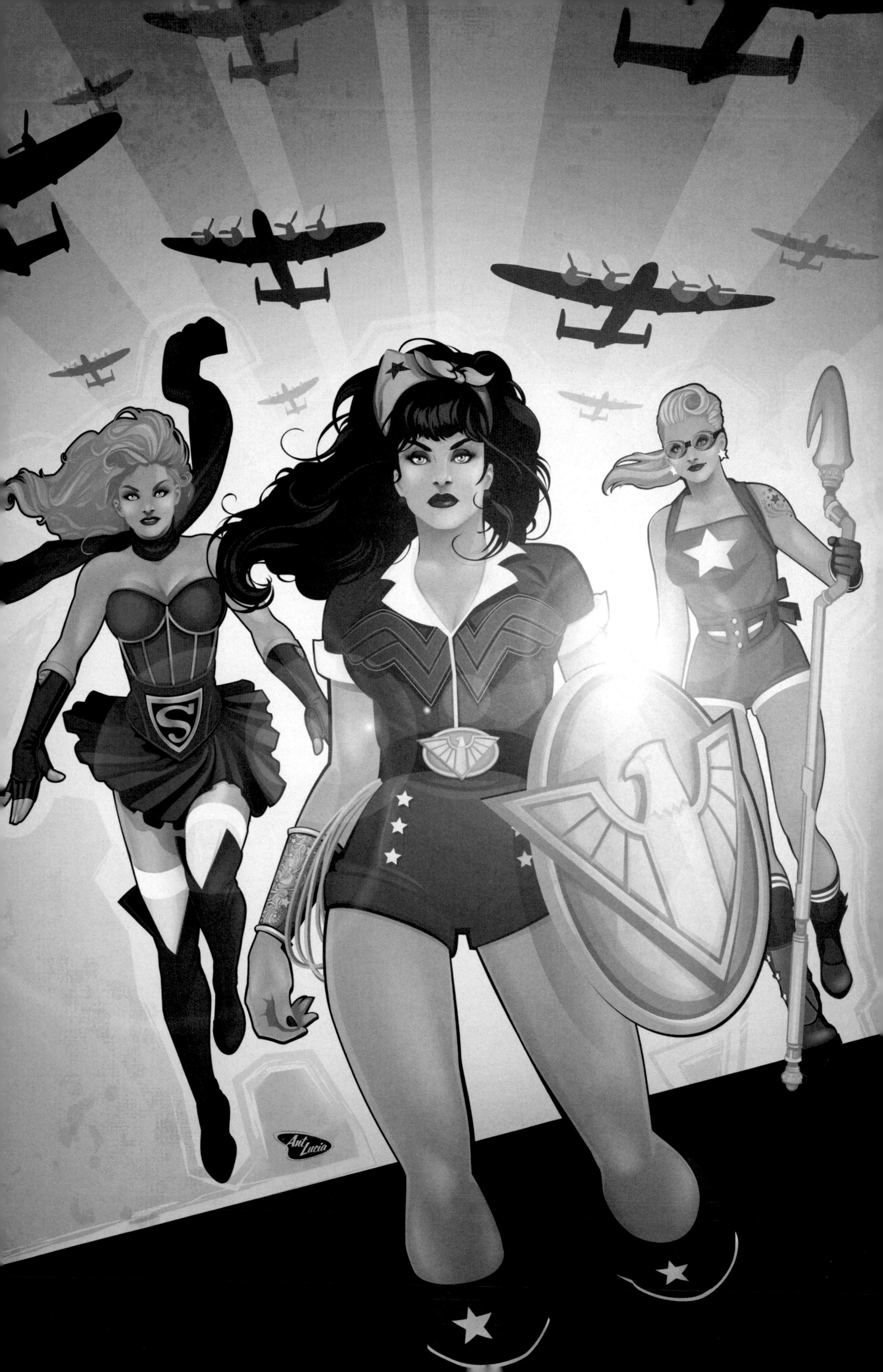
Ant Lucia

ALLIES
PART TWO

MARGUERITE BENNETT
Writer

**LAURA BRAGA
SANDY JARRELL
M.L. SANAPO
JUAN ALBARRAN**
Artists

**J. NANJAN
KELLY FITZPATRICK**
Colorists

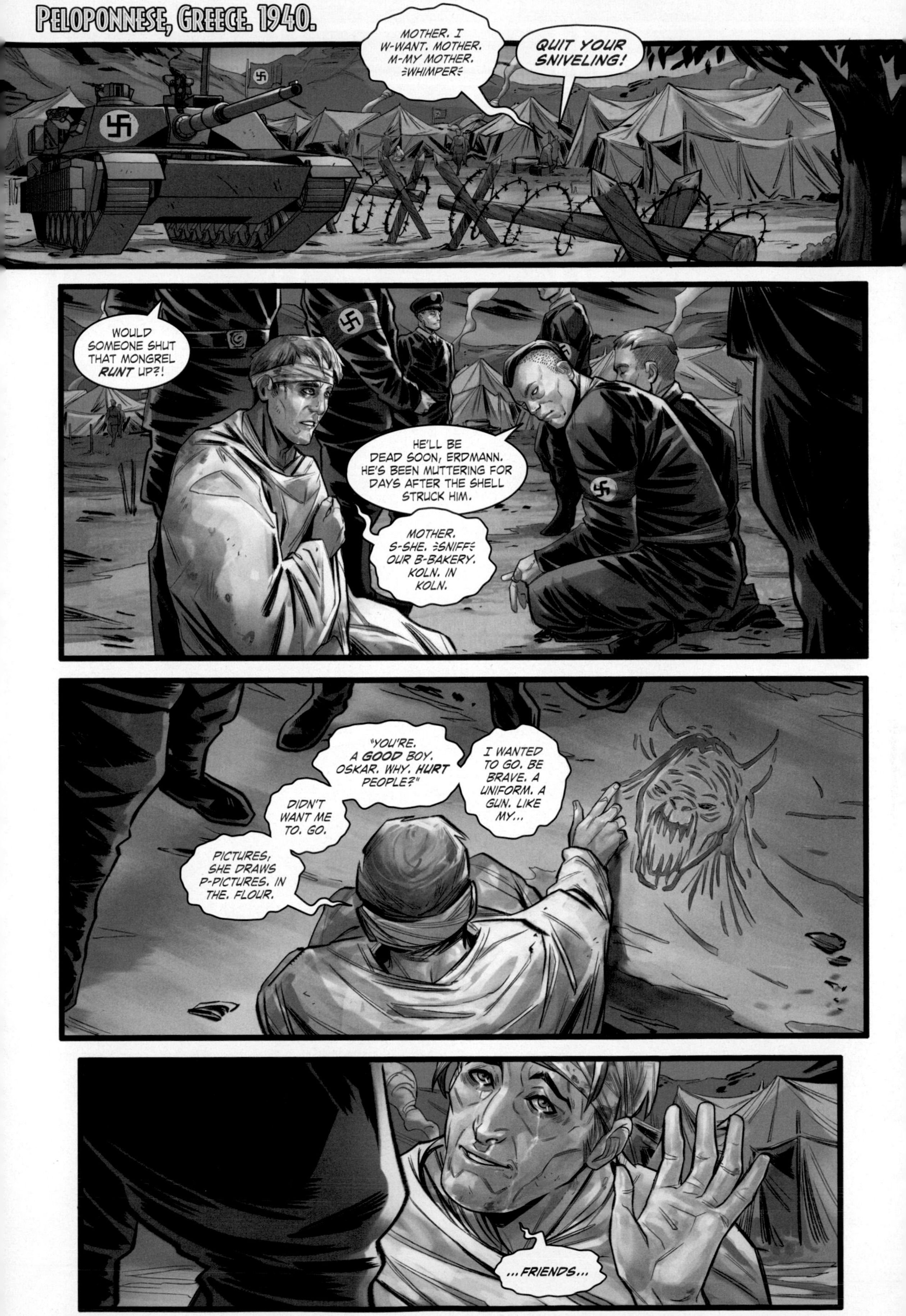
PELOPONNESE, GREECE. 1940.
MOTHER. I W-WANT. MOTHER. M-MY MOTHER. =WHIMPER=
QUIT YOUR SNIVELING!
WOULD SOMEONE SHUT THAT MONGREL RUNT UP?!
HE'LL BE DEAD SOON, ERDMANN. HE'S BEEN MUTTERING FOR DAYS AFTER THE SHELL STRUCK HIM.
MOTHER. S-SHE. =SNIFF= OUR B-BAKERY. KOLN. IN KOLN.
"YOU'RE. A GOOD BOY. OSKAR. WHY. HURT PEOPLE?"
I WANTED TO GO. BE BRAVE. A UNIFORM. A GUN. LIKE MY...
DIDN'T WANT ME TO. GO.
PICTURES, SHE DRAWS P-PICTURES. IN THE. FLOUR.
...FRIENDS...

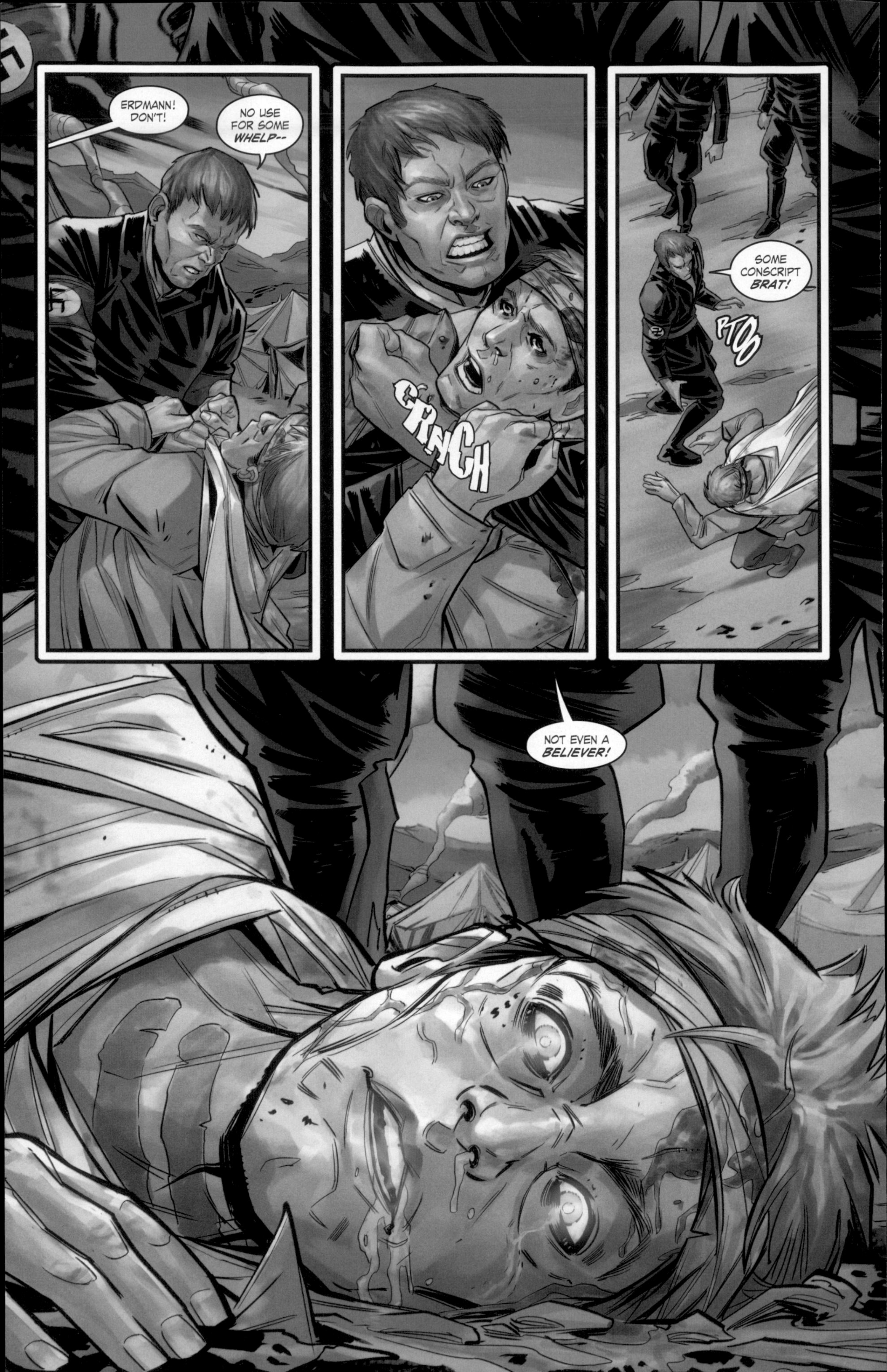
ERDMANN! DON'T!
NO USE FOR SOME WHELP--
CRNCH
SOME CONSCRIPT BRAT!
PTOO
NOT EVEN A BELIEVER!

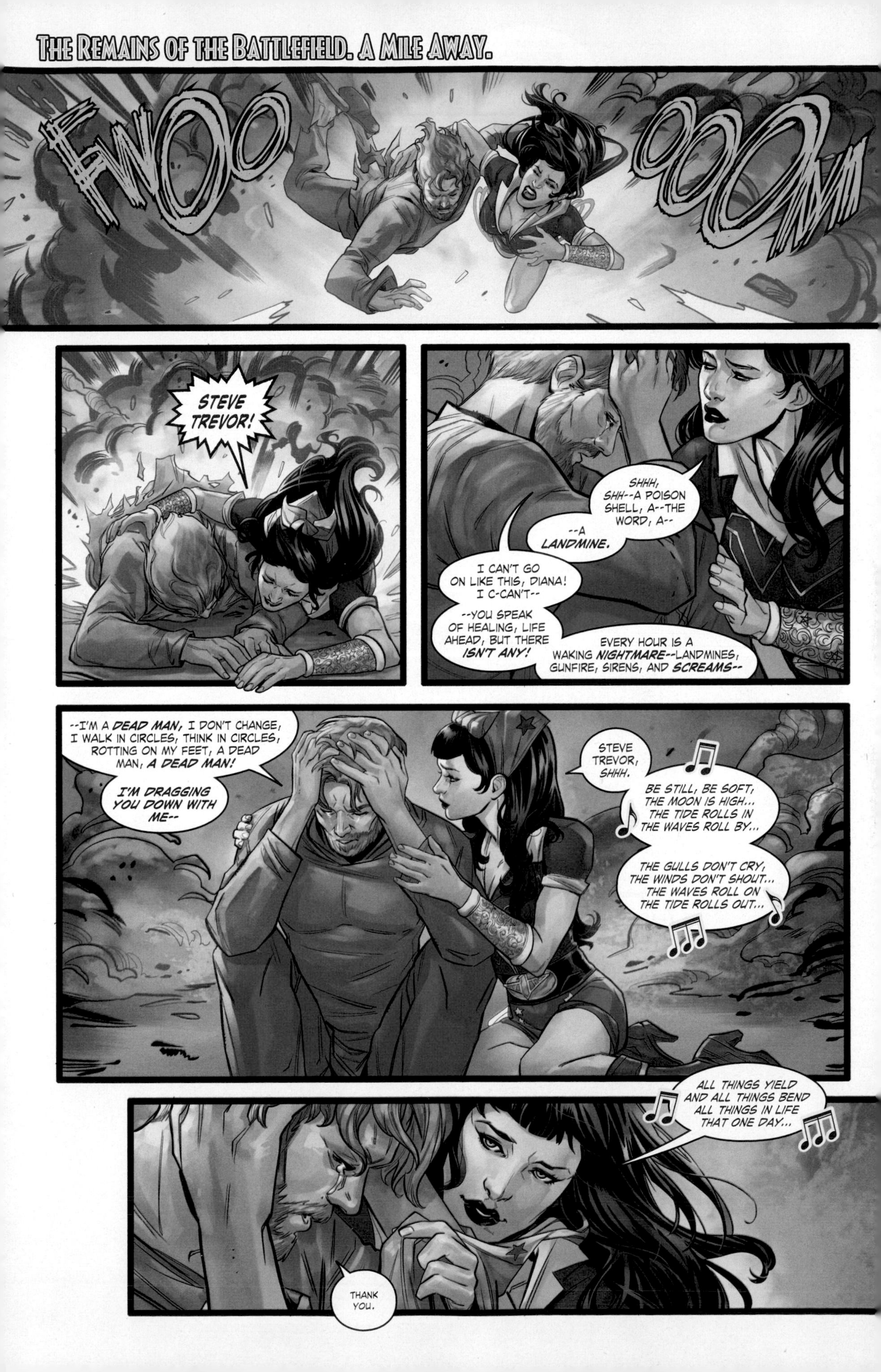
THE REMAINS OF THE BATTLEFIELD. A MILE AWAY.
FWOOOOOOOM
STEVE TREVOR!
SHHH, SHH--A POISON SHELL, A--THE WORD, A--
--A LANDMINE.
I CAN'T GO ON LIKE THIS, DIANA! I C-CAN'T--
--YOU SPEAK OF HEALING, LIFE AHEAD, BUT THERE ISN'T ANY!
EVERY HOUR IS A WAKING NIGHTMARE--LANDMINES, GUNFIRE, SIRENS, AND SCREAMS--
--I'M A DEAD MAN, I DON'T CHANGE, I WALK IN CIRCLES, THINK IN CIRCLES, ROTTING ON MY FEET, A DEAD MAN, A DEAD MAN!
I'M DRAGGING YOU DOWN WITH ME--
STEVE TREVOR, SHHH.
BE STILL, BE SOFT, THE MOON IS HIGH... THE TIDE ROLLS IN THE WAVES ROLL BY...
THE GULLS DON'T CRY, THE WINDS DON'T SHOUT... THE WAVES ROLL ON THE TIDE ROLLS OUT...
ALL THINGS YIELD AND ALL THINGS BEND ALL THINGS IN LIFE THAT ONE DAY...
THANK YOU.

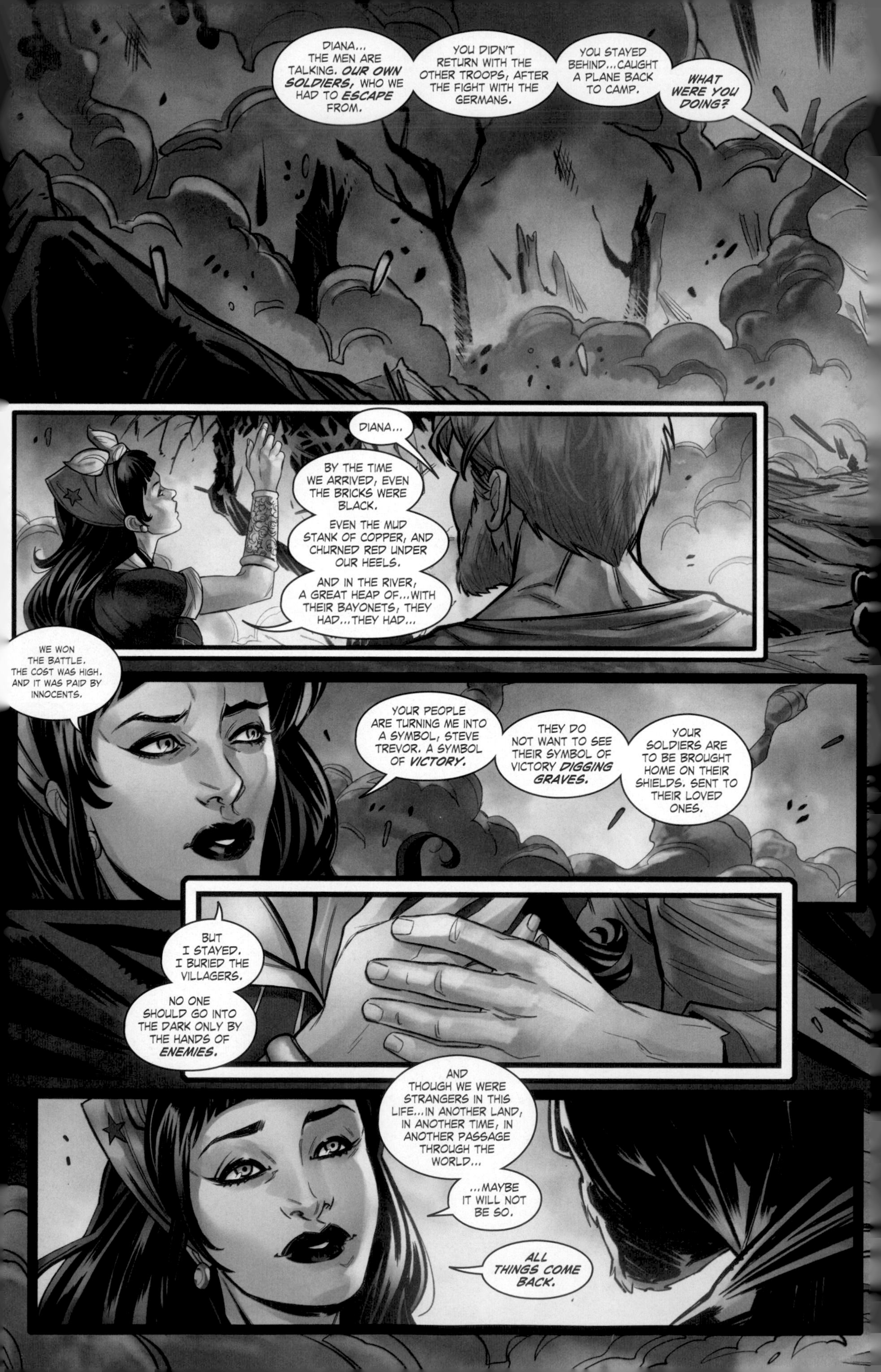
DIANA... THE MEN ARE TALKING. OUR OWN SOLDIERS, WHO WE HAD TO ESCAPE FROM.
YOU DIDN'T RETURN WITH THE OTHER TROOPS, AFTER THE FIGHT WITH THE GERMANS.
YOU STAYED BEHIND...CAUGHT A PLANE BACK TO CAMP.
WHAT WERE YOU DOING?
DIANA...
BY THE TIME WE ARRIVED, EVEN THE BRICKS WERE BLACK.
EVEN THE MUD STANK OF COPPER, AND CHURNED RED UNDER OUR HEELS.
AND IN THE RIVER, A GREAT HEAP OF...WITH THEIR BAYONETS, THEY HAD...THEY HAD...
WE WON THE BATTLE. THE COST WAS HIGH. AND IT WAS PAID BY INNOCENTS.
YOUR PEOPLE ARE TURNING ME INTO A SYMBOL, STEVE TREVOR. A SYMBOL OF VICTORY.
THEY DO NOT WANT TO SEE THEIR SYMBOL OF VICTORY DIGGING GRAVES.
YOUR SOLDIERS ARE TO BE BROUGHT HOME ON THEIR SHIELDS. SENT TO THEIR LOVED ONES.
BUT I STAYED. I BURIED THE VILLAGERS.
NO ONE SHOULD GO INTO THE DARK ONLY BY THE HANDS OF ENEMIES.
AND THOUGH WE WERE STRANGERS IN THIS LIFE...IN ANOTHER LAND, IN ANOTHER TIME, IN ANOTHER PASSAGE THROUGH THE WORLD...
...MAYBE IT WILL NOT BE SO.
ALL THINGS COME BACK.

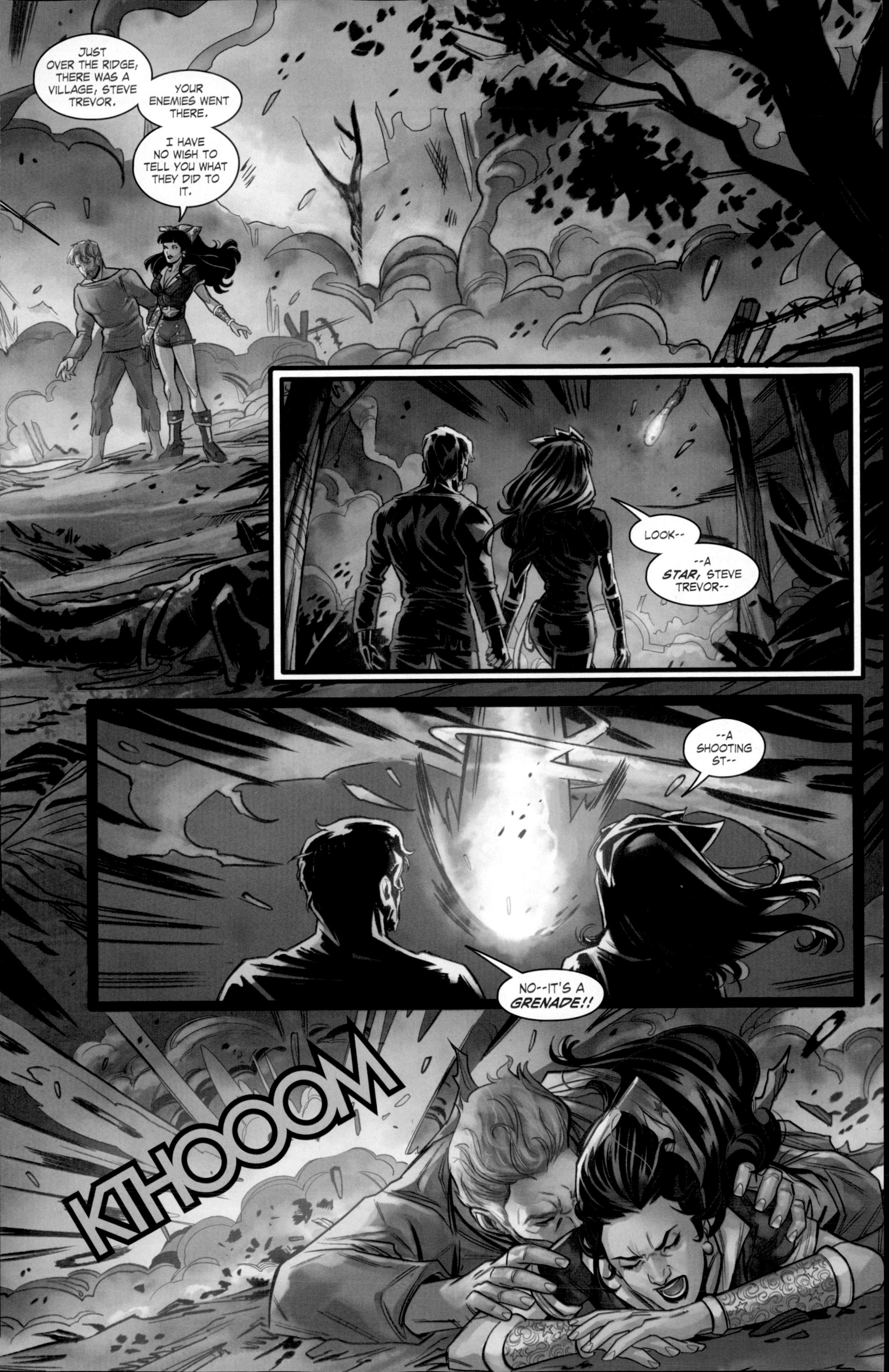
JUST OVER THE RIDGE, THERE WAS A VILLAGE, STEVE TREVOR.
YOUR ENEMIES WENT THERE.
I HAVE NO WISH TO TELL YOU WHAT THEY DID TO IT.
LOOK--
--A STAR, STEVE TREVOR--
--A SHOOTING ST--
NO--IT'S A GRENADE!!
KTHOOOM

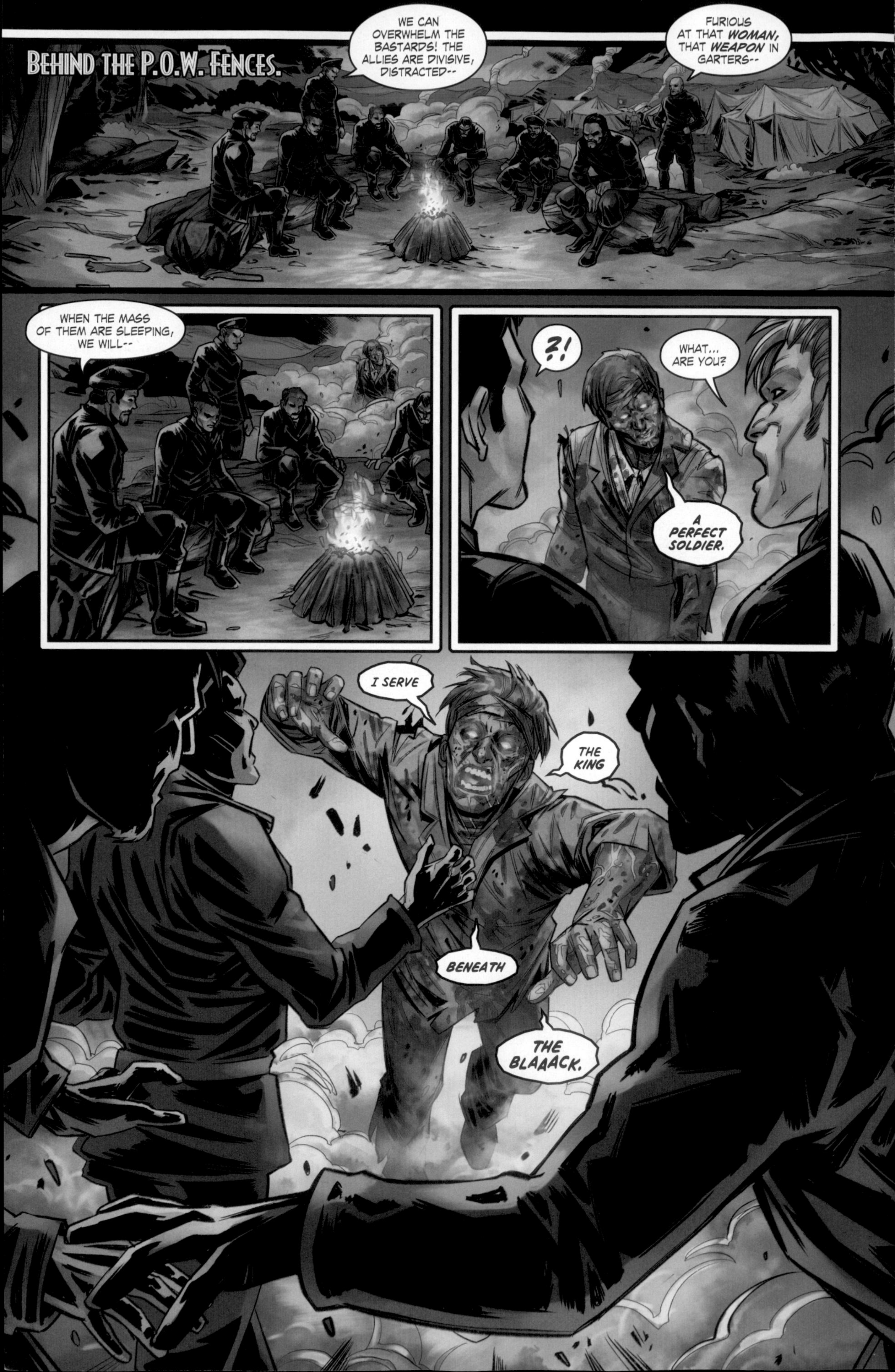
BEHIND THE P.O.W. FENCES.
WE CAN OVERWHELM THE BASTARDS! THE ALLIES ARE DIVISIVE, DISTRACTED--
FURIOUS AT THAT WOMAN, THAT WEAPON IN GARTERS--
WHEN THE MASS OF THEM ARE SLEEPING, WE WILL--
?!
WHAT... ARE YOU?
A PERFECT SOLDIER.
I SERVE
THE KING
BENEATH
THE BLAAACK.

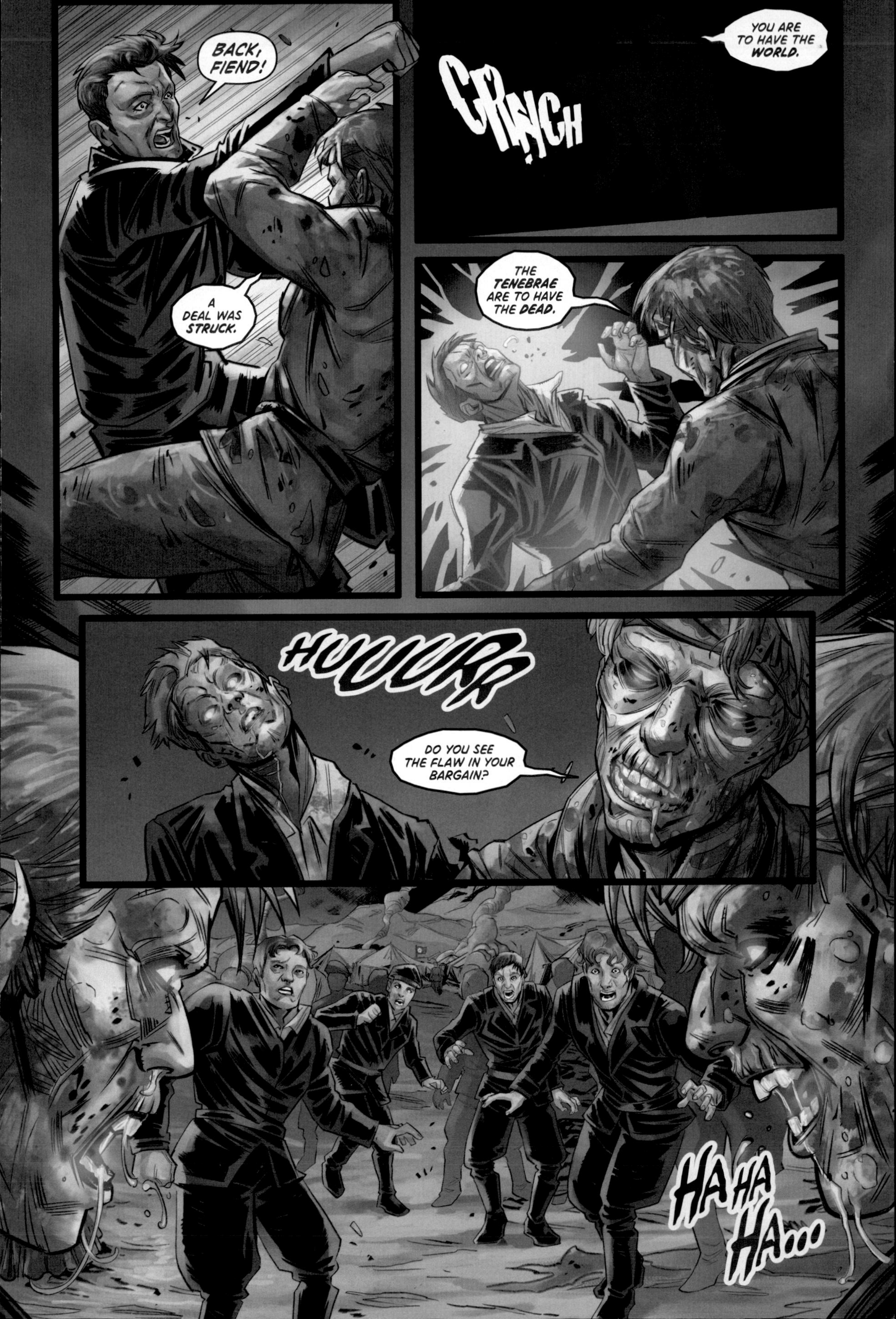
BACK, FIEND!
A DEAL WAS STRUCK.
CRNCH
YOU ARE TO HAVE THE WORLD.
THE TENEBRAE ARE TO HAVE THE DEAD.
HUUURR
DO YOU SEE THE FLAW IN YOUR BARGAIN?
HA HA HA...

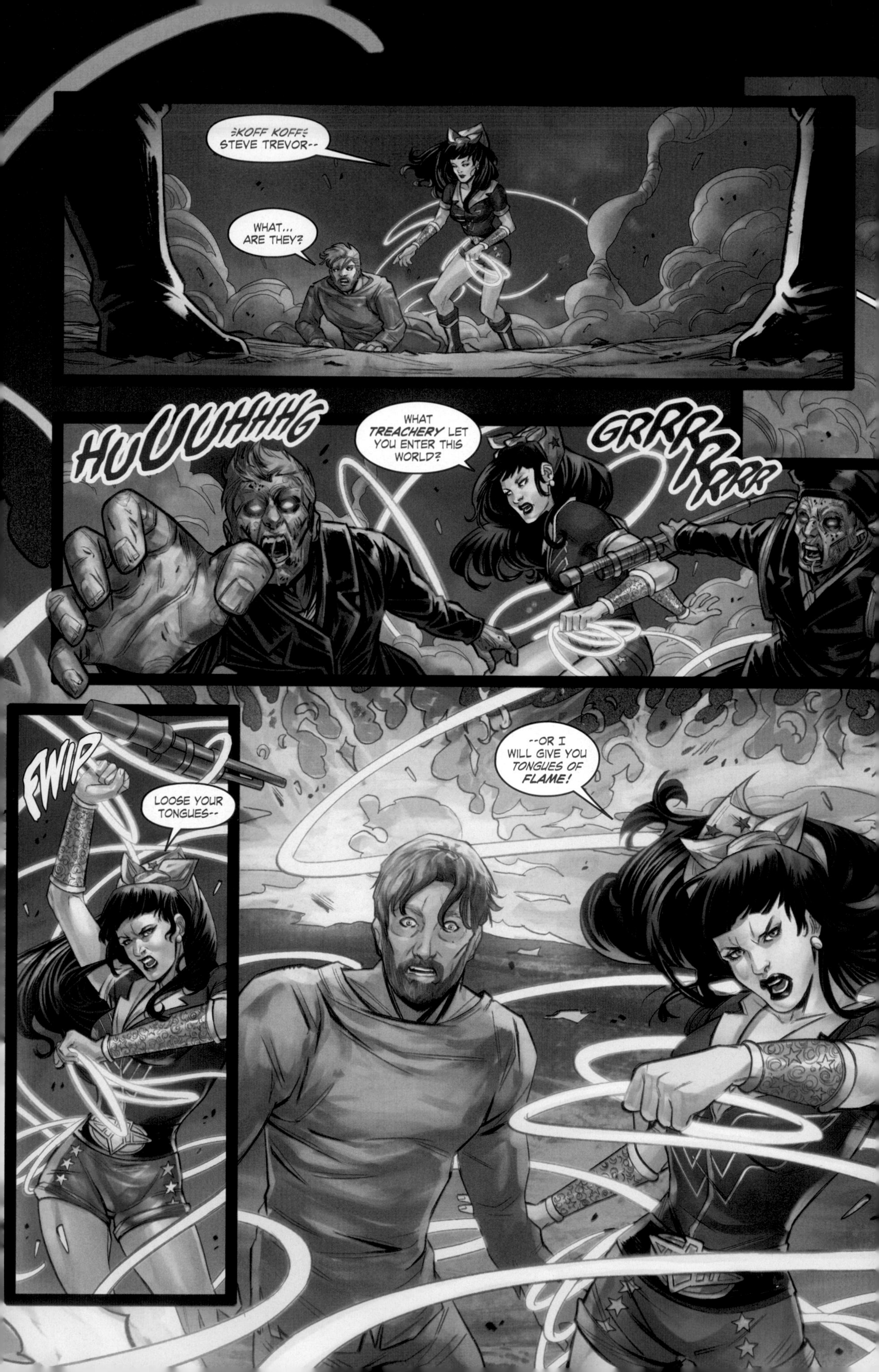

KOFF KOFF
STEVE TREVOR--
WHAT... ARE THEY?
HUUUHHHG
WHAT **TREACHERY** LET YOU ENTER THIS WORLD?
GRRRRRRR
FWIP
LOOSE YOUR TONGUES--
--OR I WILL GIVE YOU **TONGUES OF FLAME!**

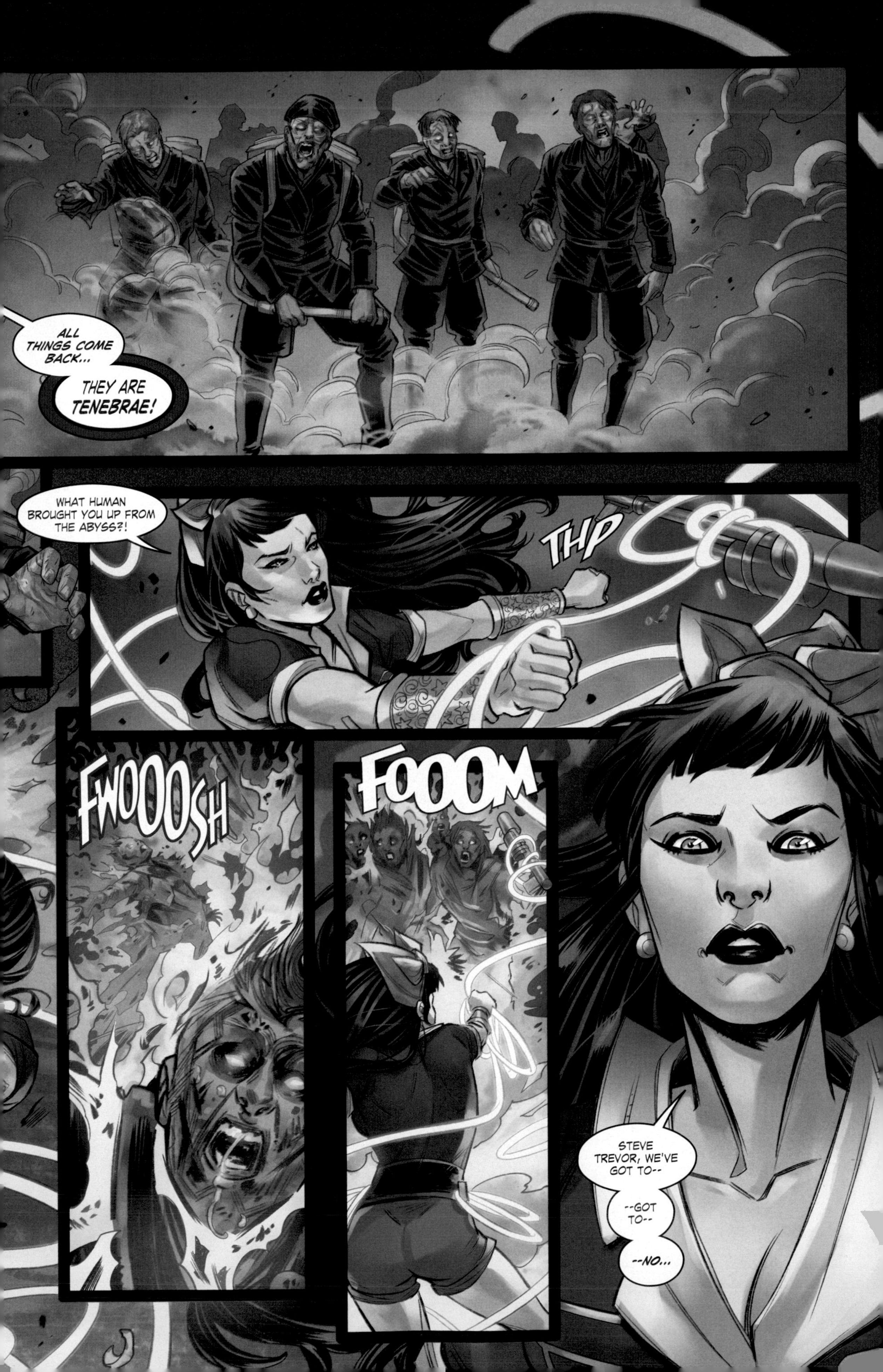
ALL THINGS COME BACK...
THEY ARE TENEBRAE!
WHAT HUMAN BROUGHT YOU UP FROM THE ABYSS?!
THP
FWOOOSH
FOOOM
STEVE TREVOR, WE'VE GOT TO--
--GOT TO--
--NO...

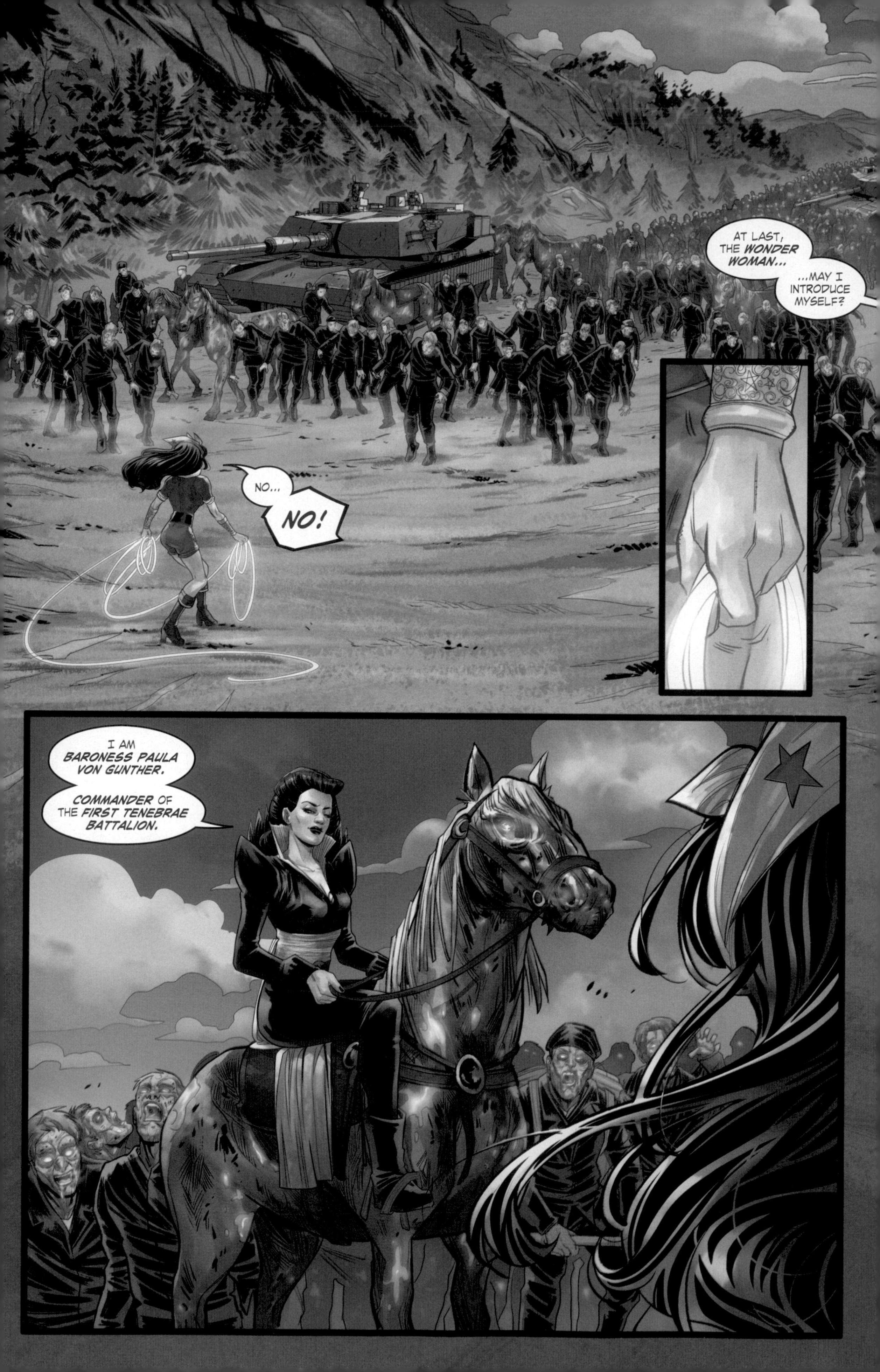
AT LAST, THE WONDER WOMAN...
...MAY I INTRODUCE MYSELF?
NO...
NO!
I AM BARONESS PAULA VON GUNTHER.
COMMANDER OF THE FIRST TENEBRAE BATTALION.
...

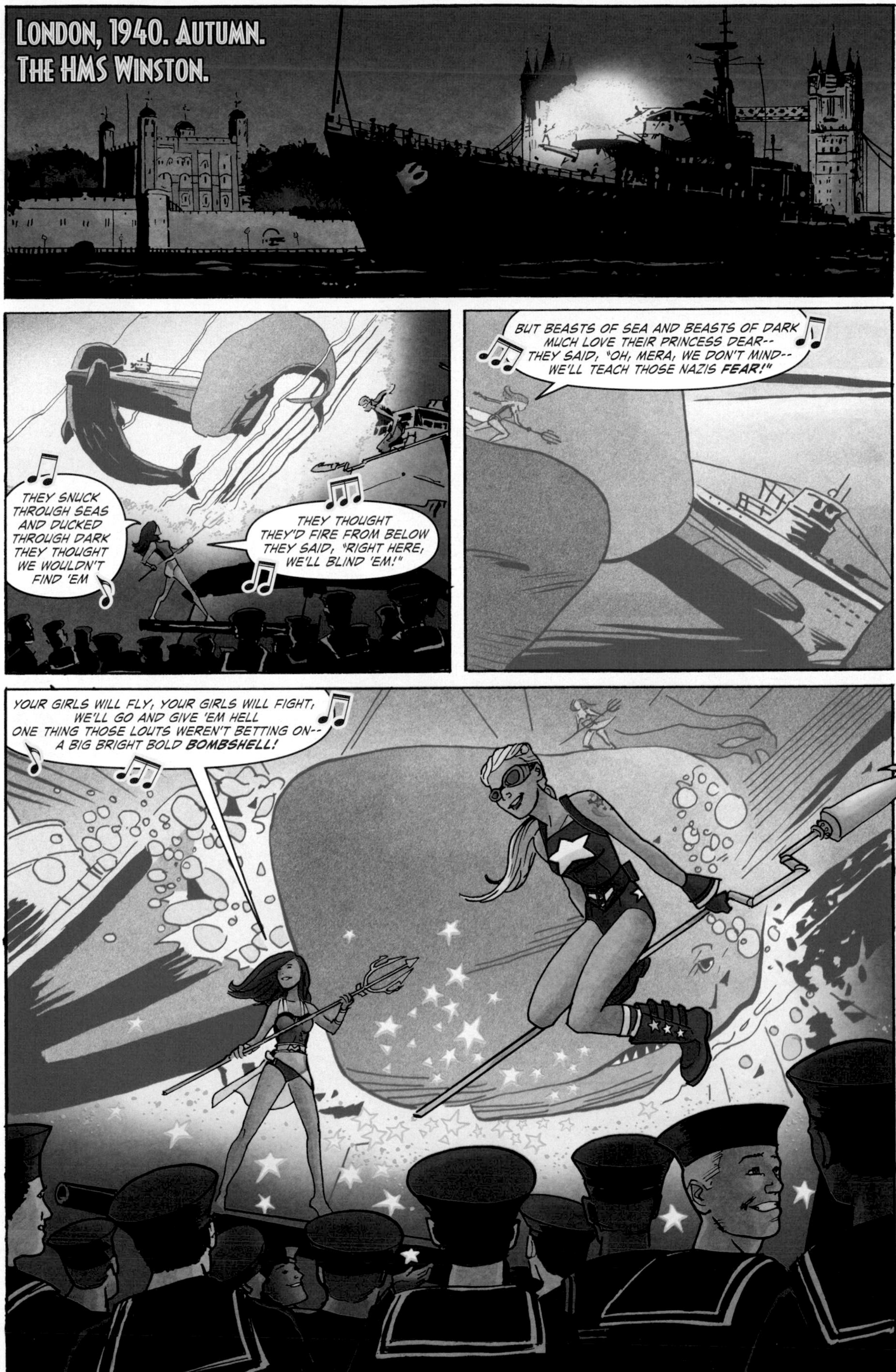
LONDON, 1940. AUTUMN.
THE HMS WINSTON.
THEY SNUCK THROUGH SEAS AND DUCKED THROUGH DARK THEY THOUGHT WE WOULDN'T FIND 'EM
THEY THOUGHT THEY'D FIRE FROM BELOW THEY SAID, "RIGHT HERE, WE'LL BLIND 'EM!"
BUT BEASTS OF SEA AND BEASTS OF DARK MUCH LOVE THEIR PRINCESS DEAR-- THEY SAID, "OH, MERA, WE DON'T MIND-- WE'LL TEACH THOSE NAZIS FEAR!"
YOUR GIRLS WILL FLY, YOUR GIRLS WILL FIGHT, WE'LL GO AND GIVE 'EM HELL ONE THING THOSE LOUTS WEREN'T BETTING ON-- A BIG BRIGHT BOLD BOMBSHELL!

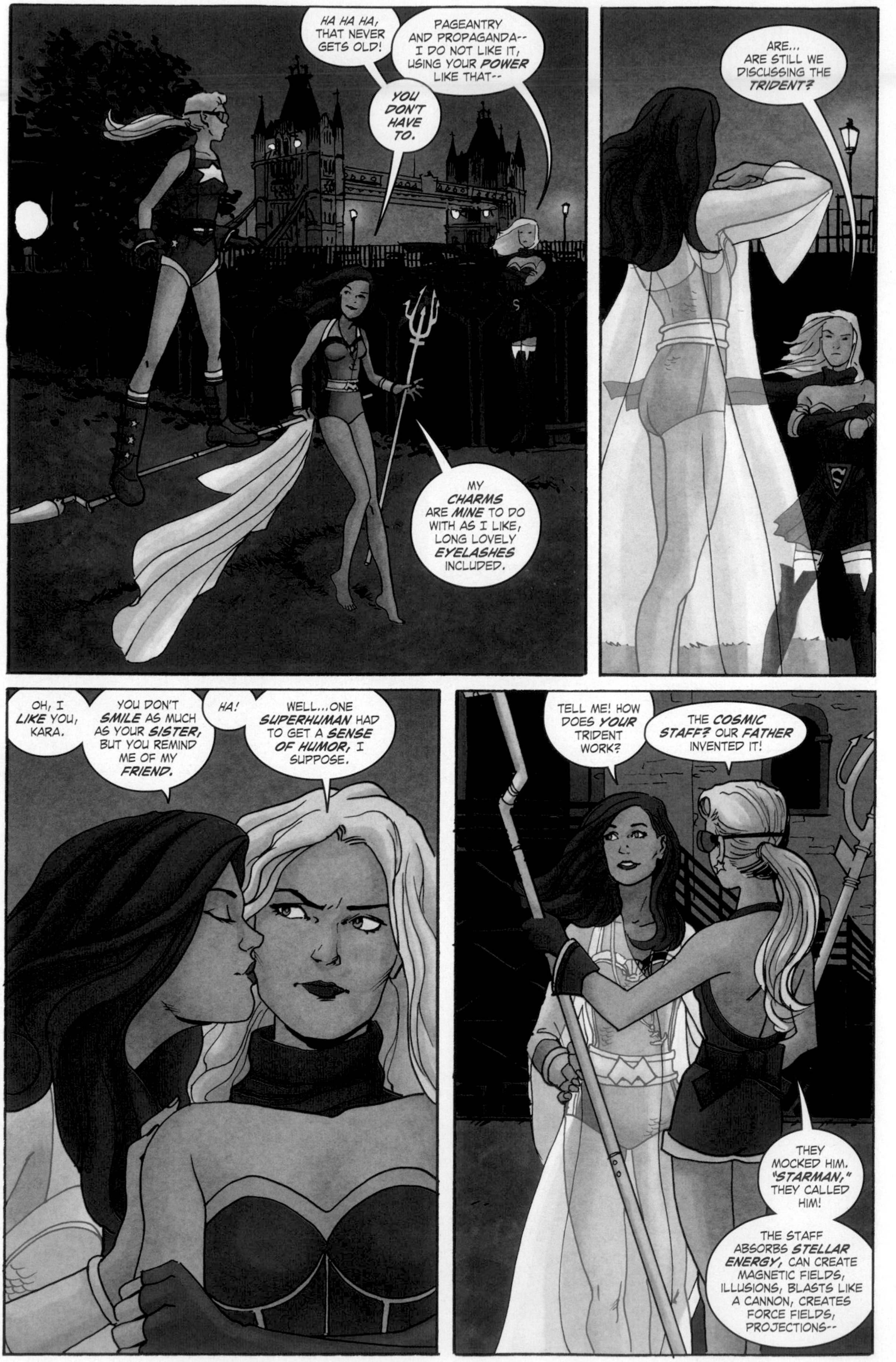
HA HA HA, THAT NEVER GETS OLD!
PAGEANTRY AND PROPAGANDA-- I DO NOT LIKE IT, USING YOUR POWER LIKE THAT--
YOU DON'T HAVE TO.
MY CHARMS ARE MINE TO DO WITH AS I LIKE, LONG LOVELY EYELASHES INCLUDED.
ARE... ARE STILL WE DISCUSSING THE TRIDENT?
OH, I LIKE YOU, KARA.
YOU DON'T SMILE AS MUCH AS YOUR SISTER, BUT YOU REMIND ME OF MY FRIEND.
HA!
WELL...ONE SUPERHUMAN HAD TO GET A SENSE OF HUMOR, I SUPPOSE.
TELL ME! HOW DOES YOUR TRIDENT WORK?
THE COSMIC STAFF? OUR FATHER INVENTED IT!
THEY MOCKED HIM. "STARMAN," THEY CALLED HIM!
THE STAFF ABSORBS STELLAR ENERGY, CAN CREATE MAGNETIC FIELDS, ILLUSIONS, BLASTS LIKE A CANNON, CREATES FORCE FIELDS, PROJECTIONS--

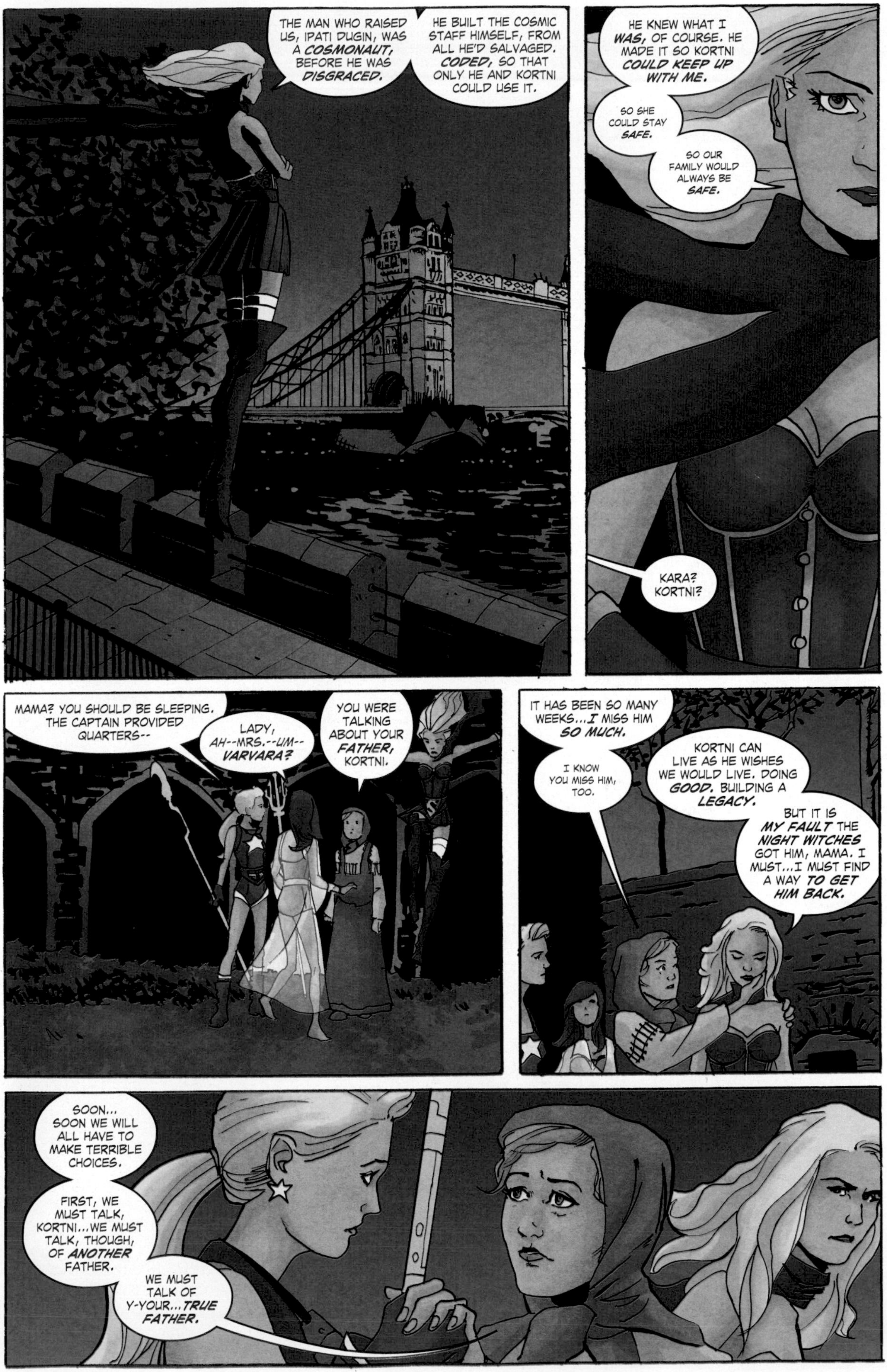
THE MAN WHO RAISED US, IPATI DUGIN, WAS A COSMONAUT, BEFORE HE WAS DISGRACED.
HE BUILT THE COSMIC STAFF HIMSELF, FROM ALL HE'D SALVAGED. CODED, SO THAT ONLY HE AND KORTNI COULD USE IT.
HE KNEW WHAT I WAS, OF COURSE. HE MADE IT SO KORTNI COULD KEEP UP WITH ME.
SO SHE COULD STAY SAFE.
SO OUR FAMILY WOULD ALWAYS BE SAFE.
KARA? KORTNI?
MAMA? YOU SHOULD BE SLEEPING. THE CAPTAIN PROVIDED QUARTERS--
LADY, AH--MRS.--UM--VARVARA?
YOU WERE TALKING ABOUT YOUR FATHER, KORTNI.
IT HAS BEEN SO MANY WEEKS...I MISS HIM SO MUCH.
I KNOW YOU MISS HIM, TOO.
KORTNI CAN LIVE AS HE WISHES WE WOULD LIVE. DOING GOOD. BUILDING A LEGACY.
BUT IT IS MY FAULT THE NIGHT WITCHES GOT HIM, MAMA. I MUST...I MUST FIND A WAY TO GET HIM BACK.
SOON... SOON WE WILL ALL HAVE TO MAKE TERRIBLE CHOICES.
FIRST, WE MUST TALK, KORTNI...WE MUST TALK, THOUGH, OF ANOTHER FATHER.
WE MUST TALK OF Y-YOUR...TRUE FATHER.

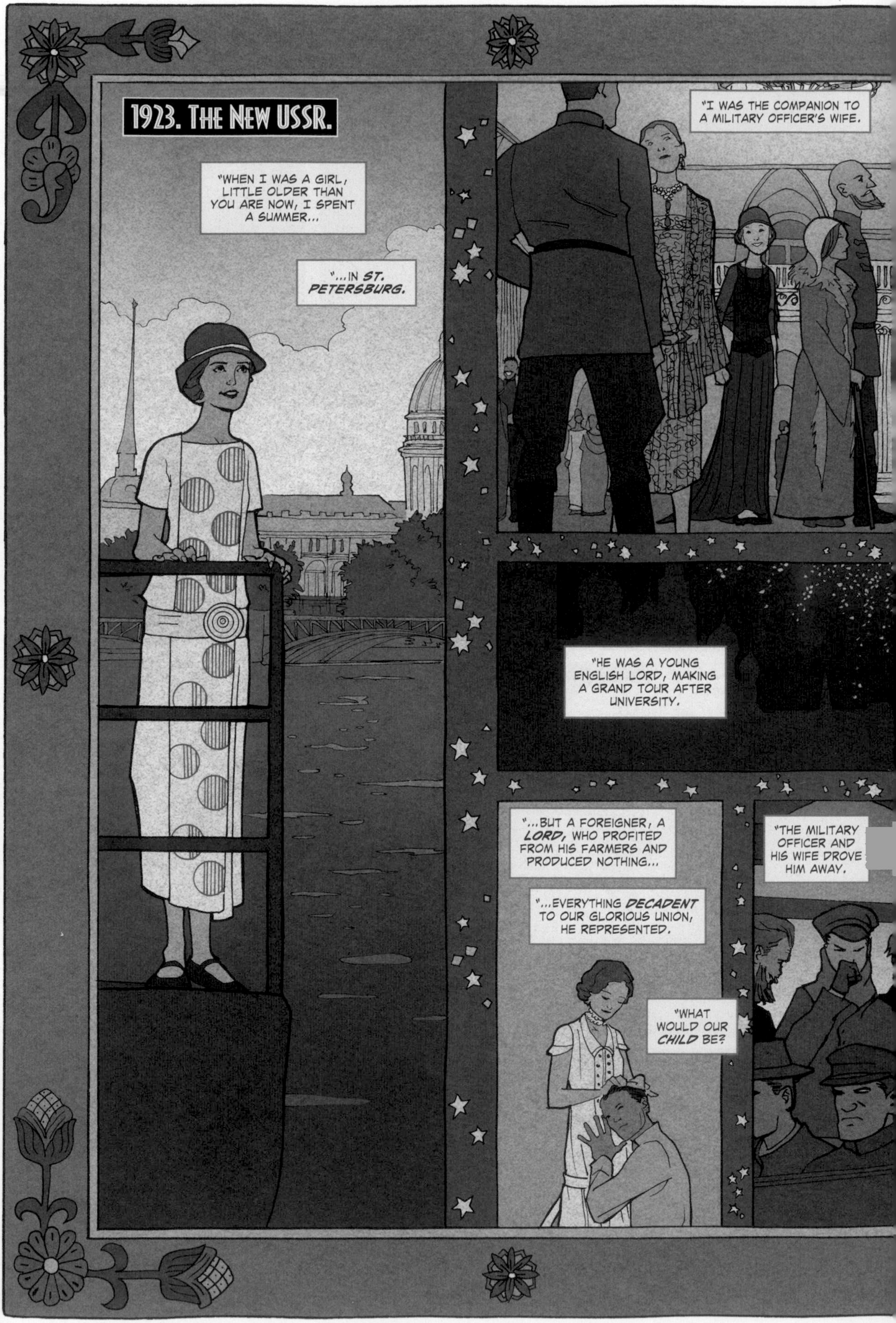
1923. THE NEW USSR.
"WHEN I WAS A GIRL, LITTLE OLDER THAN YOU ARE NOW, I SPENT A SUMMER...
"...IN ST. PETERSBURG.
"I WAS THE COMPANION TO A MILITARY OFFICER'S WIFE.
"HE WAS A YOUNG ENGLISH LORD, MAKING A GRAND TOUR AFTER UNIVERSITY.
"...BUT A FOREIGNER, A LORD, WHO PROFITED FROM HIS FARMERS AND PRODUCED NOTHING...
"...EVERYTHING DECADENT TO OUR GLORIOUS UNION, HE REPRESENTED.
"WHAT WOULD OUR CHILD BE?
"THE MILITARY OFFICER AND HIS WIFE DROVE HIM AWAY.

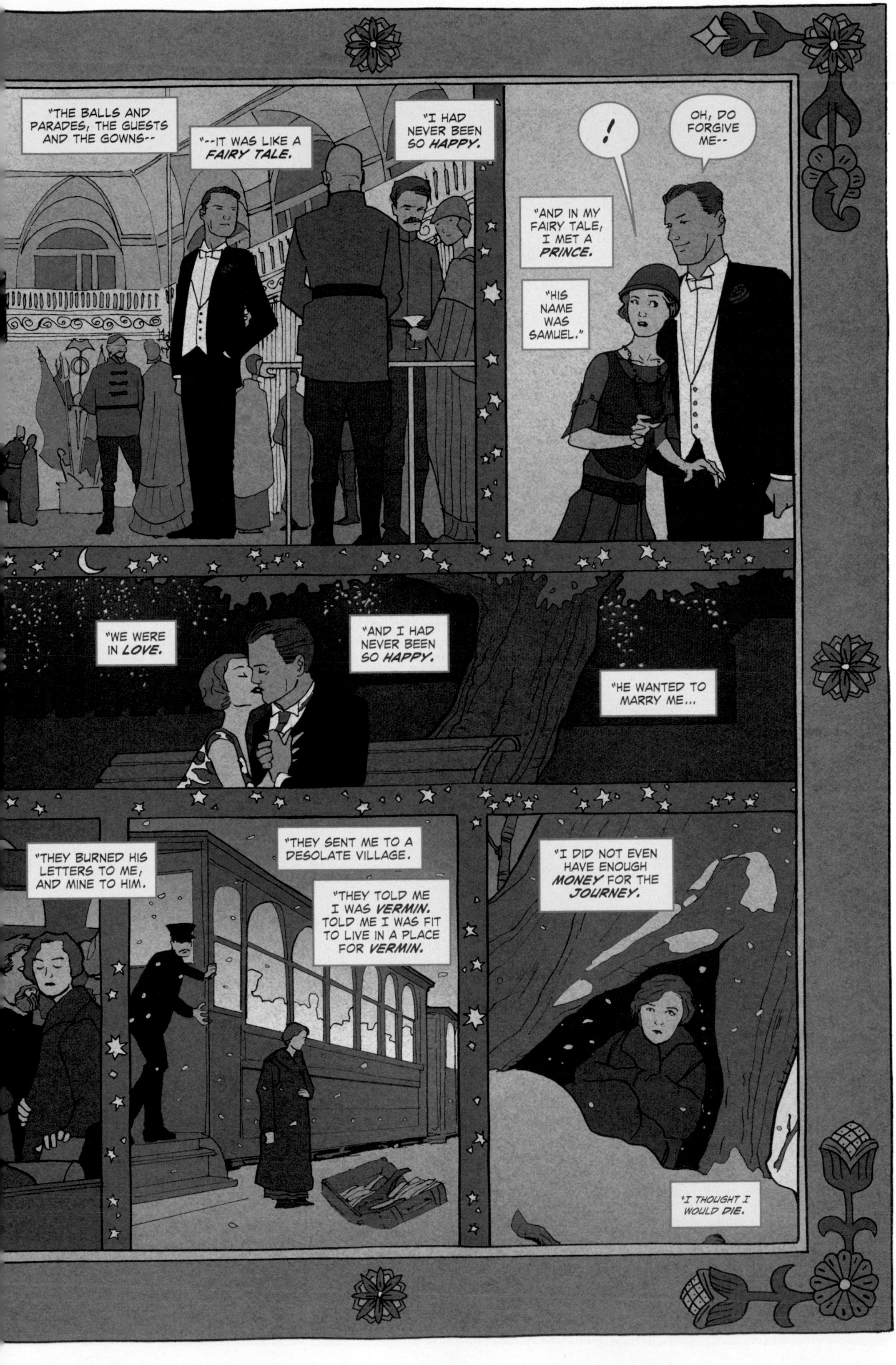
"THE BALLS AND PARADES, THE GUESTS AND THE GOWNS--
"--IT WAS LIKE A FAIRY TALE.
"I HAD NEVER BEEN SO HAPPY.
!
OH, DO FORGIVE ME--
"AND IN MY FAIRY TALE, I MET A PRINCE.
"HIS NAME WAS SAMUEL."
"WE WERE IN LOVE.
"AND I HAD NEVER BEEN SO HAPPY.
"HE WANTED TO MARRY ME...
"THEY BURNED HIS LETTERS TO ME, AND MINE TO HIM.
"THEY SENT ME TO A DESOLATE VILLAGE.
"THEY TOLD ME I WAS VERMIN. TOLD ME I WAS FIT TO LIVE IN A PLACE FOR VERMIN.
"I DID NOT EVEN HAVE ENOUGH MONEY FOR THE JOURNEY.
"I THOUGHT I WOULD DIE.

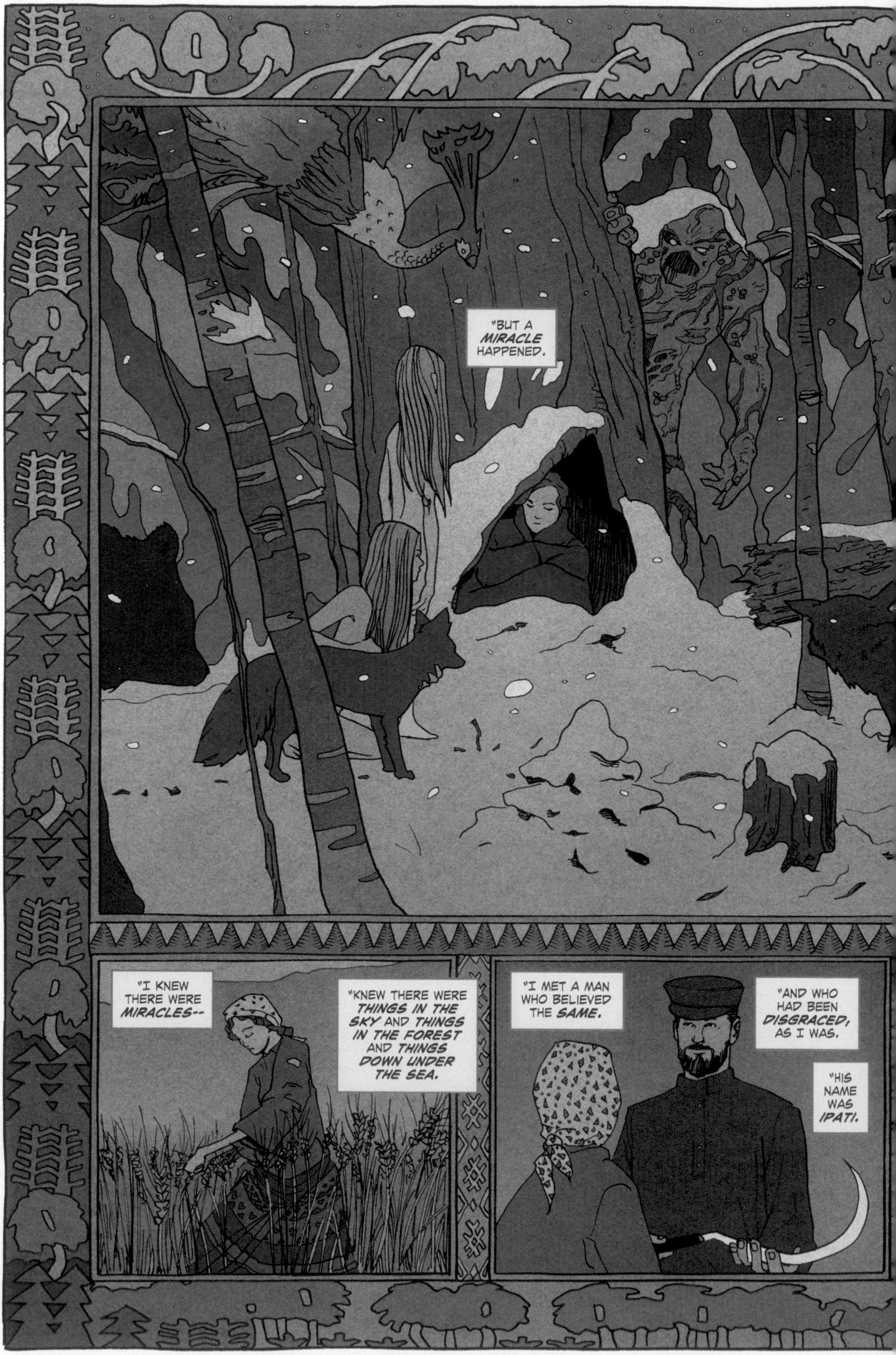
"BUT A MIRACLE HAPPENED.
"I KNEW THERE WERE MIRACLES--
"KNEW THERE WERE THINGS IN THE SKY AND THINGS IN THE FOREST AND THINGS DOWN UNDER THE SEA.
"I MET A MAN WHO BELIEVED THE SAME.
"AND WHO HAD BEEN DISGRACED, AS I WAS.
"HIS NAME WAS IPATI.

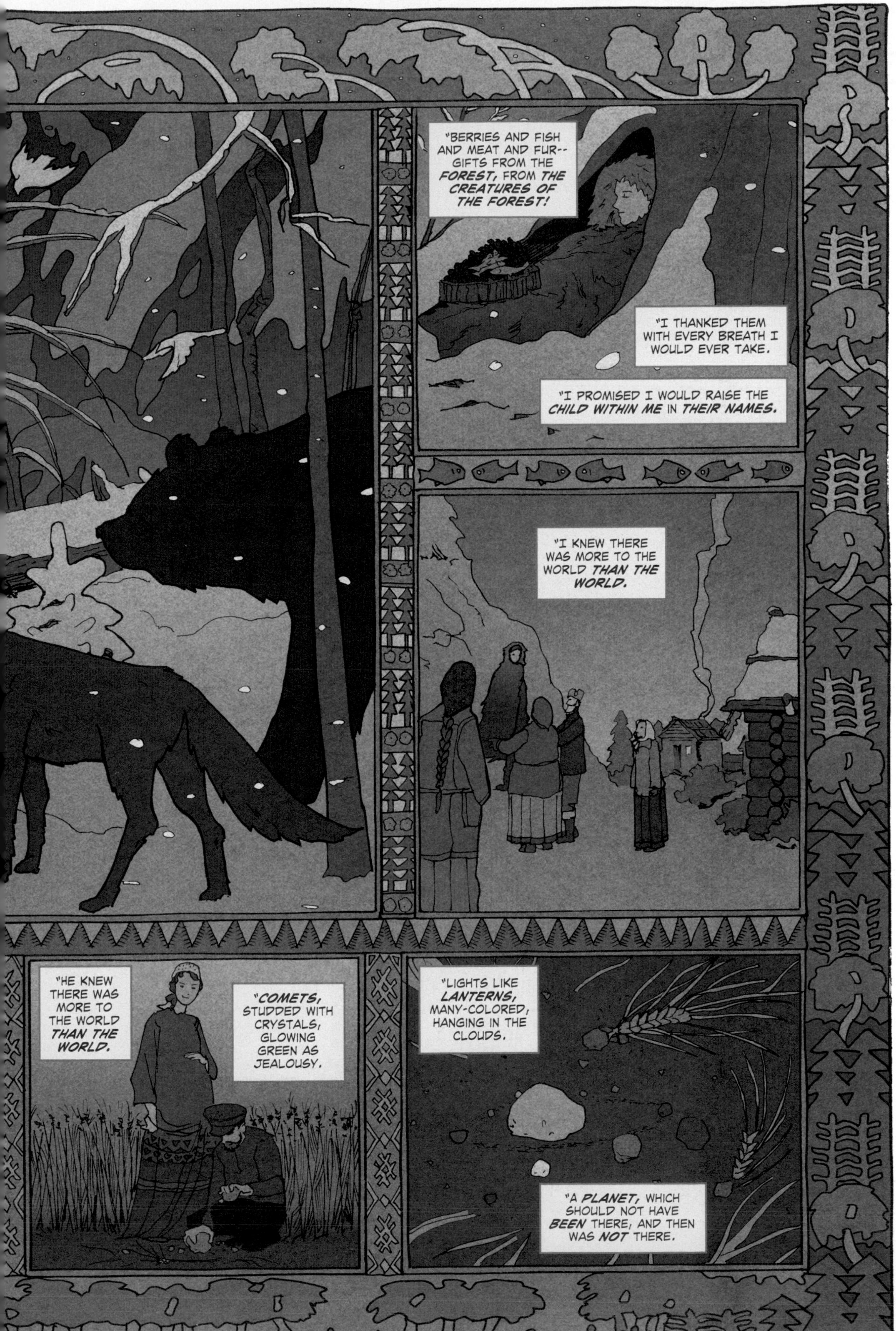
"BERRIES AND FISH AND MEAT AND FUR-- GIFTS FROM THE FOREST, FROM THE CREATURES OF THE FOREST!
"I THANKED THEM WITH EVERY BREATH I WOULD EVER TAKE.
"I PROMISED I WOULD RAISE THE CHILD WITHIN ME IN THEIR NAMES.
"I KNEW THERE WAS MORE TO THE WORLD THAN THE WORLD.
"HE KNEW THERE WAS MORE TO THE WORLD THAN THE WORLD.
"COMETS, STUDDED WITH CRYSTALS, GLOWING GREEN AS JEALOUSY.
"LIGHTS LIKE LANTERNS, MANY-COLORED, HANGING IN THE CLOUDS.
"A PLANET, WHICH SHOULD NOT HAVE BEEN THERE, AND THEN WAS NOT THERE.

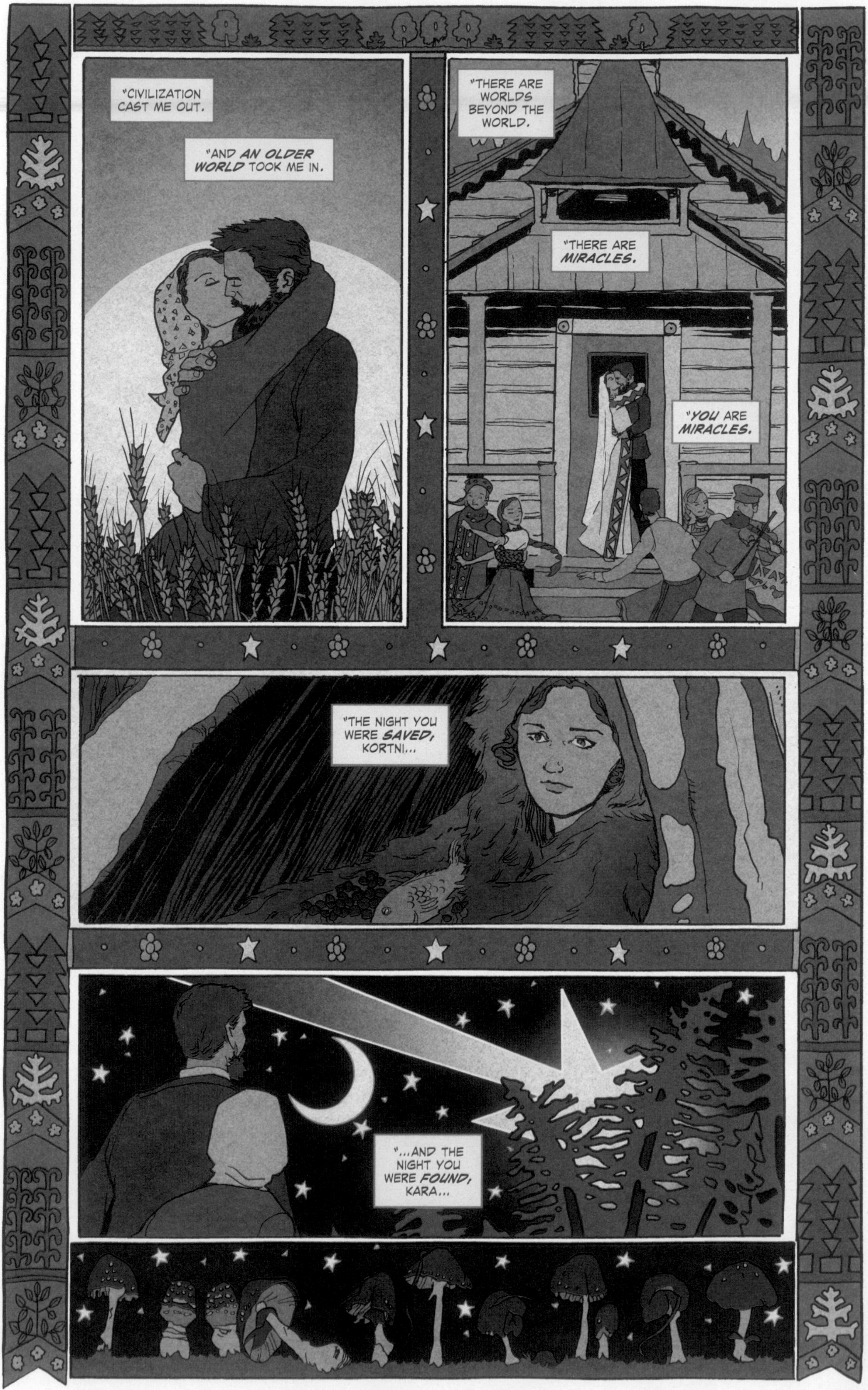
"CIVILIZATION CAST ME OUT.
"AND AN OLDER WORLD TOOK ME IN.
"THERE ARE WORLDS BEYOND THE WORLD.
"THERE ARE MIRACLES.
"YOU ARE MIRACLES.
"THE NIGHT YOU WERE SAVED, KORTNI...
"...AND THE NIGHT YOU WERE FOUND, KARA...

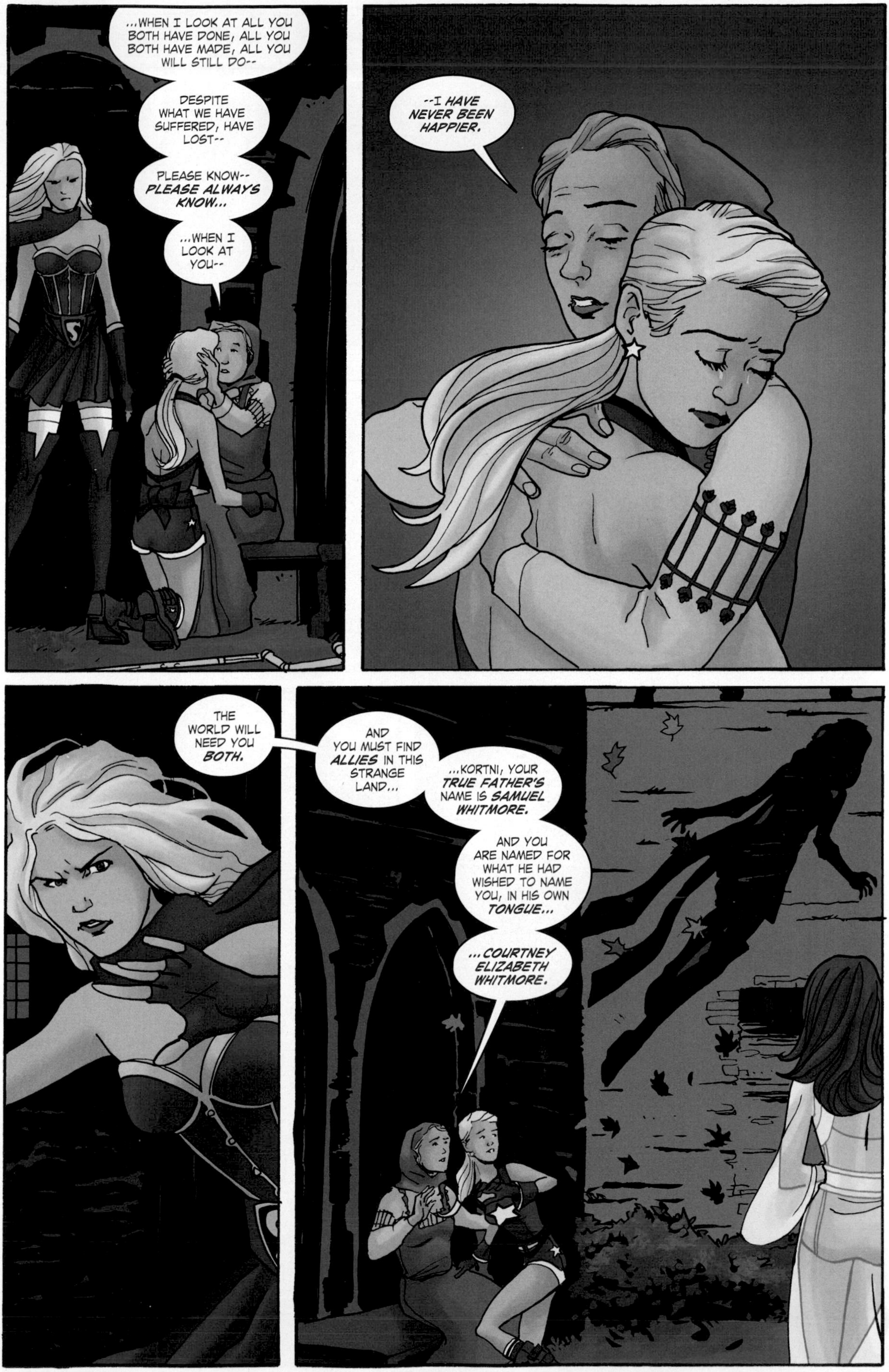
...WHEN I LOOK AT ALL YOU BOTH HAVE DONE, ALL YOU BOTH HAVE MADE, ALL YOU WILL STILL DO--
DESPITE WHAT WE HAVE SUFFERED, HAVE LOST--
PLEASE KNOW-- *PLEASE ALWAYS KNOW...*
...WHEN I LOOK AT YOU--
--I *HAVE NEVER BEEN HAPPIER.*
THE WORLD WILL NEED YOU *BOTH.*
AND YOU MUST FIND *ALLIES* IN THIS STRANGE LAND...
...KORTNI, YOUR *TRUE FATHER'S* NAME IS *SAMUEL WHITMORE.*
AND YOU ARE NAMED FOR WHAT HE HAD WISHED TO NAME YOU, IN HIS OWN *TONGUE...*
...COURTNEY ELIZABETH WHITMORE.

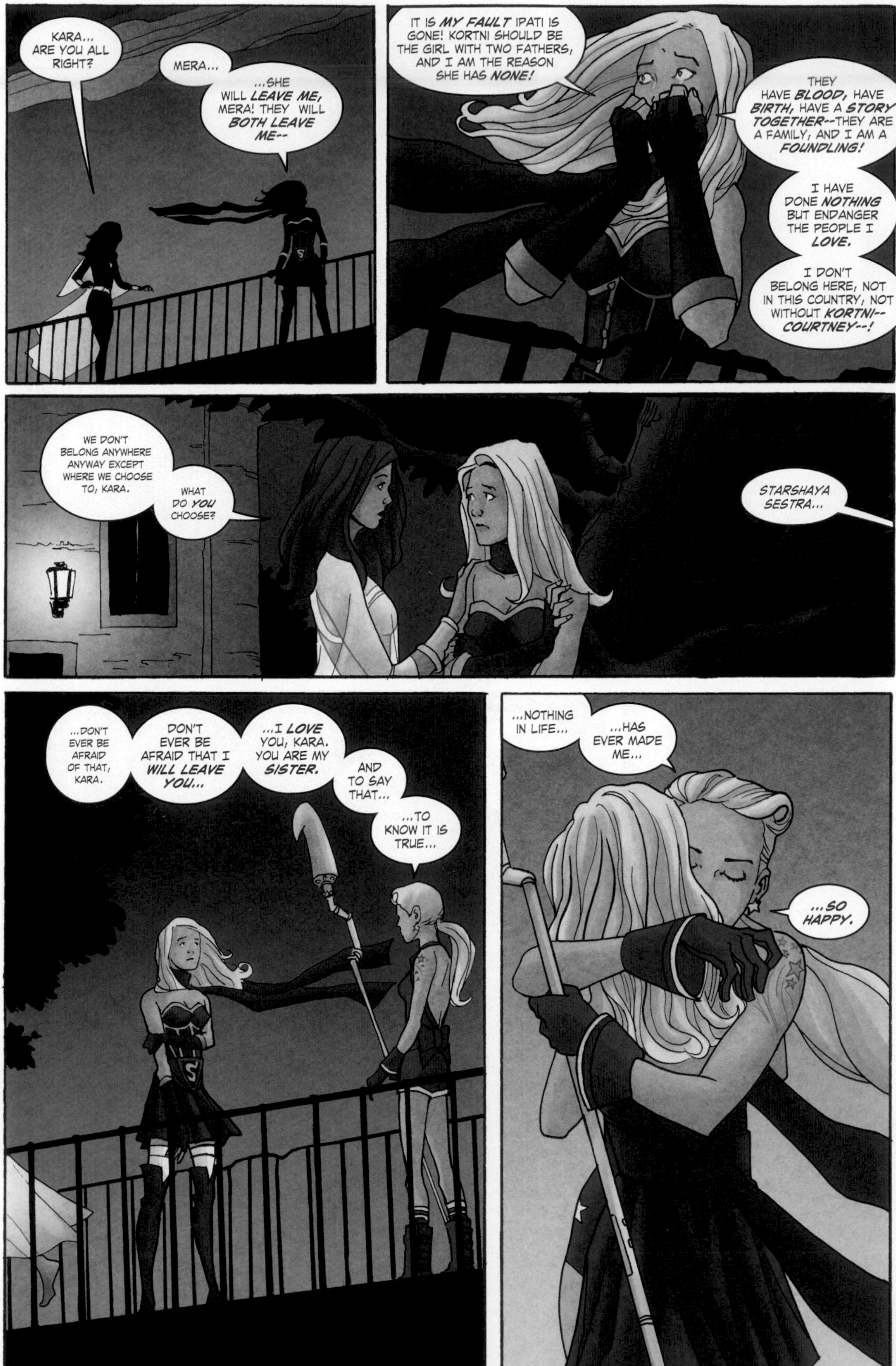
KARA... ARE YOU ALL RIGHT?
MERA...
...SHE WILL LEAVE ME, MERA! THEY WILL BOTH LEAVE ME--
IT IS MY FAULT IPATI IS GONE! KORTNI SHOULD BE THE GIRL WITH TWO FATHERS, AND I AM THE REASON SHE HAS NONE!
THEY HAVE BLOOD, HAVE BIRTH, HAVE A STORY TOGETHER--THEY ARE A FAMILY, AND I AM A FOUNDLING!
I HAVE DONE NOTHING BUT ENDANGER THE PEOPLE I LOVE.
I DON'T BELONG HERE, NOT IN THIS COUNTRY, NOT WITHOUT KORTNI--COURTNEY--!
WE DON'T BELONG ANYWHERE ANYWAY EXCEPT WHERE WE CHOOSE TO, KARA.
WHAT DO YOU CHOOSE?
STARSHAYA SESTRA...
...DON'T EVER BE AFRAID OF THAT, KARA.
DON'T EVER BE AFRAID THAT I WILL LEAVE YOU...
...I LOVE YOU, KARA. YOU ARE MY SISTER.
AND TO SAY THAT...
...TO KNOW IT IS TRUE...
...NOTHING IN LIFE...
...HAS EVER MADE ME...
...SO HAPPY.

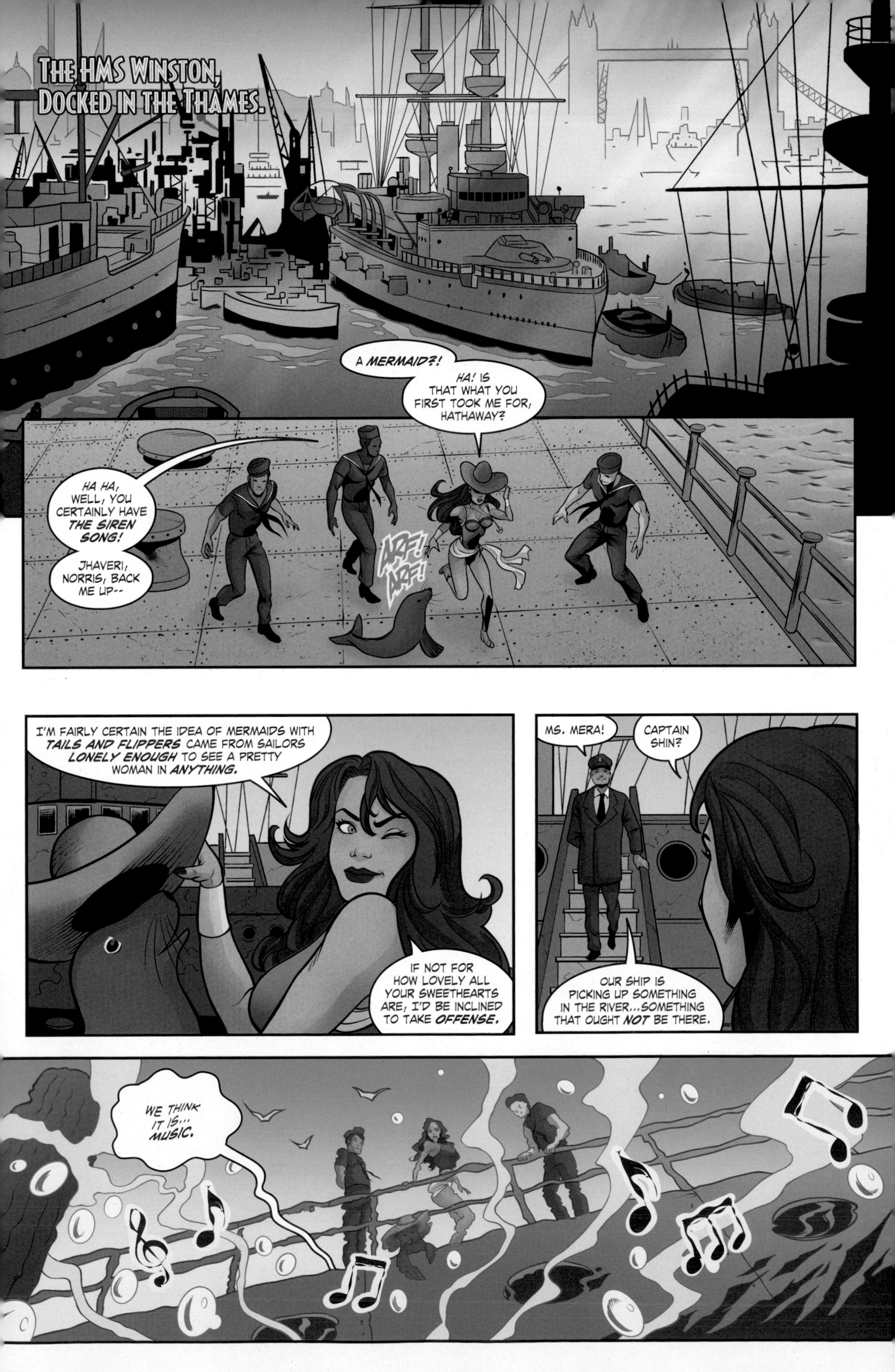
The HMS Winston, Docked in the Thames.
A *MERMAID?!*
HA! IS THAT WHAT YOU FIRST TOOK ME FOR, HATHAWAY?
HA HA, WELL, YOU CERTAINLY HAVE ***THE SIREN SONG!***
JHAVERI, NORRIS, BACK ME UP--
ARF! ARF!
I'M FAIRLY CERTAIN THE IDEA OF MERMAIDS WITH ***TAILS AND FLIPPERS*** CAME FROM SAILORS ***LONELY ENOUGH*** TO SEE A PRETTY WOMAN IN ***ANYTHING.***
IF NOT FOR HOW LOVELY ALL YOUR SWEETHEARTS ARE, I'D BE INCLINED TO TAKE ***OFFENSE.***
MS. MERA!
CAPTAIN SHIN?
OUR SHIP IS PICKING UP SOMETHING IN THE RIVER...SOMETHING THAT OUGHT ***NOT*** BE THERE.
*WE THINK IT IS... **MUSIC.***

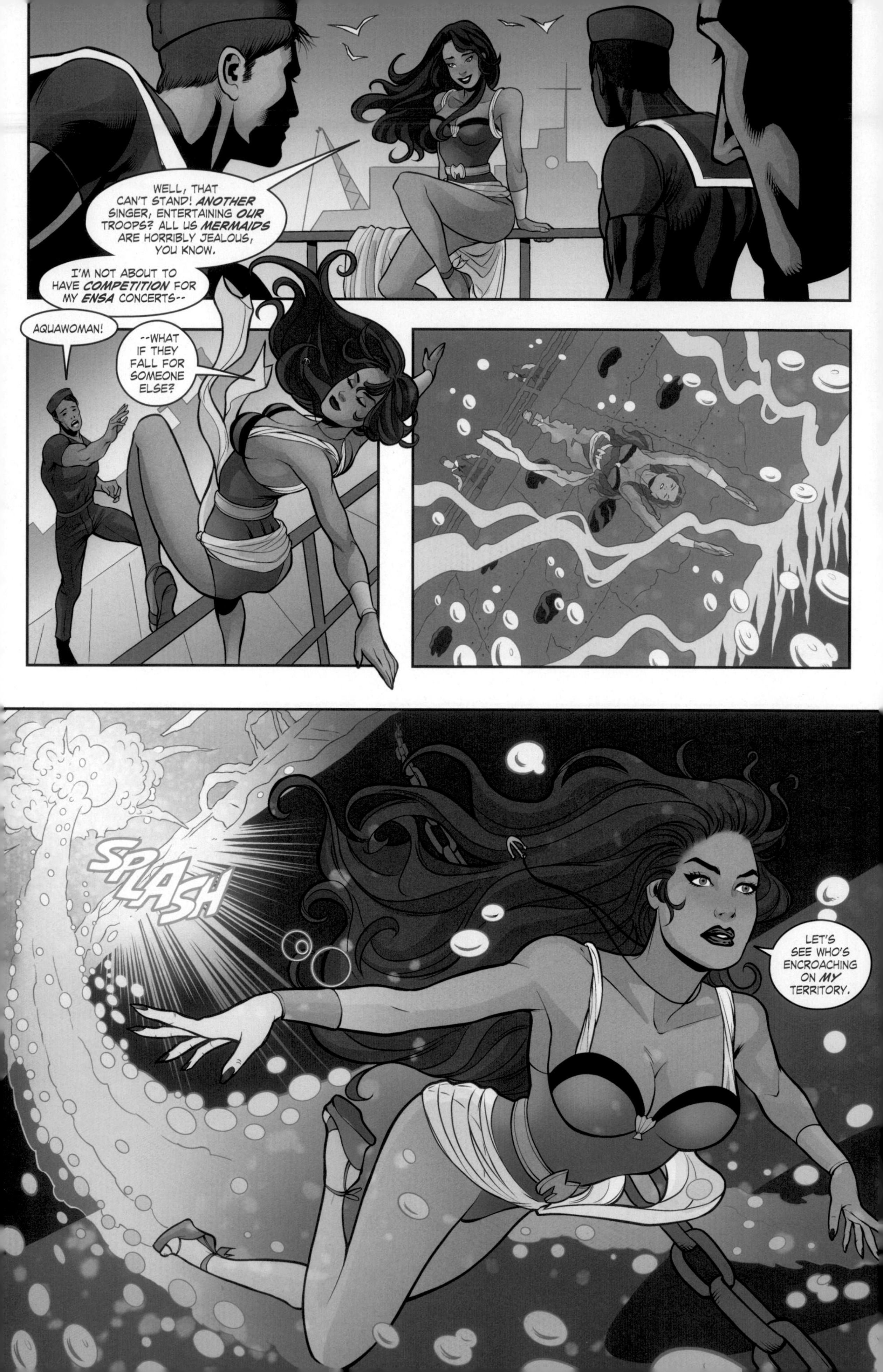
WELL, THAT CAN'T STAND! ***ANOTHER*** SINGER, ENTERTAINING ***OUR*** TROOPS? ALL US ***MERMAIDS*** ARE HORRIBLY JEALOUS, YOU KNOW.
I'M NOT ABOUT TO HAVE ***COMPETITION*** FOR MY ***ENSA*** CONCERTS--
AQUAWOMAN!
--WHAT IF THEY FALL FOR SOMEONE ELSE?
SPLASH
LET'S SEE WHO'S ENCROACHING ON ***MY*** TERRITORY.

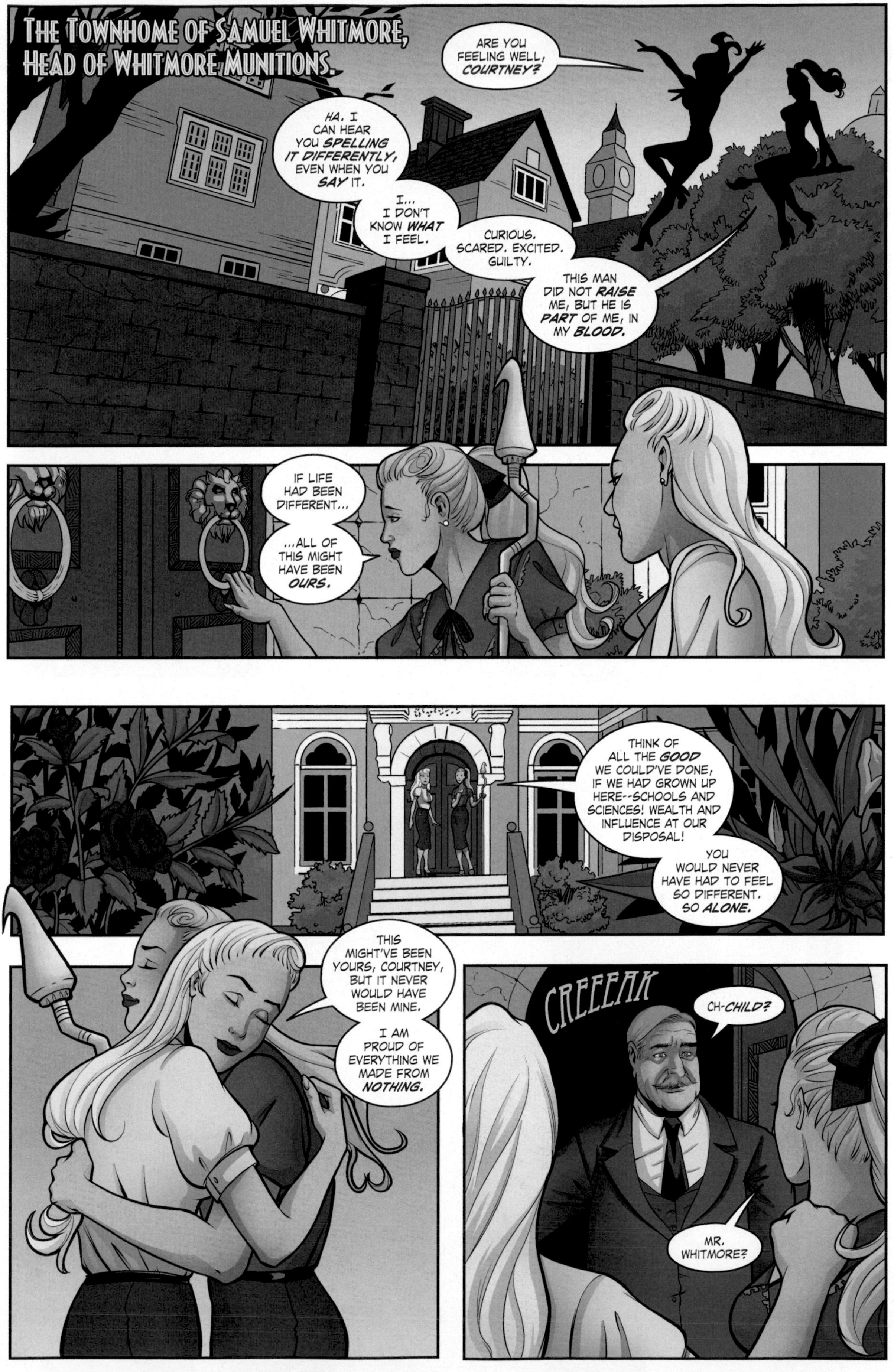
THE TOWNHOME OF SAMUEL WHITMORE, HEAD OF WHITMORE MUNITIONS.
ARE YOU FEELING WELL, COURTNEY?
HA. I CAN HEAR YOU SPELLING IT DIFFERENTLY, EVEN WHEN YOU SAY IT.
I... I DON'T KNOW WHAT I FEEL.
CURIOUS. SCARED. EXCITED. GUILTY.
THIS MAN DID NOT RAISE ME, BUT HE IS PART OF ME, IN MY BLOOD.
IF LIFE HAD BEEN DIFFERENT...
...ALL OF THIS MIGHT HAVE BEEN OURS.
THINK OF ALL THE GOOD WE COULD'VE DONE, IF WE HAD GROWN UP HERE--SCHOOLS AND SCIENCES! WEALTH AND INFLUENCE AT OUR DISPOSAL!
YOU WOULD NEVER HAVE HAD TO FEEL SO DIFFERENT. SO ALONE.
THIS MIGHT'VE BEEN YOURS, COURTNEY, BUT IT NEVER WOULD HAVE BEEN MINE.
I AM PROUD OF EVERYTHING WE MADE FROM NOTHING.
CREEEAK
CH-CHILD?
MR. WHITMORE?

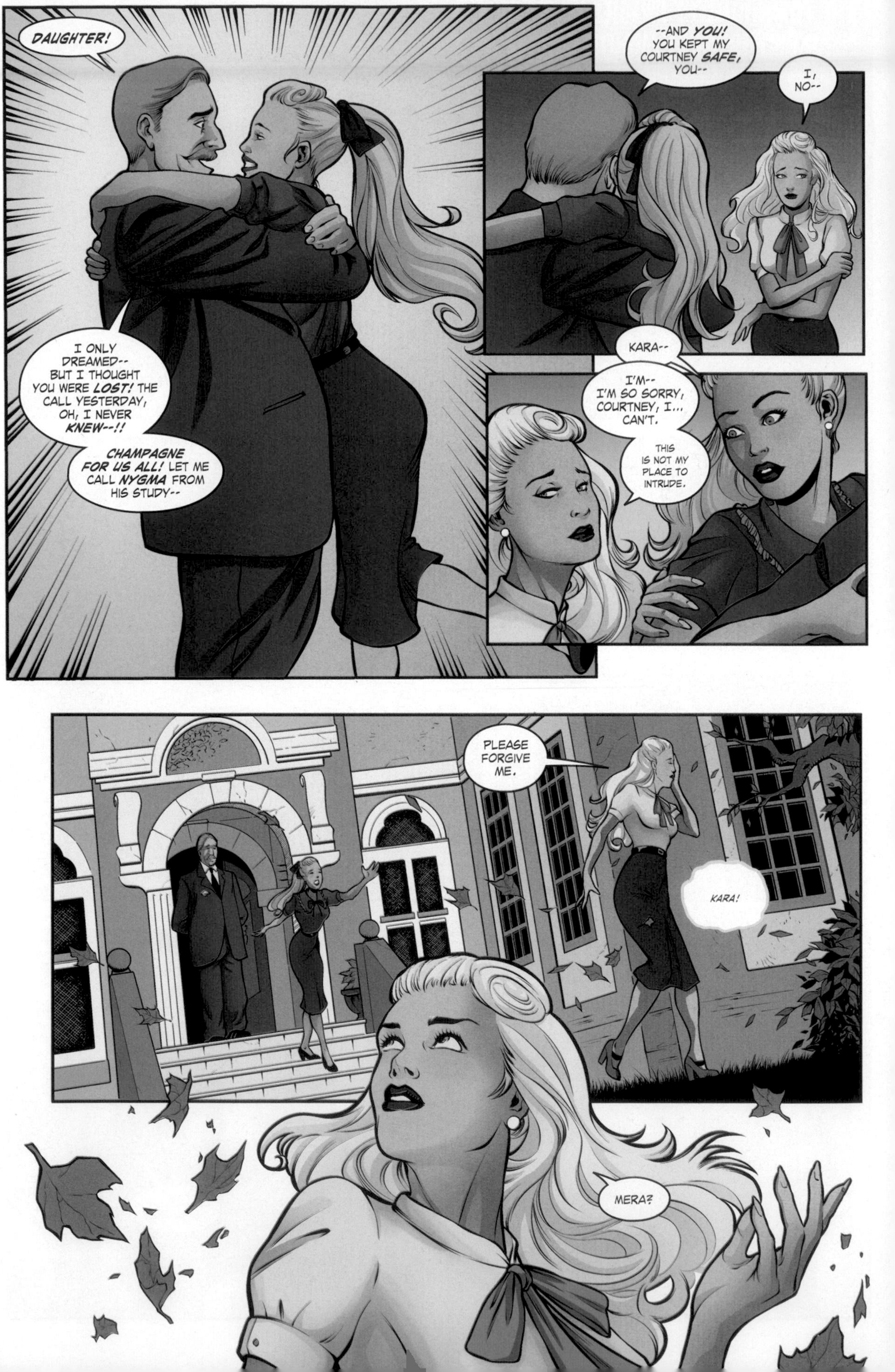
DAUGHTER!
I ONLY DREAMED-- BUT I THOUGHT YOU WERE LOST! THE CALL YESTERDAY, OH, I NEVER KNEW--!!
CHAMPAGNE FOR US ALL! LET ME CALL NYGMA FROM HIS STUDY--
--AND YOU! YOU KEPT MY COURTNEY SAFE, YOU--
I, NO--
KARA--
I'M-- I'M SO SORRY, COURTNEY, I... CAN'T.
THIS IS NOT MY PLACE TO INTRUDE.
PLEASE FORGIVE ME.
KARA!
MERA?

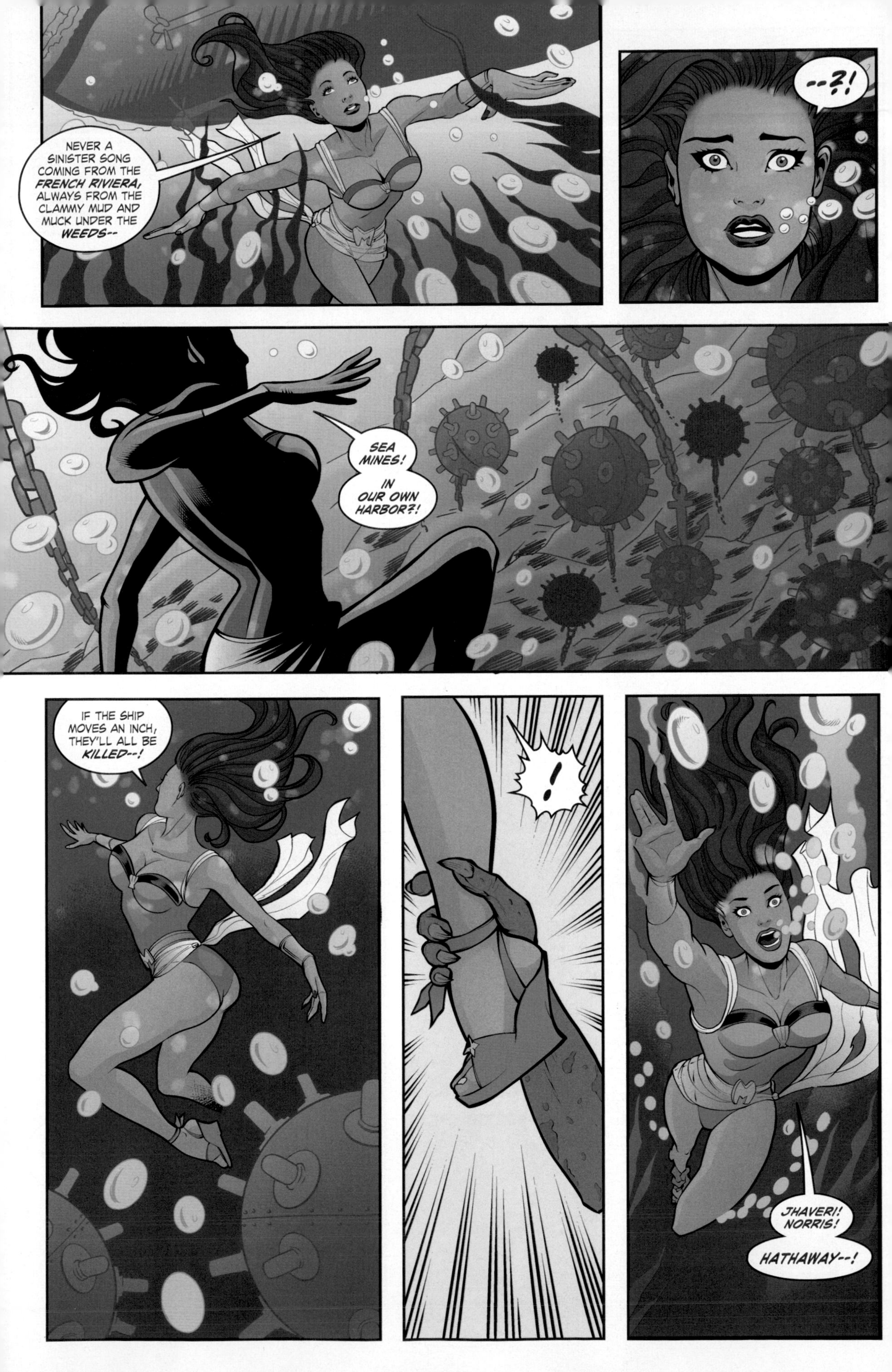
NEVER A SINISTER SONG COMING FROM THE FRENCH RIVIERA, ALWAYS FROM THE CLAMMY MUD AND MUCK UNDER THE WEEDS--
--?!
SEA MINES!
IN OUR OWN HARBOR?!
IF THE SHIP MOVES AN INCH, THEY'LL ALL BE KILLED--!
!
JHAVERI! NORRIS!
HATHAWAY--!

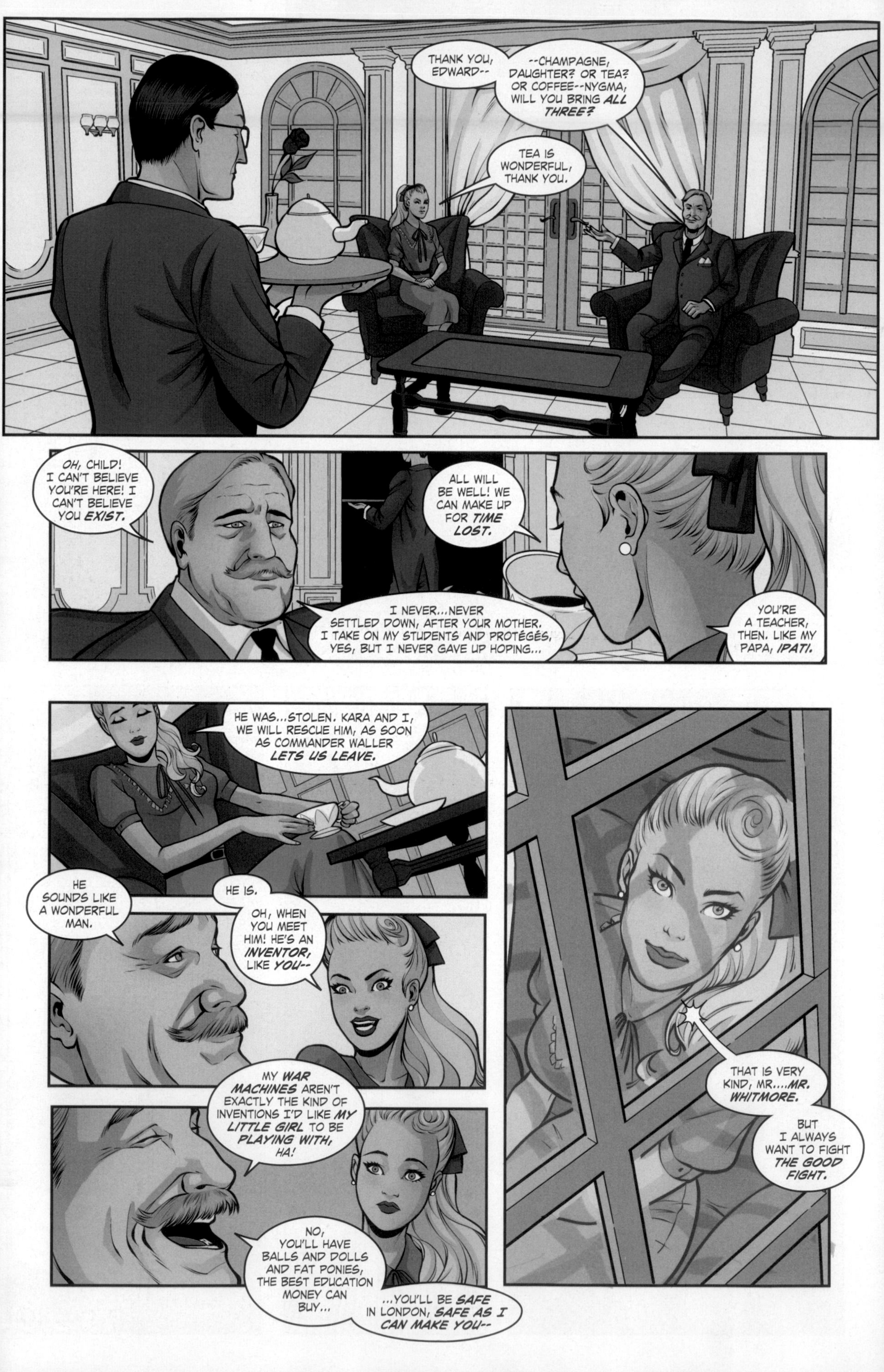
THANK YOU, EDWARD--
--CHAMPAGNE, DAUGHTER? OR TEA? OR COFFEE--NYGMA, WILL YOU BRING ALL THREE?
TEA IS WONDERFUL, THANK YOU.
OH, CHILD! I CAN'T BELIEVE YOU'RE HERE! I CAN'T BELIEVE YOU EXIST.
ALL WILL BE WELL! WE CAN MAKE UP FOR TIME LOST.
I NEVER...NEVER SETTLED DOWN, AFTER YOUR MOTHER. I TAKE ON MY STUDENTS AND PROTÉGÉS, YES, BUT I NEVER GAVE UP HOPING...
YOU'RE A TEACHER, THEN. LIKE MY PAPA, IPATI.
HE WAS...STOLEN. KARA AND I, WE WILL RESCUE HIM, AS SOON AS COMMANDER WALLER LETS US LEAVE.
HE SOUNDS LIKE A WONDERFUL MAN.
HE IS.
OH, WHEN YOU MEET HIM! HE'S AN INVENTOR, LIKE YOU--
MY WAR MACHINES AREN'T EXACTLY THE KIND OF INVENTIONS I'D LIKE MY LITTLE GIRL TO BE PLAYING WITH, HA!
NO, YOU'LL HAVE BALLS AND DOLLS AND FAT PONIES, THE BEST EDUCATION MONEY CAN BUY...
...YOU'LL BE SAFE IN LONDON, SAFE AS I CAN MAKE YOU--
THAT IS VERY KIND, MR....MR. WHITMORE.
BUT I ALWAYS WANT TO FIGHT THE GOOD FIGHT.

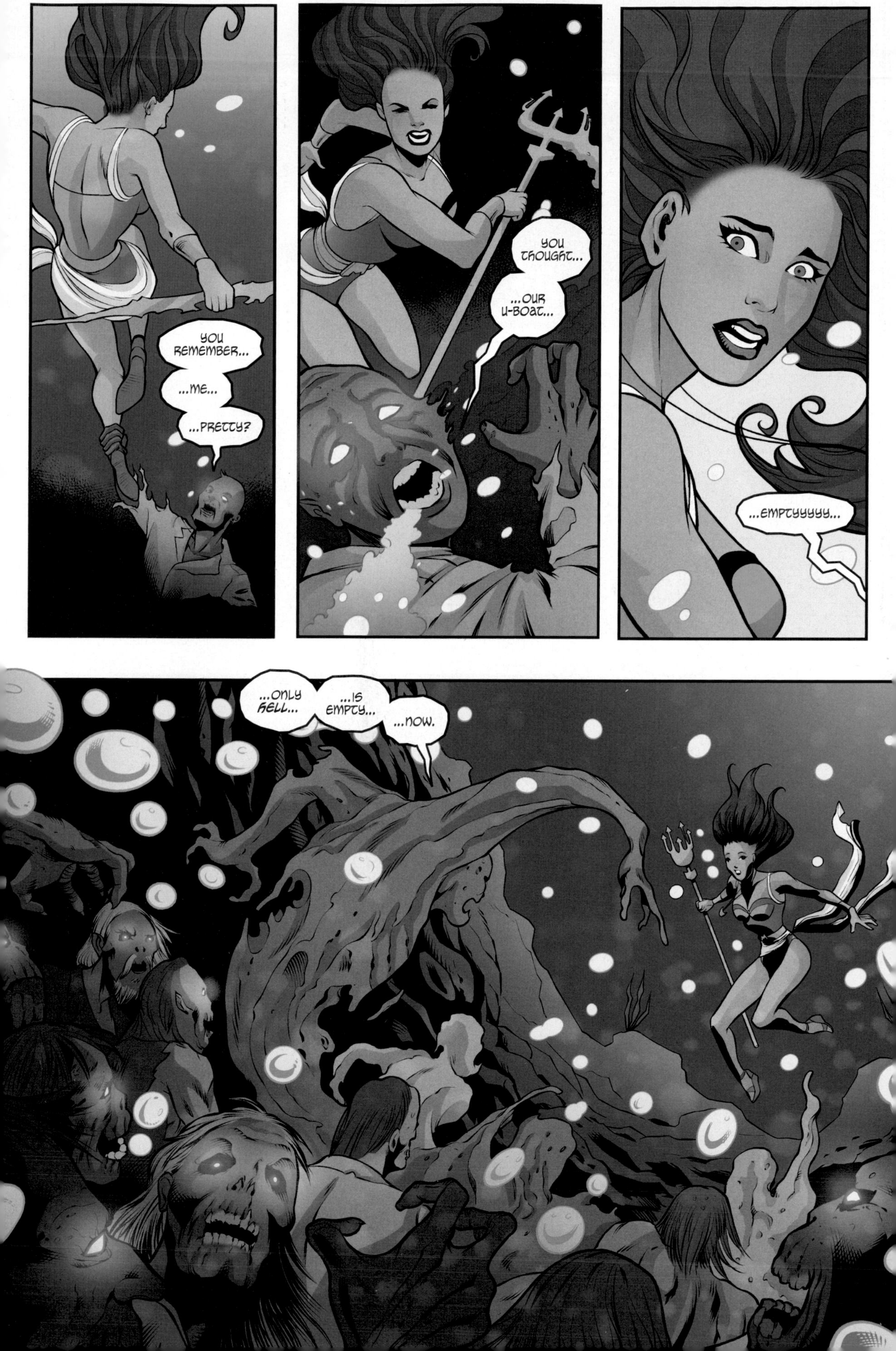
YOU REMEMBER...
...ME...
...PRETTY?
YOU THOUGHT...
...OUR U-BOAT...
...EMPTYYYYY...
...ONLY HELL...
...IS EMPTY...
...NOW.

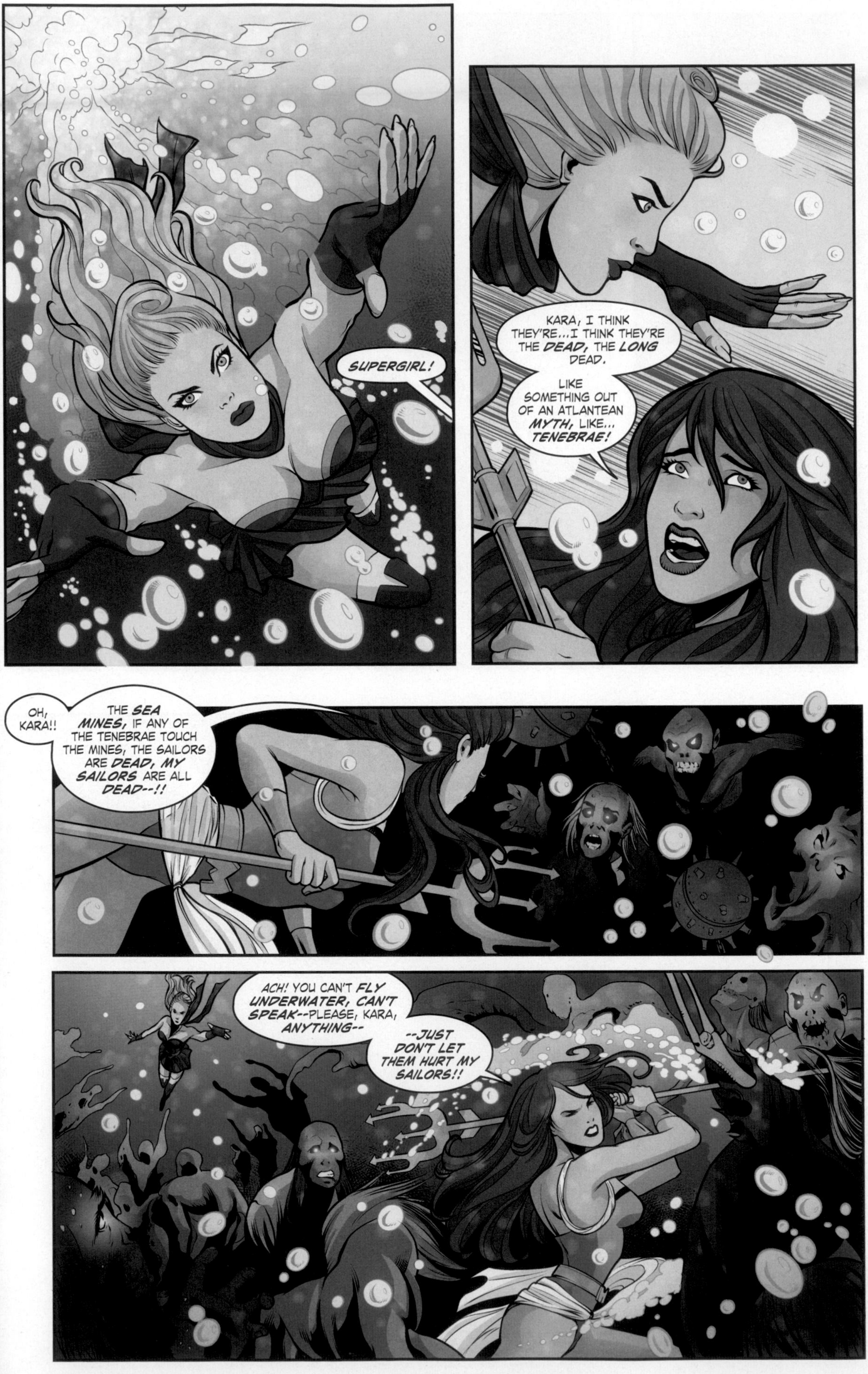
SUPERGIRL!
KARA, I THINK THEY'RE...I THINK THEY'RE THE DEAD, THE LONG DEAD.
LIKE SOMETHING OUT OF AN ATLANTEAN MYTH, LIKE... TENEBRAE!
OH, KARA!!
THE SEA MINES, IF ANY OF THE TENEBRAE TOUCH THE MINES, THE SAILORS ARE DEAD, MY SAILORS ARE ALL DEAD--!!
ACH! YOU CAN'T FLY UNDERWATER, CAN'T SPEAK--PLEASE, KARA, ANYTHING--
--JUST DON'T LET THEM HURT MY SAILORS!!

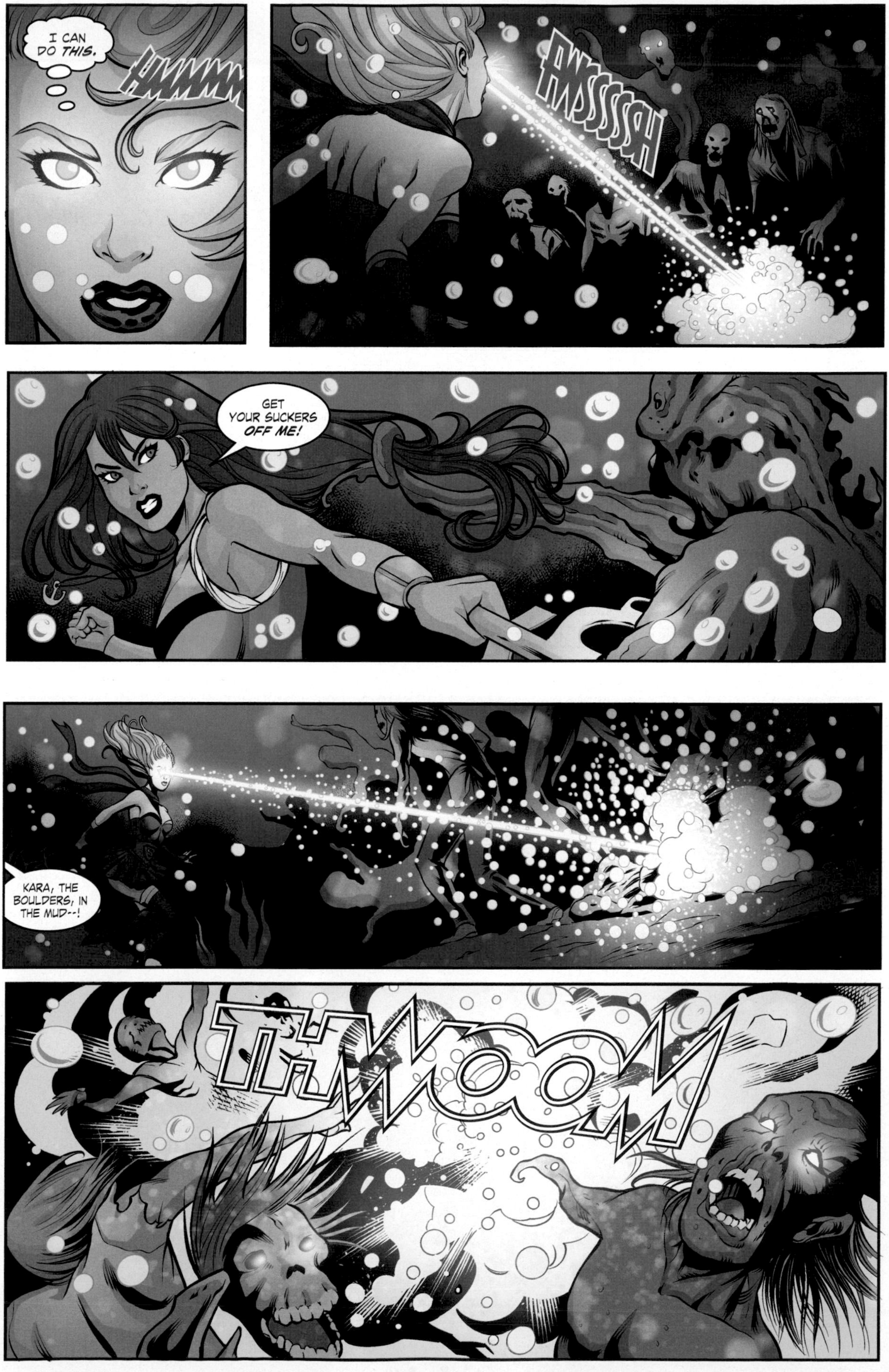
I CAN DO THIS.
HMMMM
FWSSSSSH
GET YOUR SUCKERS OFF ME!
KARA, THE BOULDERS, IN THE MUD--!
THWOOM

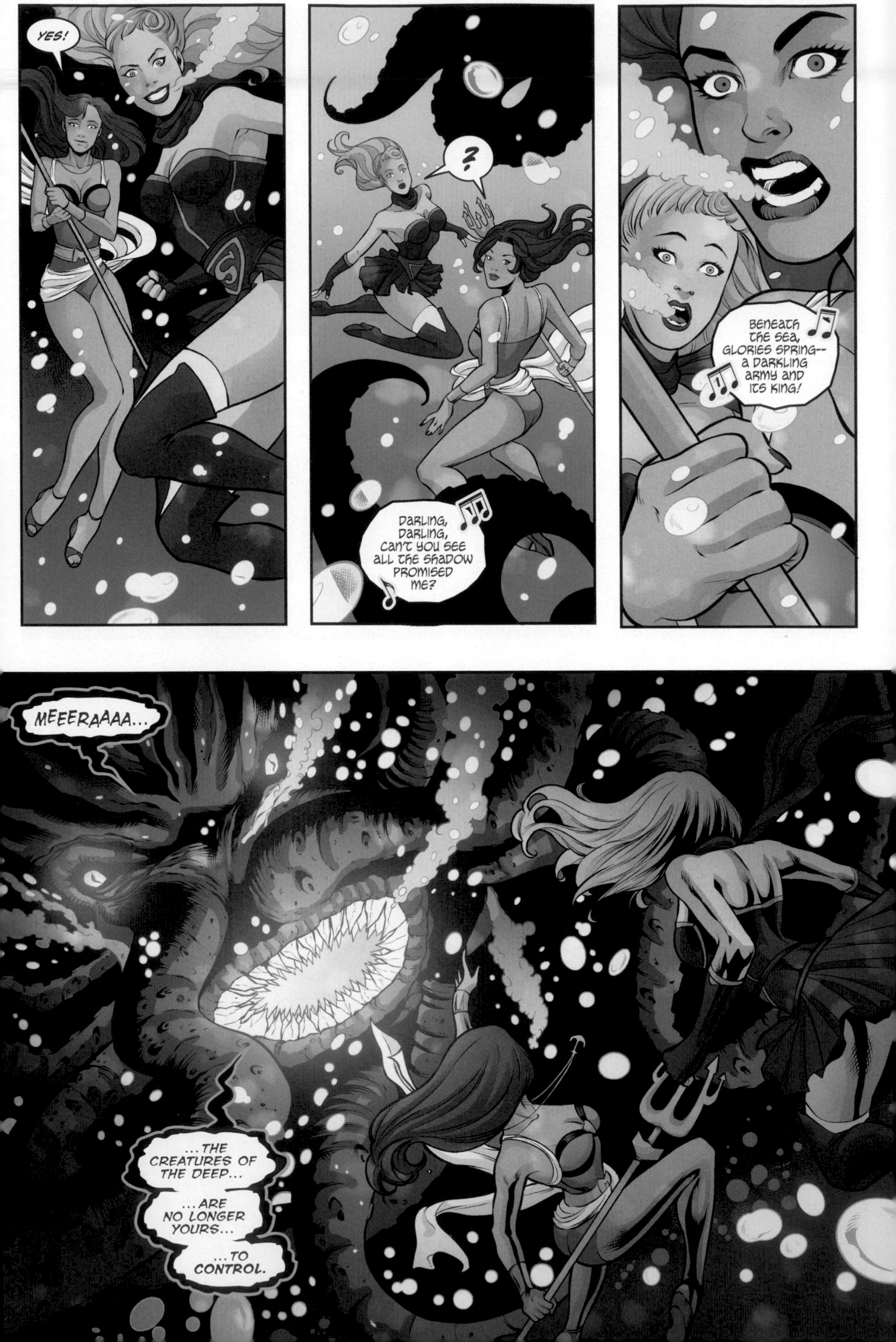
YES!
?
DARLING, DARLING, CAN'T YOU SEE ALL THE SHADOW PROMISED ME?
BENEATH THE SEA, GLORIES SPRING-- A DARKLING ARMY AND ITS KING!
MEEERAAAA...
...THE CREATURES OF THE DEEP...
...ARE NO LONGER YOURS...
...TO CONTROL.

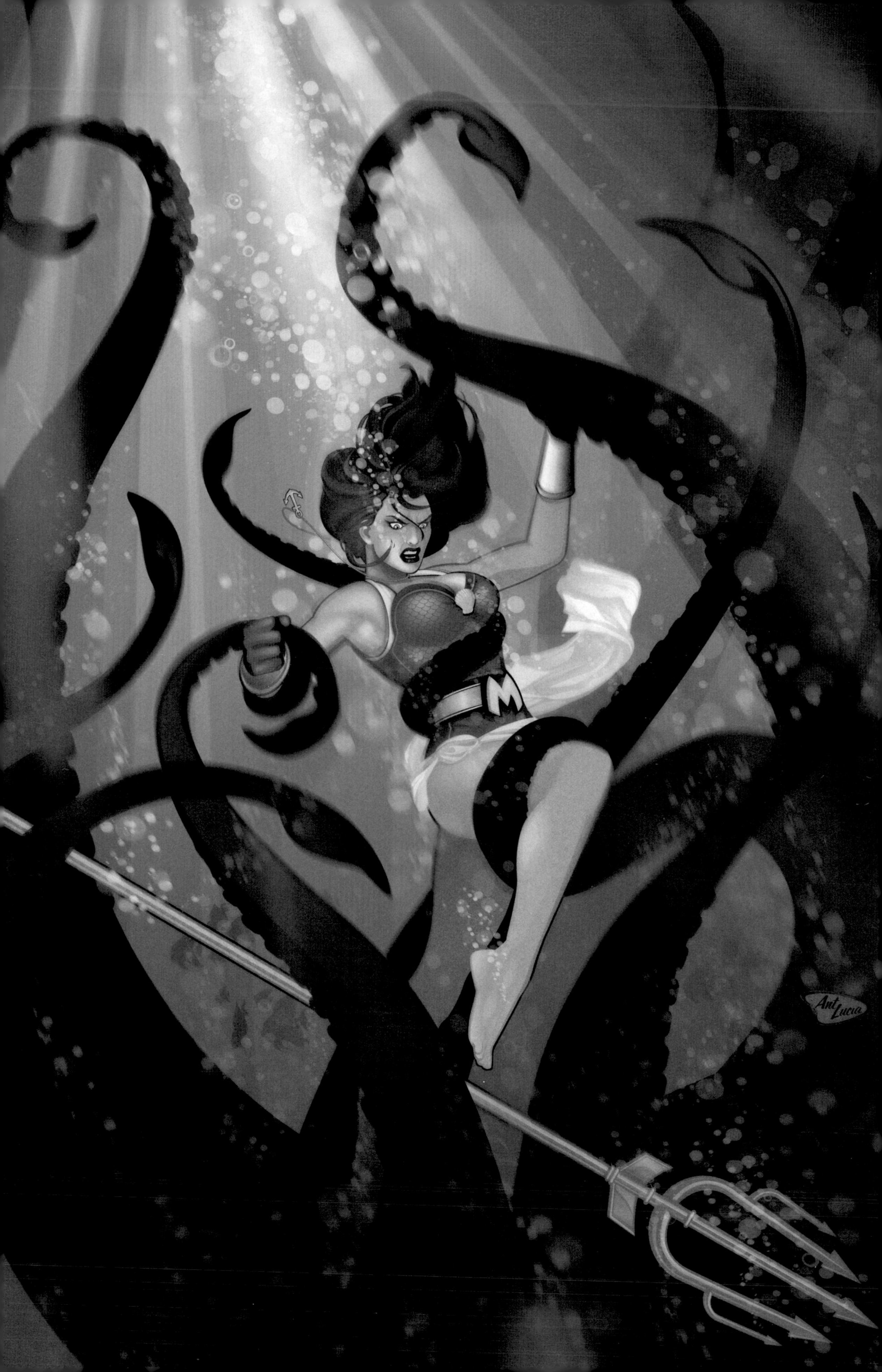
Ant Lucia

ALLIES AND ENEMIES
PART ONE

MARGUERITE BENNETT
Writer

MIRKA ANDOLFO
LAURA BRAGA
Artists

J. NANJAN
Colorist

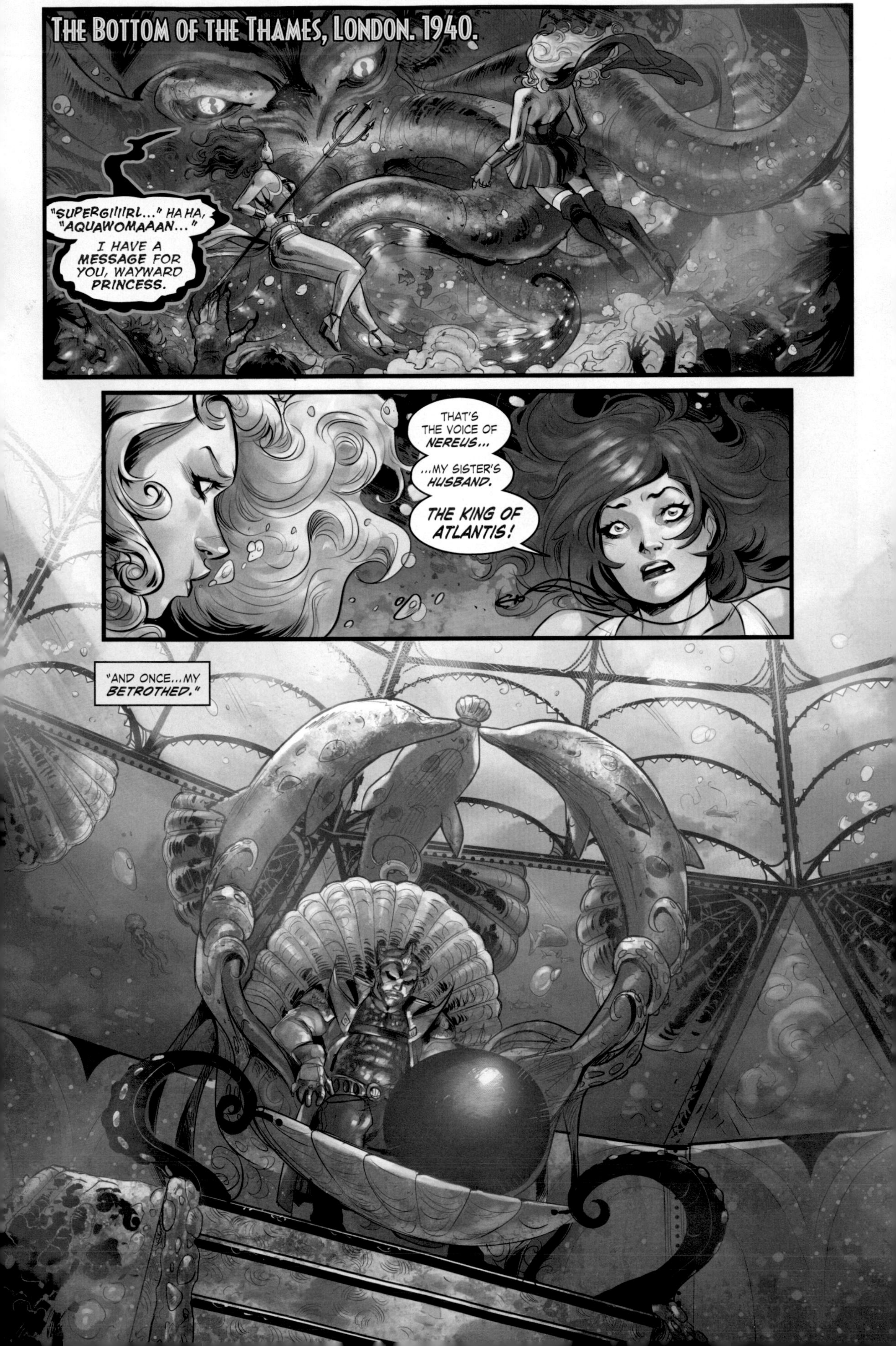
The Bottom of the Thames, London. 1940.
"SUPERGIIIIRL..." HA HA, "AQUAWOMAAAN..."
I HAVE A MESSAGE FOR YOU, WAYWARD PRINCESS.
THAT'S THE VOICE OF NEREUS...
...MY SISTER'S HUSBAND.
THE KING OF ATLANTIS!
"AND ONCE...MY BETROTHED."

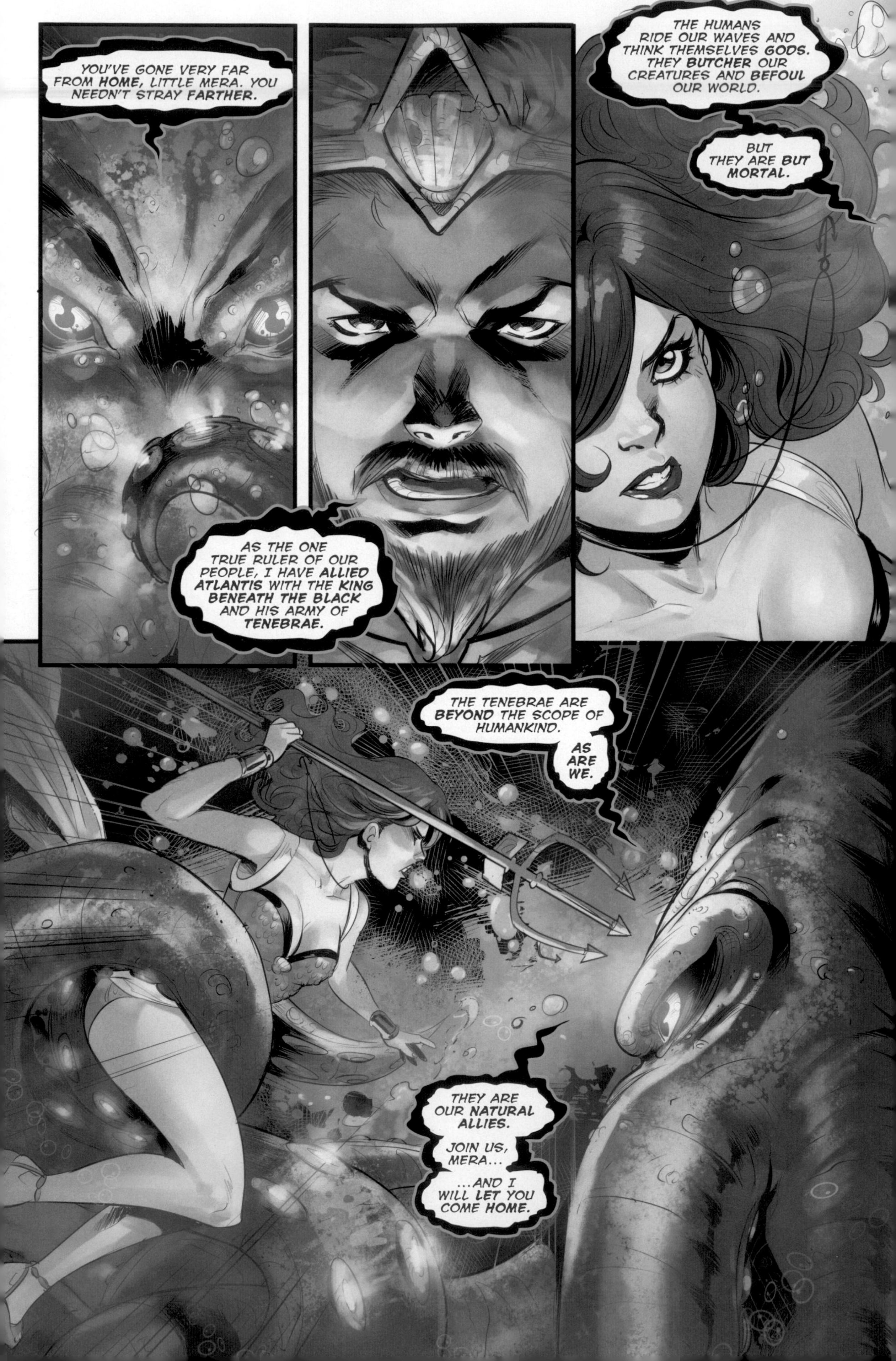
YOU'VE GONE VERY FAR FROM HOME, LITTLE MERA. YOU NEEDN'T STRAY FARTHER.
AS THE ONE TRUE RULER OF OUR PEOPLE, I HAVE ALLIED ATLANTIS WITH THE KING BENEATH THE BLACK AND HIS ARMY OF TENEBRAE.
THE HUMANS RIDE OUR WAVES AND THINK THEMSELVES GODS. THEY BUTCHER OUR CREATURES AND BEFOUL OUR WORLD.
BUT THEY ARE BUT MORTAL.
THE TENEBRAE ARE BEYOND THE SCOPE OF HUMANKIND.
AS ARE WE.
THEY ARE OUR NATURAL ALLIES.
JOIN US, MERA...
...AND I WILL LET YOU COME HOME.

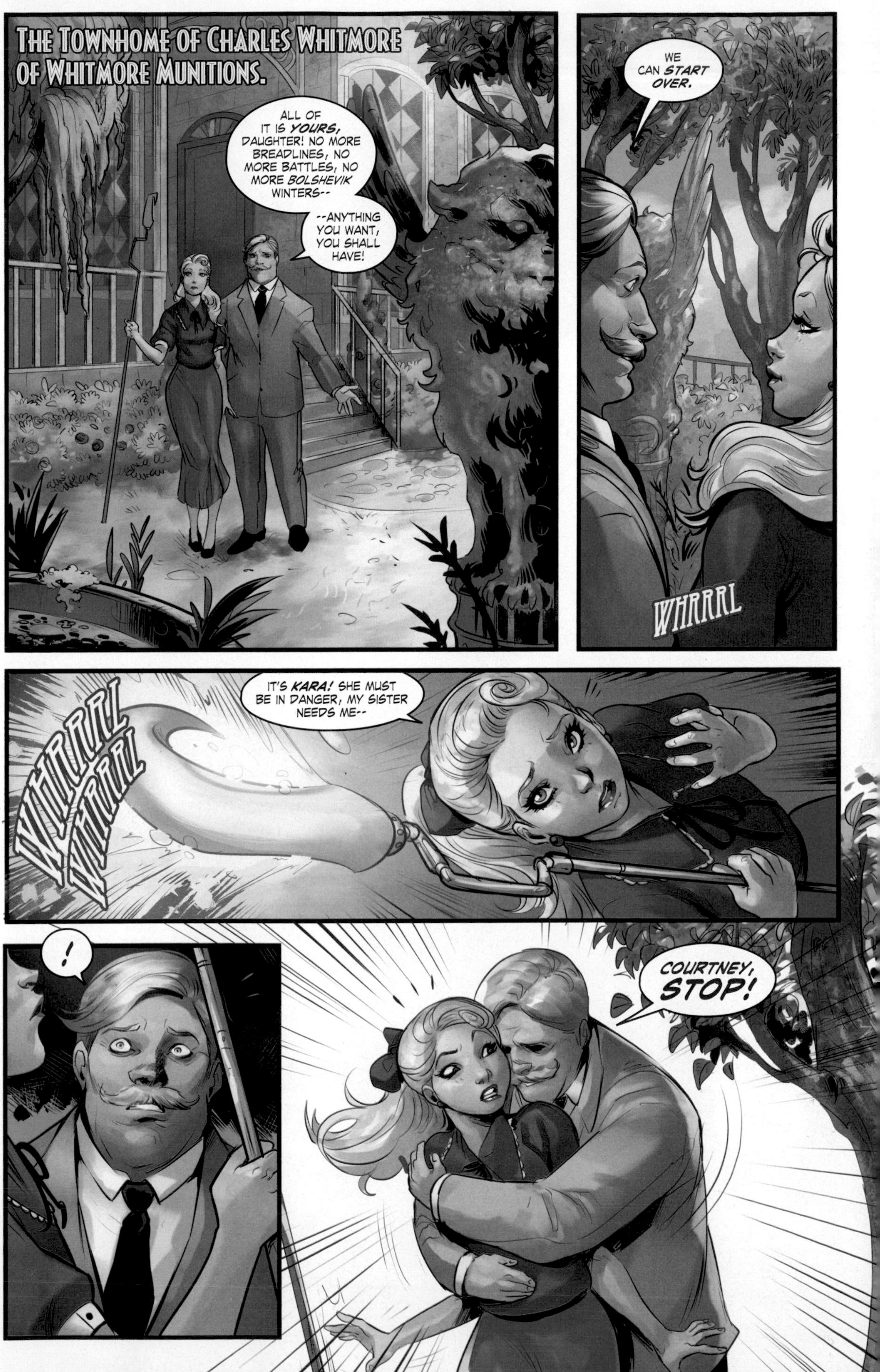
THE TOWNHOME OF CHARLES WHITMORE OF WHITMORE MUNITIONS.
ALL OF IT IS YOURS, DAUGHTER! NO MORE BREADLINES, NO MORE BATTLES, NO MORE BOLSHEVIK WINTERS--
--ANYTHING YOU WANT, YOU SHALL HAVE!
WE CAN START OVER.
WHRRRL
IT'S KARA! SHE MUST BE IN DANGER, MY SISTER NEEDS ME--
WHRRRL WHRRRL
!
COURTNEY, STOP!

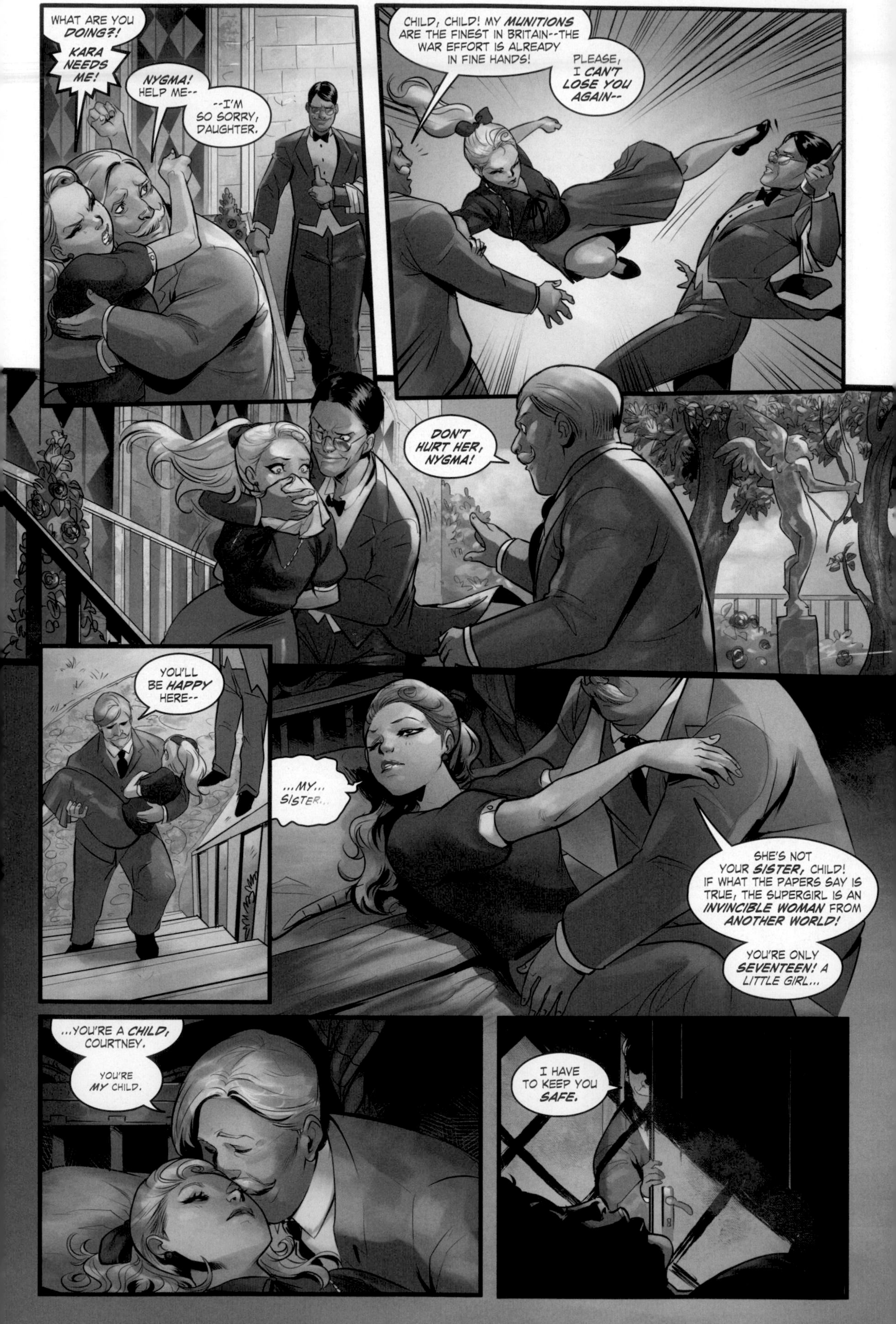
WHAT ARE YOU DOING?! KARA NEEDS ME!
NYGMA! HELP ME--
--I'M SO SORRY, DAUGHTER.
CHILD, CHILD! MY MUNITIONS ARE THE FINEST IN BRITAIN--THE WAR EFFORT IS ALREADY IN FINE HANDS!
PLEASE, I CAN'T LOSE YOU AGAIN--
DON'T HURT HER, NYGMA!
YOU'LL BE HAPPY HERE--
...MY... SISTER...
SHE'S NOT YOUR SISTER, CHILD! IF WHAT THE PAPERS SAY IS TRUE, THE SUPERGIRL IS AN INVINCIBLE WOMAN FROM ANOTHER WORLD!
YOU'RE ONLY SEVENTEEN! A LITTLE GIRL...
...YOU'RE A CHILD, COURTNEY.
YOU'RE MY CHILD.
I HAVE TO KEEP YOU SAFE.

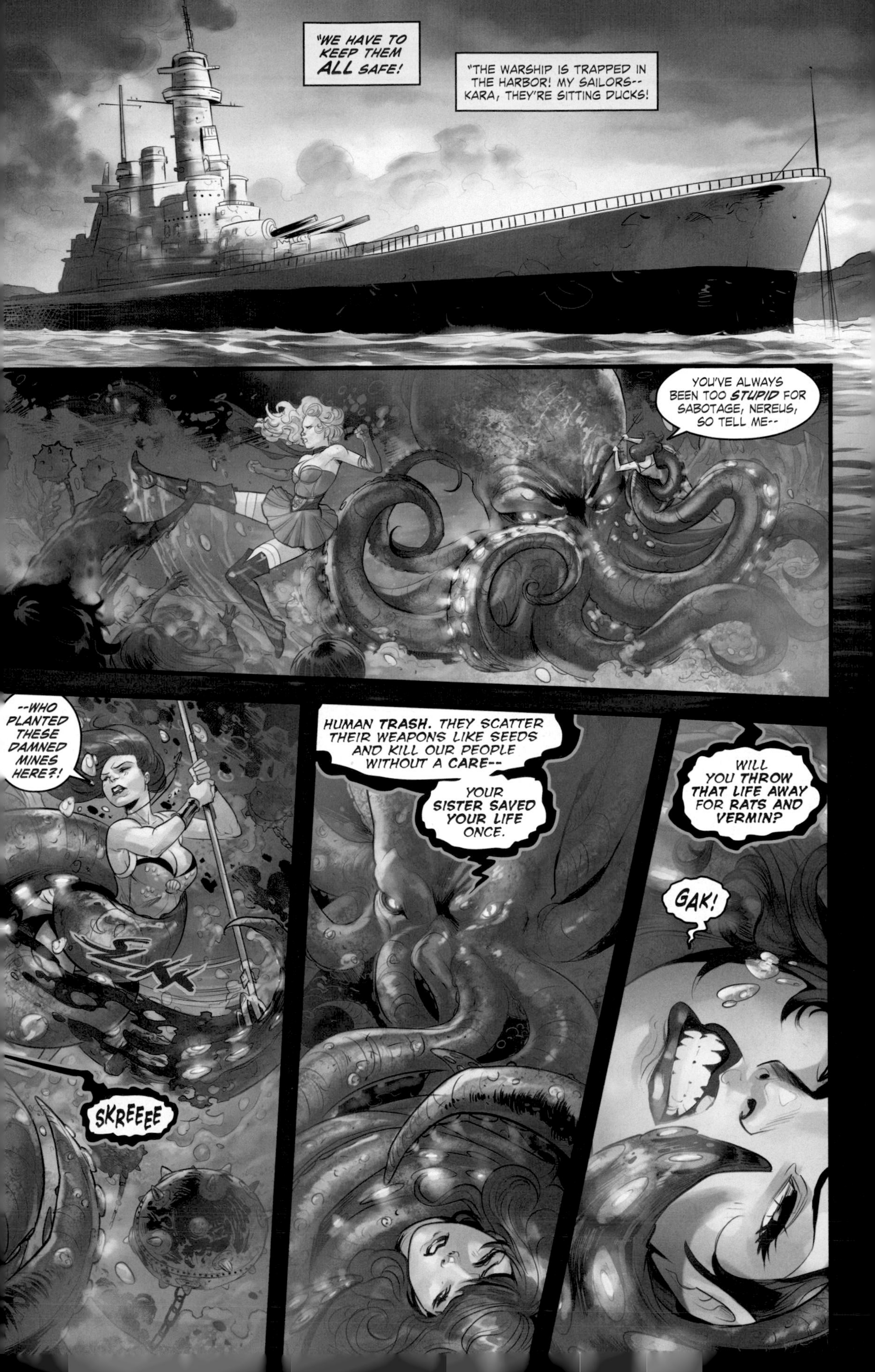
"WE HAVE TO KEEP THEM ALL SAFE!
"THE WARSHIP IS TRAPPED IN THE HARBOR! MY SAILORS-- KARA, THEY'RE SITTING DUCKS!
YOU'VE ALWAYS BEEN TOO STUPID FOR SABOTAGE, NEREUS, SO TELL ME--
--WHO PLANTED THESE DAMNED MINES HERE?!
SKREEEE
HUMAN TRASH. THEY SCATTER THEIR WEAPONS LIKE SEEDS AND KILL OUR PEOPLE WITHOUT A CARE--
YOUR SISTER SAVED YOUR LIFE ONCE.
WILL YOU THROW THAT LIFE AWAY FOR RATS AND VERMIN?
GAK!

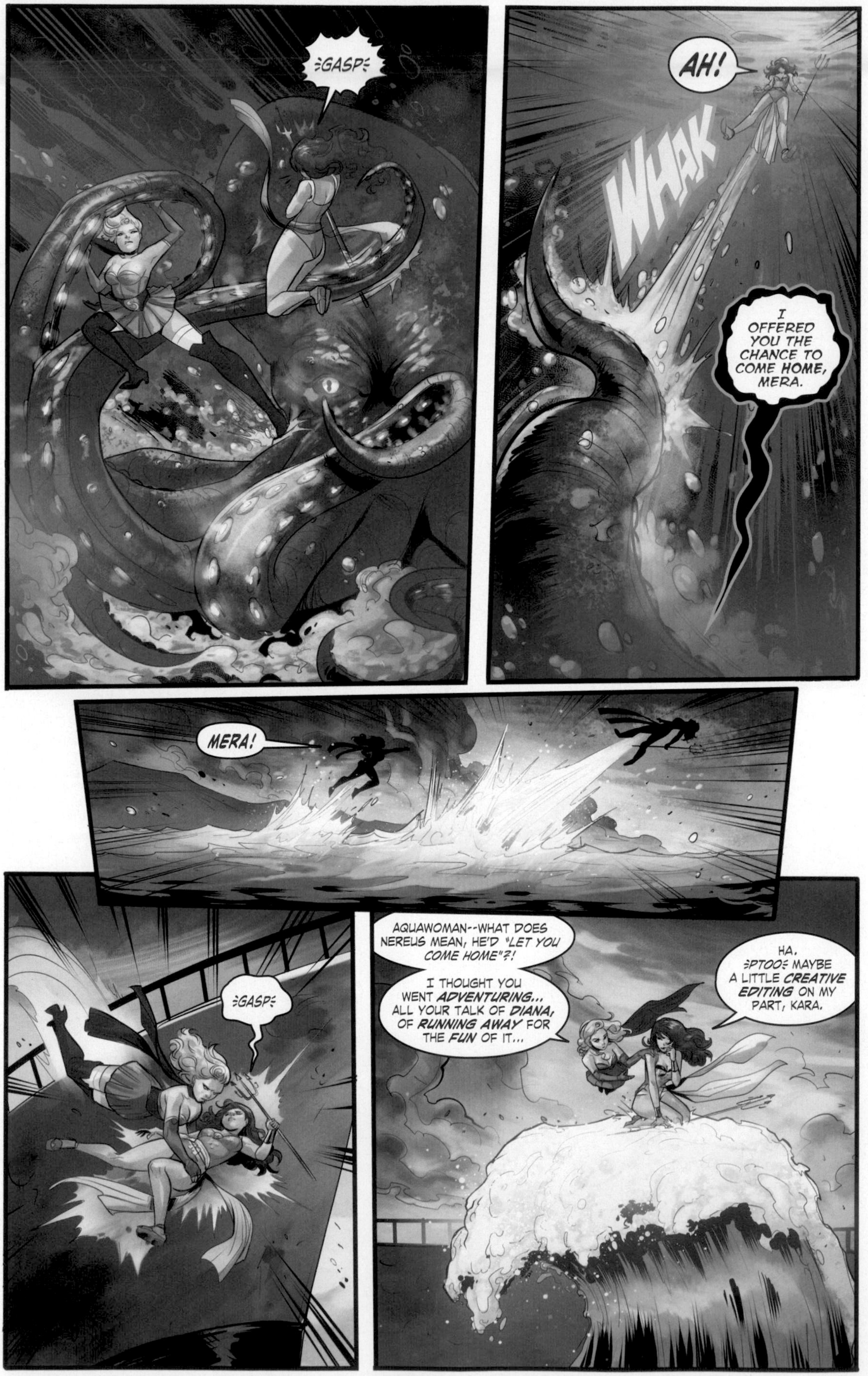
GASP
AH!
WHAK
I OFFERED YOU THE CHANCE TO COME HOME, MERA.
MERA!
GASP
AQUAWOMAN--WHAT DOES NEREUS MEAN, HE'D "LET YOU COME HOME"?!
I THOUGHT YOU WENT ADVENTURING... ALL YOUR TALK OF DIANA, OF RUNNING AWAY FOR THE FUN OF IT...
HA. PTOO MAYBE A LITTLE CREATIVE EDITING ON MY PART, KARA.

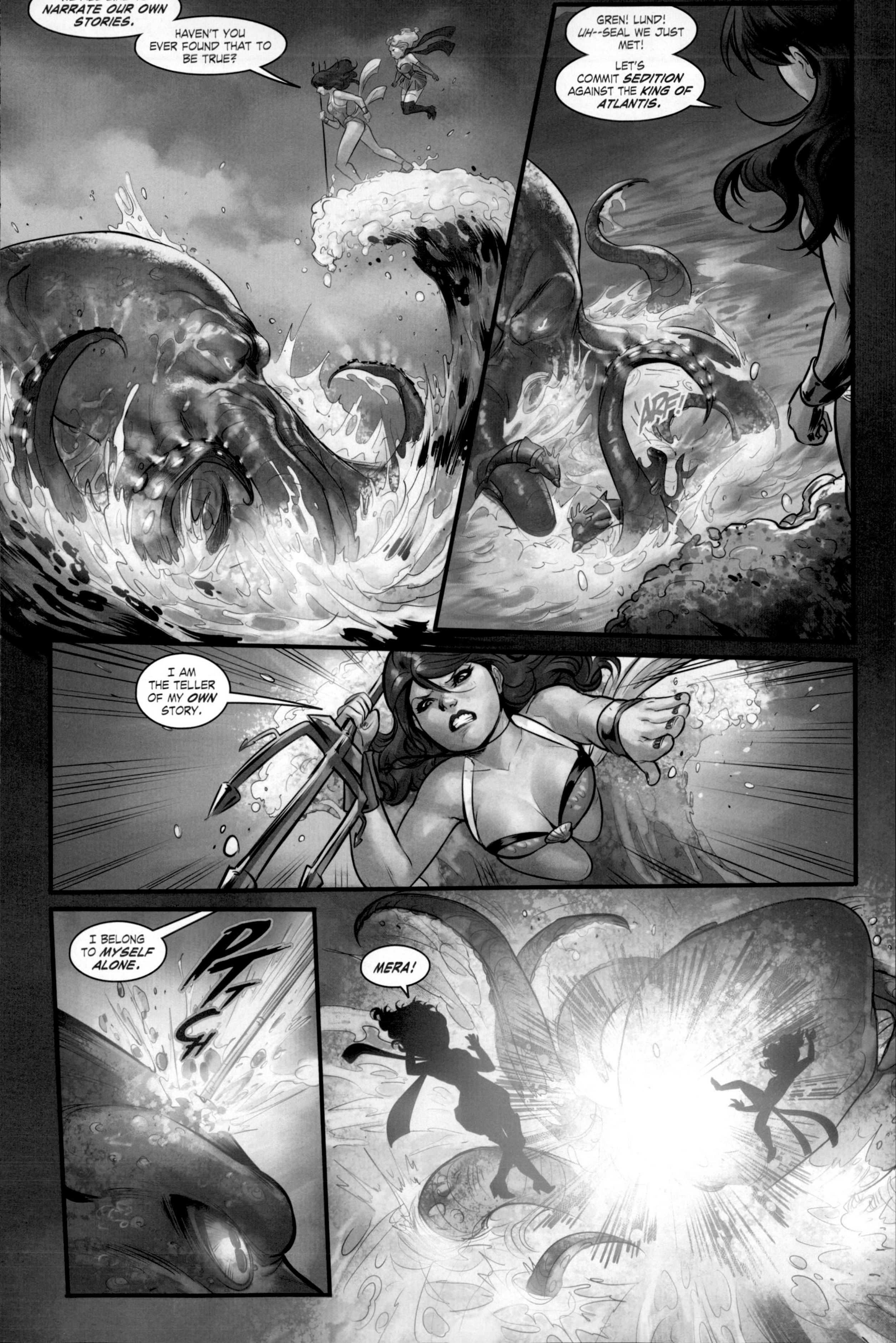
WE ALL LIKE TO NARRATE OUR OWN STORIES.
HAVEN'T YOU EVER FOUND THAT TO BE TRUE?
GREN! LUND! UH--SEAL WE JUST MET!
LET'S COMMIT SEDITION AGAINST THE KING OF ATLANTIS.
ARF!
I AM THE TELLER OF MY OWN STORY.
I BELONG TO MYSELF ALONE.
PTTCH
MERA!

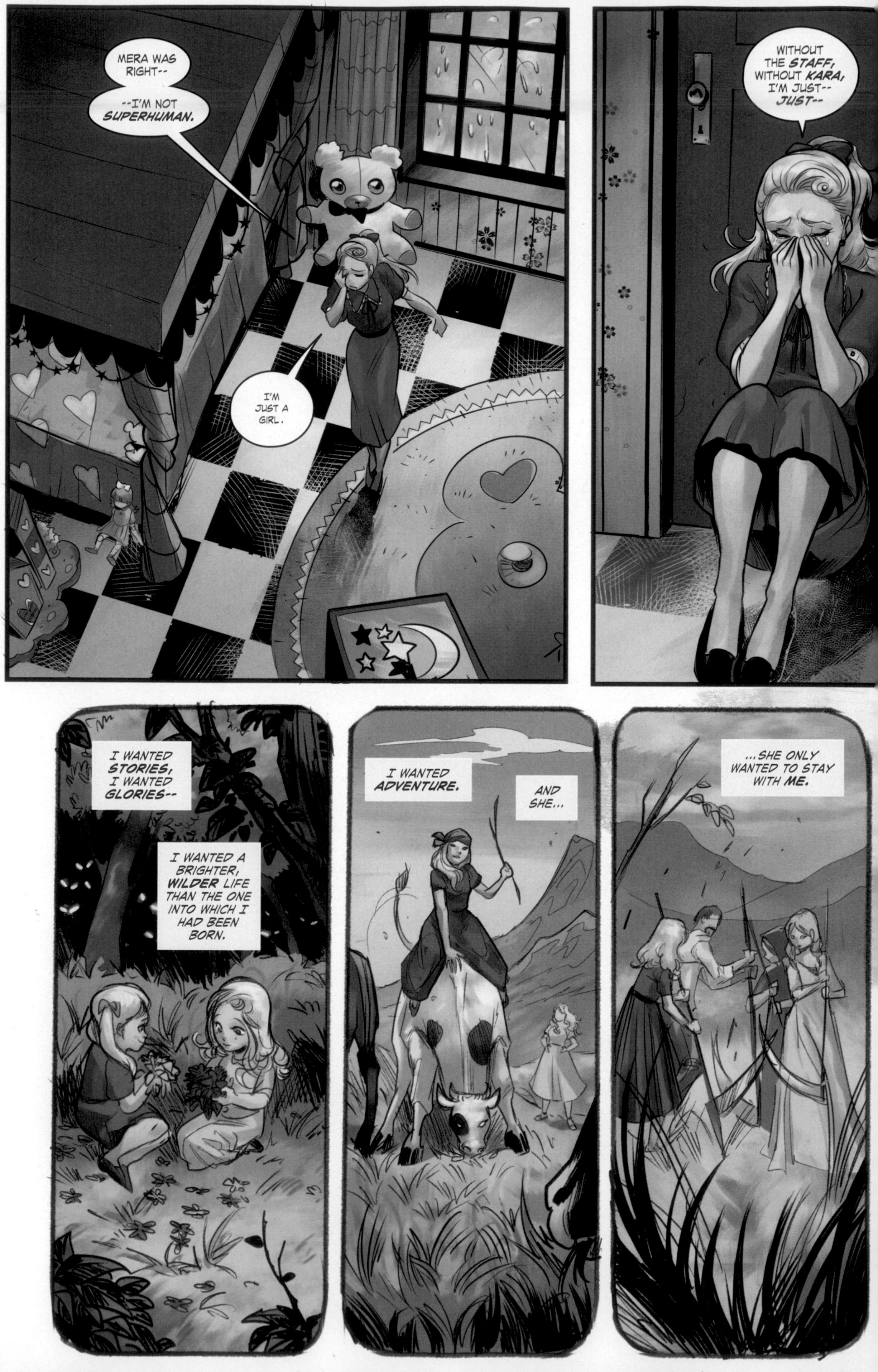
MERA WAS RIGHT--
--I'M NOT SUPERHUMAN.
I'M JUST A GIRL.
WITHOUT THE STAFF, WITHOUT KARA, I'M JUST-- JUST--
I WANTED STORIES, I WANTED GLORIES--
I WANTED A BRIGHTER, WILDER LIFE THAN THE ONE INTO WHICH I HAD BEEN BORN.
I WANTED ADVENTURE.
AND SHE...
...SHE ONLY WANTED TO STAY WITH ME.

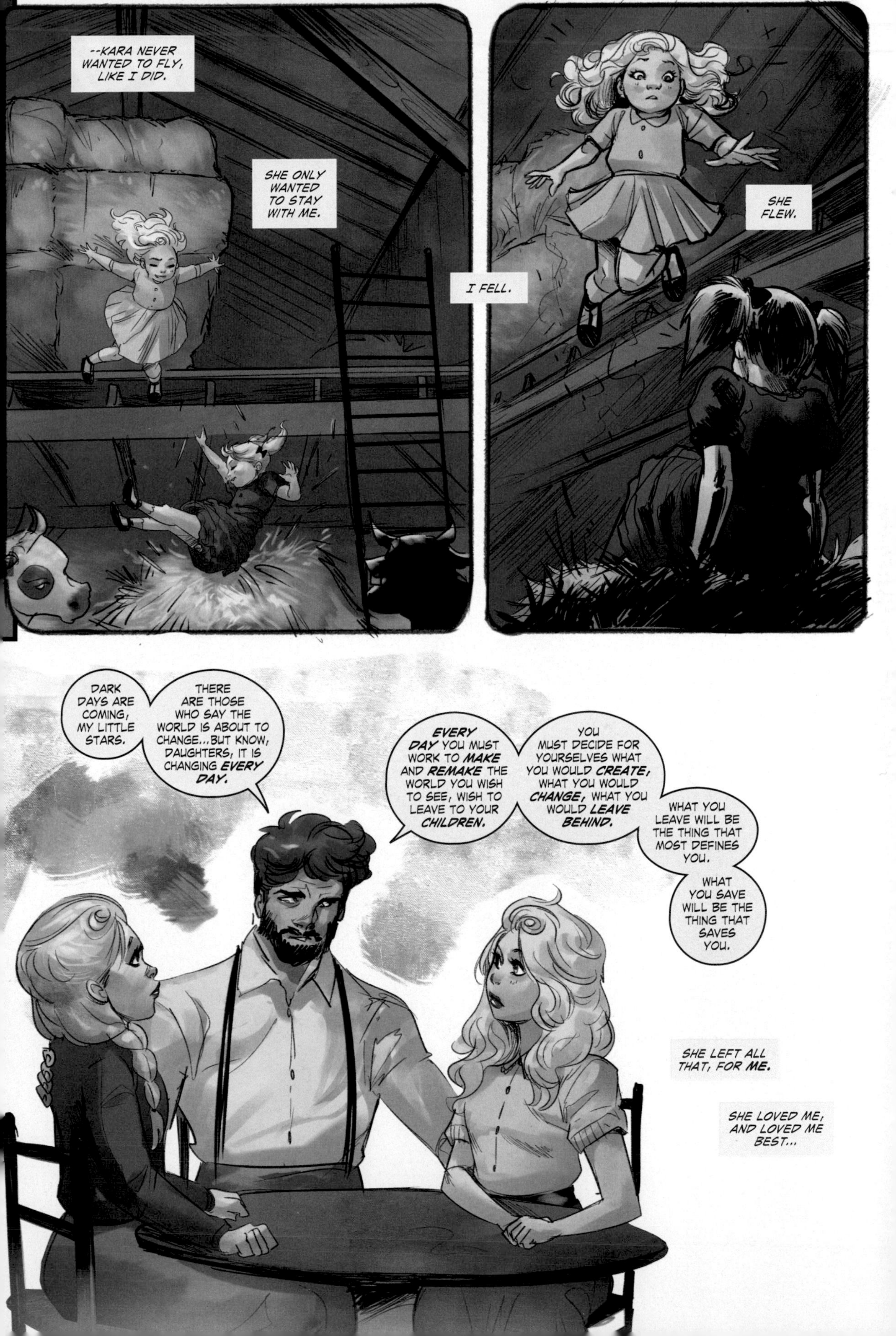
--KARA NEVER WANTED TO FLY, LIKE I DID.
SHE ONLY WANTED TO STAY WITH ME.
I FELL.
SHE FLEW.
DARK DAYS ARE COMING, MY LITTLE STARS.
THERE ARE THOSE WHO SAY THE WORLD IS ABOUT TO CHANGE...BUT KNOW, DAUGHTERS, IT IS CHANGING EVERY DAY.
EVERY DAY YOU MUST WORK TO MAKE AND REMAKE THE WORLD YOU WISH TO SEE, WISH TO LEAVE TO YOUR CHILDREN.
YOU MUST DECIDE FOR YOURSELVES WHAT YOU WOULD CREATE, WHAT YOU WOULD CHANGE, WHAT YOU WOULD LEAVE BEHIND.
WHAT YOU LEAVE WILL BE THE THING THAT MOST DEFINES YOU.
WHAT YOU SAVE WILL BE THE THING THAT SAVES YOU.
SHE LEFT ALL THAT, FOR ME.
SHE LOVED ME, AND LOVED ME BEST...

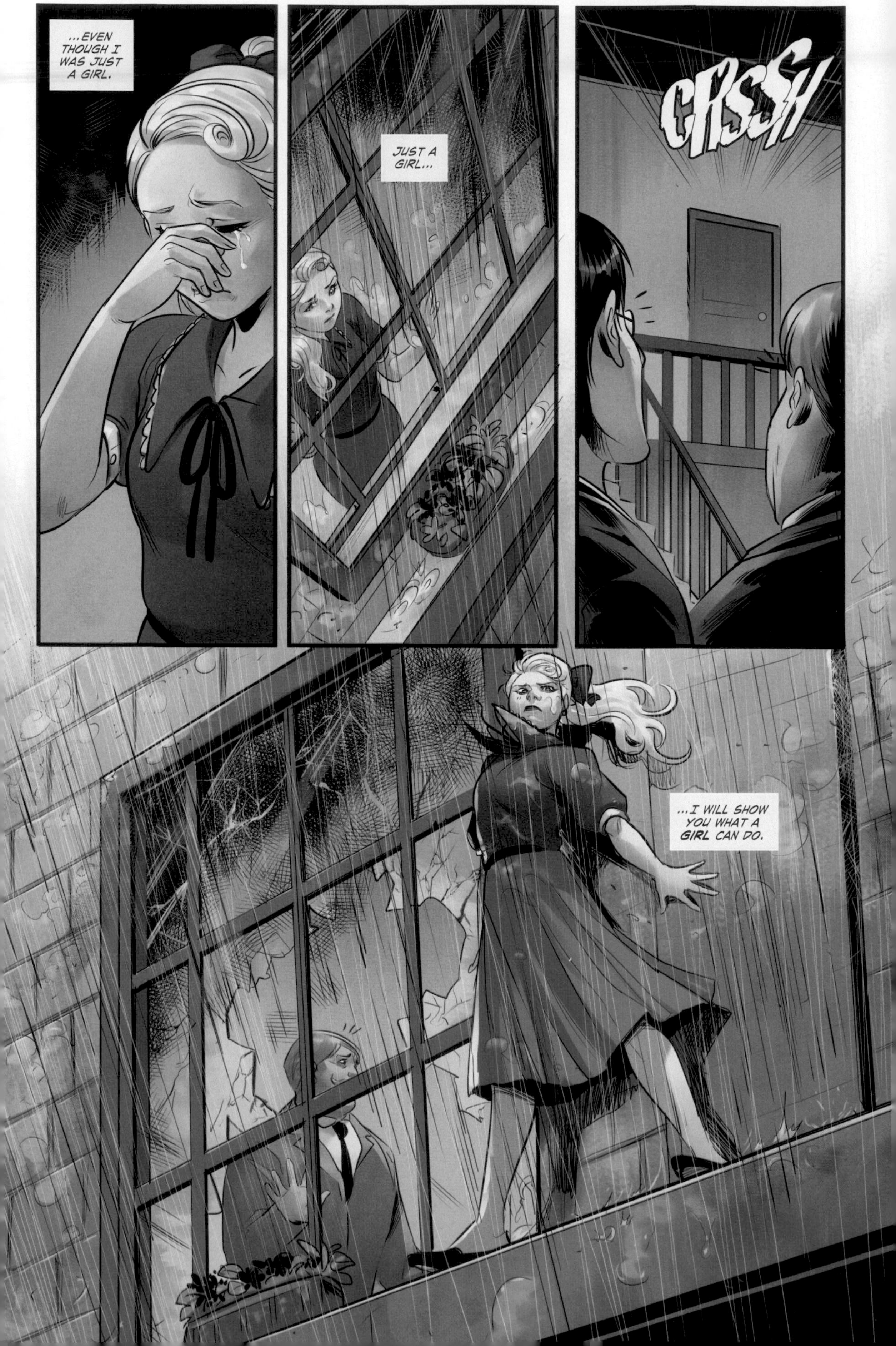
...EVEN THOUGH I WAS JUST A GIRL.
JUST A GIRL...
CRSSH
...I WILL SHOW YOU WHAT A GIRL CAN DO.

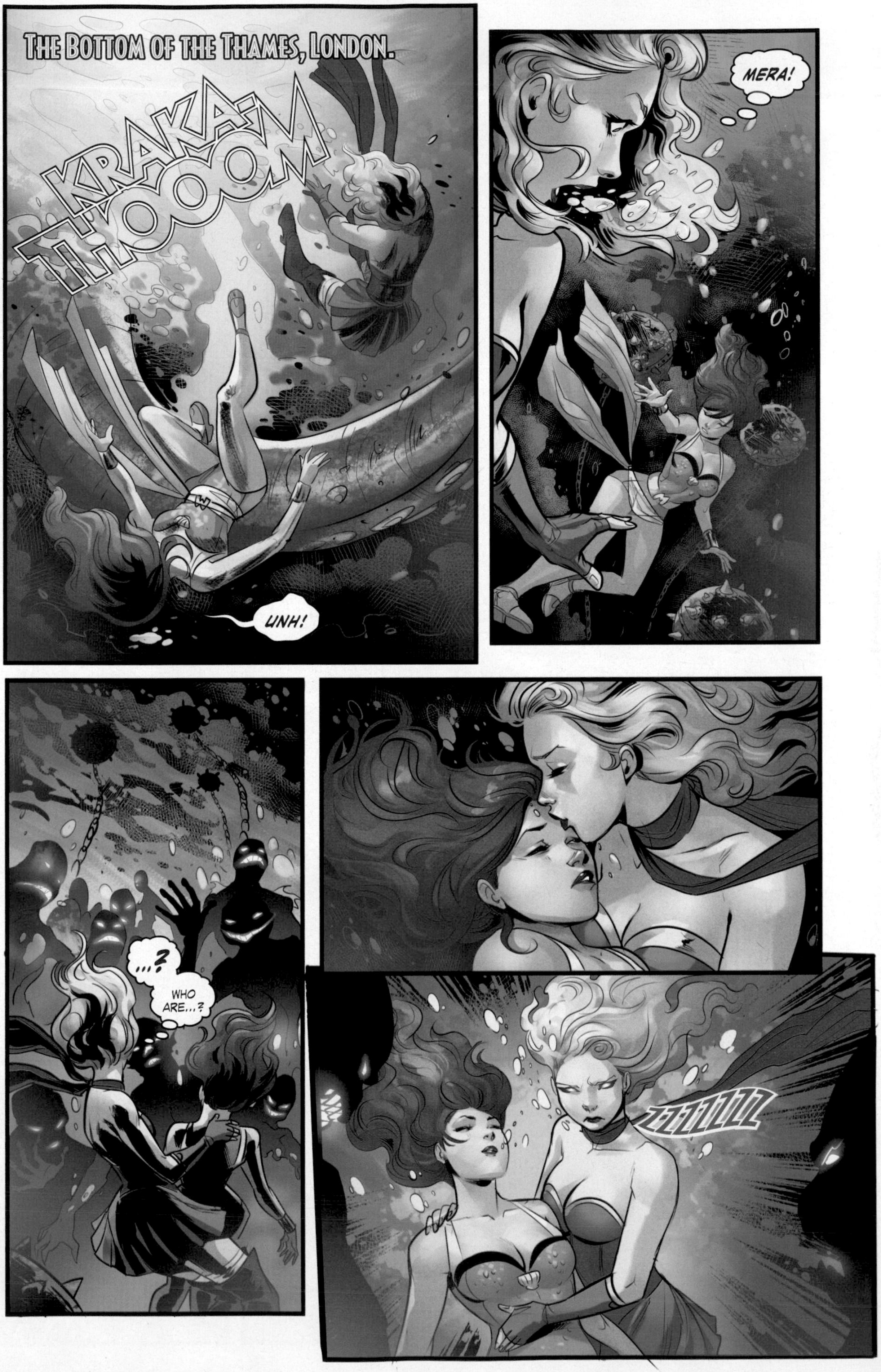
THE BOTTOM OF THE THAMES, LONDON.
KRAKA-THOOOOM
UNH!
MERA!
...?
WHO ARE...?
ZZZZZZZZ

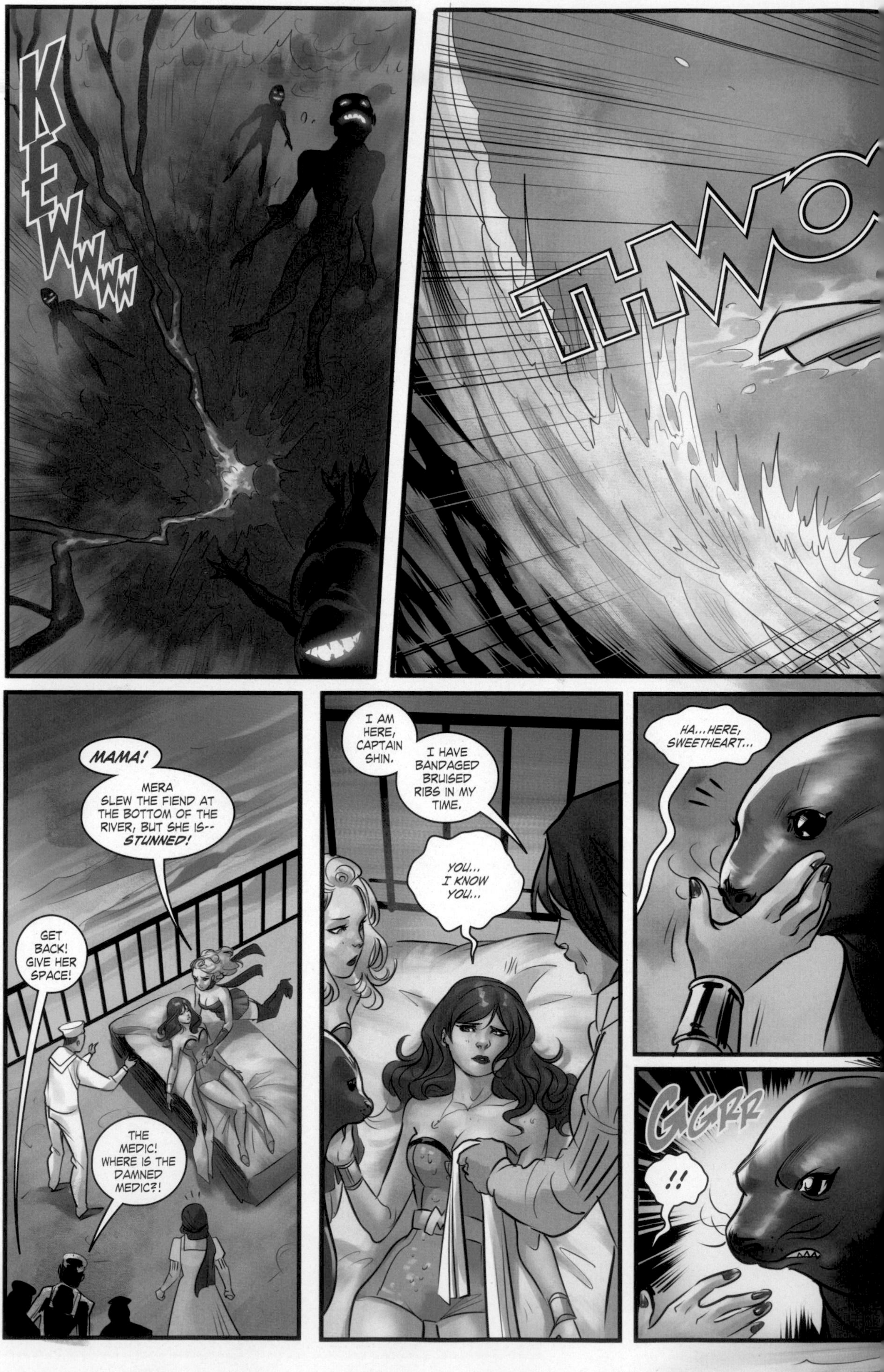
KEWWWWW
THWO
MAMA!
MERA SLEW THE FIEND AT THE BOTTOM OF THE RIVER, BUT SHE IS-- STUNNED!
GET BACK! GIVE HER SPACE!
THE MEDIC! WHERE IS THE DAMNED MEDIC?!
I AM HERE, CAPTAIN SHIN.
I HAVE BANDAGED BRUISED RIBS IN MY TIME.
YOU... I KNOW YOU...
HA...HERE, SWEETHEART...
GGRR
!!

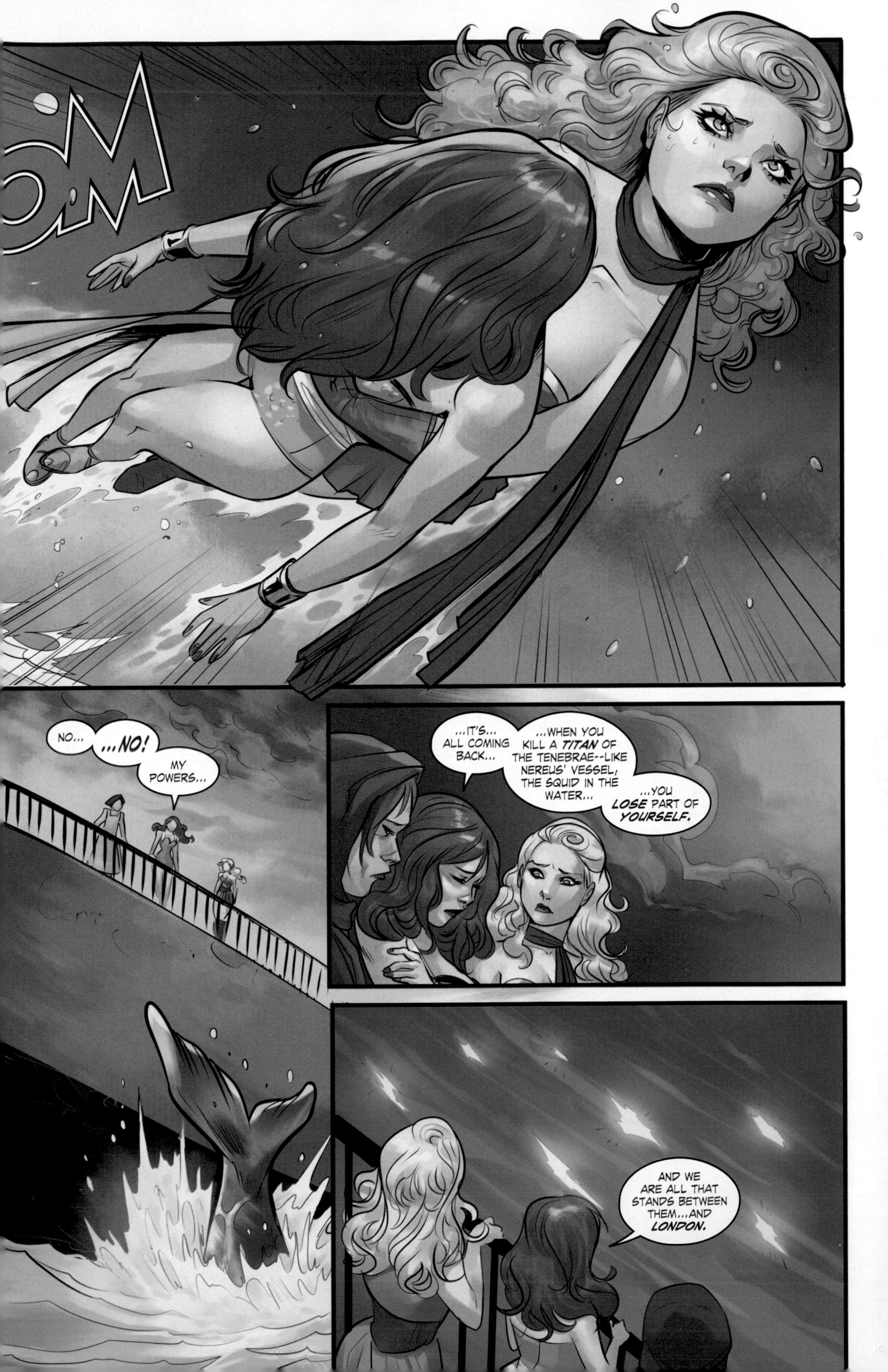

NO...
...NO!
MY POWERS...
...IT'S... ALL COMING BACK...
...WHEN YOU KILL A TITAN OF THE TENEBRAE--LIKE NEREUS' VESSEL, THE SQUID IN THE WATER...
...YOU LOSE PART OF YOURSELF.
AND WE ARE ALL THAT STANDS BETWEEN THEM...AND LONDON.

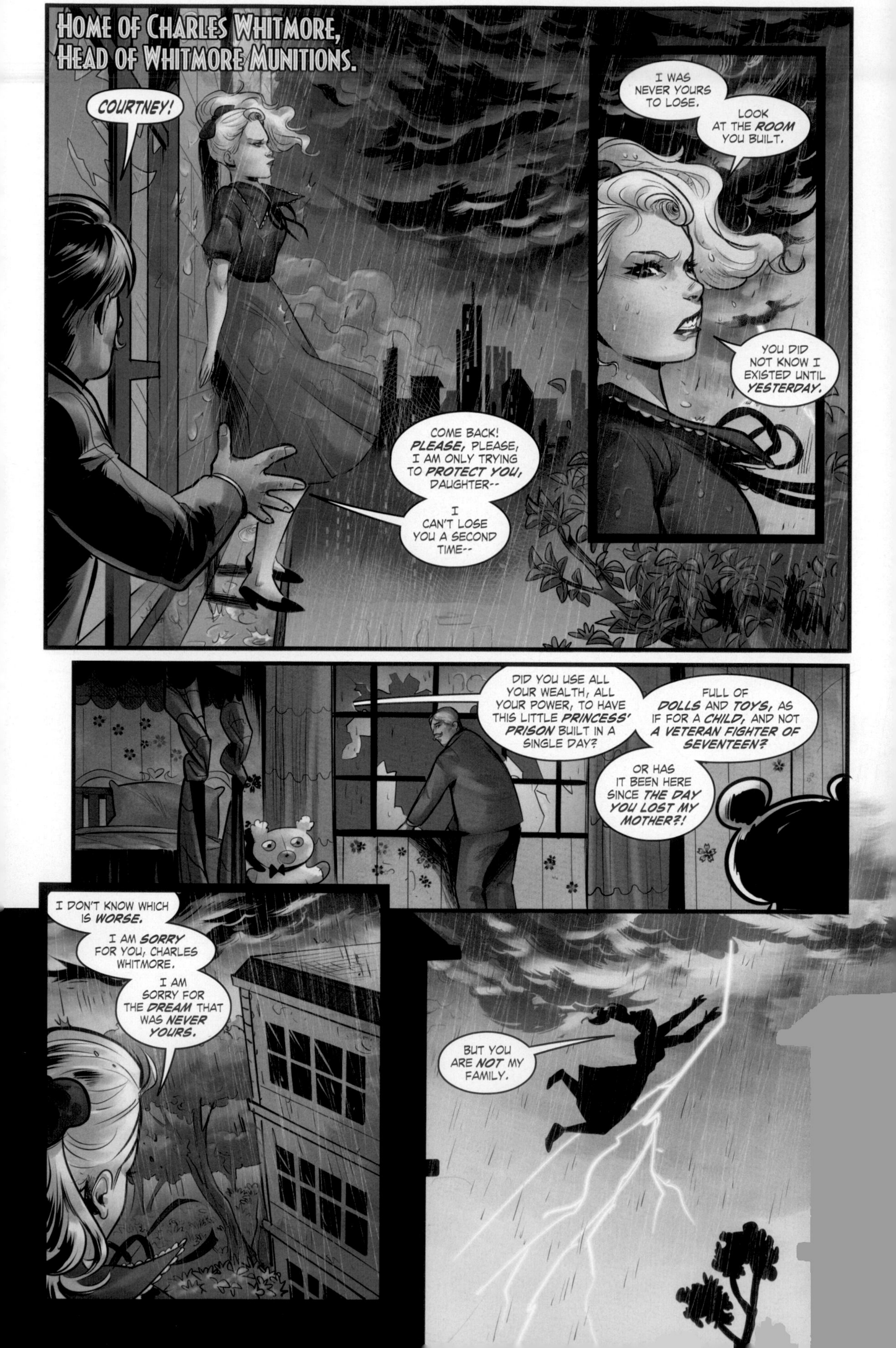
HOME OF CHARLES WHITMORE, HEAD OF WHITMORE MUNITIONS.
COURTNEY!
I WAS NEVER YOURS TO LOSE.
LOOK AT THE ROOM YOU BUILT.
YOU DID NOT KNOW I EXISTED UNTIL YESTERDAY.
COME BACK! PLEASE, PLEASE, I AM ONLY TRYING TO PROTECT YOU, DAUGHTER--
I CAN'T LOSE YOU A SECOND TIME--
DID YOU USE ALL YOUR WEALTH, ALL YOUR POWER, TO HAVE THIS LITTLE PRINCESS' PRISON BUILT IN A SINGLE DAY?
FULL OF DOLLS AND TOYS, AS IF FOR A CHILD, AND NOT A VETERAN FIGHTER OF SEVENTEEN?
OR HAS IT BEEN HERE SINCE THE DAY YOU LOST MY MOTHER?!
I DON'T KNOW WHICH IS WORSE.
I AM SORRY FOR YOU, CHARLES WHITMORE.
I AM SORRY FOR THE DREAM THAT WAS NEVER YOURS.
BUT YOU ARE NOT MY FAMILY.

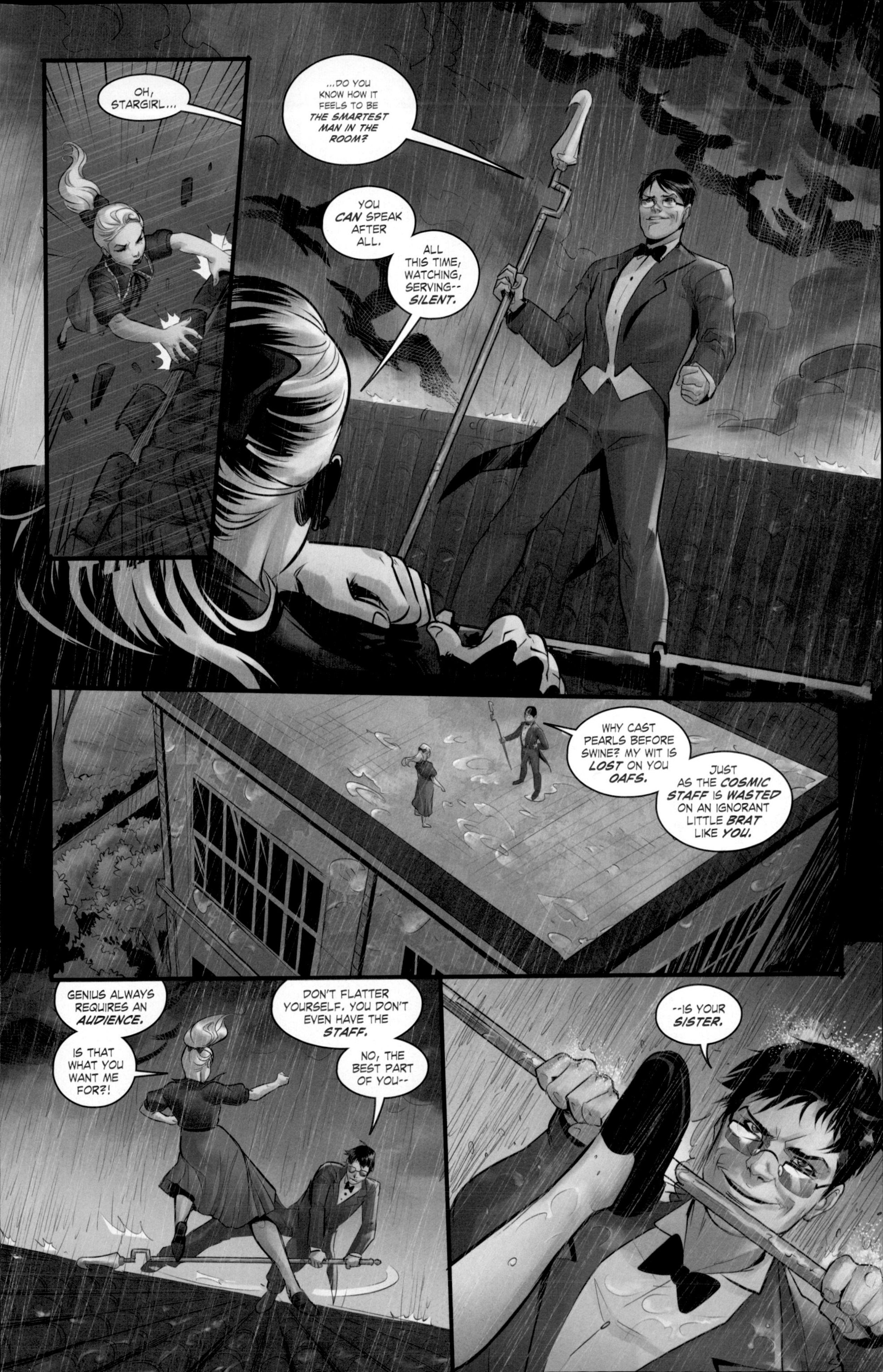
OH, STARGIRL...
...DO YOU KNOW HOW IT FEELS TO BE THE SMARTEST MAN IN THE ROOM?
YOU CAN SPEAK AFTER ALL.
ALL THIS TIME, WATCHING, SERVING-- SILENT.
WHY CAST PEARLS BEFORE SWINE? MY WIT IS LOST ON YOU OAFS.
JUST AS THE COSMIC STAFF IS WASTED ON AN IGNORANT LITTLE BRAT LIKE YOU.
GENIUS ALWAYS REQUIRES AN AUDIENCE.
IS THAT WHAT YOU WANT ME FOR?!
DON'T FLATTER YOURSELF. YOU DON'T EVEN HAVE THE STAFF.
NO, THE BEST PART OF YOU--
--IS YOUR SISTER.

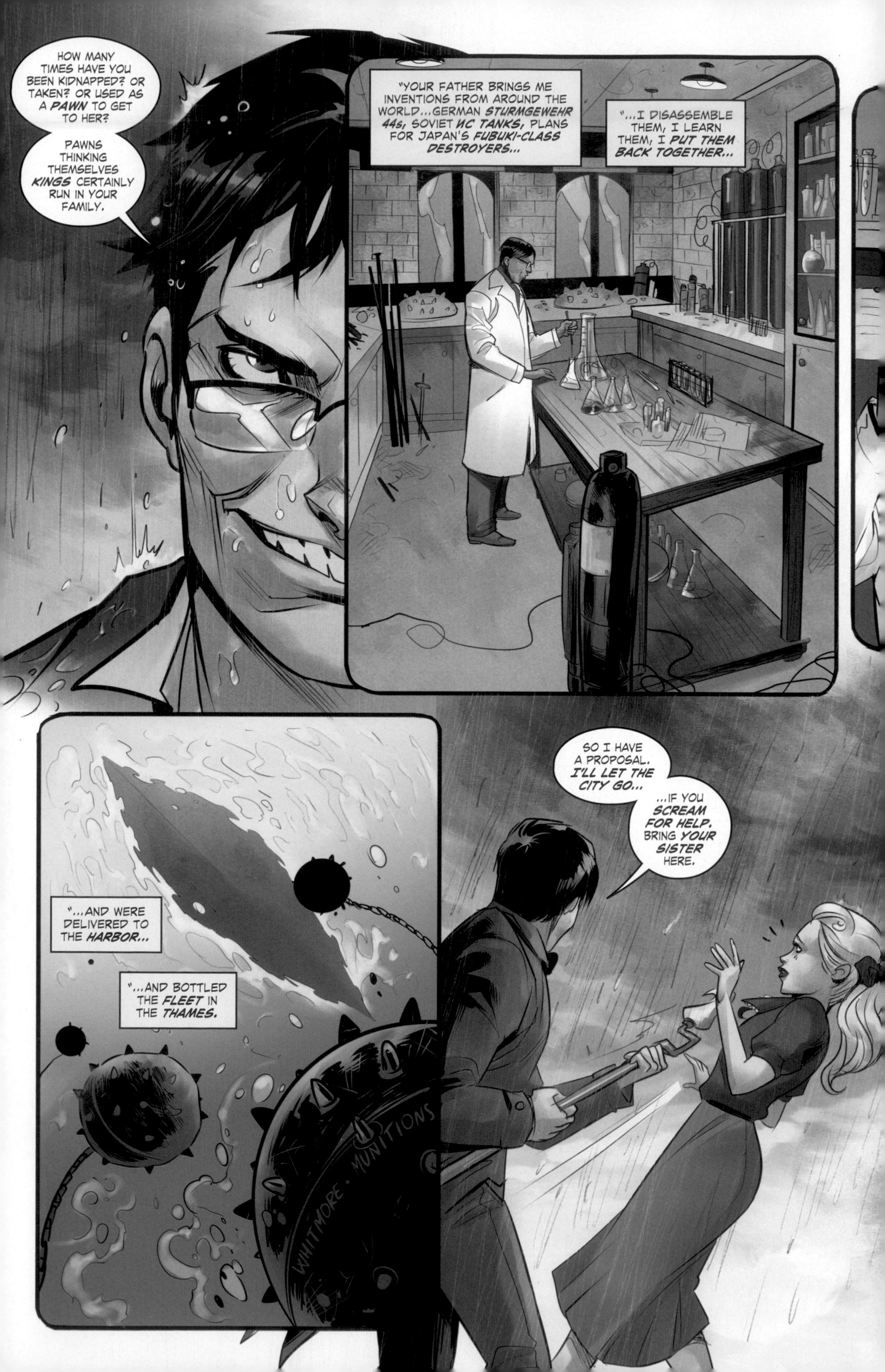
HOW MANY TIMES HAVE YOU BEEN KIDNAPPED? OR TAKEN? OR USED AS A PAWN TO GET TO HER?
PAWNS THINKING THEMSELVES KINGS CERTAINLY RUN IN YOUR FAMILY.
"YOUR FATHER BRINGS ME INVENTIONS FROM AROUND THE WORLD...GERMAN STURMGEWEHR 44s, SOVIET UC TANKS, PLANS FOR JAPAN'S FUBUKI-CLASS DESTROYERS...
"...I DISASSEMBLE THEM, I LEARN THEM, I PUT THEM BACK TOGETHER...
"...AND WERE DELIVERED TO THE HARBOR...
"...AND BOTTLED THE FLEET IN THE THAMES.
WHITMORE · MUNITIONS
SO I HAVE A PROPOSAL. I'LL LET THE CITY GO...
...IF YOU SCREAM FOR HELP. BRING YOUR SISTER HERE.

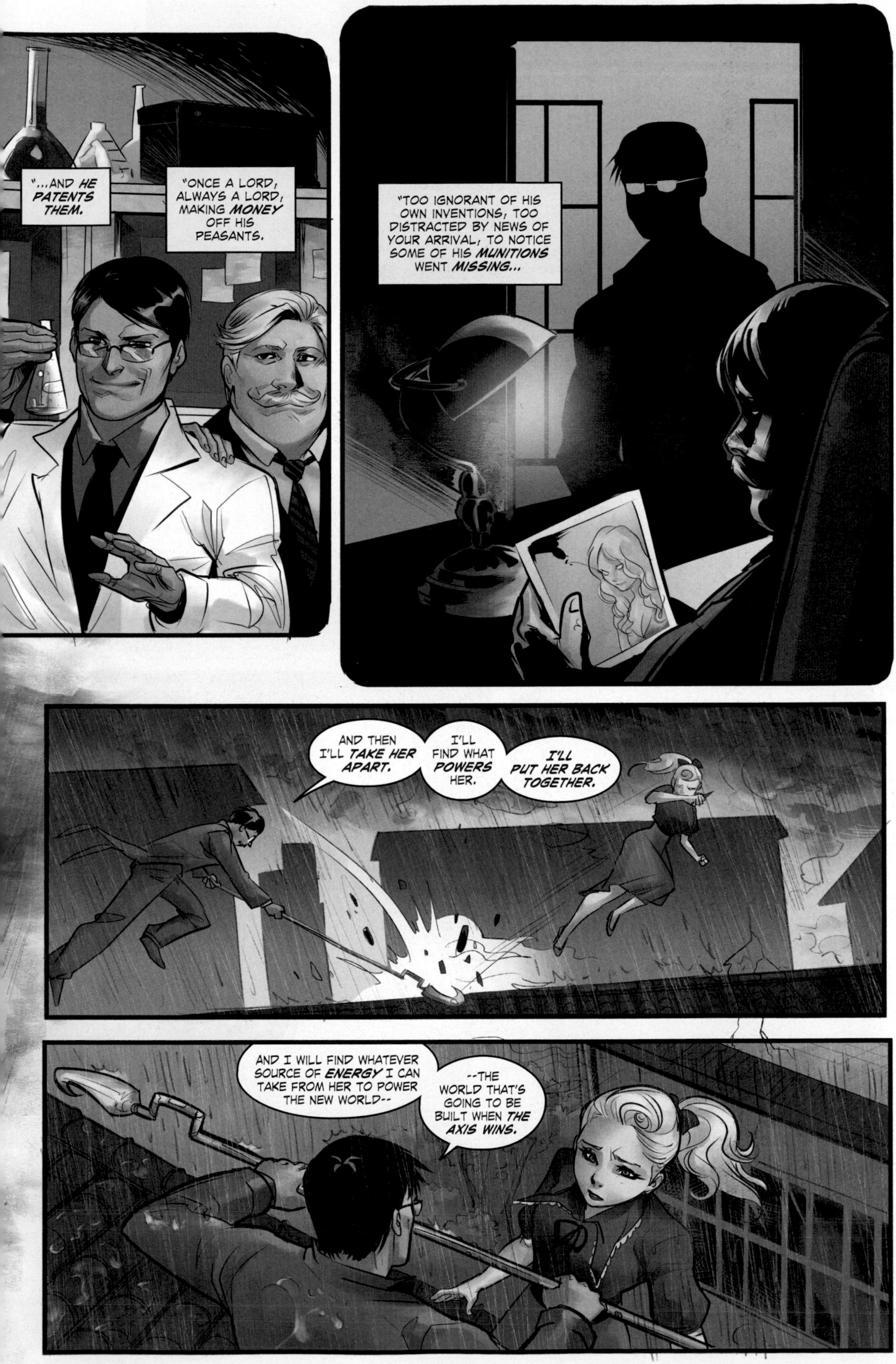
"...AND HE PATENTS THEM.
"ONCE A LORD, ALWAYS A LORD, MAKING MONEY OFF HIS PEASANTS.
"TOO IGNORANT OF HIS OWN INVENTIONS, TOO DISTRACTED BY NEWS OF YOUR ARRIVAL, TO NOTICE SOME OF HIS MUNITIONS WENT MISSING...
AND THEN I'LL TAKE HER APART.
I'LL FIND WHAT POWERS HER.
I'LL PUT HER BACK TOGETHER.
AND I WILL FIND WHATEVER SOURCE OF ENERGY I CAN TAKE FROM HER TO POWER THE NEW WORLD--
--THE WORLD THAT'S GOING TO BE BUILT WHEN THE AXIS WINS.

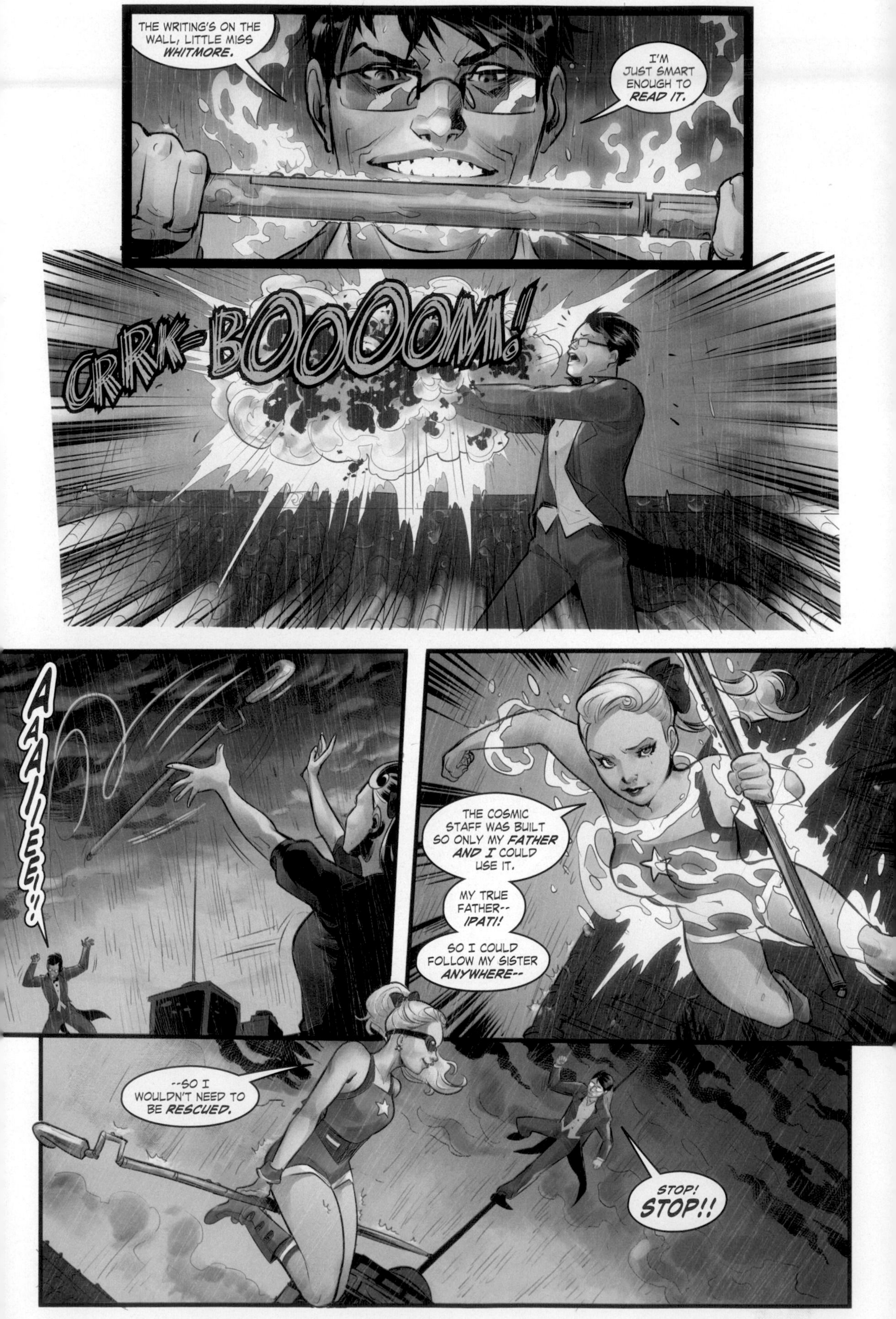
THE WRITING'S ON THE WALL, LITTLE MISS WHITMORE.
I'M JUST SMART ENOUGH TO READ IT.
CRRK-BOOOOOM!
AAAIIEEE!!
THE COSMIC STAFF WAS BUILT SO ONLY MY FATHER AND I COULD USE IT.
MY TRUE FATHER-- IPATI!
SO I COULD FOLLOW MY SISTER ANYWHERE--
--SO I WOULDN'T NEED TO BE RESCUED.
STOP! STOP!!

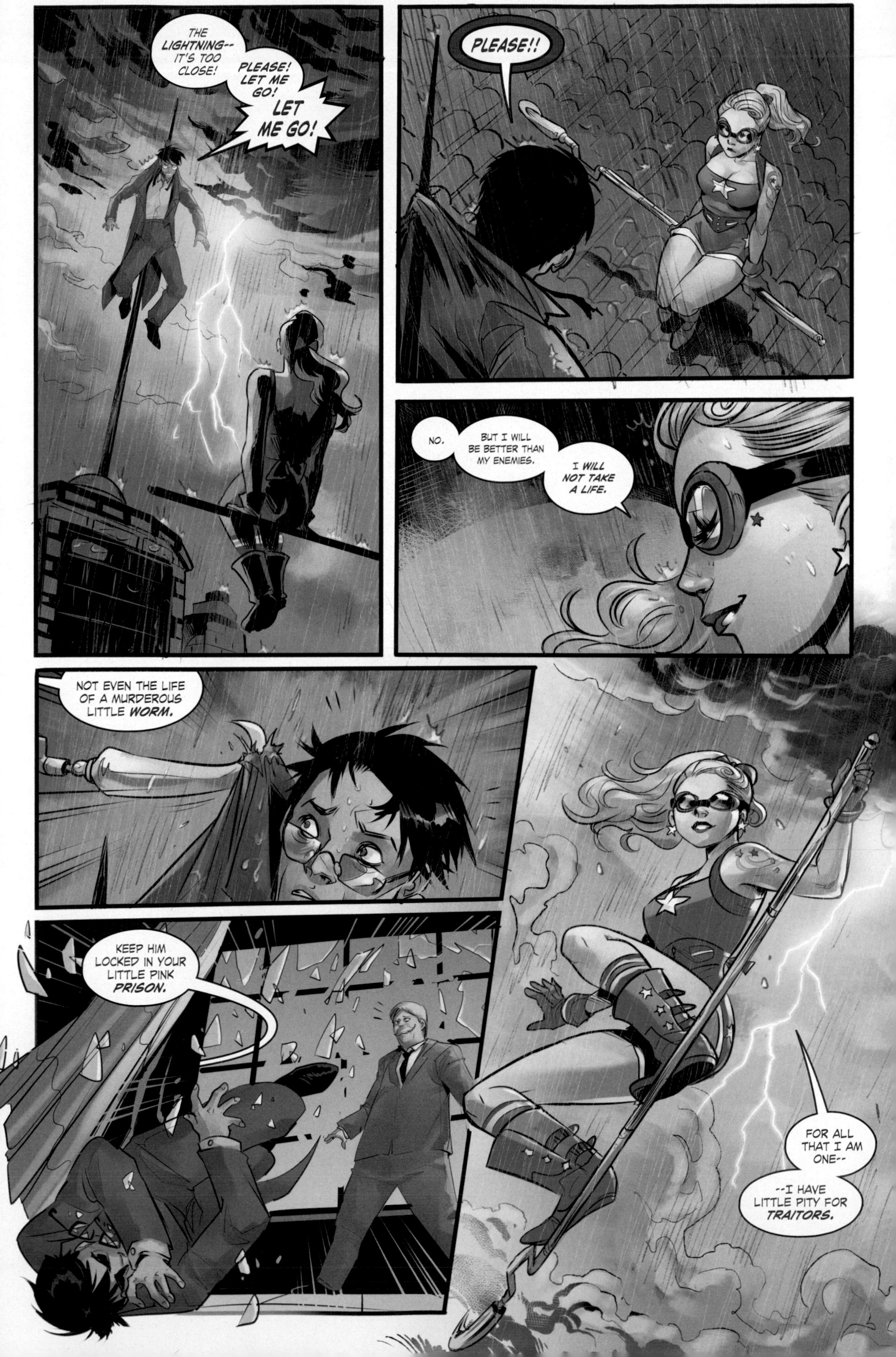
THE LIGHTNING-- IT'S TOO CLOSE!
PLEASE! LET ME GO!
LET ME GO!
PLEASE!!
NO.
BUT I WILL BE BETTER THAN MY ENEMIES.
I WILL NOT TAKE A LIFE.
NOT EVEN THE LIFE OF A MURDEROUS LITTLE WORM.
KEEP HIM LOCKED IN YOUR LITTLE PINK PRISON.
FOR ALL THAT I AM ONE--
--I HAVE LITTLE PITY FOR TRAITORS.

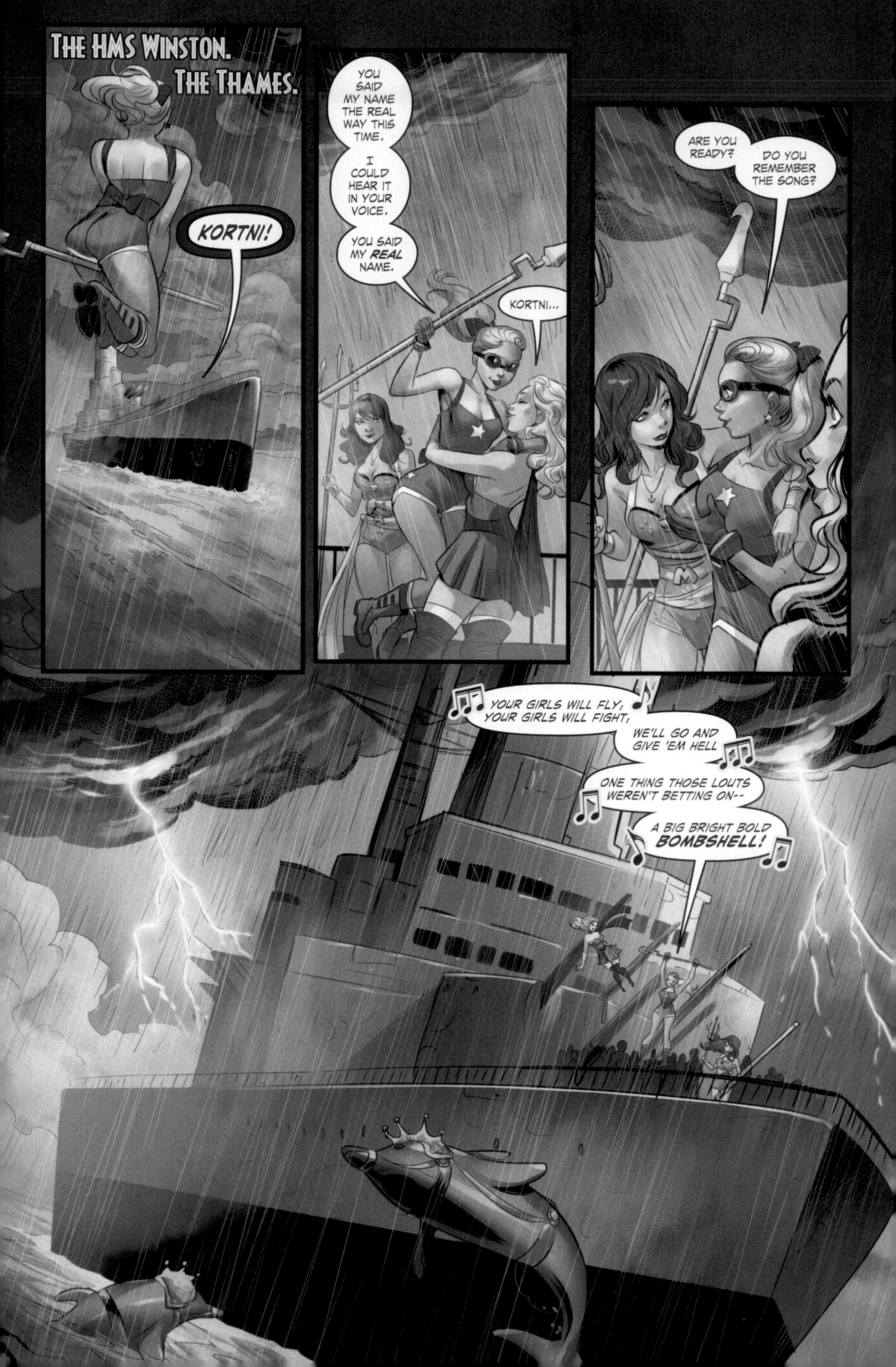
THE HMS WINSTON.
THE THAMES.
KORTNI!
YOU SAID MY NAME THE REAL WAY THIS TIME.
I COULD HEAR IT IN YOUR VOICE.
YOU SAID MY REAL NAME.
KORTNI...
ARE YOU READY?
DO YOU REMEMBER THE SONG?
YOUR GIRLS WILL FLY, YOUR GIRLS WILL FIGHT,
WE'LL GO AND GIVE 'EM HELL
ONE THING THOSE LOUTS WEREN'T BETTING ON--
A BIG BRIGHT BOLD BOMBSHELL!

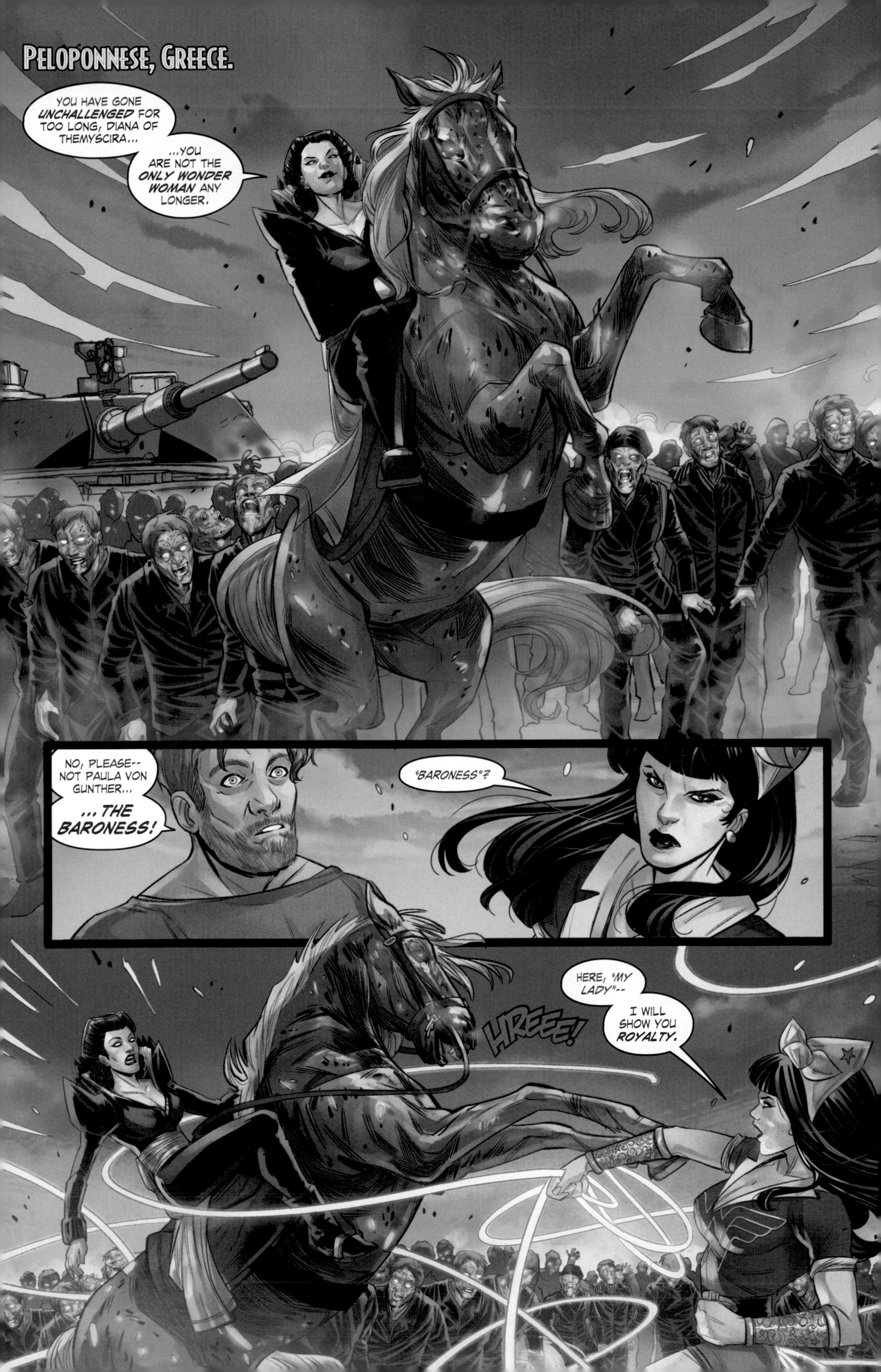
PELOPONNESE, GREECE.
YOU HAVE GONE UNCHALLENGED FOR TOO LONG, DIANA OF THEMYSCIRA...
...YOU ARE NOT THE ONLY WONDER WOMAN ANY LONGER.
NO, PLEASE-- NOT PAULA VON GUNTHER...
...THE BARONESS!
"BARONESS"?
HREEE!
HERE, "MY LADY"--
I WILL SHOW YOU ROYALTY.

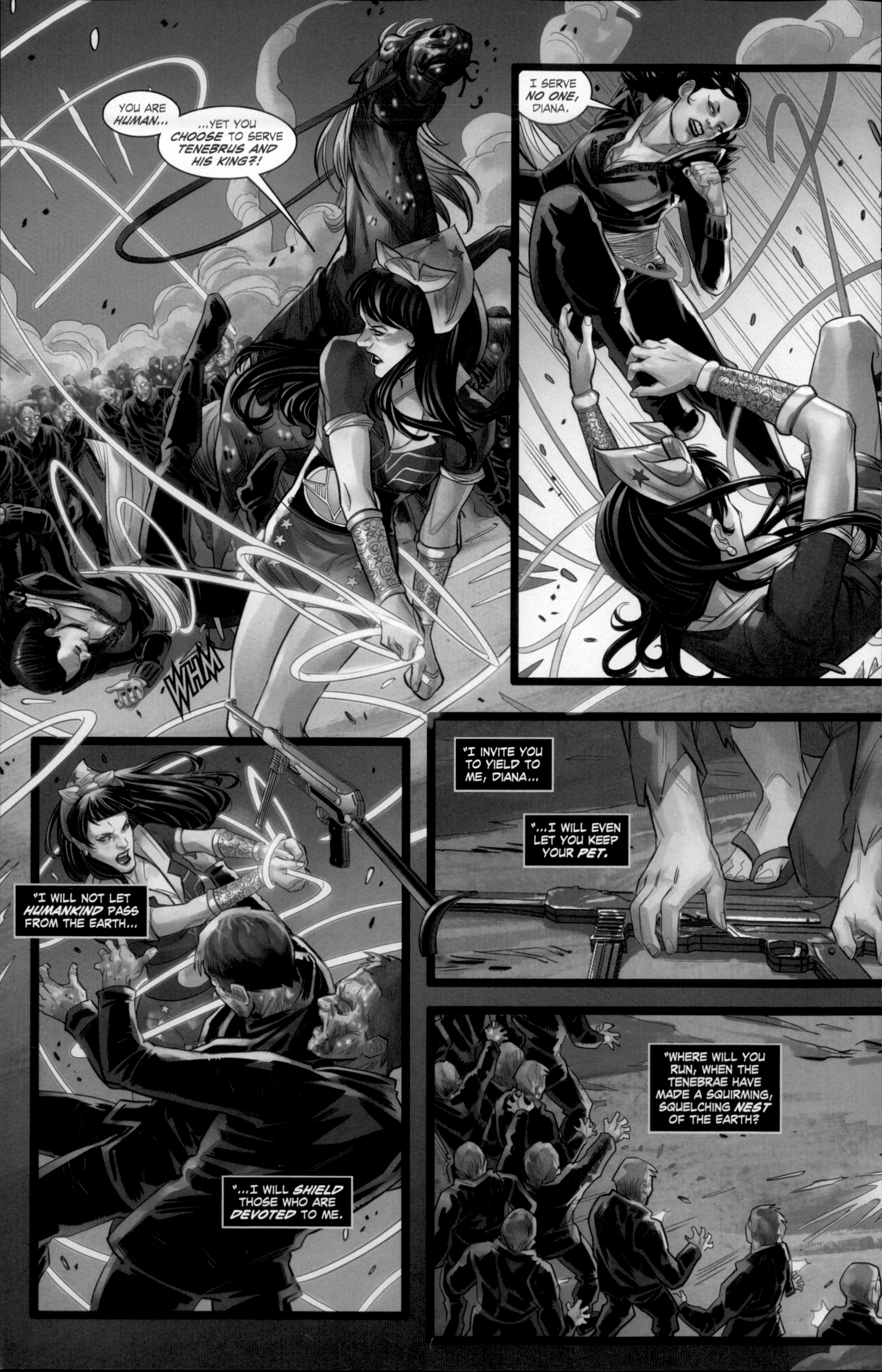

YOU ARE *HUMAN*...
...YET YOU *CHOOSE* TO SERVE *TENEBRUS AND HIS KING?!*
I SERVE *NO ONE*, DIANA.
WHM
"I WILL NOT LET *HUMANKIND* PASS FROM THE EARTH...
"...I WILL *SHIELD* THOSE WHO ARE *DEVOTED* TO ME.
"I INVITE YOU TO YIELD TO ME, DIANA...
"...I WILL EVEN LET YOU KEEP YOUR *PET*.
"WHERE WILL YOU RUN, WHEN THE TENEBRAE HAVE MADE A SQUIRMING, SQUELCHING *NEST* OF THE EARTH?

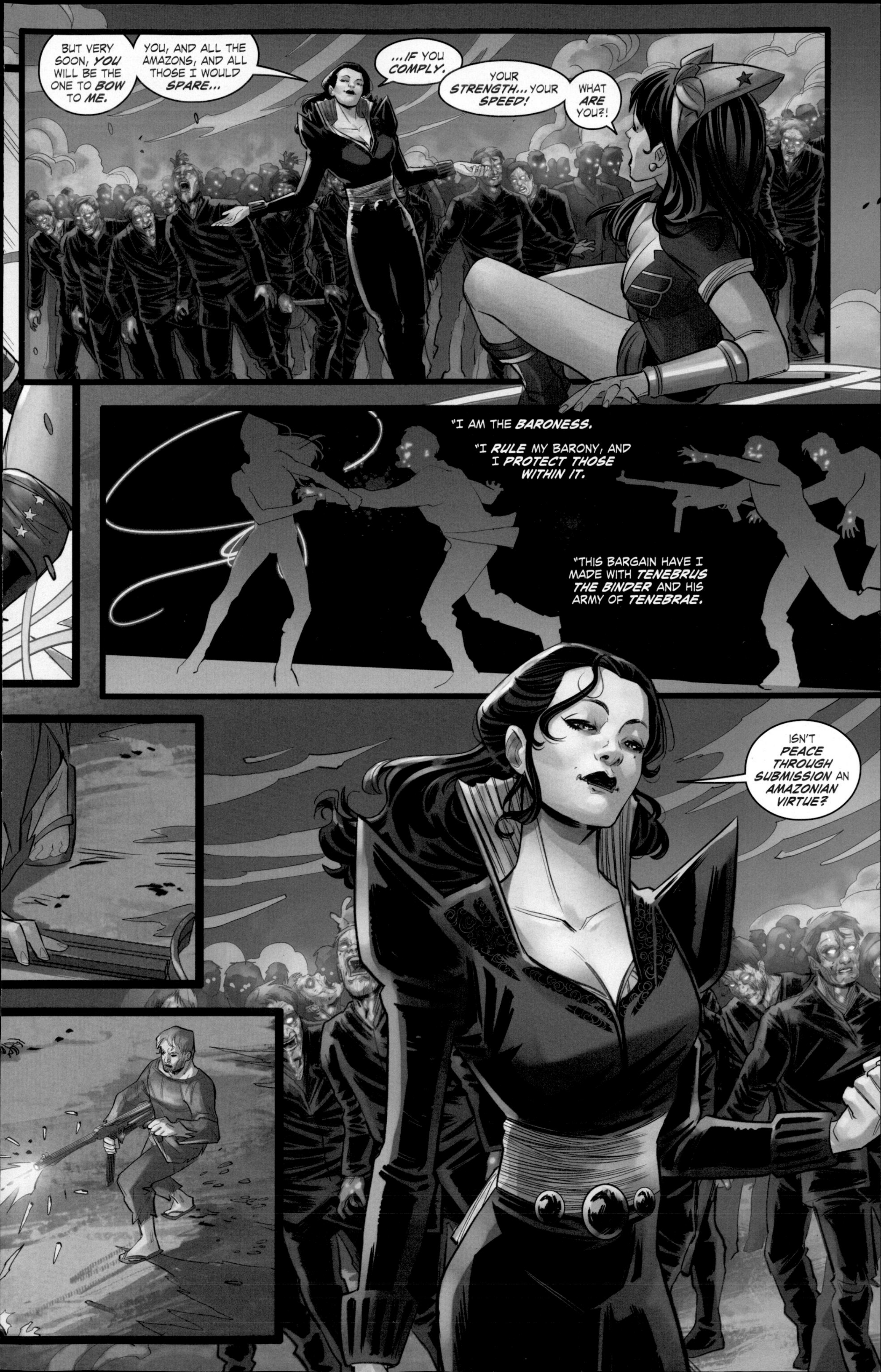
BUT VERY SOON, YOU WILL BE THE ONE TO BOW TO ME.
YOU, AND ALL THE AMAZONS, AND ALL THOSE I WOULD SPARE...
...IF YOU COMPLY.
YOUR STRENGTH... YOUR SPEED!
WHAT ARE YOU?!
"I AM THE BARONESS.
"I RULE MY BARONY, AND I PROTECT THOSE WITHIN IT.
"THIS BARGAIN HAVE I MADE WITH TENEBRUS THE BINDER AND HIS ARMY OF TENEBRAE.
ISN'T PEACE THROUGH SUBMISSION AN AMAZONIAN VIRTUE?

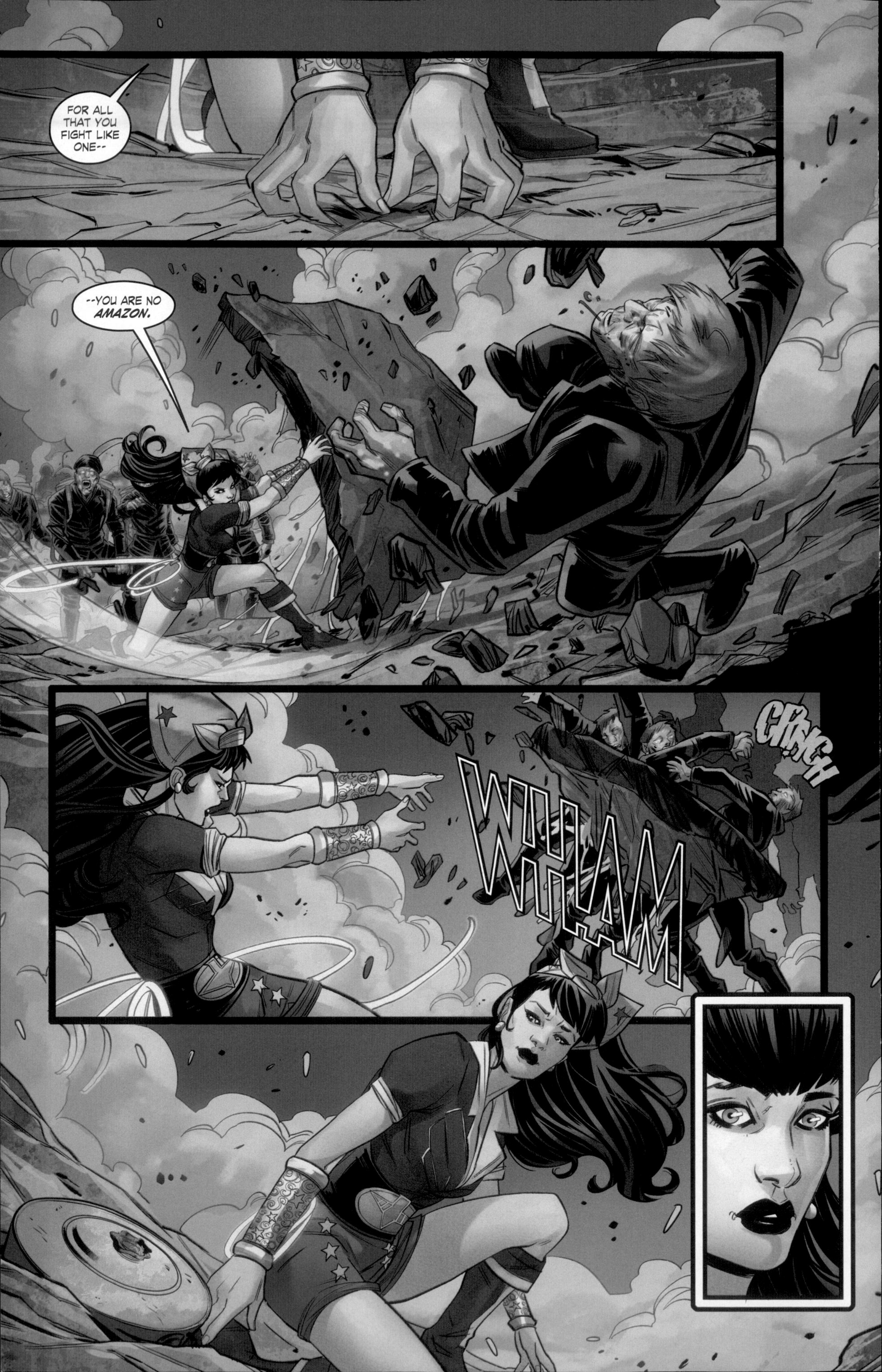
FOR ALL THAT YOU FIGHT LIKE ONE--
--YOU ARE NO AMAZON.
WHAM
WHAM
CRNCH

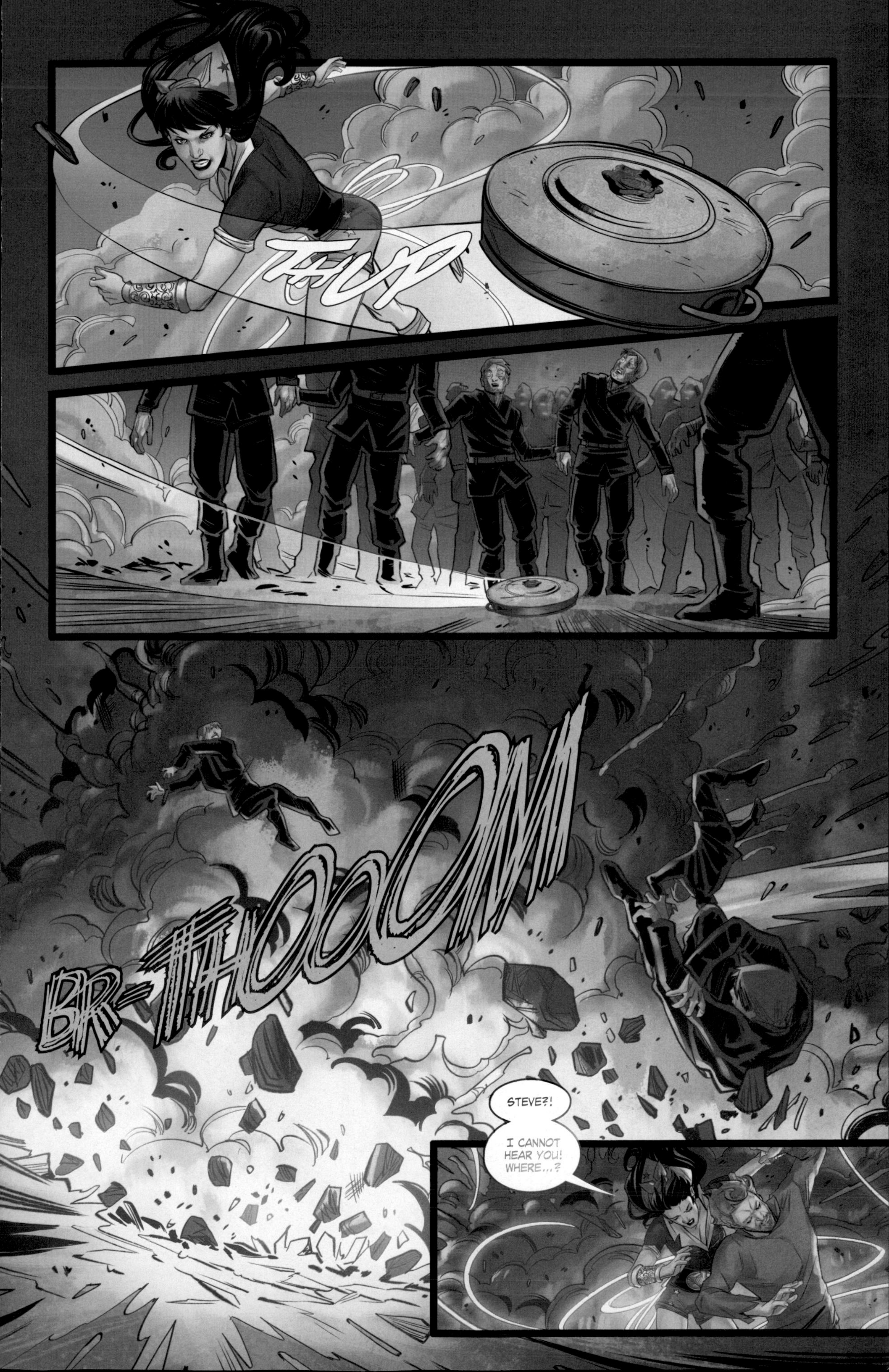
THUD
BR-THOOOOM
STEVE?!
I CANNOT HEAR YOU! WHERE...?

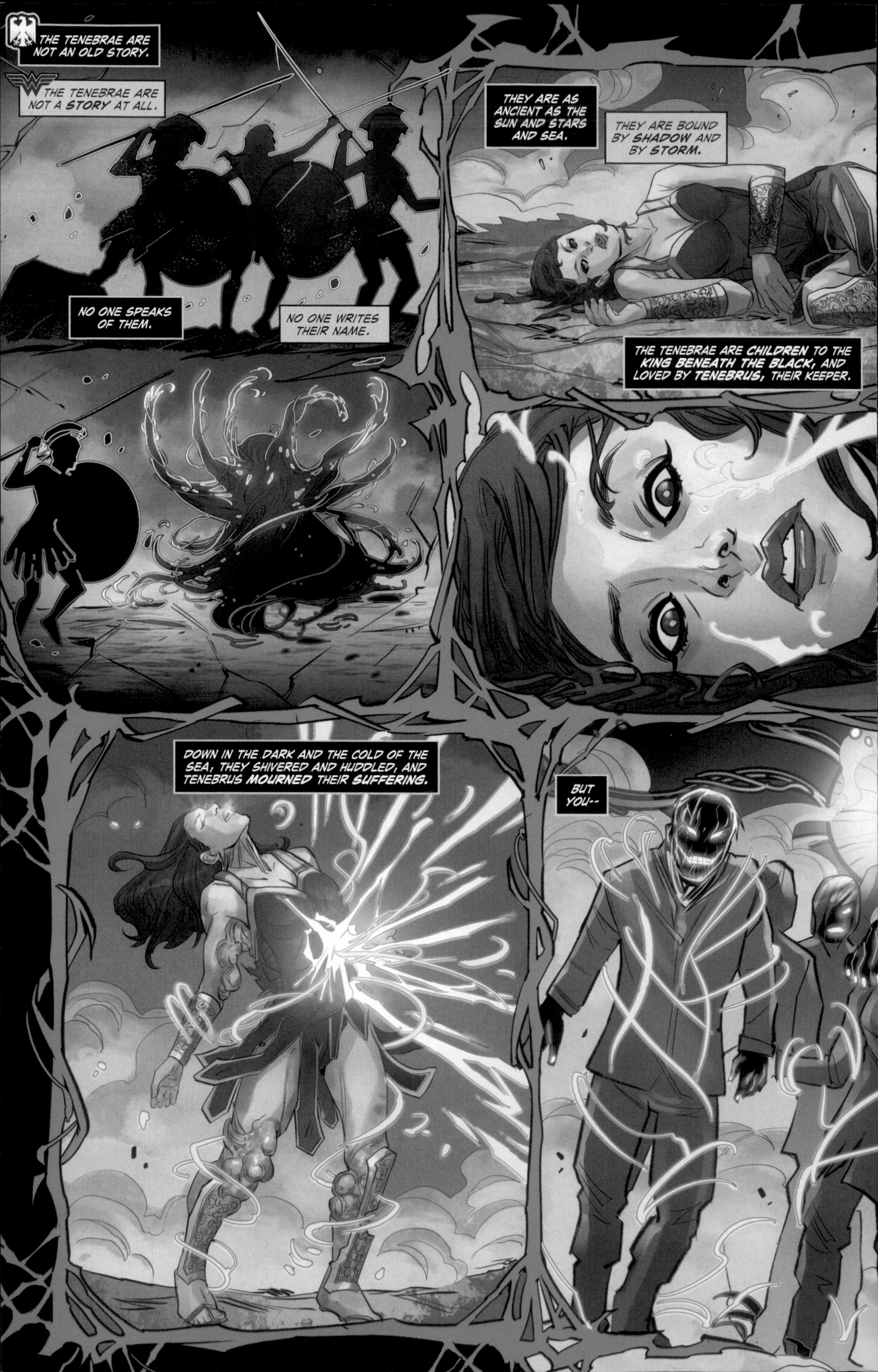

THE TENEBRAE ARE NOT AN OLD STORY.
THE TENEBRAE ARE NOT A STORY AT ALL.
NO ONE SPEAKS OF THEM.
NO ONE WRITES THEIR NAME.
THEY ARE AS ANCIENT AS THE SUN AND STARS AND SEA.
THEY ARE BOUND BY SHADOW AND BY STORM.
THE TENEBRAE ARE CHILDREN TO THE KING BENEATH THE BLACK, AND LOVED BY TENEBRUS, THEIR KEEPER.
DOWN IN THE DARK AND THE COLD OF THE SEA, THEY SHIVERED AND HUDDLED, AND TENEBRUS MOURNED THEIR SUFFERING.
BUT YOU--

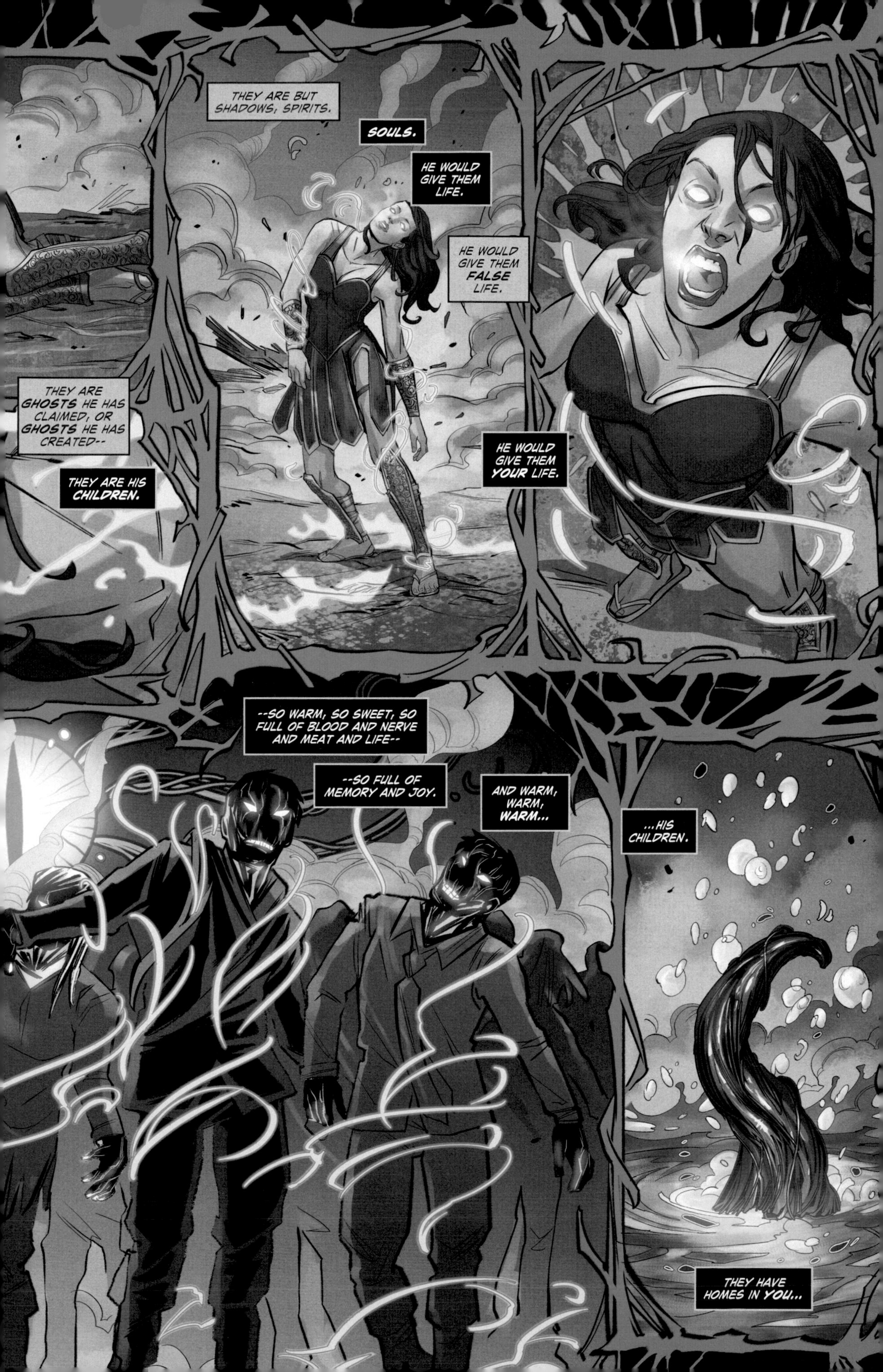
THEY ARE BUT SHADOWS, SPIRITS.
SOULS.
HE WOULD GIVE THEM LIFE.
HE WOULD GIVE THEM FALSE LIFE.
THEY ARE GHOSTS HE HAS CLAIMED, OR GHOSTS HE HAS CREATED--
THEY ARE HIS CHILDREN.
HE WOULD GIVE THEM YOUR LIFE.
--SO WARM, SO SWEET, SO FULL OF BLOOD AND NERVE AND MEAT AND LIFE--
--SO FULL OF MEMORY AND JOY.
AND WARM, WARM, WARM...
...HIS CHILDREN.
THEY HAVE HOMES IN YOU...

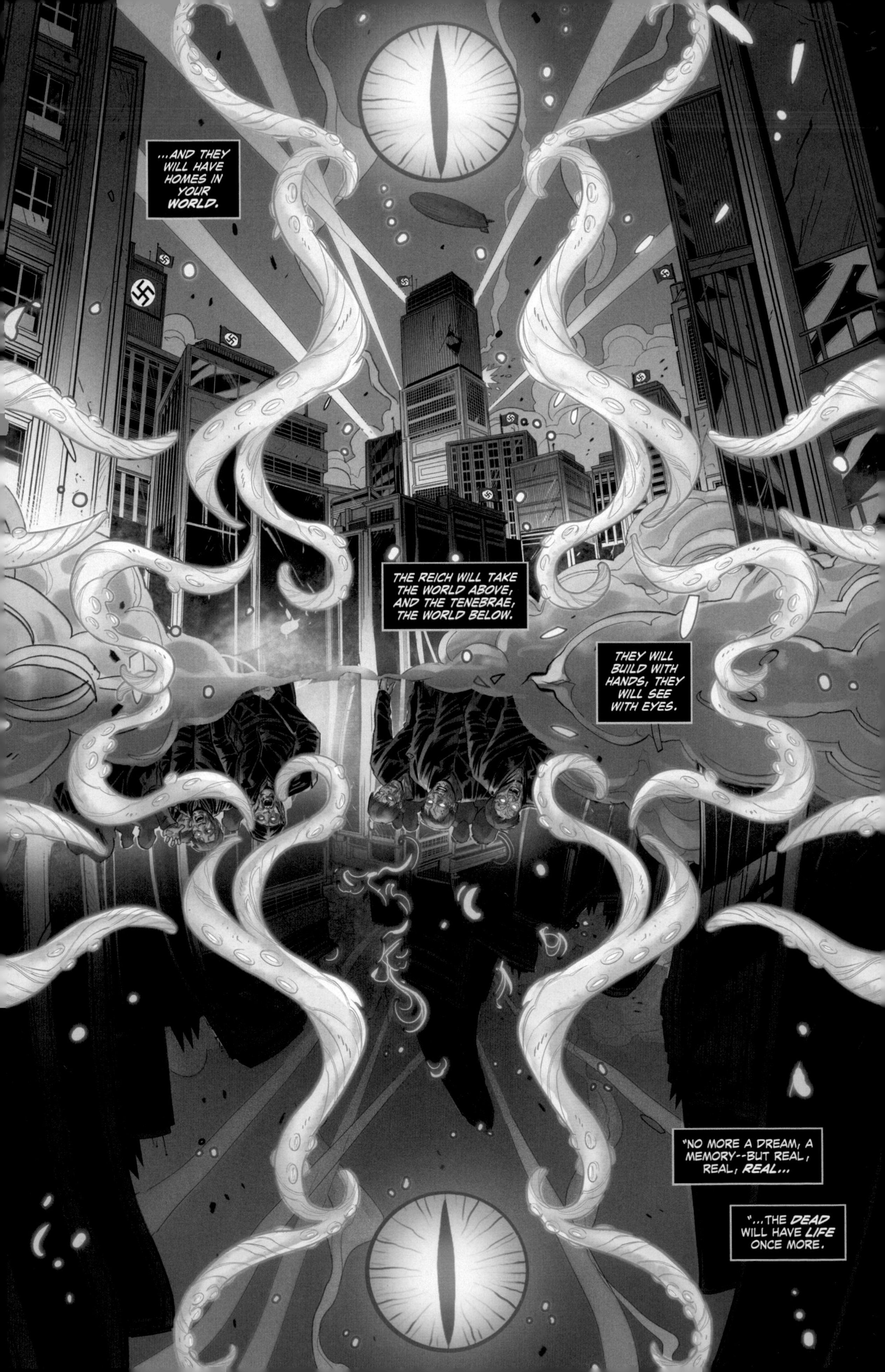
...AND THEY WILL HAVE HOMES IN YOUR WORLD.
THE REICH WILL TAKE THE WORLD ABOVE, AND THE TENEBRAE, THE WORLD BELOW.
THEY WILL BUILD WITH HANDS, THEY WILL SEE WITH EYES.
"NO MORE A DREAM, A MEMORY--BUT REAL, REAL, REAL...
"...THE DEAD WILL HAVE LIFE ONCE MORE.

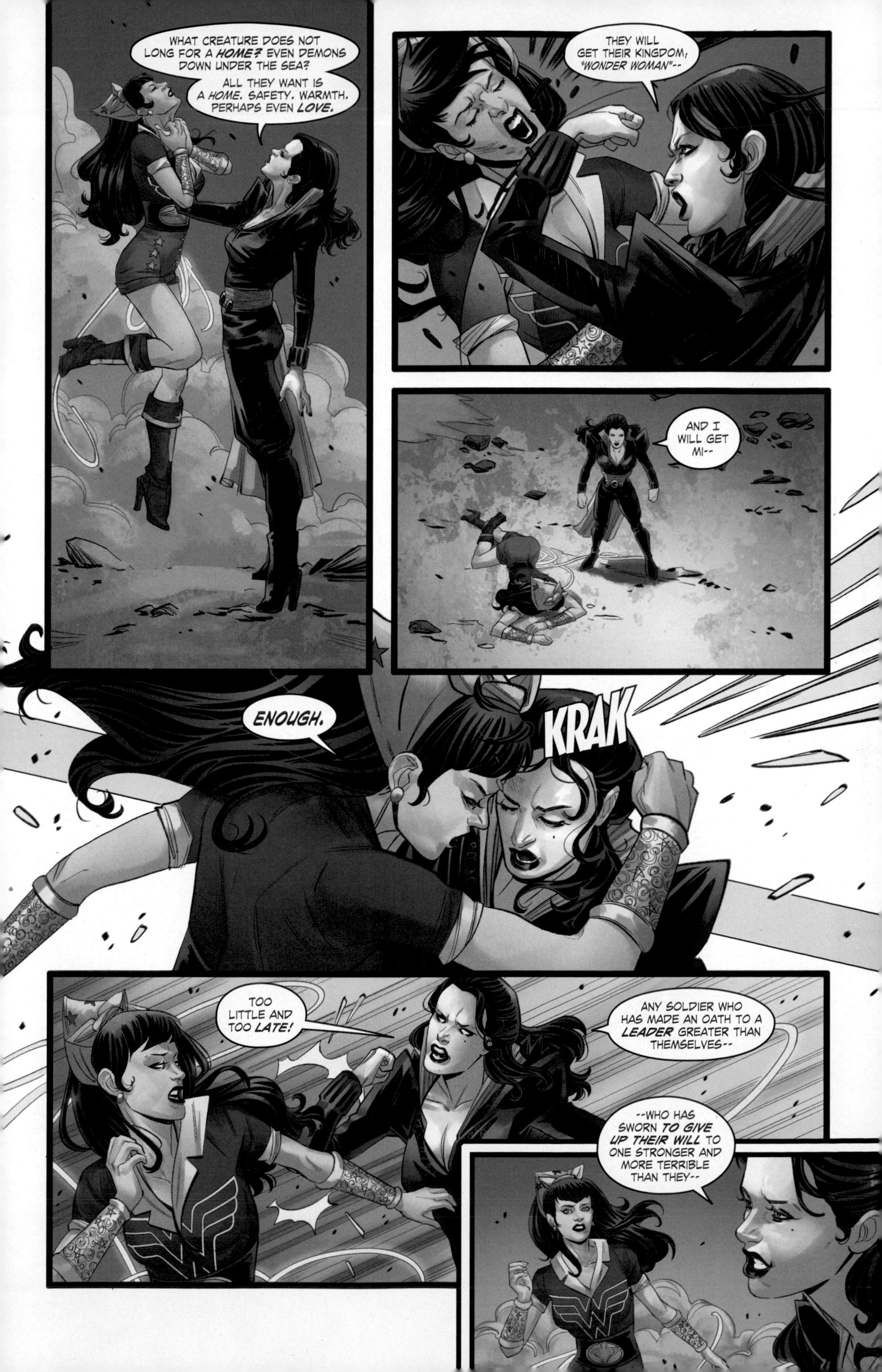
WHAT CREATURE DOES NOT LONG FOR A HOME? EVEN DEMONS DOWN UNDER THE SEA?
ALL THEY WANT IS A HOME. SAFETY. WARMTH. PERHAPS EVEN LOVE.
THEY WILL GET THEIR KINGDOM, "WONDER WOMAN"--
AND I WILL GET MI--
ENOUGH.
KRAK
TOO LITTLE AND TOO LATE!
ANY SOLDIER WHO HAS MADE AN OATH TO A LEADER GREATER THAN THEMSELVES--
--WHO HAS SWORN TO GIVE UP THEIR WILL TO ONE STRONGER AND MORE TERRIBLE THAN THEY--

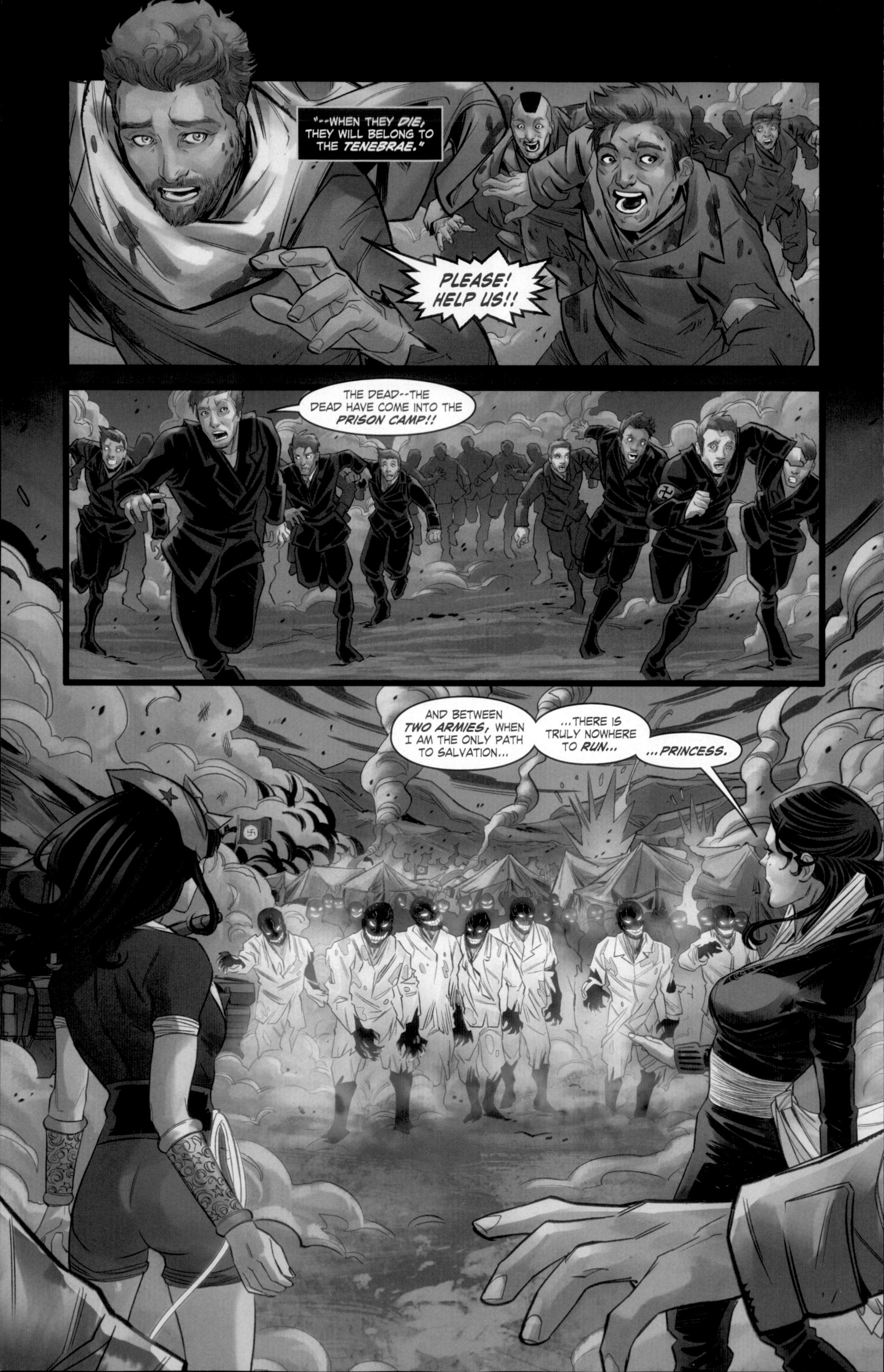
"--WHEN THEY DIE, THEY WILL BELONG TO THE TENEBRAE."
PLEASE! HELP US!!
THE DEAD--THE DEAD HAVE COME INTO THE PRISON CAMP!!
AND BETWEEN TWO ARMIES, WHEN I AM THE ONLY PATH TO SALVATION...
...THERE IS TRULY NOWHERE TO RUN...
...PRINCESS.

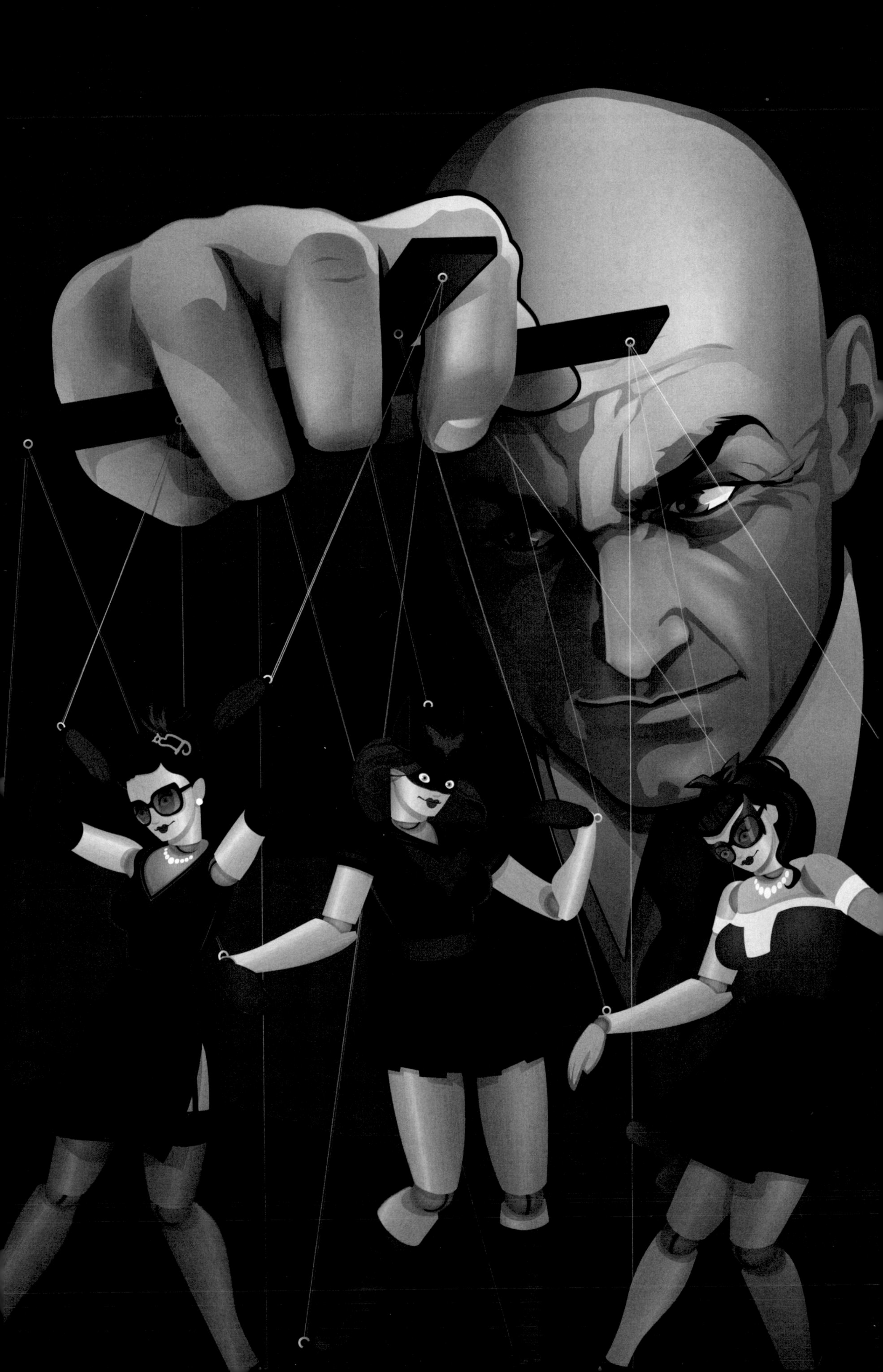

ALLIES AND ENEMIES
PART TWO

MARGUERITE BENNETT
Writer

LAURA BRAGA
MARGUERITE SAUVAGE
Artists

J. NANJAN
JEREMY LAWSON
Colorists

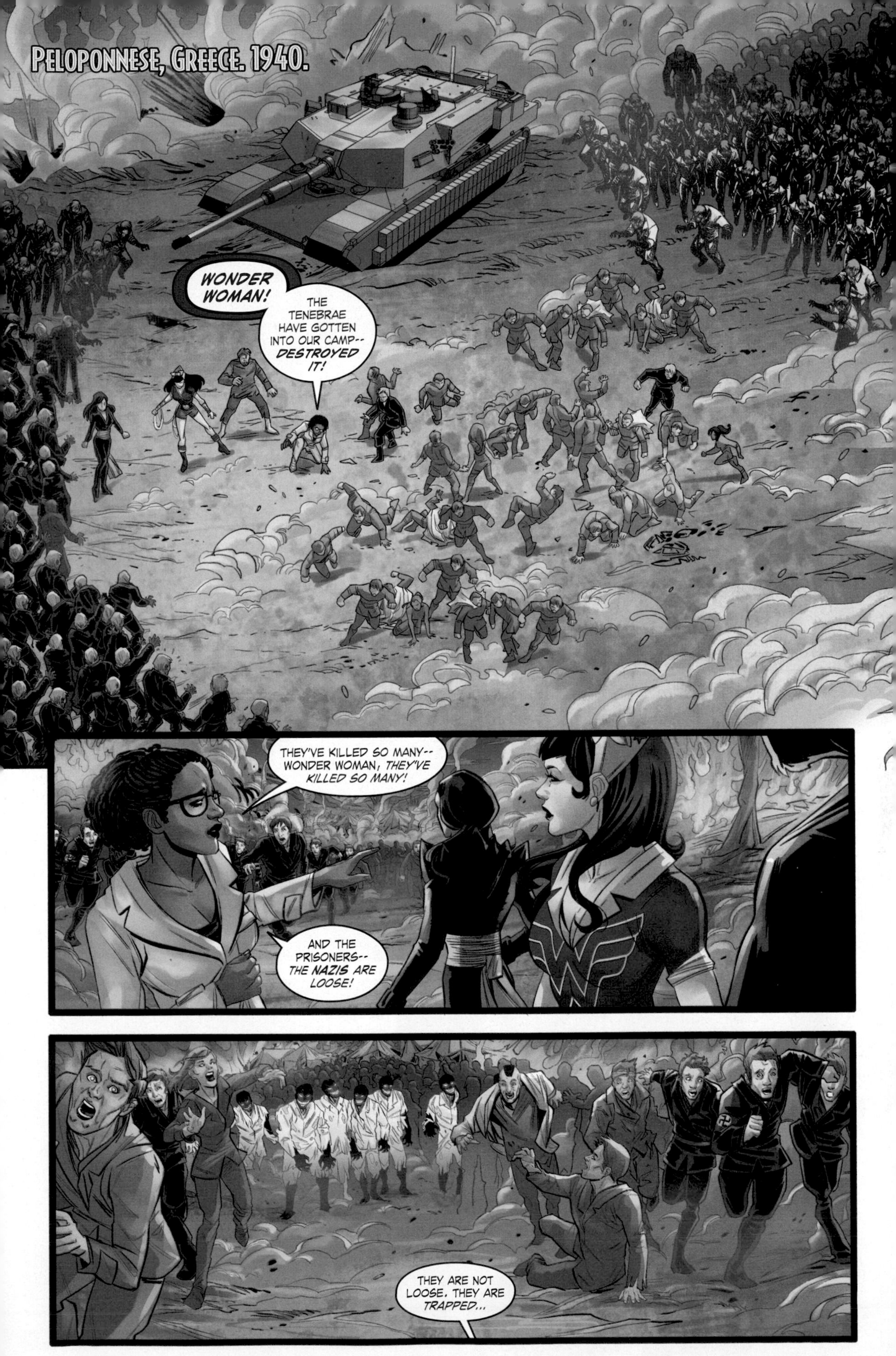
PELOPONNESE, GREECE. 1940.
WONDER WOMAN!
THE TENEBRAE HAVE GOTTEN INTO OUR CAMP-- DESTROYED IT!
THEY'VE KILLED SO MANY-- WONDER WOMAN, THEY'VE KILLED SO MANY!
AND THE PRISONERS-- THE NAZIS ARE LOOSE!
THEY ARE NOT LOOSE. THEY ARE TRAPPED...

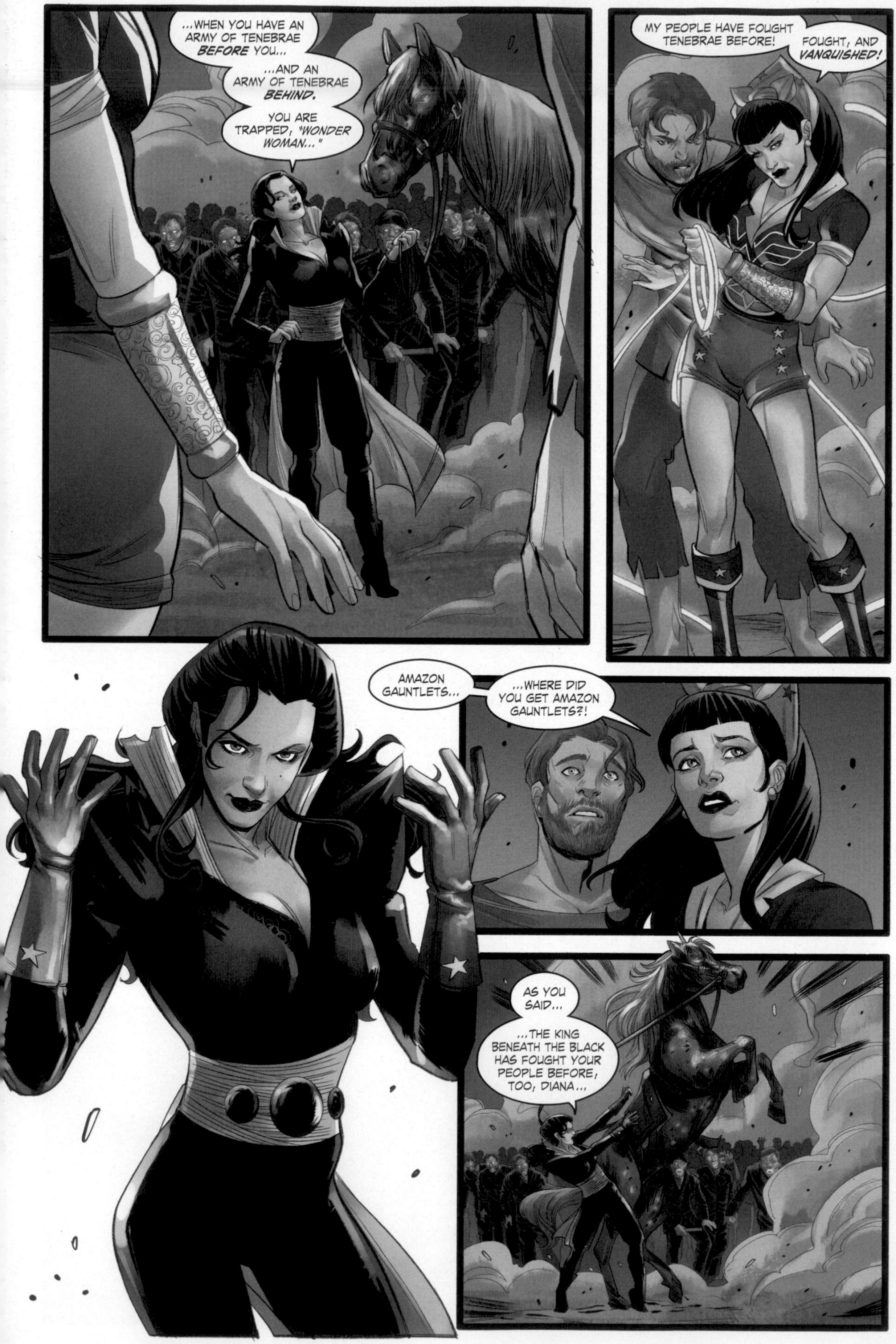
...WHEN YOU HAVE AN ARMY OF TENEBRAE BEFORE YOU...
...AND AN ARMY OF TENEBRAE BEHIND.
YOU ARE TRAPPED, "WONDER WOMAN..."
MY PEOPLE HAVE FOUGHT TENEBRAE BEFORE!
FOUGHT, AND VANQUISHED!
AMAZON GAUNTLETS...
...WHERE DID YOU GET AMAZON GAUNTLETS?!
AS YOU SAID...
...THE KING BENEATH THE BLACK HAS FOUGHT YOUR PEOPLE BEFORE, TOO, DIANA...

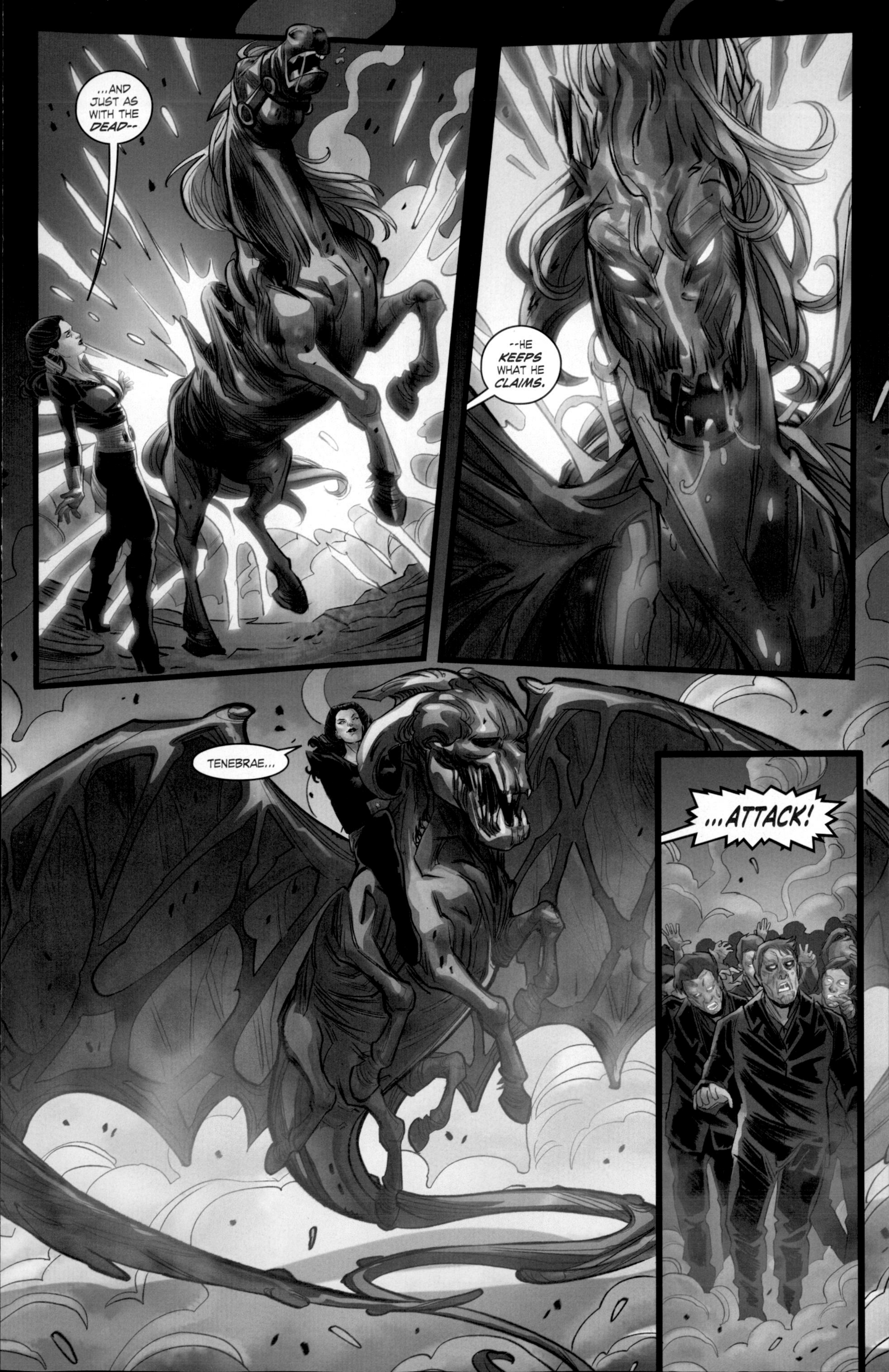
...AND JUST AS WITH THE DEAD--
--HE KEEPS WHAT HE CLAIMS.
TENEBRAE...
...ATTACK!

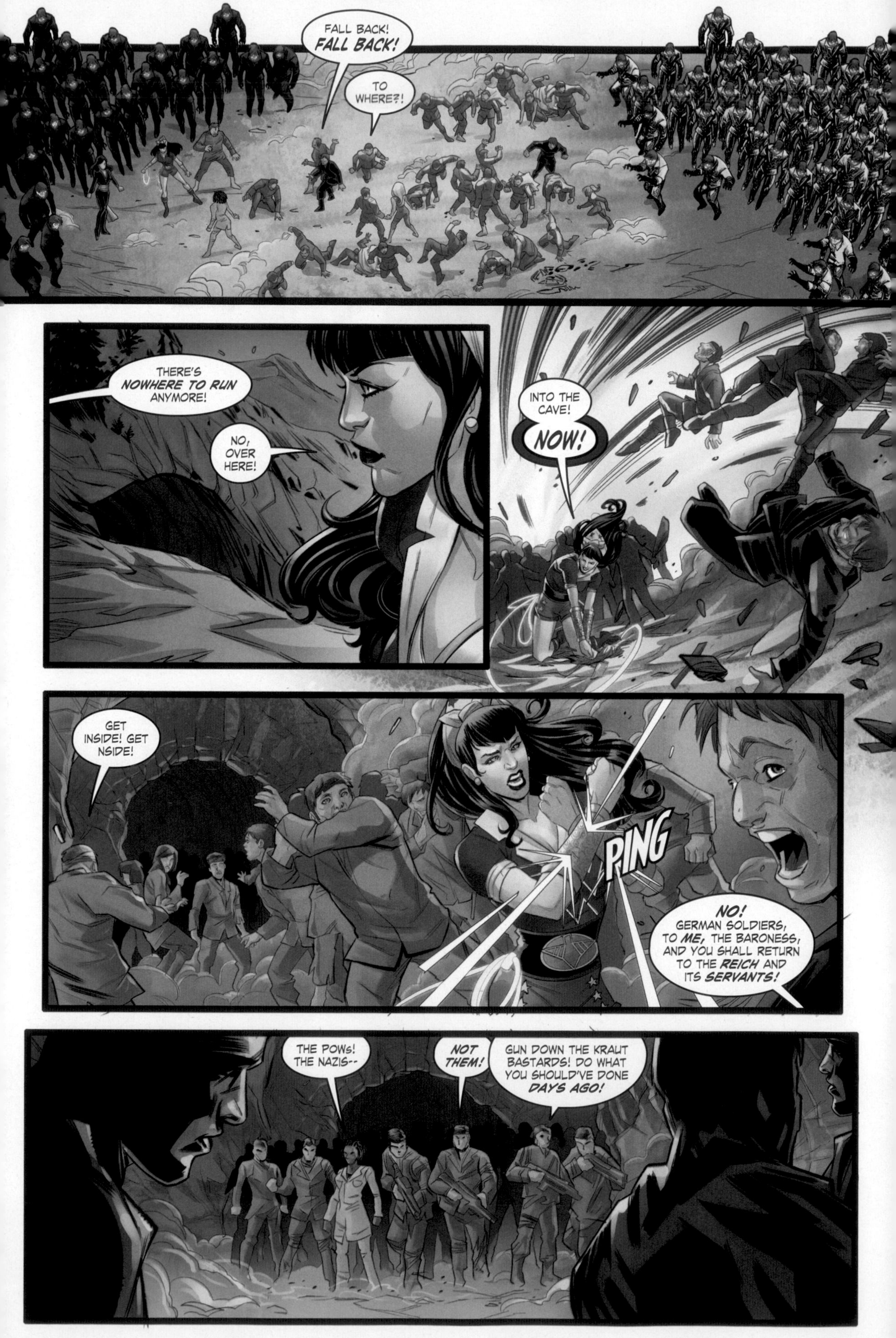
FALL BACK! FALL BACK!
TO WHERE?!
THERE'S NOWHERE TO RUN ANYMORE!
NO, OVER HERE!
INTO THE CAVE! NOW!
GET INSIDE! GET NSIDE!
PING
NO! GERMAN SOLDIERS, TO ME, THE BARONESS, AND YOU SHALL RETURN TO THE REICH AND ITS SERVANTS!
THE POWs! THE NAZIS--
NOT THEM!
GUN DOWN THE KRAUT BASTARDS! DO WHAT YOU SHOULD'VE DONE DAYS AGO!

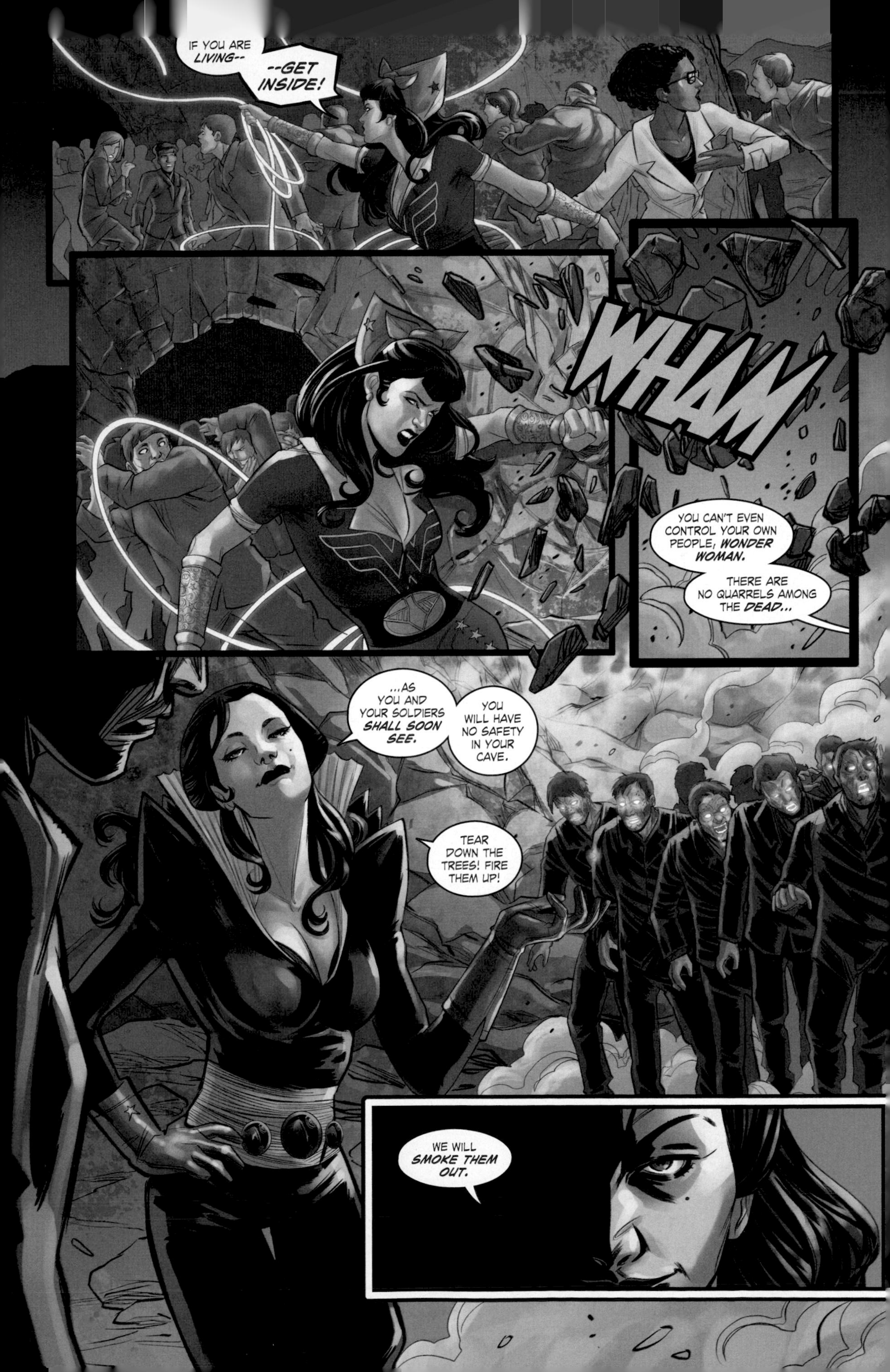
IF YOU ARE LIVING--
--GET INSIDE!
WHAM
YOU CAN'T EVEN CONTROL YOUR OWN PEOPLE, WONDER WOMAN.
THERE ARE NO QUARRELS AMONG THE DEAD...
...AS YOU AND YOUR SOLDIERS SHALL SOON SEE.
YOU WILL HAVE NO SAFETY IN YOUR CAVE.
TEAR DOWN THE TREES! FIRE THEM UP!
WE WILL SMOKE THEM OUT.

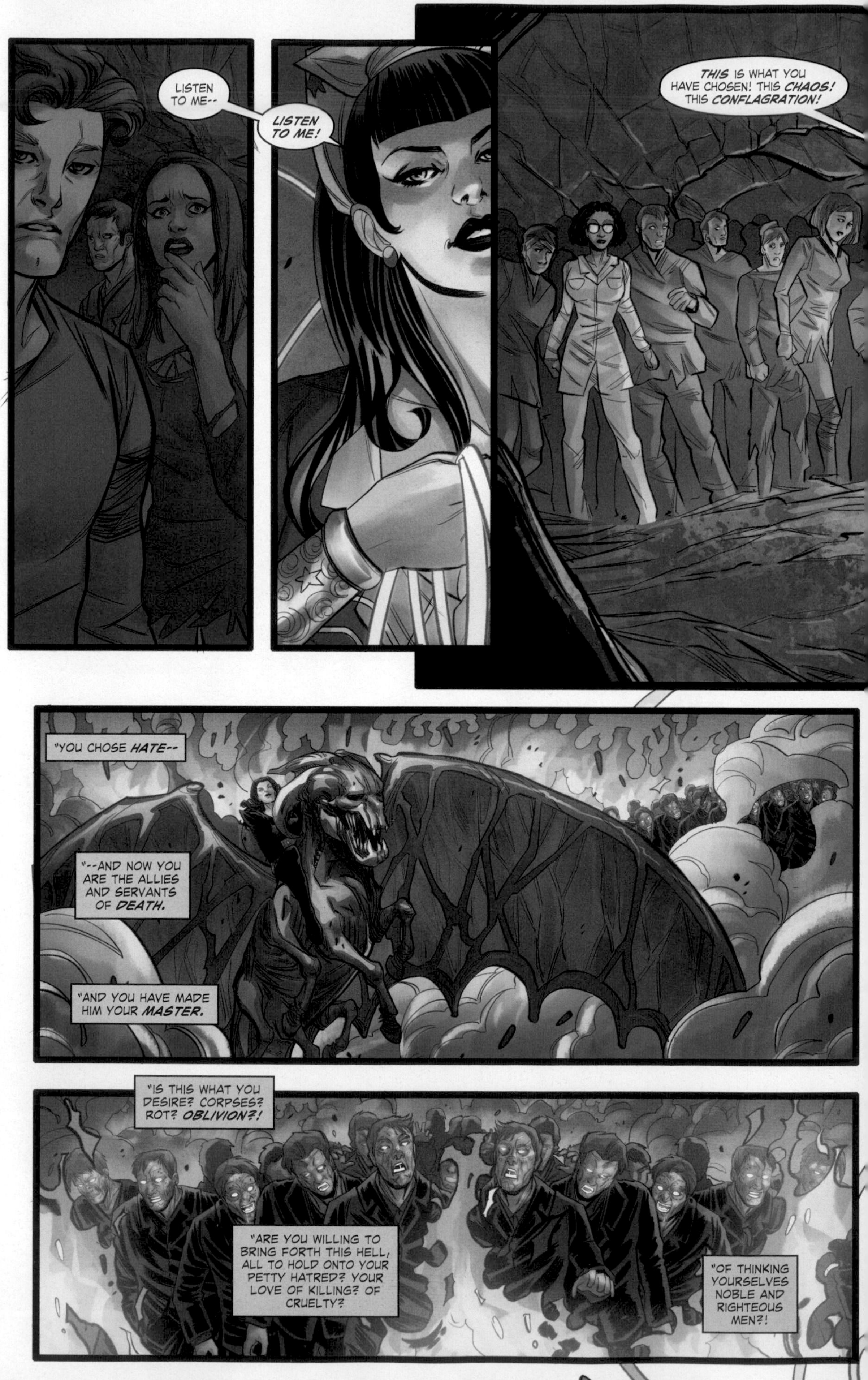
LISTEN TO ME--
LISTEN TO ME!
THIS IS WHAT YOU HAVE CHOSEN! THIS CHAOS! THIS CONFLAGRATION!
"YOU CHOSE HATE--
"--AND NOW YOU ARE THE ALLIES AND SERVANTS OF DEATH.
"AND YOU HAVE MADE HIM YOUR MASTER.
"IS THIS WHAT YOU DESIRE? CORPSES? ROT? OBLIVION?!
"ARE YOU WILLING TO BRING FORTH THIS HELL, ALL TO HOLD ONTO YOUR PETTY HATRED? YOUR LOVE OF KILLING? OF CRUELTY?
"OF THINKING YOURSELVES NOBLE AND RIGHTEOUS MEN?!

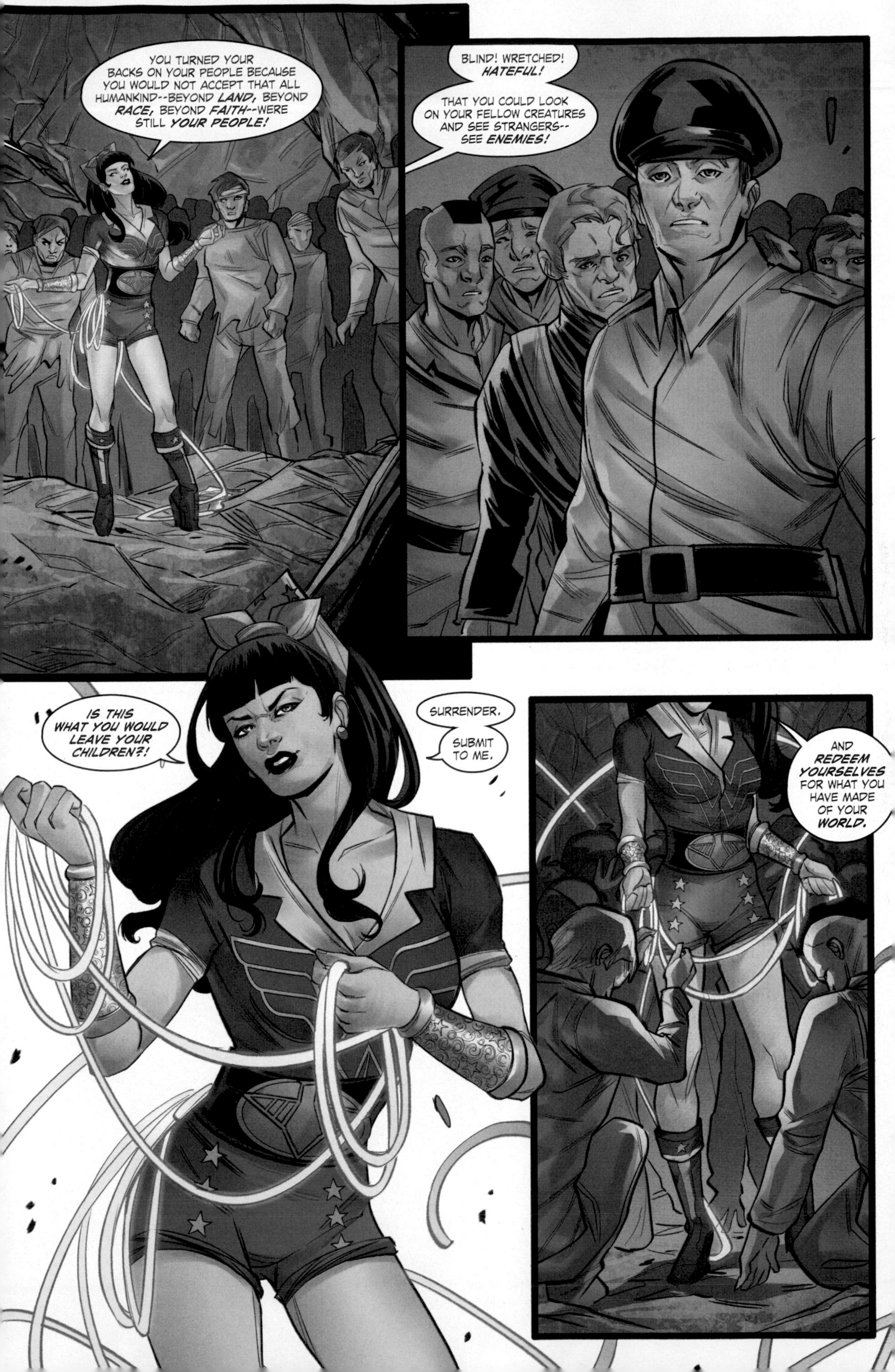
YOU TURNED YOUR BACKS ON YOUR PEOPLE BECAUSE YOU WOULD NOT ACCEPT THAT ALL HUMANKIND--BEYOND LAND, BEYOND RACE, BEYOND FAITH--WERE STILL YOUR PEOPLE!
BLIND! WRETCHED! HATEFUL!
THAT YOU COULD LOOK ON YOUR FELLOW CREATURES AND SEE STRANGERS--SEE ENEMIES!
IS THIS WHAT YOU WOULD LEAVE YOUR CHILDREN?!
SURRENDER.
SUBMIT TO ME.
AND REDEEM YOURSELVES FOR WHAT YOU HAVE MADE OF YOUR WORLD.

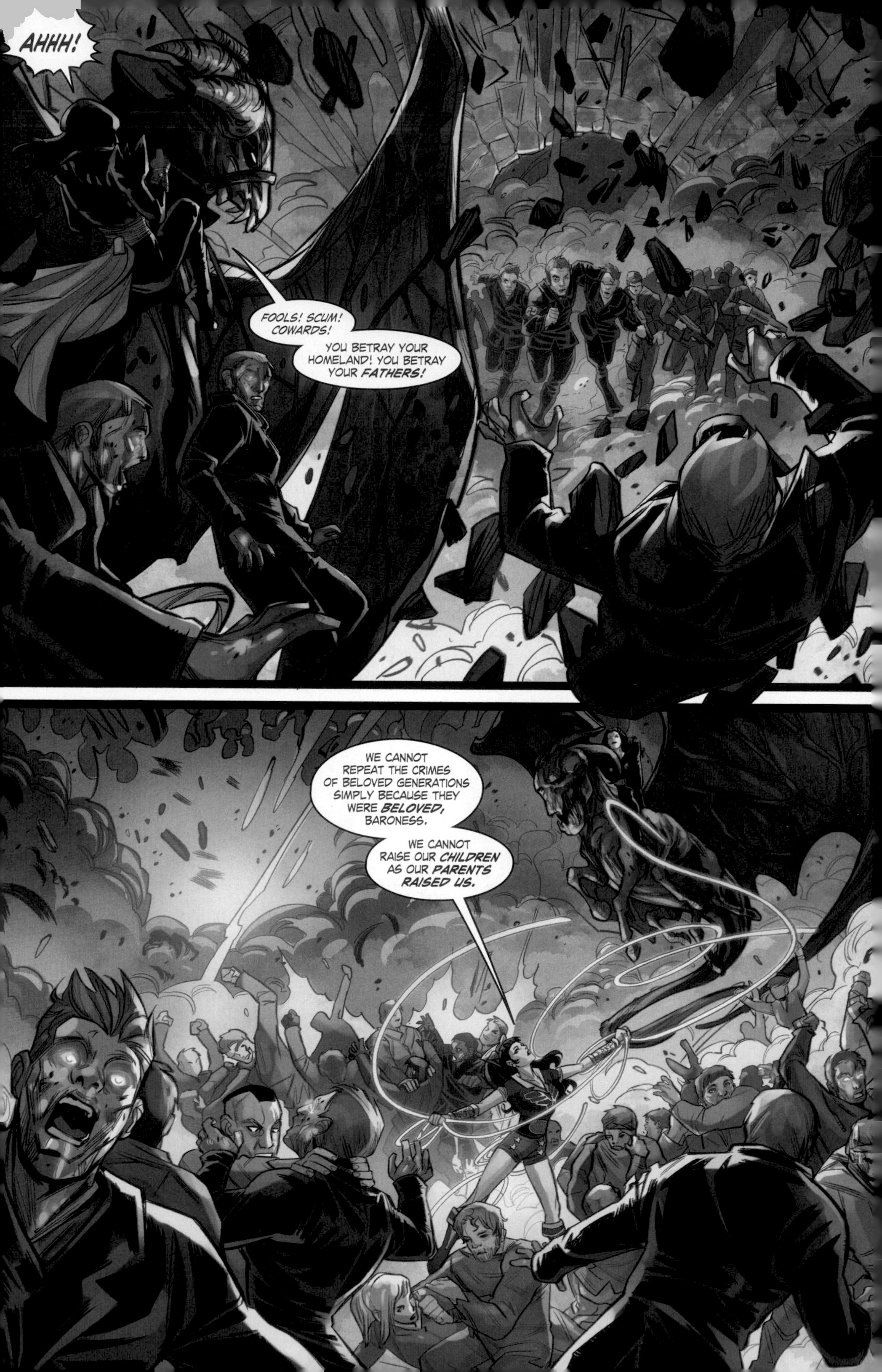
AHHH!
FOOLS! SCUM! COWARDS!
YOU BETRAY YOUR HOMELAND! YOU BETRAY YOUR FATHERS!
WE CANNOT REPEAT THE CRIMES OF BELOVED GENERATIONS SIMPLY BECAUSE THEY WERE BELOVED, BARONESS.
WE CANNOT RAISE OUR CHILDREN AS OUR PARENTS RAISED US.

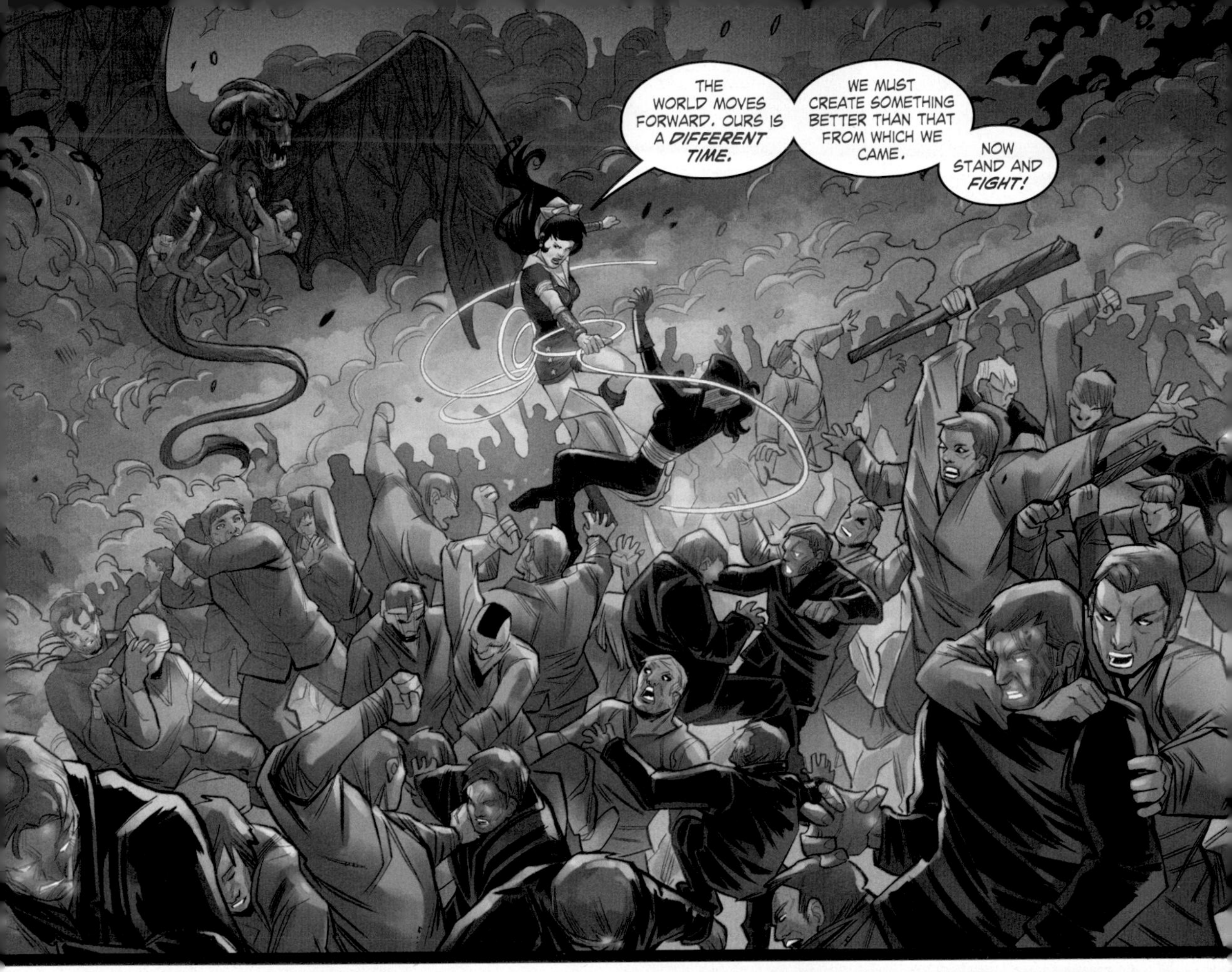
THE WORLD MOVES FORWARD. OURS IS A DIFFERENT TIME.
WE MUST CREATE SOMETHING BETTER THAN THAT FROM WHICH WE CAME.
NOW STAND AND FIGHT!

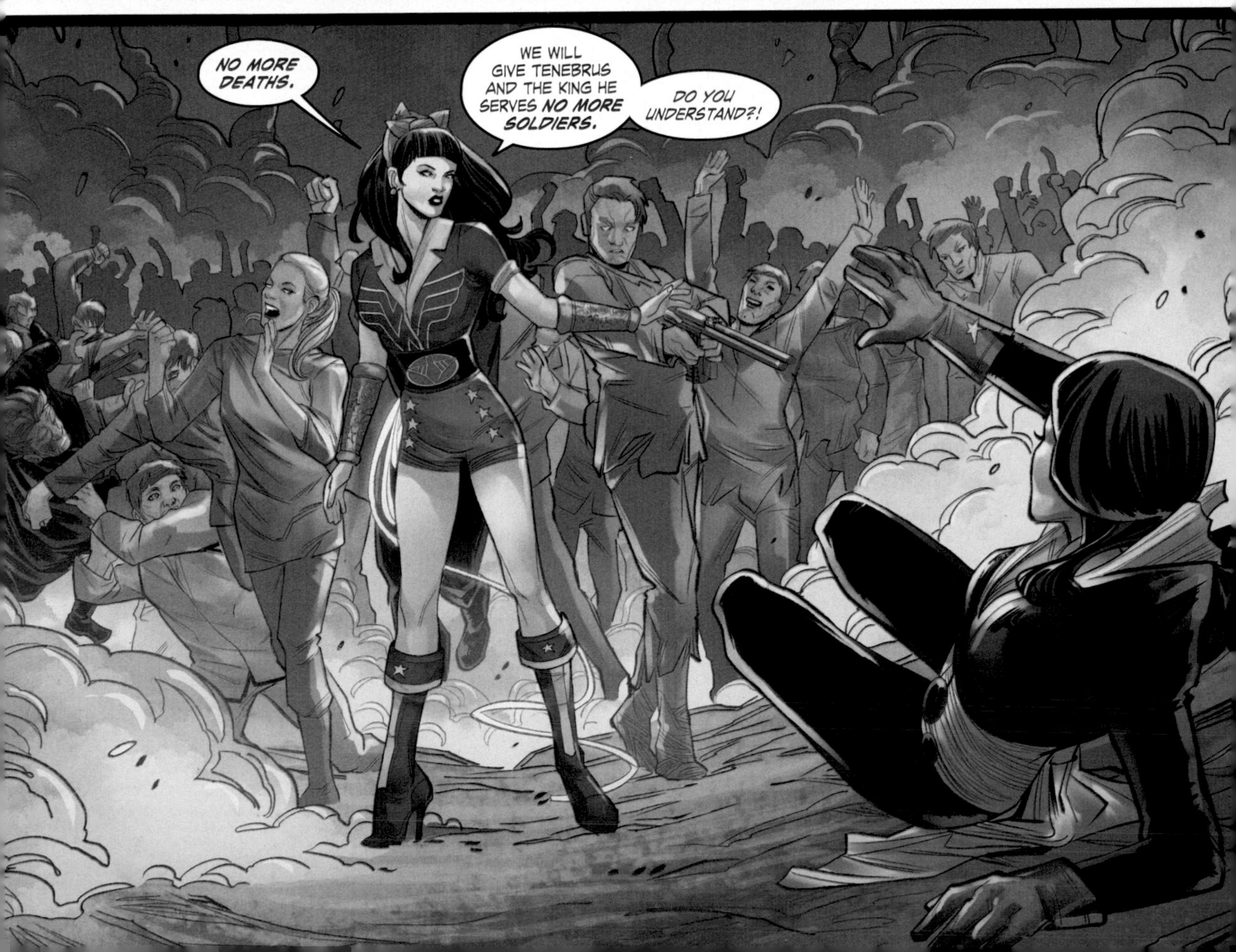
NO MORE DEATHS.
WE WILL GIVE TENEBRUS AND THE KING HE SERVES NO MORE SOLDIERS.
DO YOU UNDERSTAND?!

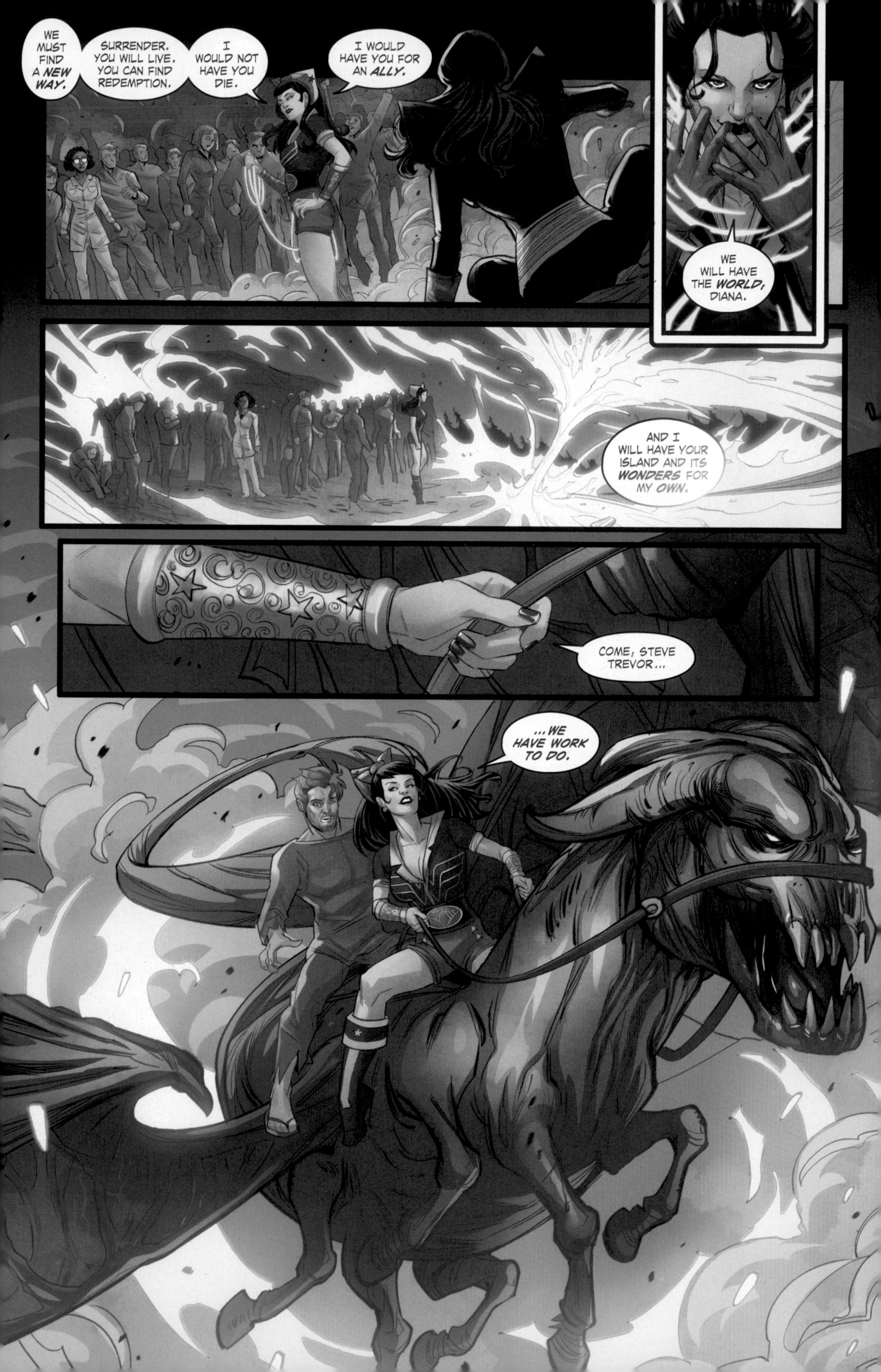
WE MUST FIND A NEW WAY.
SURRENDER. YOU WILL LIVE. YOU CAN FIND REDEMPTION.
I WOULD NOT HAVE YOU DIE.
I WOULD HAVE YOU FOR AN ALLY.
WE WILL HAVE THE WORLD, DIANA.
AND I WILL HAVE YOUR ISLAND AND ITS WONDERS FOR MY OWN.
COME, STEVE TREVOR...
...WE HAVE WORK TO DO.

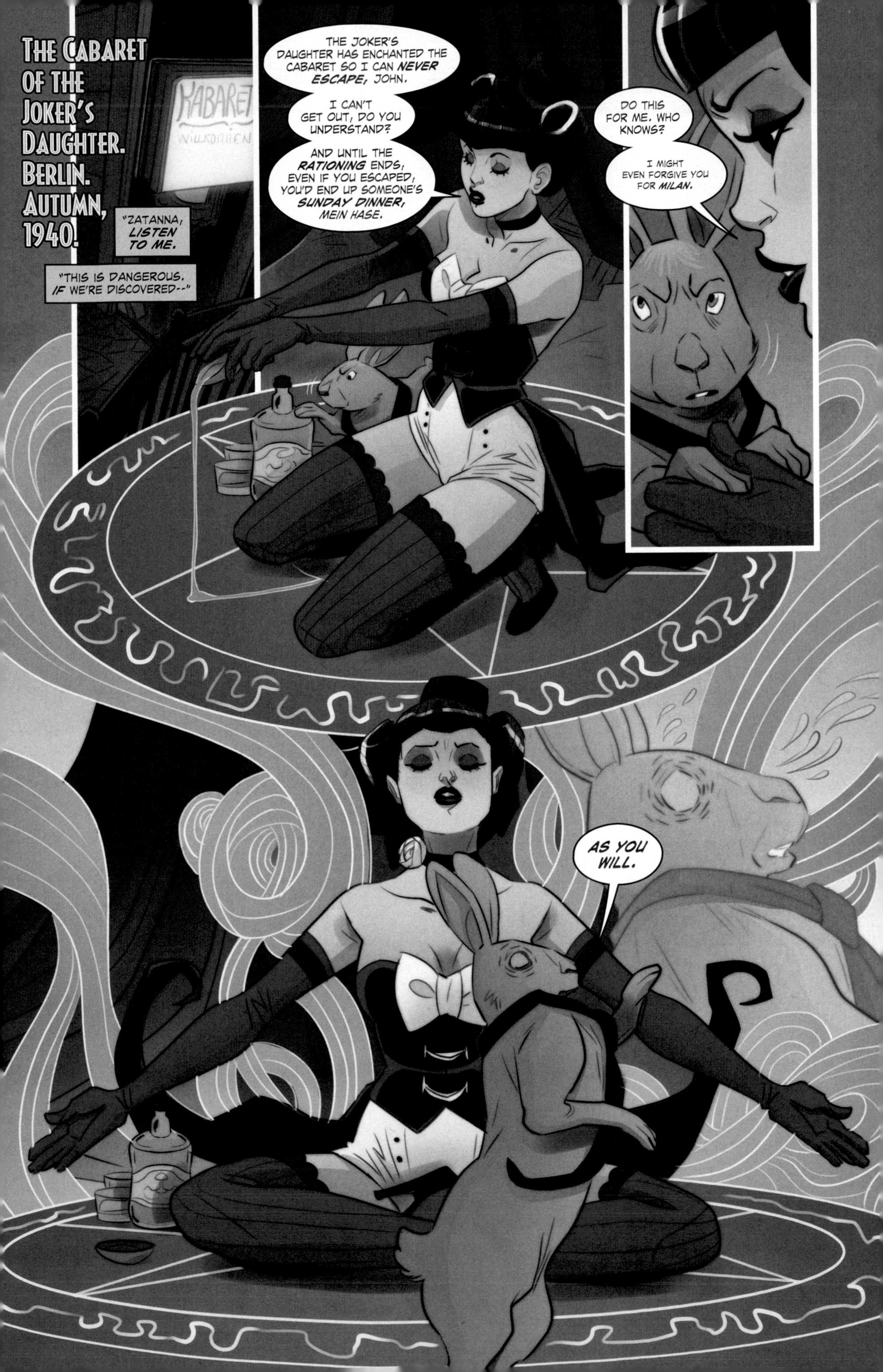
THE CABARET OF THE JOKER'S DAUGHTER. BERLIN. AUTUMN, 1940.
KABARET
WILLKOMMEN
"ZATANNA, LISTEN TO ME.
"THIS IS DANGEROUS. IF WE'RE DISCOVERED--"
THE JOKER'S DAUGHTER HAS ENCHANTED THE CABARET SO I CAN NEVER ESCAPE, JOHN.
I CAN'T GET OUT, DO YOU UNDERSTAND?
AND UNTIL THE RATIONING ENDS, EVEN IF YOU ESCAPED, YOU'D END UP SOMEONE'S SUNDAY DINNER, MEIN HASE.
DO THIS FOR ME. WHO KNOWS?
I MIGHT EVEN FORGIVE YOU FOR MILAN.
AS YOU WILL.

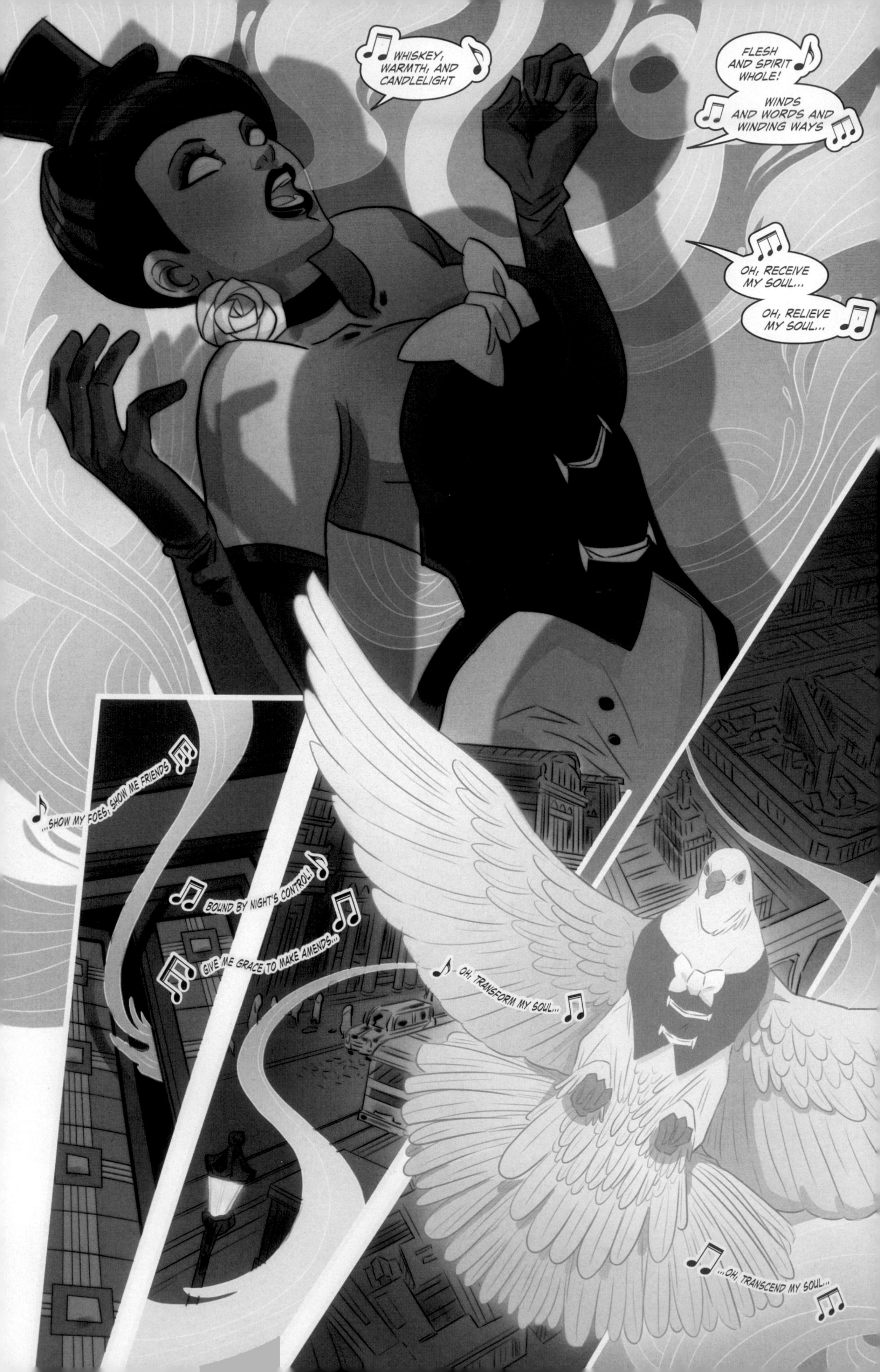
WHISKEY, WARMTH, AND CANDLELIGHT
FLESH AND SPIRIT WHOLE!
WINDS AND WORDS AND WINDING WAYS
OH, RECEIVE MY SOUL...
OH, RELIEVE MY SOUL...
...SHOW MY FOES, SHOW ME FRIENDS
BOUND BY NIGHT'S CONTROL!
GIVE ME GRACE TO MAKE AMENDS...
OH, TRANSFORM MY SOUL...
...OH, TRANSCEND MY SOUL...

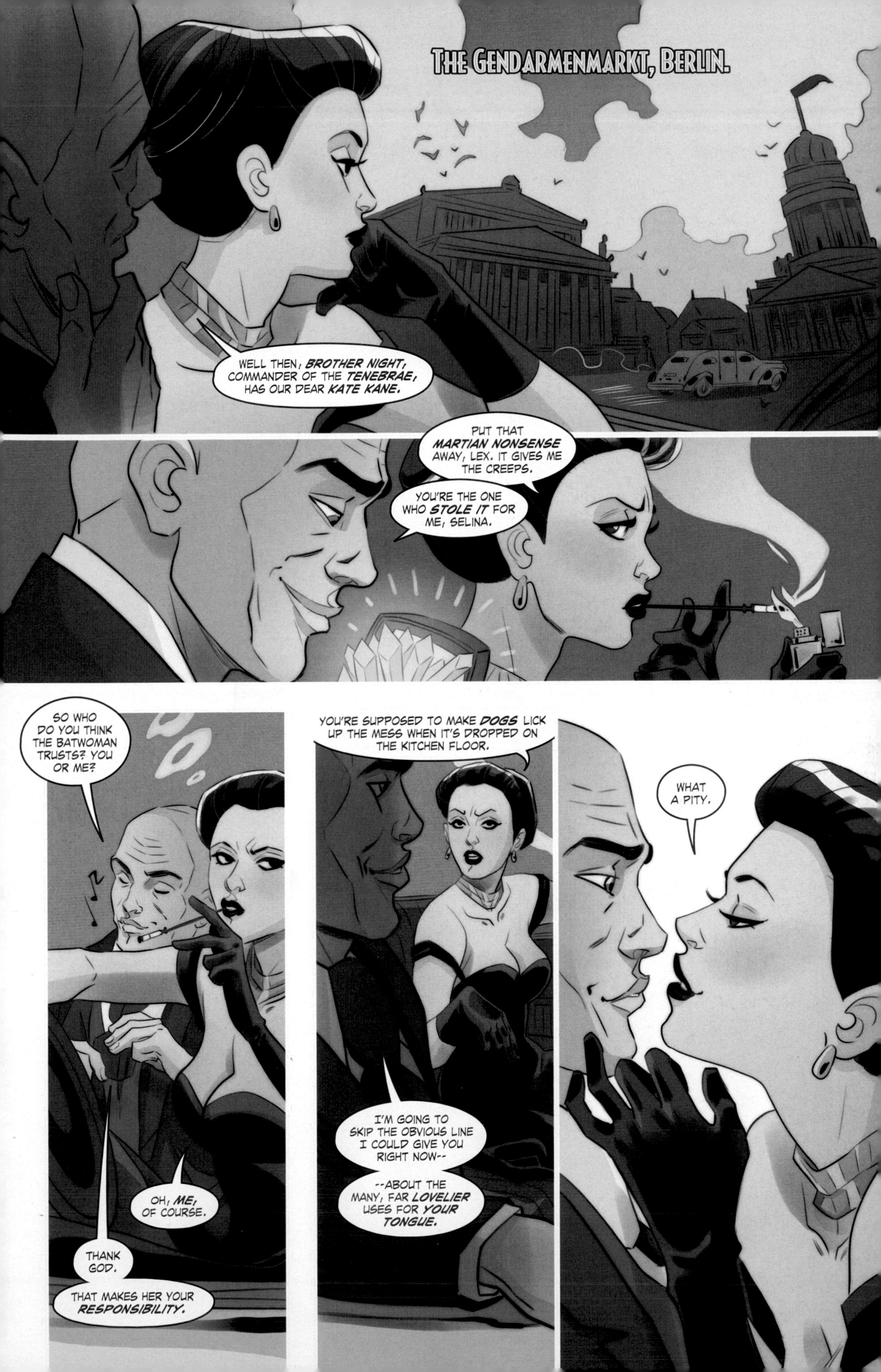
THE GENDARMENMARKT, BERLIN.
WELL THEN, BROTHER NIGHT, COMMANDER OF THE TENEBRAE, HAS OUR DEAR KATE KANE.
PUT THAT MARTIAN NONSENSE AWAY, LEX. IT GIVES ME THE CREEPS.
YOU'RE THE ONE WHO STOLE IT FOR ME, SELINA.
SO WHO DO YOU THINK THE BATWOMAN TRUSTS? YOU OR ME?
OH, ME, OF COURSE.
THANK GOD.
THAT MAKES HER YOUR RESPONSIBILITY.
YOU'RE SUPPOSED TO MAKE DOGS LICK UP THE MESS WHEN IT'S DROPPED ON THE KITCHEN FLOOR.
I'M GOING TO SKIP THE OBVIOUS LINE I COULD GIVE YOU RIGHT NOW--
--ABOUT THE MANY, FAR LOVELIER USES FOR YOUR TONGUE.
WHAT A PITY.

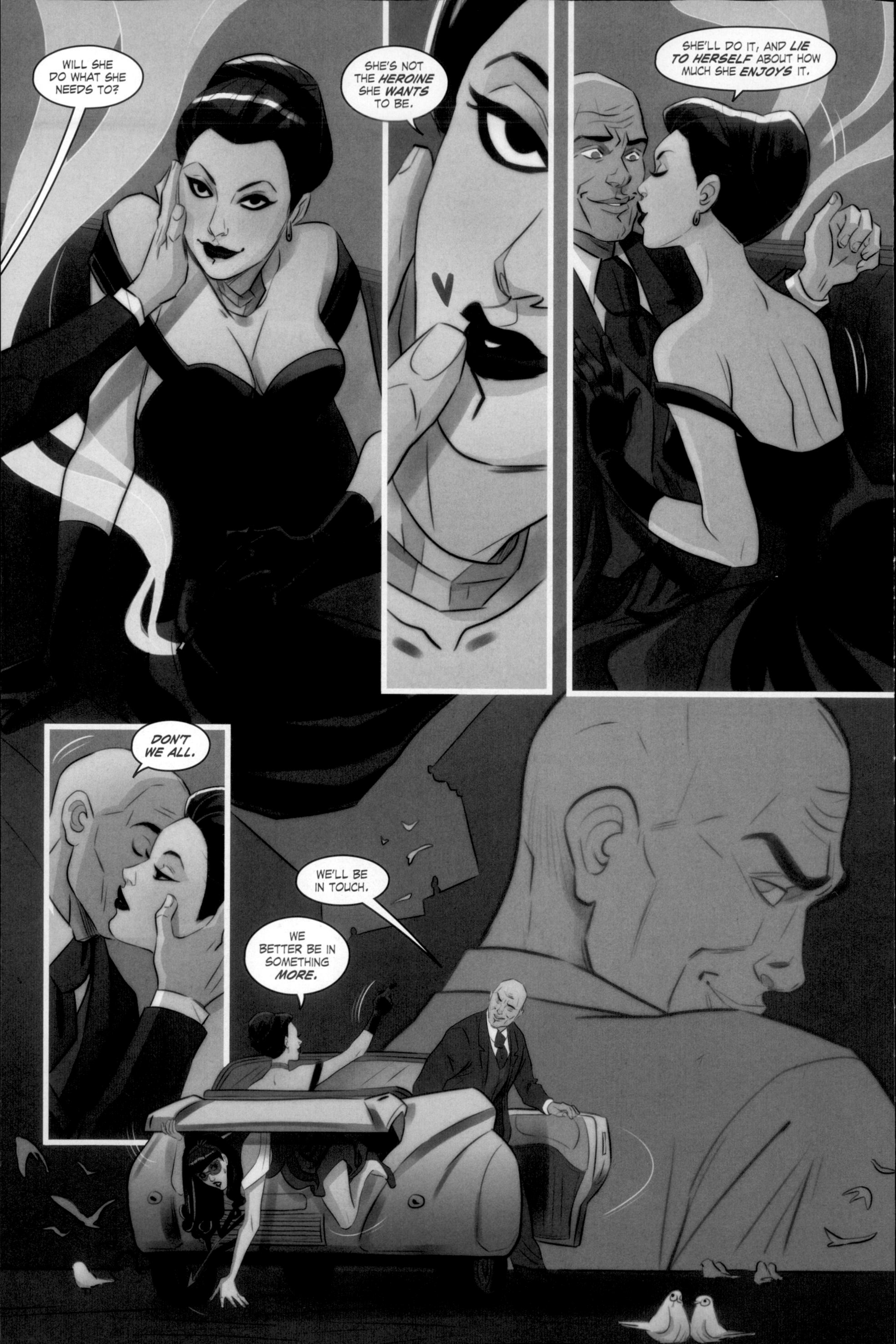
WILL SHE DO WHAT SHE NEEDS TO?
SHE'S NOT THE HEROINE SHE WANTS TO BE.
SHE'LL DO IT, AND LIE TO HERSELF ABOUT HOW MUCH SHE ENJOYS IT.
DON'T WE ALL.
WE'LL BE IN TOUCH.
WE BETTER BE IN SOMETHING MORE.

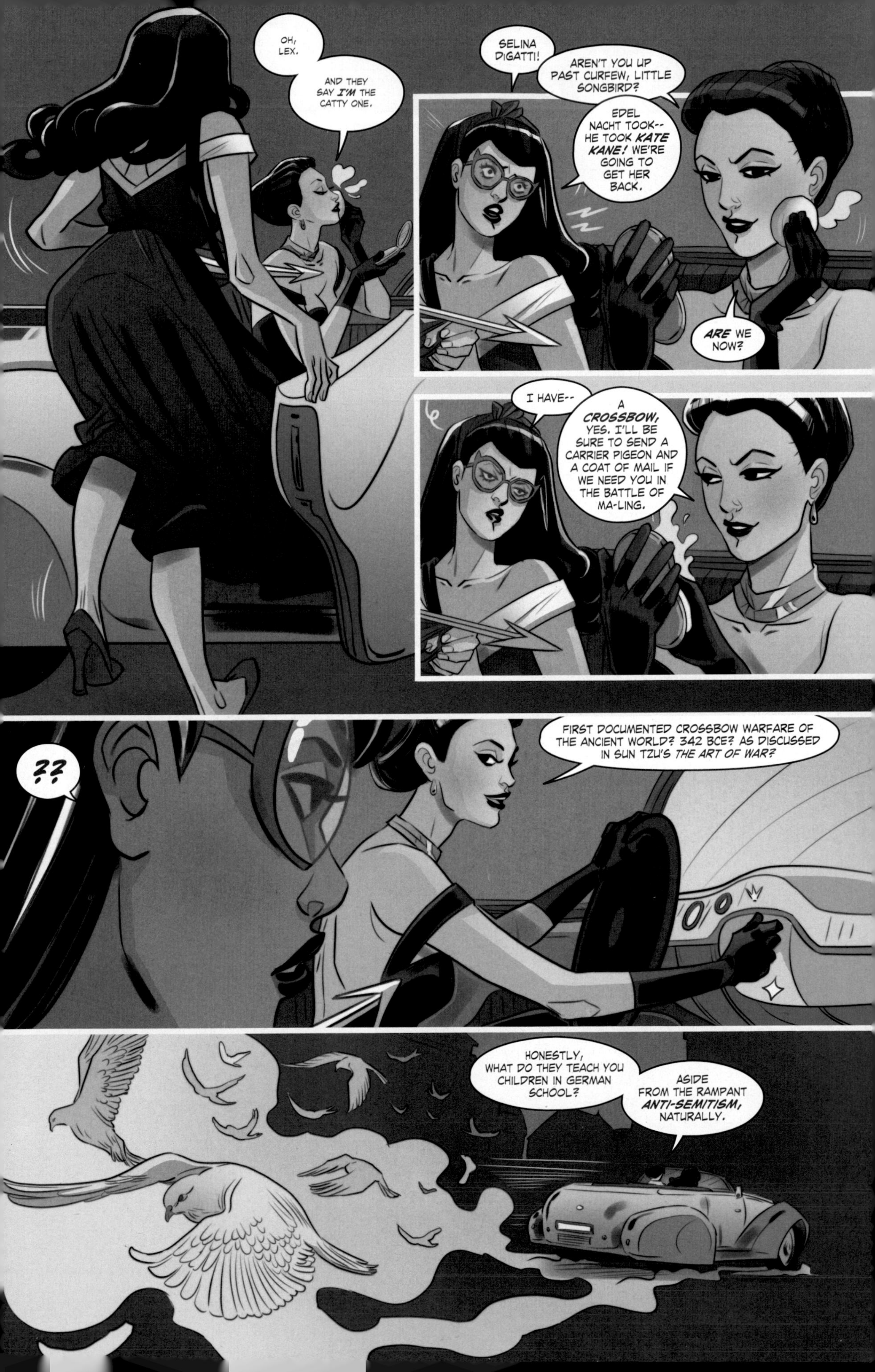

OH, LEX.
AND THEY SAY *I'M* THE CATTY ONE.
SELINA DIGATTI!
AREN'T YOU UP PAST CURFEW, LITTLE SONGBIRD?
EDEL NACHT TOOK-- HE TOOK *KATE KANE!* WE'RE GOING TO GET HER BACK.
ARE WE NOW?
I HAVE--
A *CROSSBOW,* YES. I'LL BE SURE TO SEND A CARRIER PIGEON AND A COAT OF MAIL IF WE NEED YOU IN THE BATTLE OF MA-LING.
??
FIRST DOCUMENTED CROSSBOW WARFARE OF THE ANCIENT WORLD? 342 BCE? AS DISCUSSED IN SUN TZU'S *THE ART OF WAR?*
HONESTLY, WHAT DO THEY TEACH YOU CHILDREN IN GERMAN SCHOOL?
ASIDE FROM THE RAMPANT *ANTI-SEMITISM,* NATURALLY.

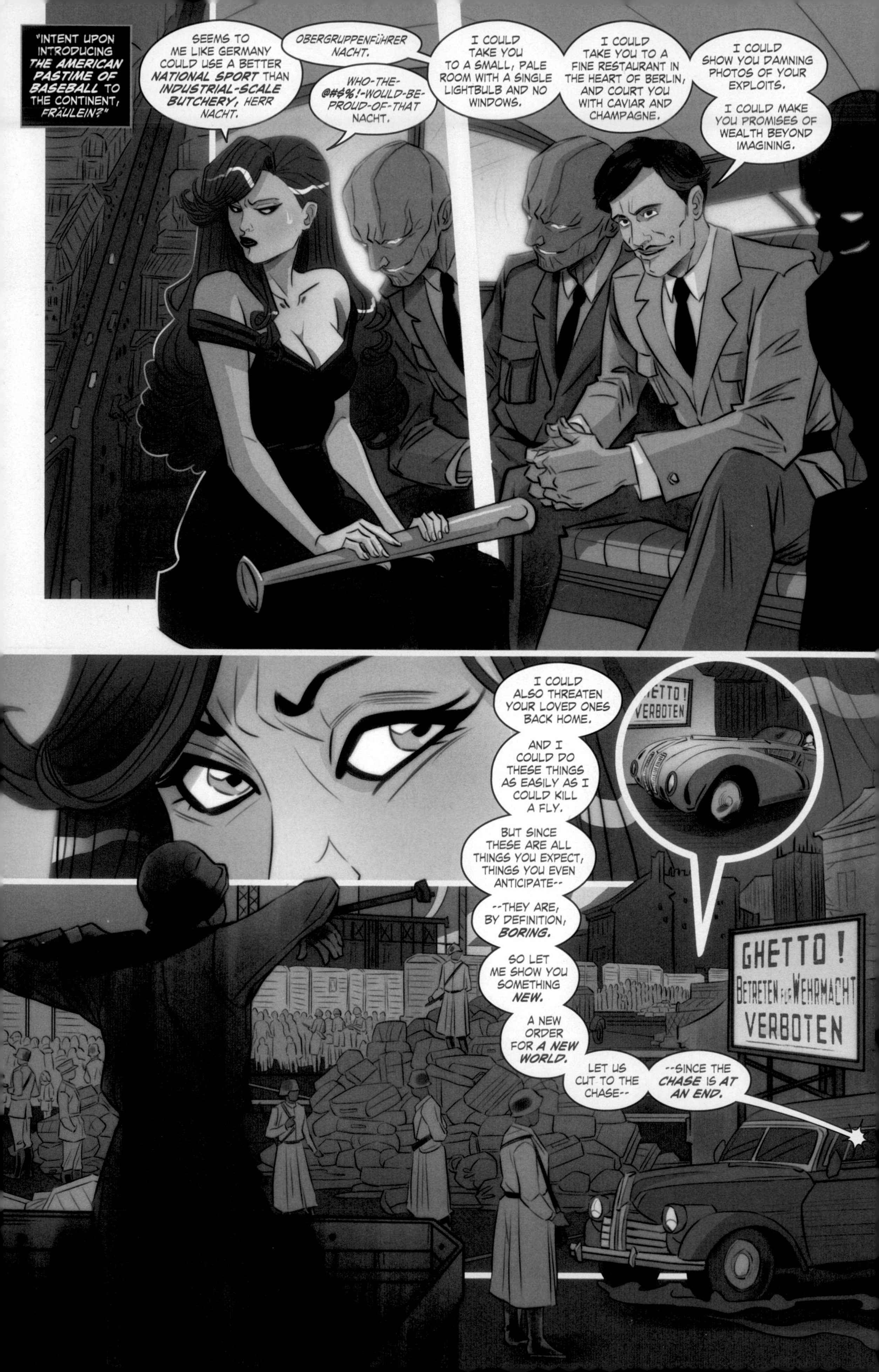
"INTENT UPON INTRODUCING THE AMERICAN PASTIME OF BASEBALL TO THE CONTINENT, FRÄULEIN?"
SEEMS TO ME LIKE GERMANY COULD USE A BETTER NATIONAL SPORT THAN INDUSTRIAL-SCALE BUTCHERY, HERR NACHT.
OBERGRUPPENFÜHRER NACHT.
WHO-THE-@#$%!-WOULD-BE-PROUD-OF-THAT NACHT.
I COULD TAKE YOU TO A SMALL, PALE ROOM WITH A SINGLE LIGHTBULB AND NO WINDOWS.
I COULD TAKE YOU TO A FINE RESTAURANT IN THE HEART OF BERLIN, AND COURT YOU WITH CAVIAR AND CHAMPAGNE.
I COULD SHOW YOU DAMNING PHOTOS OF YOUR EXPLOITS.
I COULD MAKE YOU PROMISES OF WEALTH BEYOND IMAGINING.
I COULD ALSO THREATEN YOUR LOVED ONES BACK HOME.
AND I COULD DO THESE THINGS AS EASILY AS I COULD KILL A FLY.
BUT SINCE THESE ARE ALL THINGS YOU EXPECT, THINGS YOU EVEN ANTICIPATE--
--THEY ARE, BY DEFINITION, BORING.
SO LET ME SHOW YOU SOMETHING NEW.
A NEW ORDER FOR A NEW WORLD.
LET US CUT TO THE CHASE--
--SINCE THE CHASE IS AT AN END.
GHETTO! VERBOTEN
GHETTO! BETRETEN FÜR WEHRMACHT VERBOTEN

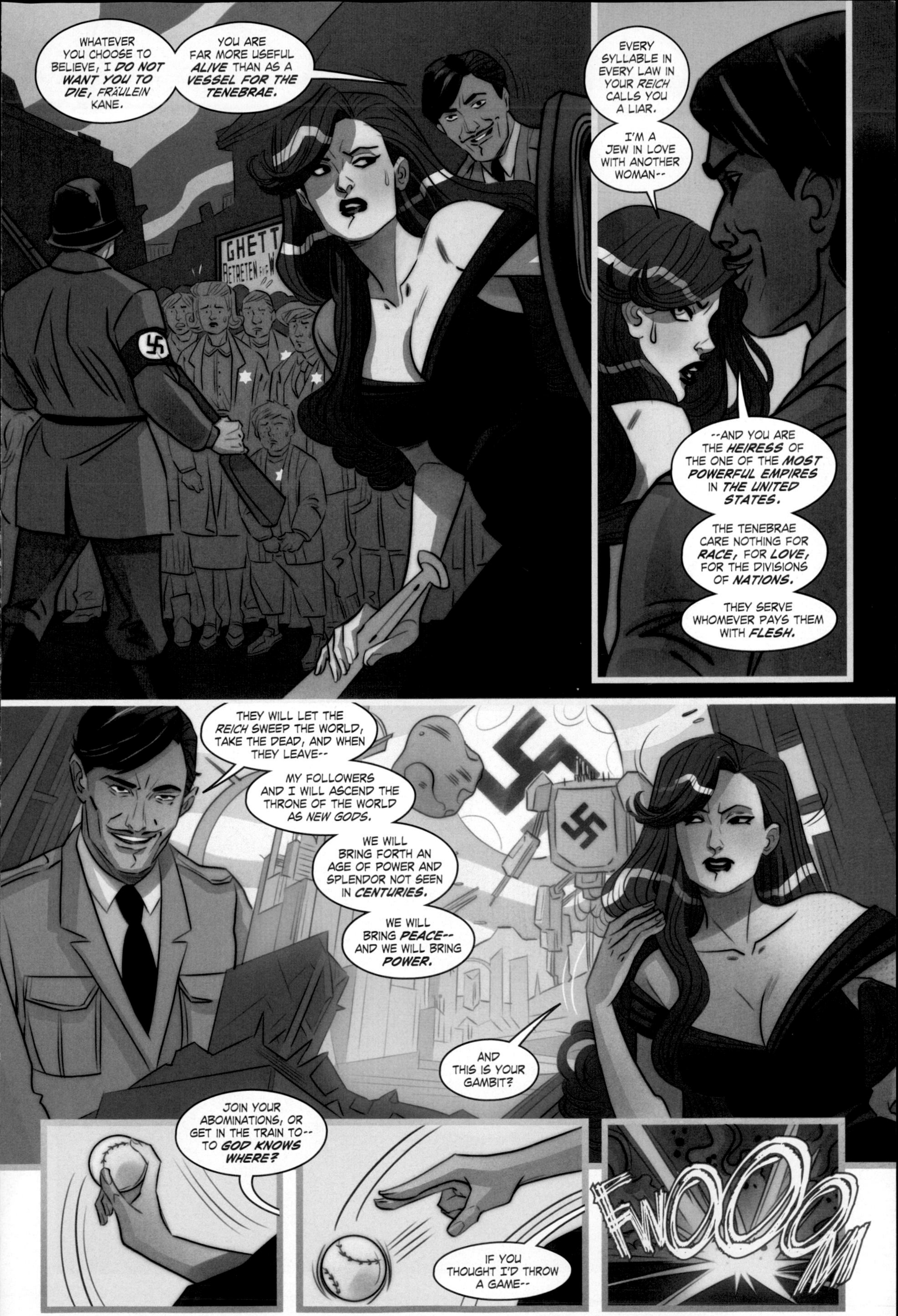
WHATEVER YOU CHOOSE TO BELIEVE, I DO NOT WANT YOU TO DIE, FRÄULEIN KANE.
YOU ARE FAR MORE USEFUL ALIVE THAN AS A VESSEL FOR THE TENEBRAE.
GHETT
EVERY SYLLABLE IN EVERY LAW IN YOUR REICH CALLS YOU A LIAR.
I'M A JEW IN LOVE WITH ANOTHER WOMAN--
--AND YOU ARE THE HEIRESS OF THE ONE OF THE MOST POWERFUL EMPIRES IN THE UNITED STATES.
THE TENEBRAE CARE NOTHING FOR RACE, FOR LOVE, FOR THE DIVISIONS OF NATIONS.
THEY SERVE WHOMEVER PAYS THEM WITH FLESH.
THEY WILL LET THE REICH SWEEP THE WORLD, TAKE THE DEAD, AND WHEN THEY LEAVE--
MY FOLLOWERS AND I WILL ASCEND THE THRONE OF THE WORLD AS NEW GODS.
WE WILL BRING FORTH AN AGE OF POWER AND SPLENDOR NOT SEEN IN CENTURIES.
WE WILL BRING PEACE-- AND WE WILL BRING POWER.
AND THIS IS YOUR GAMBIT?
JOIN YOUR ABOMINATIONS, OR GET IN THE TRAIN TO-- TO GOD KNOWS WHERE?
IF YOU THOUGHT I'D THROW A GAME--
FWOOOOM

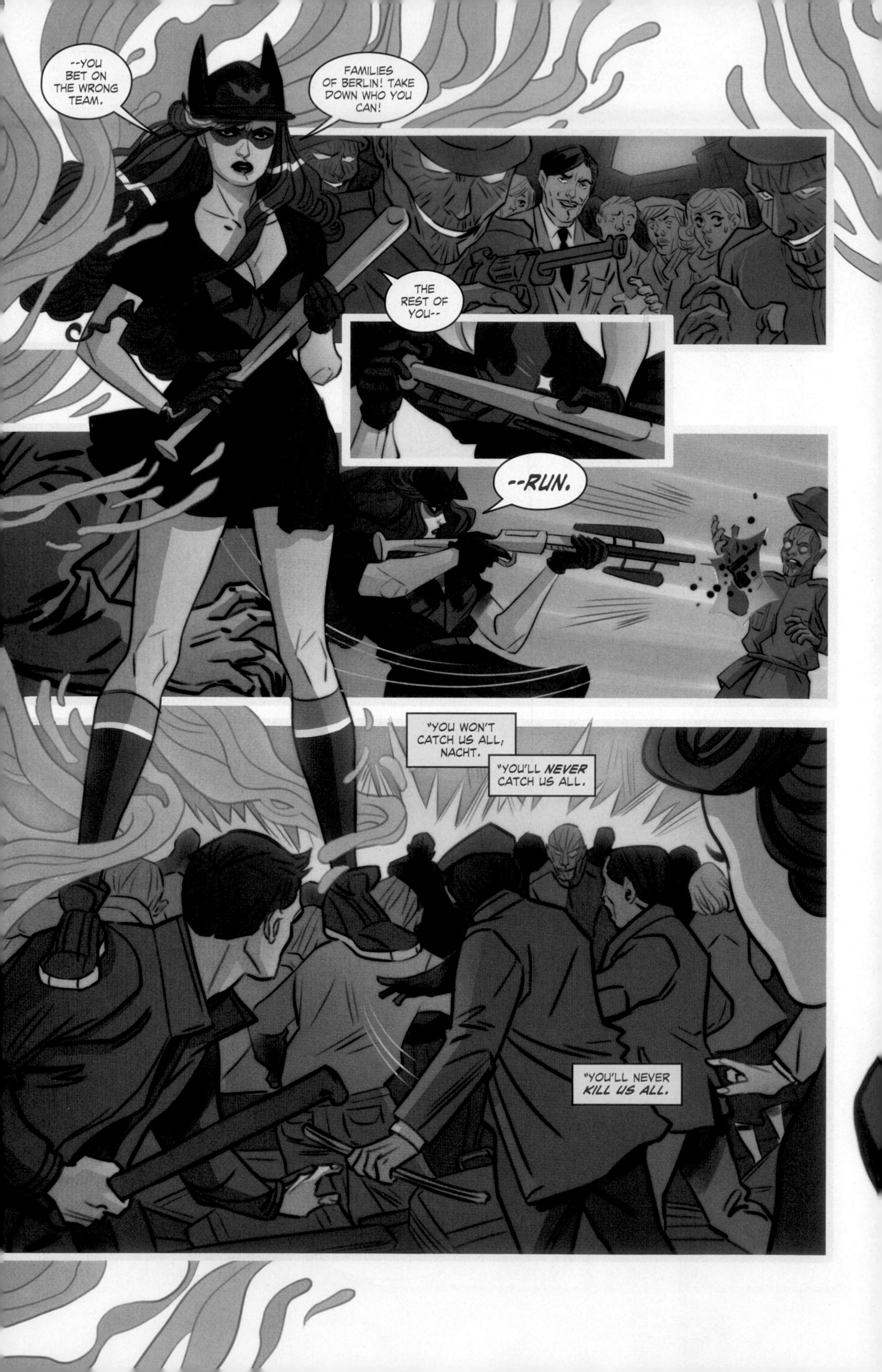
--YOU BET ON THE WRONG TEAM.
FAMILIES OF BERLIN! TAKE DOWN WHO YOU CAN!
THE REST OF YOU--
--RUN.
"YOU WON'T CATCH US ALL, NACHT.
"YOU'LL NEVER CATCH US ALL.
"YOU'LL NEVER KILL US ALL.

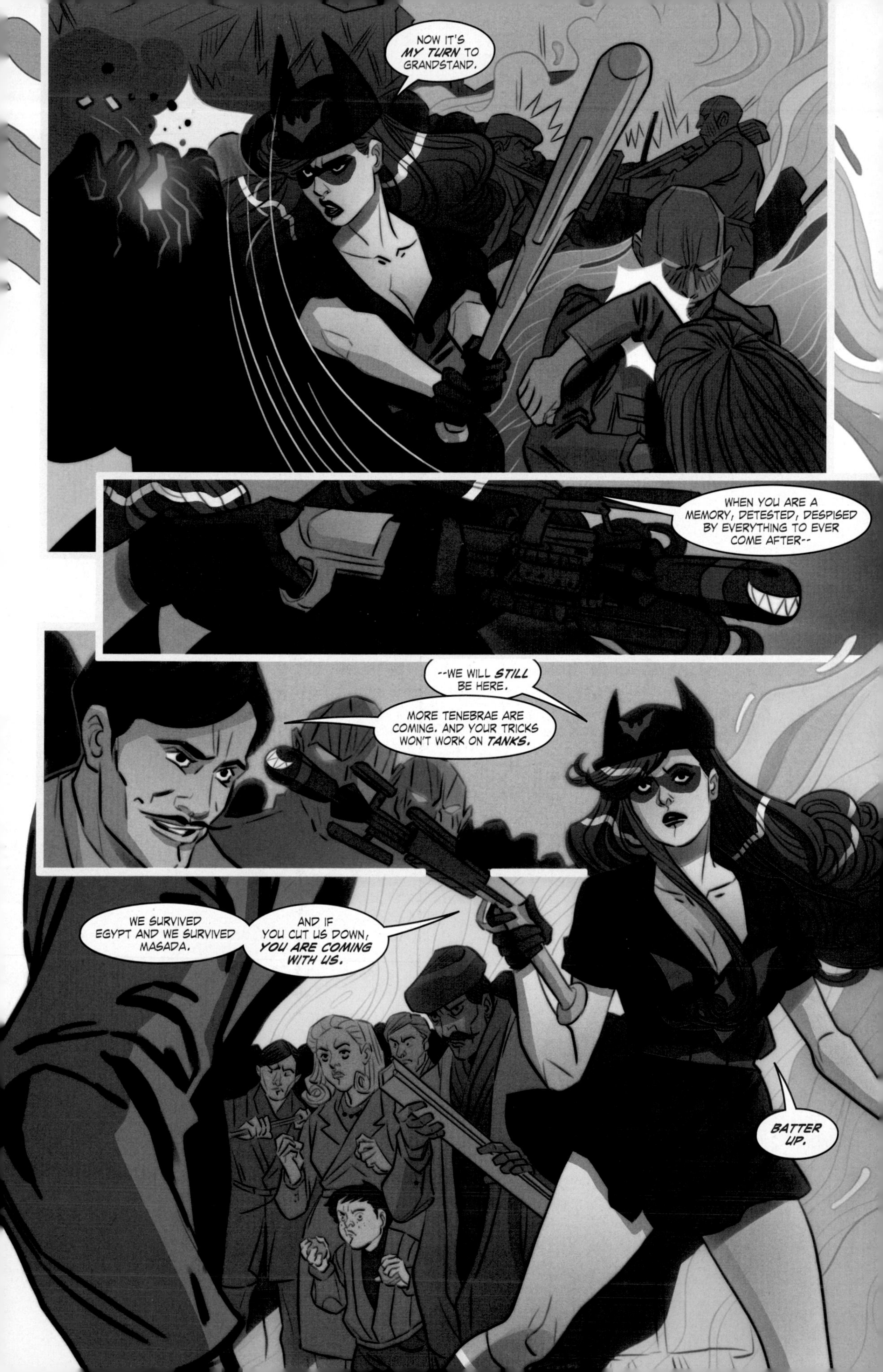
NOW IT'S MY TURN TO GRANDSTAND.
WHEN YOU ARE A MEMORY, DETESTED, DESPISED BY EVERYTHING TO EVER COME AFTER--
--WE WILL STILL BE HERE.
MORE TENEBRAE ARE COMING. AND YOUR TRICKS WON'T WORK ON TANKS.
WE SURVIVED EGYPT AND WE SURVIVED MASADA.
AND IF YOU CUT US DOWN, YOU ARE COMING WITH US.
BATTER UP.

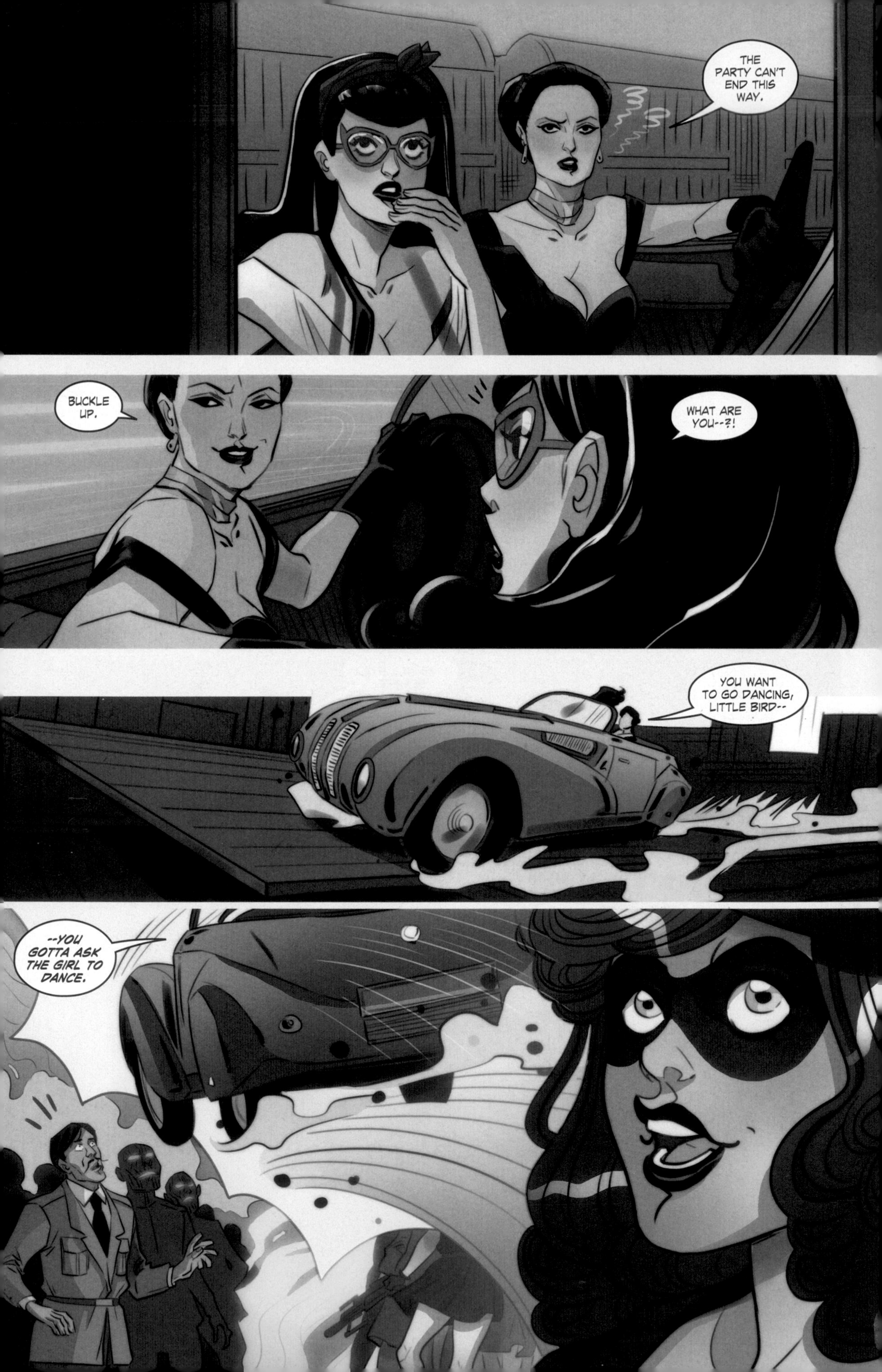
THE PARTY CAN'T END THIS WAY.
BUCKLE UP.
WHAT ARE YOU--?!
YOU WANT TO GO DANCING, LITTLE BIRD--
--YOU GOTTA ASK THE GIRL TO DANCE.

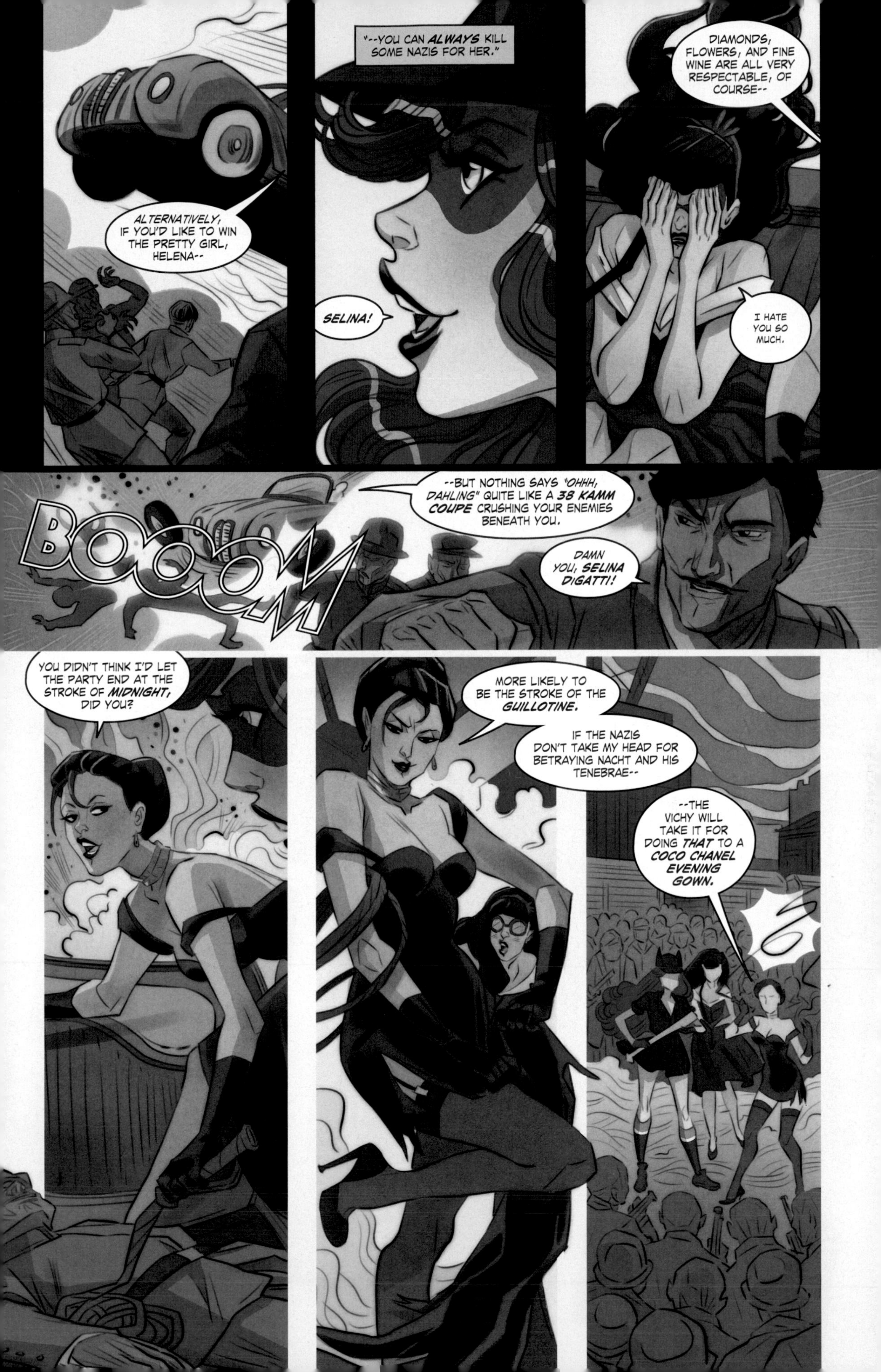
ALTERNATIVELY, IF YOU'D LIKE TO WIN THE PRETTY GIRL, HELENA--
"--YOU CAN ALWAYS KILL SOME NAZIS FOR HER."
SELINA!
DIAMONDS, FLOWERS, AND FINE WINE ARE ALL VERY RESPECTABLE, OF COURSE--
I HATE YOU SO MUCH.
BOOOOM
--BUT NOTHING SAYS "OHHH, DAHLING" QUITE LIKE A 38 KAMM COUPE CRUSHING YOUR ENEMIES BENEATH YOU.
DAMN YOU, SELINA DIGATTI!
YOU DIDN'T THINK I'D LET THE PARTY END AT THE STROKE OF MIDNIGHT, DID YOU?
MORE LIKELY TO BE THE STROKE OF THE GUILLOTINE.
IF THE NAZIS DON'T TAKE MY HEAD FOR BETRAYING NACHT AND HIS TENEBRAE--
--THE VICHY WILL TAKE IT FOR DOING THAT TO A COCO CHANEL EVENING GOWN.

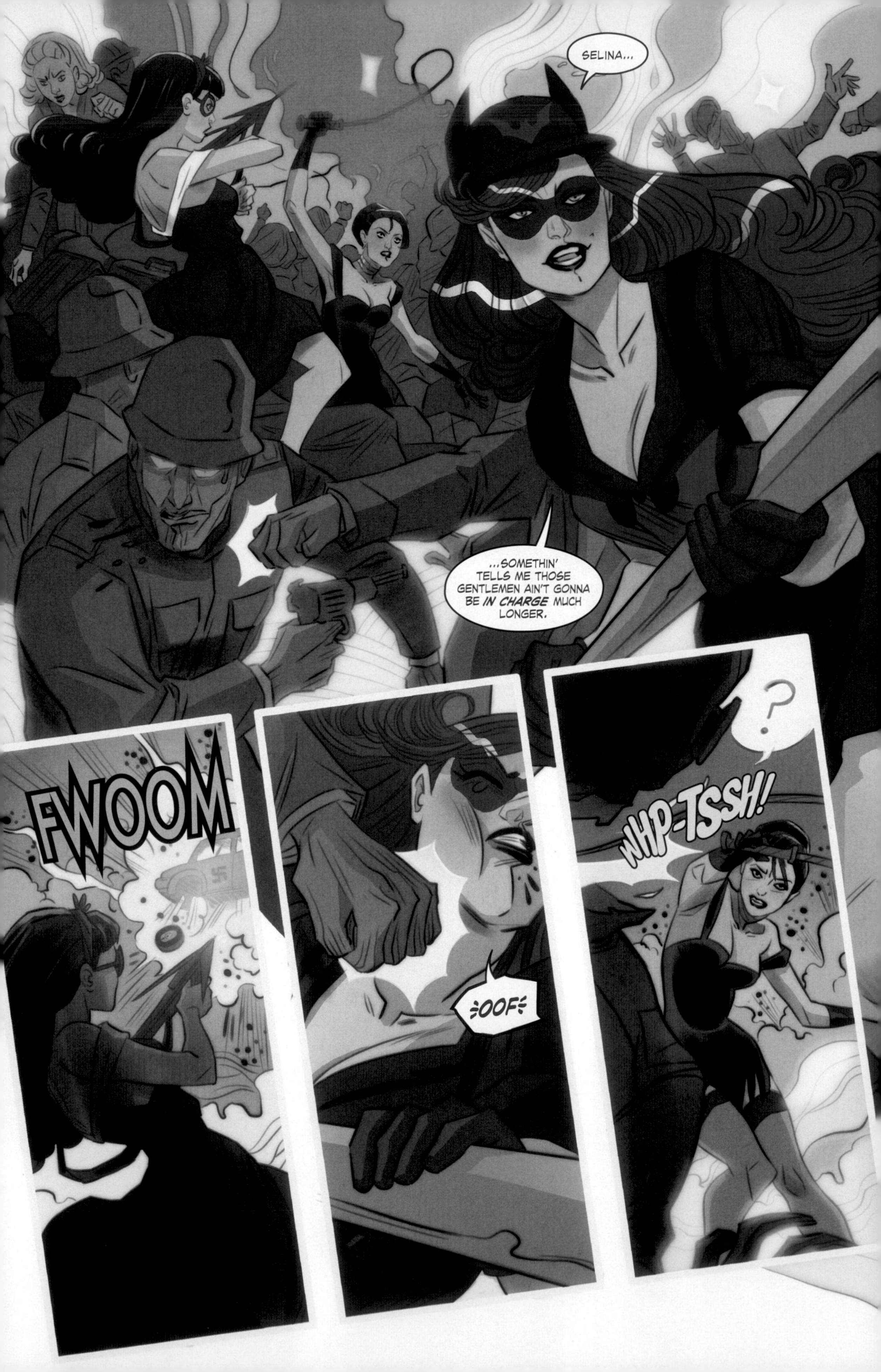
SELINA...
...SOMETHIN' TELLS ME THOSE GENTLEMEN AIN'T GONNA BE IN CHARGE MUCH LONGER.
FWOOM
OOF
?
WHP-TSSH!

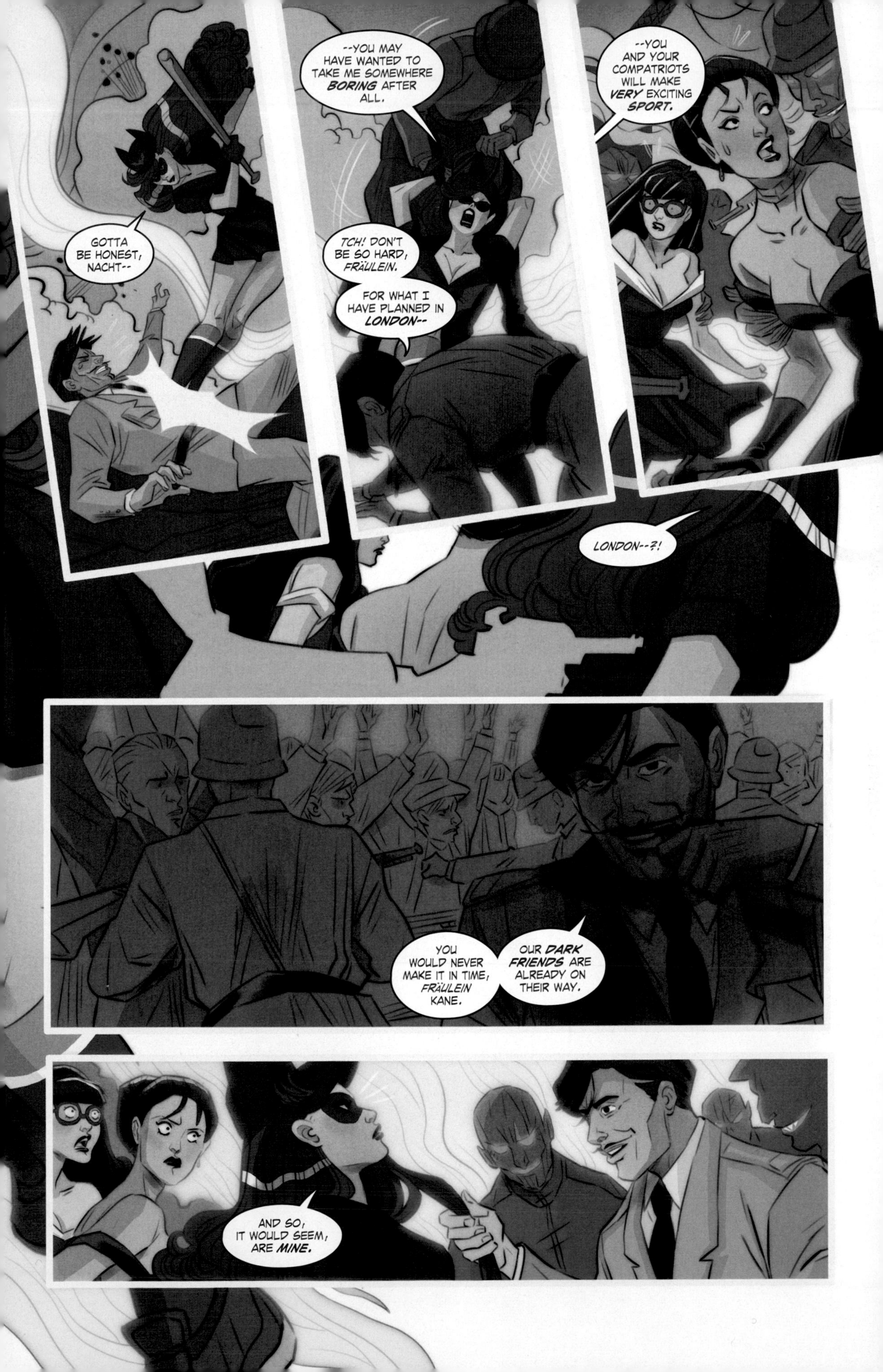
GOTTA BE HONEST, NACHT--
--YOU MAY HAVE WANTED TO TAKE ME SOMEWHERE BORING AFTER ALL.
TCH! DON'T BE SO HARD, FRÄULEIN.
FOR WHAT I HAVE PLANNED IN LONDON--
--YOU AND YOUR COMPATRIOTS WILL MAKE VERY EXCITING SPORT.
LONDON--?!
YOU WOULD NEVER MAKE IT IN TIME, FRÄULEIN KANE.
OUR DARK FRIENDS ARE ALREADY ON THEIR WAY.
AND SO, IT WOULD SEEM, ARE MINE.

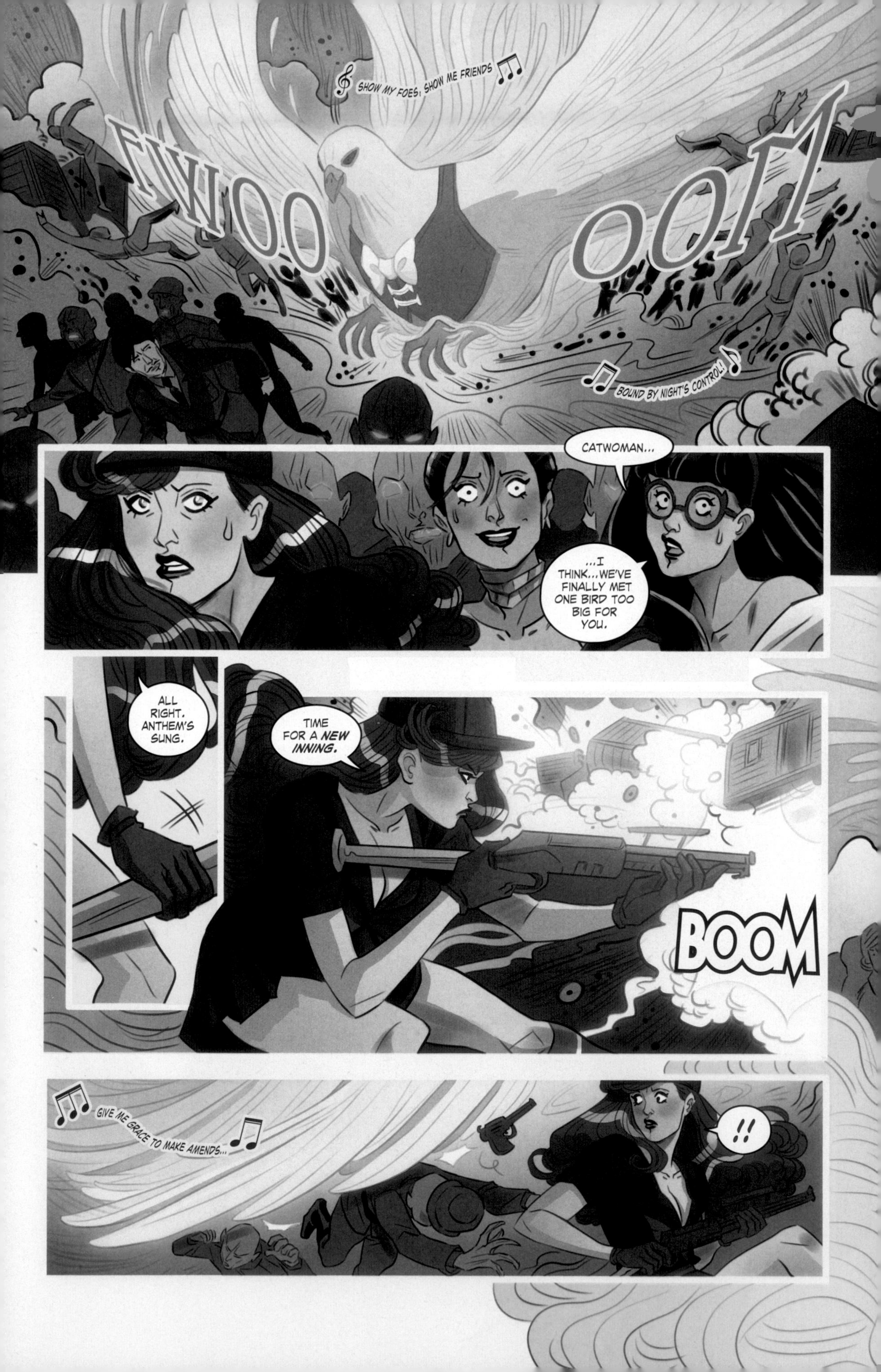

SHOW MY FOES, SHOW ME FRIENDS
FWOOM
BOUND BY NIGHT'S CONTROL!
CATWOMAN...
...I THINK...WE'VE FINALLY MET ONE BIRD TOO BIG FOR YOU.
ALL RIGHT. ANTHEM'S SUNG.
TIME FOR A *NEW INNING.*
BOOM
GIVE ME GRACE TO MAKE AMENDS...
!!

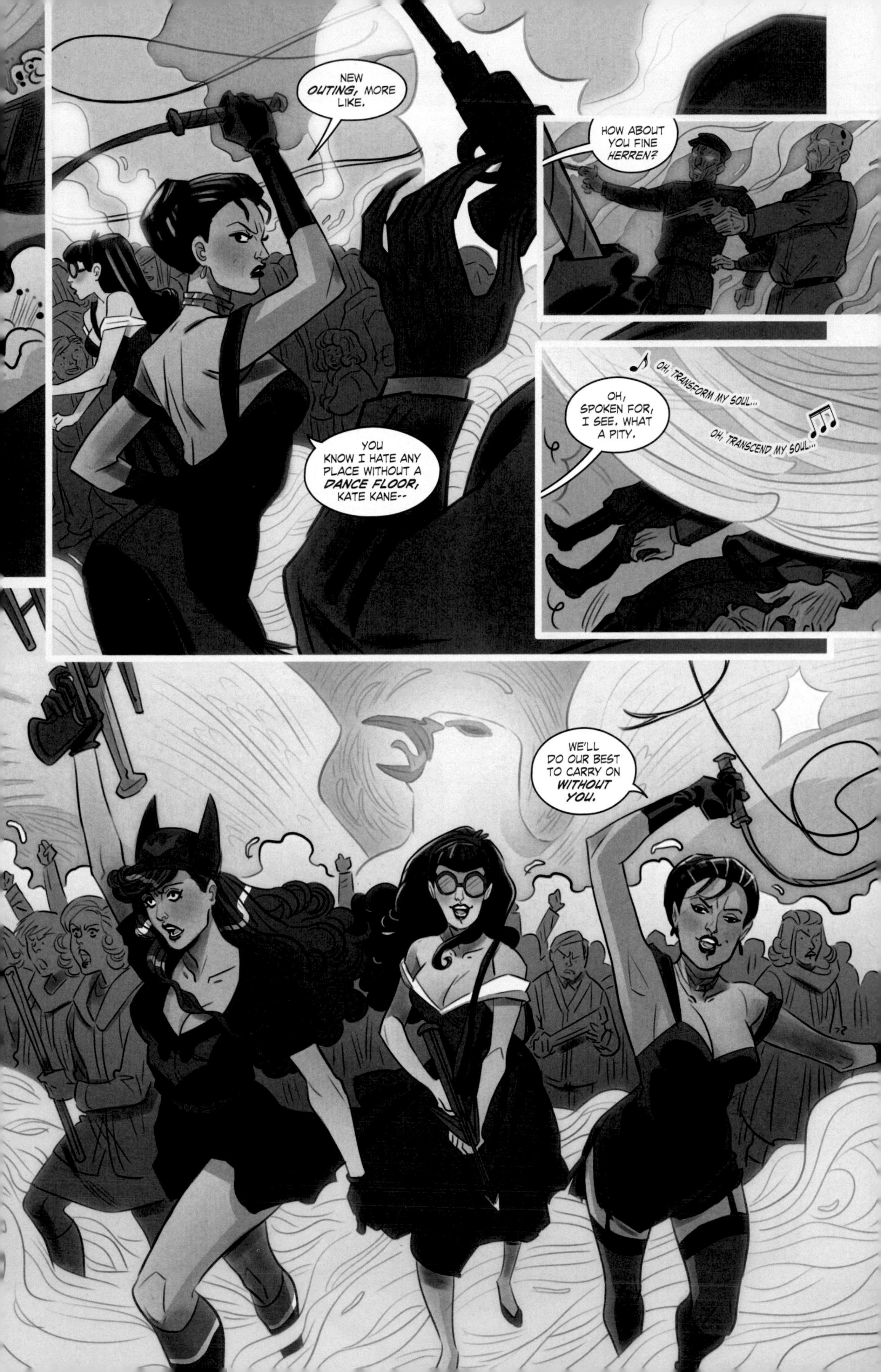
NEW OUTING, MORE LIKE.
YOU KNOW I HATE ANY PLACE WITHOUT A DANCE FLOOR, KATE KANE--
HOW ABOUT YOU FINE HERREN?
OH, SPOKEN FOR, I SEE. WHAT A PITY.
OH, TRANSFORM MY SOUL...
OH, TRANSCEND MY SOUL...
WE'LL DO OUR BEST TO CARRY ON WITHOUT YOU.

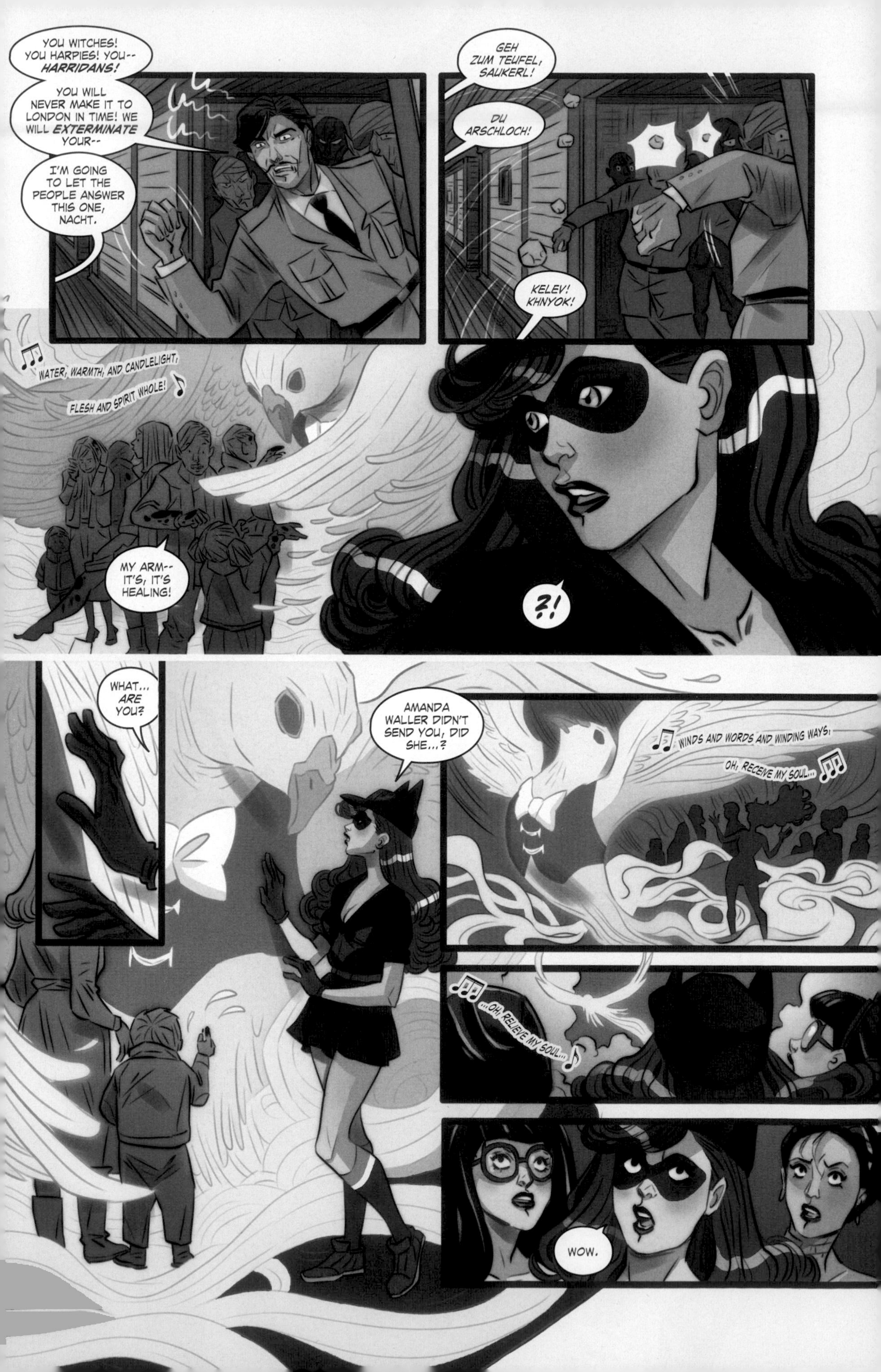
YOU WITCHES! YOU HARPIES! YOU-- HARRIDANS!
YOU WILL NEVER MAKE IT TO LONDON IN TIME! WE WILL EXTERMINATE YOUR--
I'M GOING TO LET THE PEOPLE ANSWER THIS ONE, NACHT.
GEH ZUM TEUFEL, SAUKERL!
DU ARSCHLOCH!
KELEV! KHNYOK!
WATER, WARMTH, AND CANDLELIGHT,
FLESH AND SPIRIT WHOLE!
MY ARM-- IT'S, IT'S HEALING!
?!
WHAT... ARE YOU?
AMANDA WALLER DIDN'T SEND YOU, DID SHE...?
WINDS AND WORDS AND WINDING WAYS,
OH, RECEIVE MY SOUL...
...OH, RELIEVE MY SOUL...
WOW.

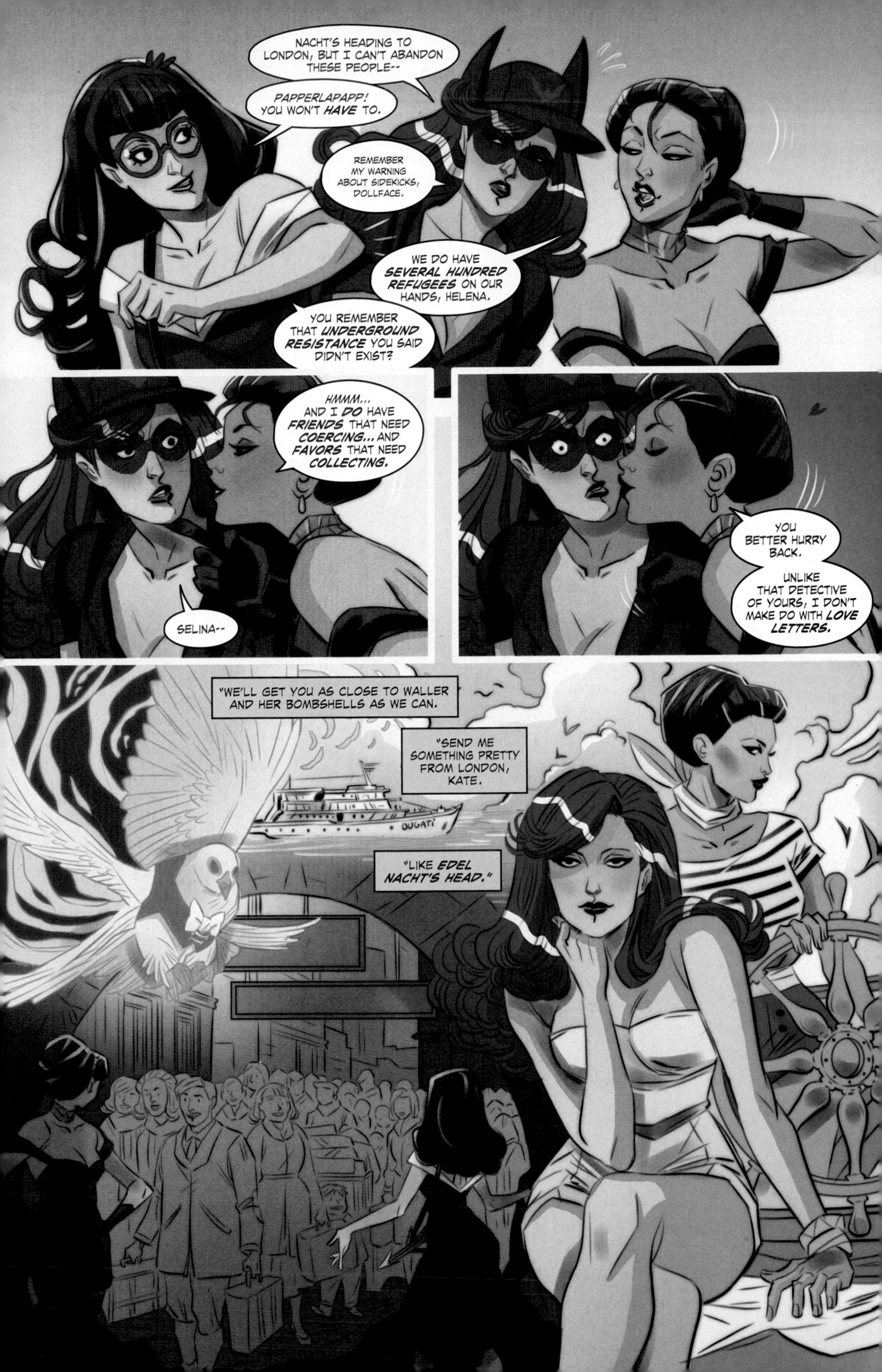

NACHT'S HEADING TO LONDON, BUT I CAN'T ABANDON THESE PEOPLE--
PAPPERLAPAPP! YOU WON'T ***HAVE*** TO.
REMEMBER MY WARNING ABOUT SIDEKICKS, DOLLFACE.
WE DO HAVE ***SEVERAL HUNDRED REFUGEES*** ON OUR HANDS, HELENA.
YOU REMEMBER THAT ***UNDERGROUND RESISTANCE*** YOU SAID DIDN'T EXIST?
HMMM... AND I ***DO*** HAVE ***FRIENDS*** THAT NEED ***COERCING...*** AND ***FAVORS*** THAT NEED ***COLLECTING.***
SELINA--
YOU BETTER HURRY BACK.
UNLIKE THAT DETECTIVE OF YOURS, I DON'T MAKE DO WITH ***LOVE LETTERS.***
"WE'LL GET YOU AS CLOSE TO WALLER AND HER BOMBSHELLS AS WE CAN.
"SEND ME SOMETHING PRETTY FROM LONDON, KATE.
"LIKE ***EDEL NACHT'S HEAD."***
DUGATI

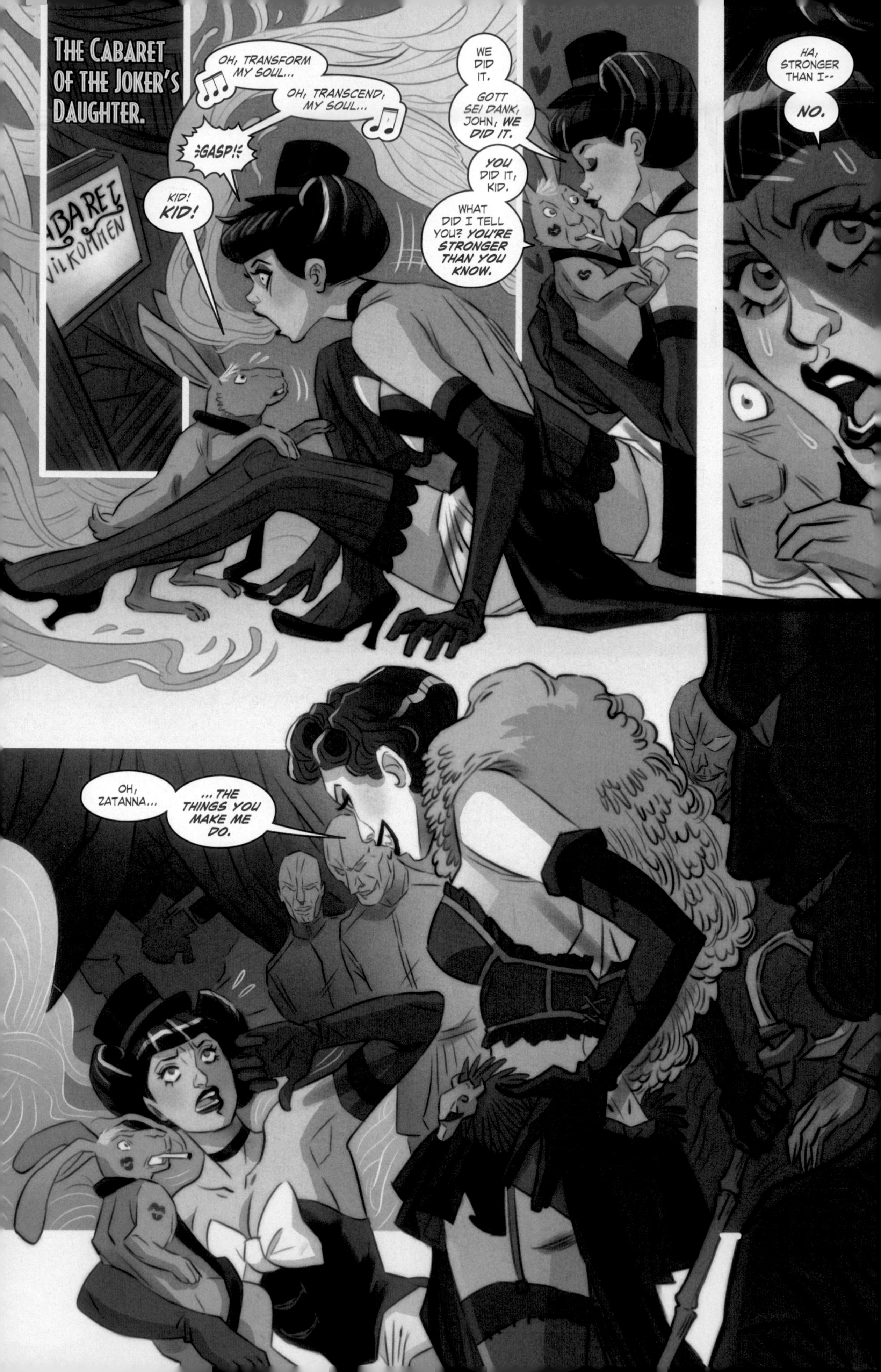
The Cabaret of the Joker's Daughter.
OH, TRANSFORM MY SOUL...
OH, TRANSCEND, MY SOUL...
GASP!
KID! KID!
CABARET WILKOMMEN
WE DID IT.
GOTT SEI DANK, JOHN, WE DID IT.
YOU DID IT, KID.
WHAT DID I TELL YOU? YOU'RE STRONGER THAN YOU KNOW.
HA, STRONGER THAN I--
NO.
OH, ZATANNA...
...THE THINGS YOU MAKE ME DO.

THE BATTLE OF BRITAIN

PART ONE

MARGUERITE BENNETT
Writer

MIRKA ANDOLFO
LAURA BRAGA
Artists

WENDY BROOME
Colorist

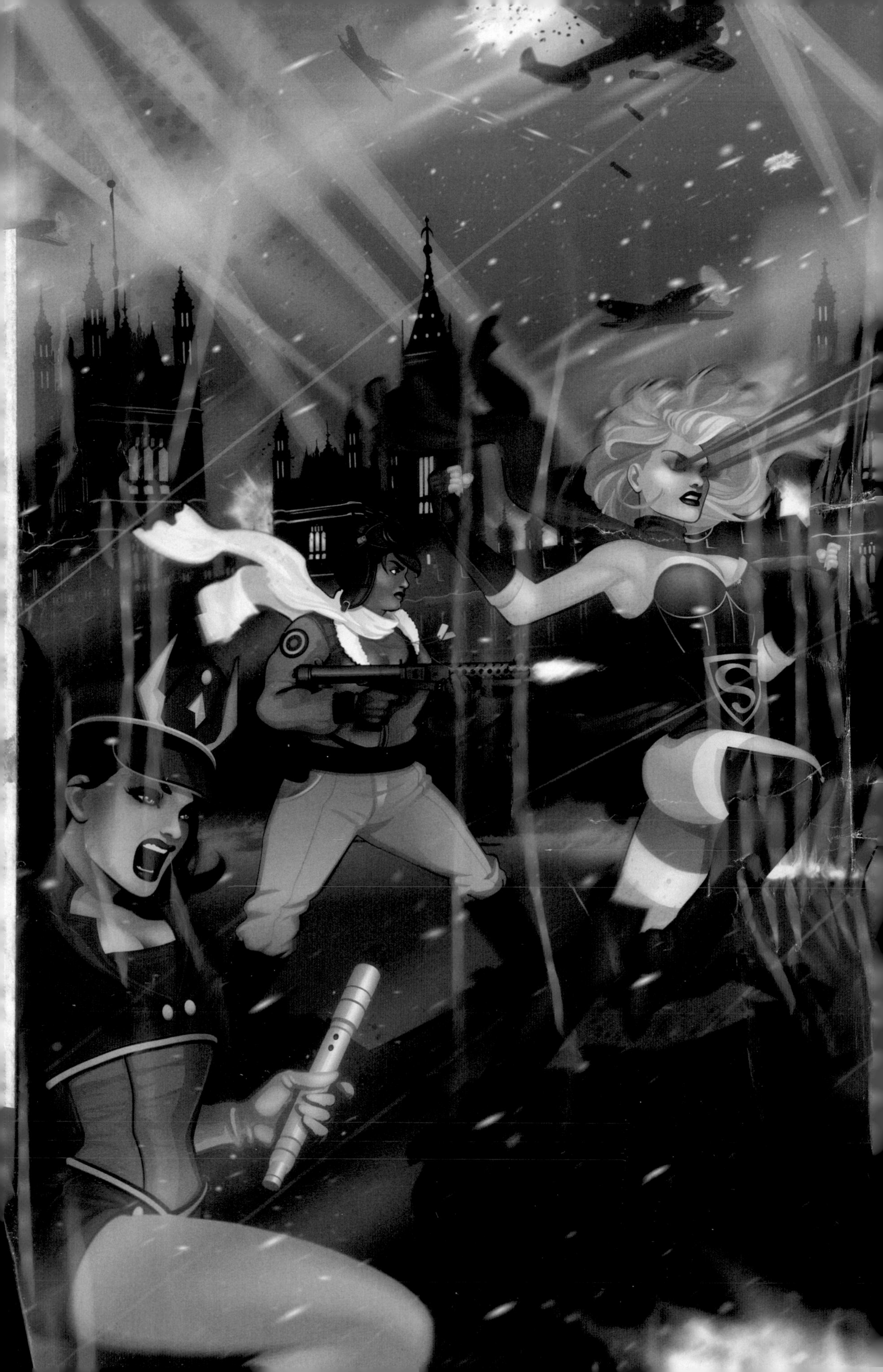

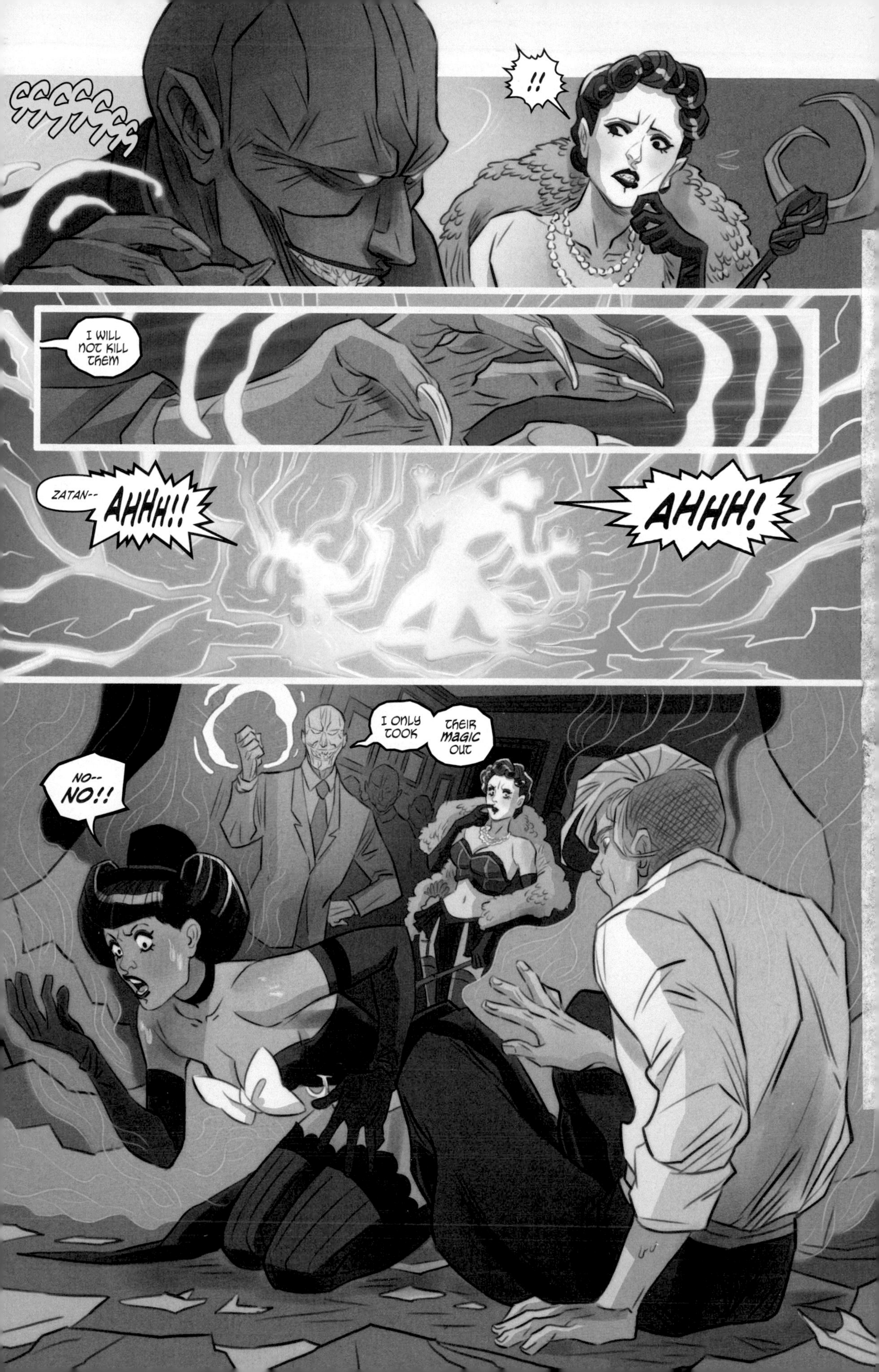
SSSSSSS
!!
I WILL NOT KILL THEM
ZATAN-- AHHH!!
AHHH!
I ONLY TOOK THEIR MAGIC OUT
NO-- NO!!

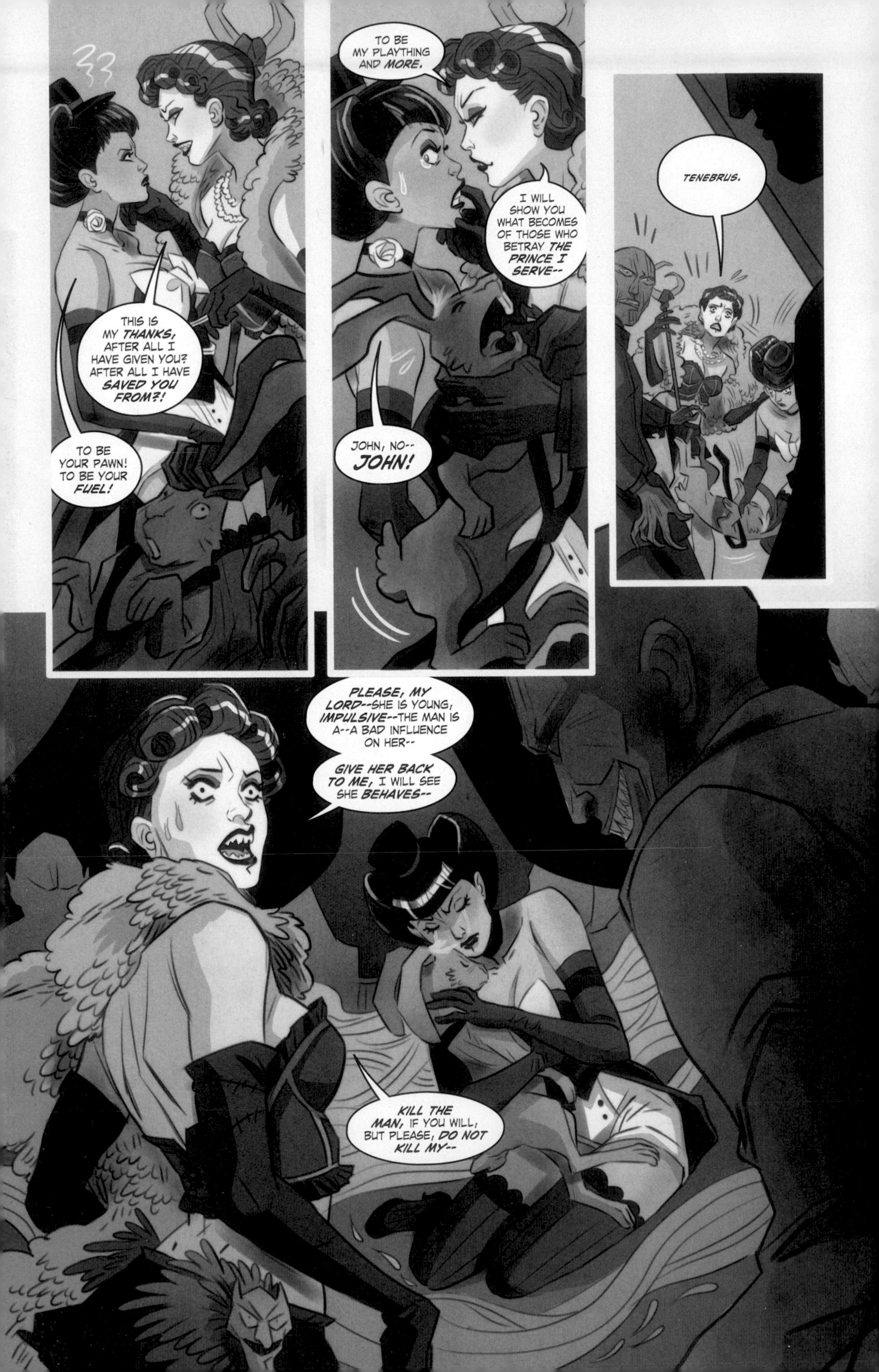
THIS IS MY THANKS, AFTER ALL I HAVE GIVEN YOU? AFTER ALL I HAVE SAVED YOU FROM?!
TO BE YOUR PAWN! TO BE YOUR FUEL!
TO BE MY PLAYTHING AND MORE.
I WILL SHOW YOU WHAT BECOMES OF THOSE WHO BETRAY THE PRINCE I SERVE--
JOHN, NO-- JOHN!
TENEBRUS.
PLEASE, MY LORD--SHE IS YOUNG, IMPULSIVE--THE MAN IS A--A BAD INFLUENCE ON HER--
GIVE HER BACK TO ME, I WILL SEE SHE BEHAVES--
KILL THE MAN, IF YOU WILL, BUT PLEASE, DO NOT KILL MY--

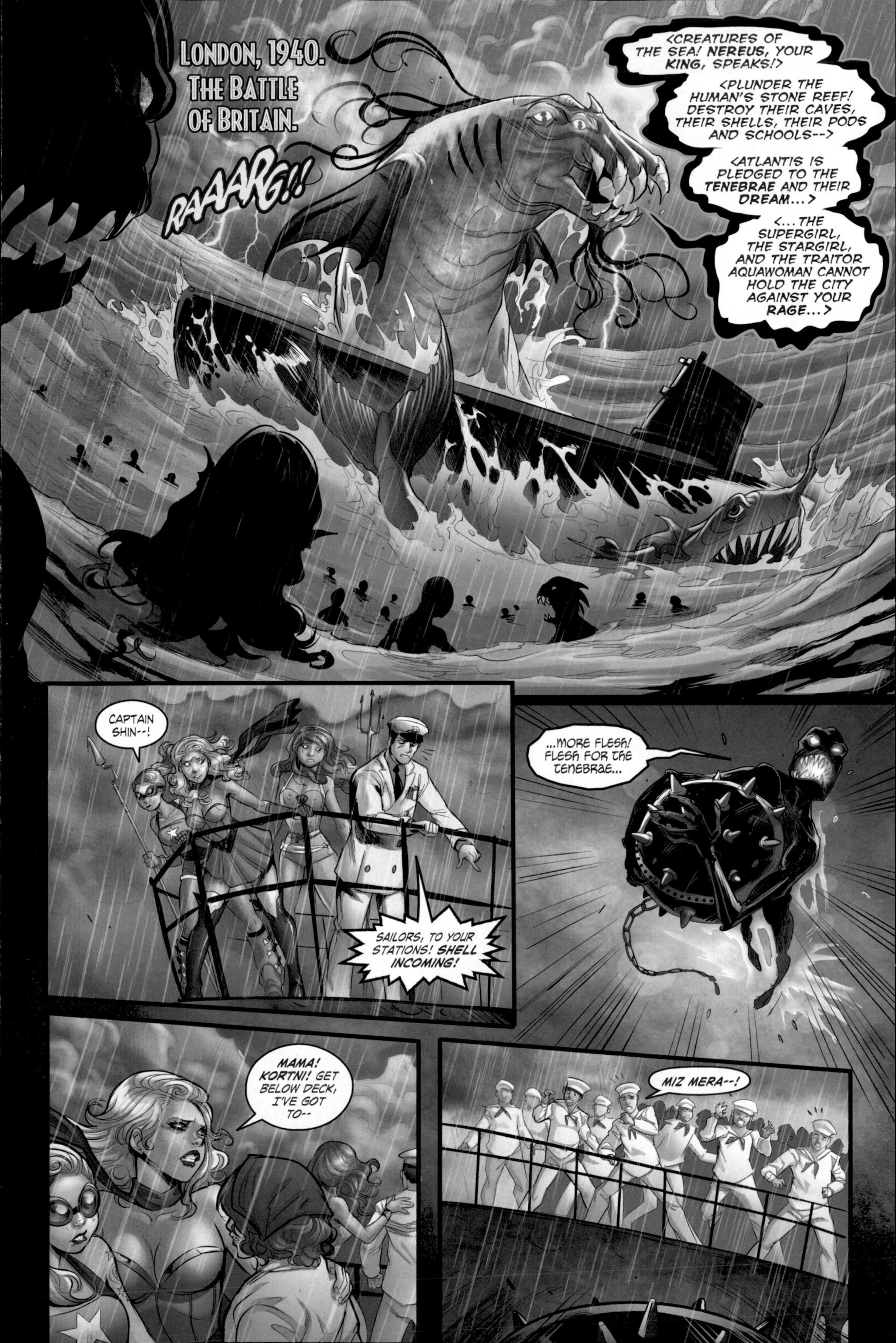
London, 1940. The Battle of Britain.
RAAARG!!
<CREATURES OF THE SEA! NEREUS, YOUR KING, SPEAKS!>
<PLUNDER THE HUMAN'S STONE REEF! DESTROY THEIR CAVES, THEIR SHELLS, THEIR PODS AND SCHOOLS-->
<ATLANTIS IS PLEDGED TO THE TENEBRAE AND THEIR DREAM...>
<...THE SUPERGIRL, THE STARGIRL, AND THE TRAITOR AQUAWOMAN CANNOT HOLD THE CITY AGAINST YOUR RAGE...>
CAPTAIN SHIN--!
SAILORS, TO YOUR STATIONS! SHELL INCOMING!
...MORE FLESH! FLESH FOR THE TENEBRAE...
MAMA! KORTNI! GET BELOW DECK, I'VE GOT TO--
MIZ MERA--!

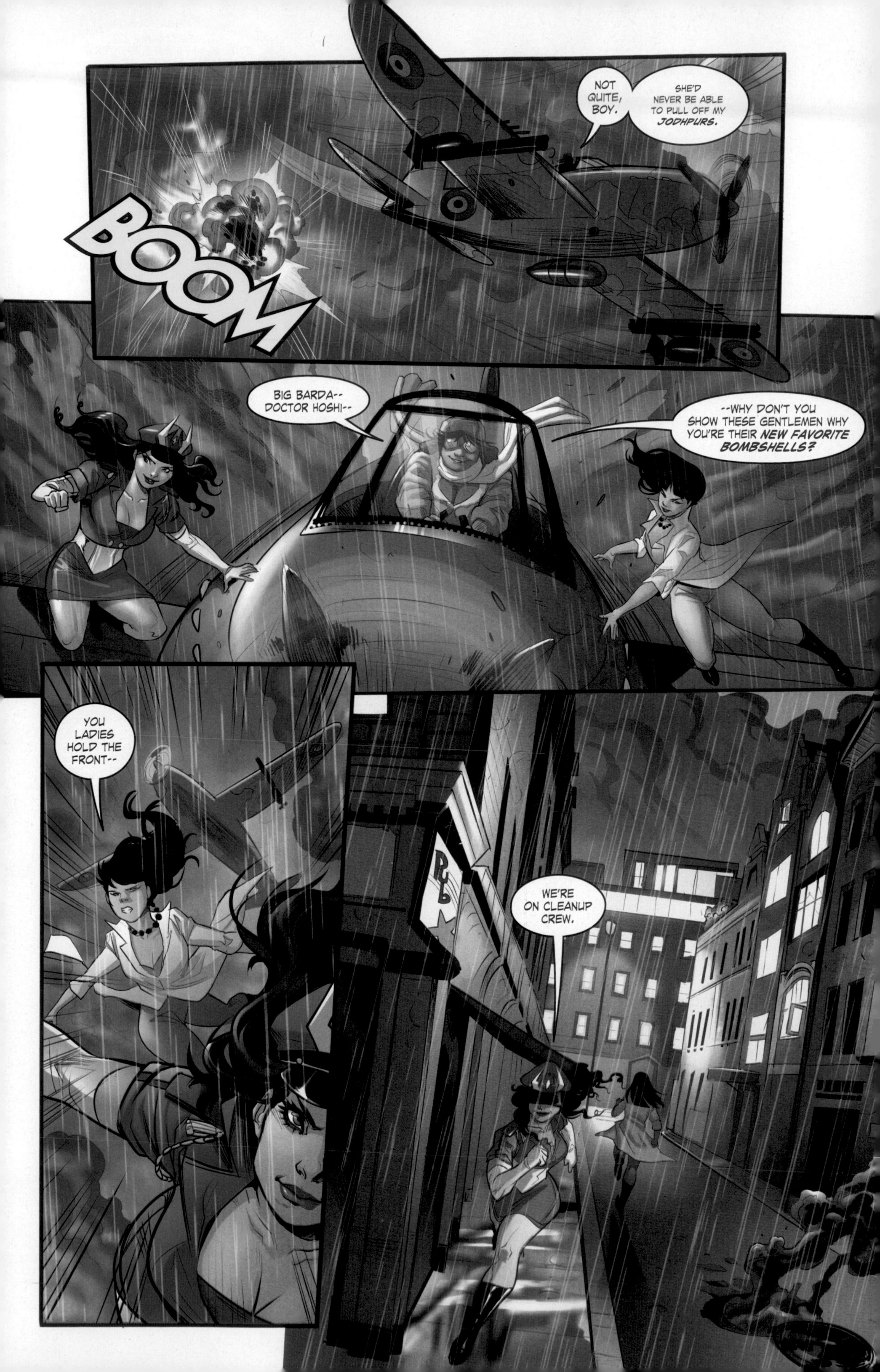
NOT QUITE, BOY.
SHE'D NEVER BE ABLE TO PULL OFF MY *JODHPURS.*
BOOM
BIG BARDA-- DOCTOR HOSHI--
--WHY DON'T YOU SHOW THESE GENTLEMEN WHY YOU'RE THEIR *NEW FAVORITE BOMBSHELLS?*
YOU LADIES HOLD THE FRONT--
PUB
WE'RE ON CLEANUP CREW.

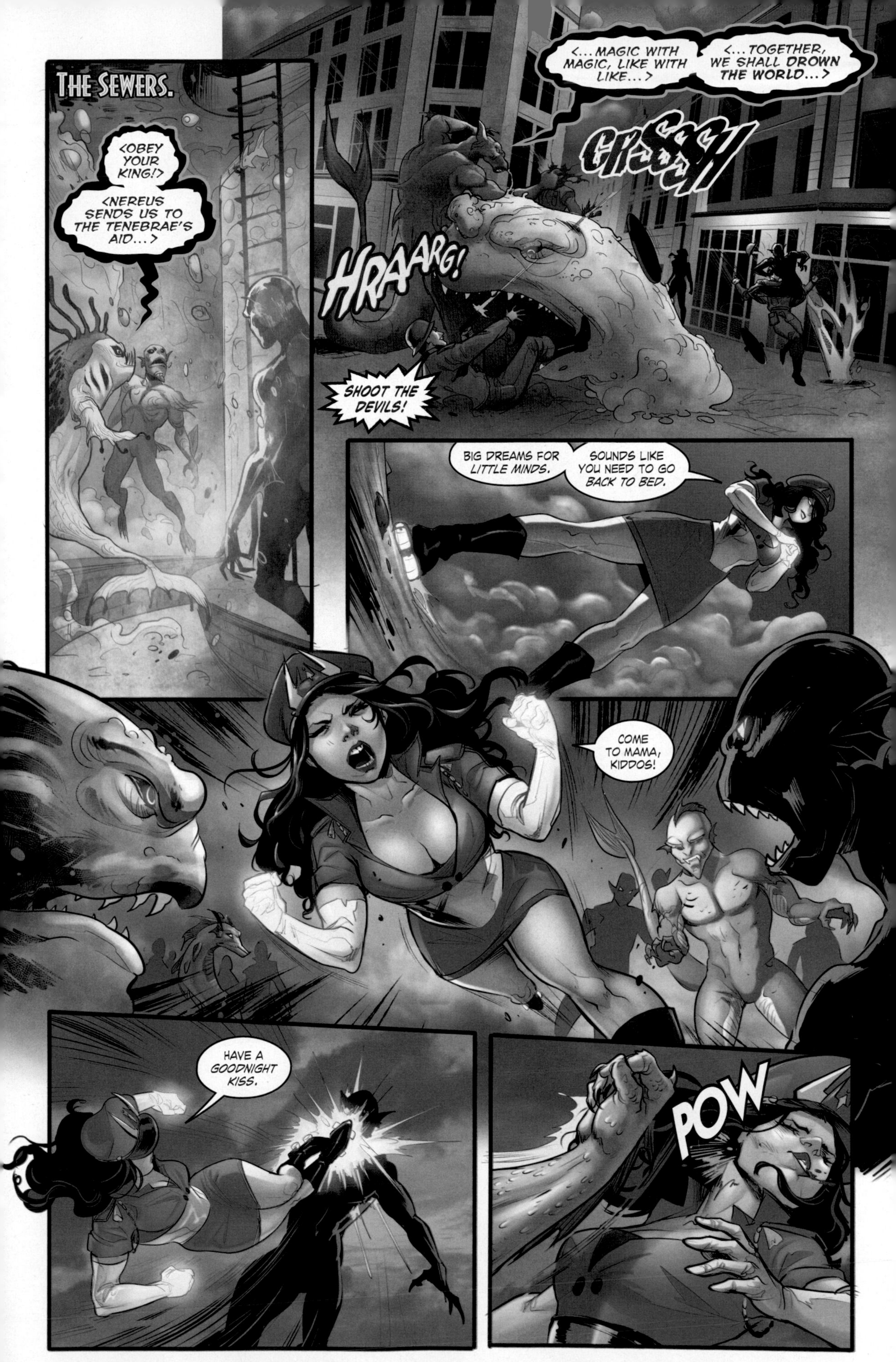
THE SEWERS.
<OBEY YOUR KING!>
<NEREUS SENDS US TO THE TENEBRAE'S AID...>
<...MAGIC WITH MAGIC, LIKE WITH LIKE...>
<...TOGETHER, WE SHALL DROWN THE WORLD...>
CRSSSH
HRAAARG!
SHOOT THE DEVILS!
BIG DREAMS FOR LITTLE MINDS.
SOUNDS LIKE YOU NEED TO GO BACK TO BED.
COME TO MAMA, KIDDOS!
HAVE A GOODNIGHT KISS.
POW

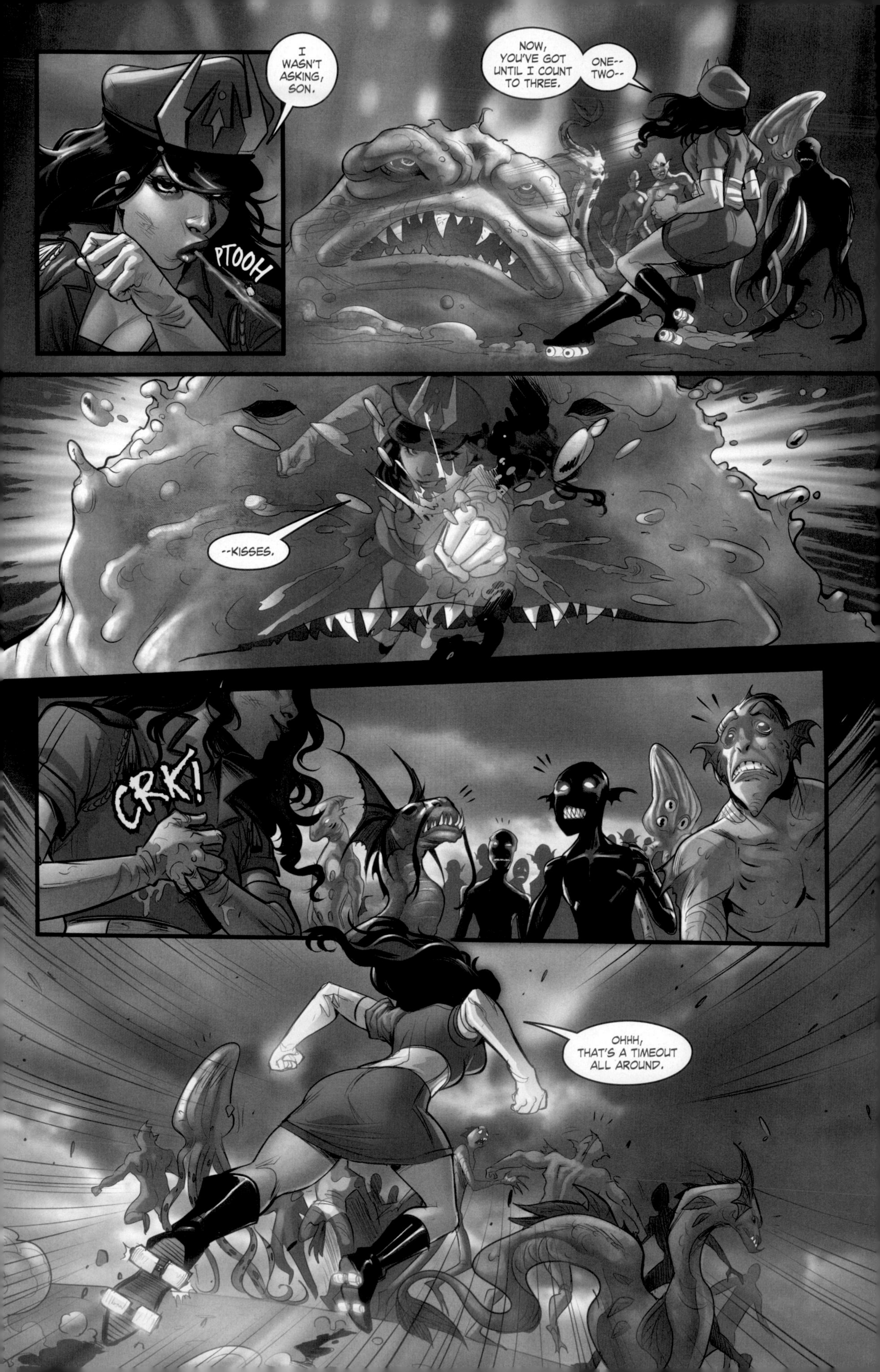
I WASN'T ASKING, SON.
PTOOH
NOW, YOU'VE GOT UNTIL I COUNT TO THREE.
ONE-- TWO--
--KISSES.
CRK!
OHHH, THAT'S A TIMEOUT ALL AROUND.

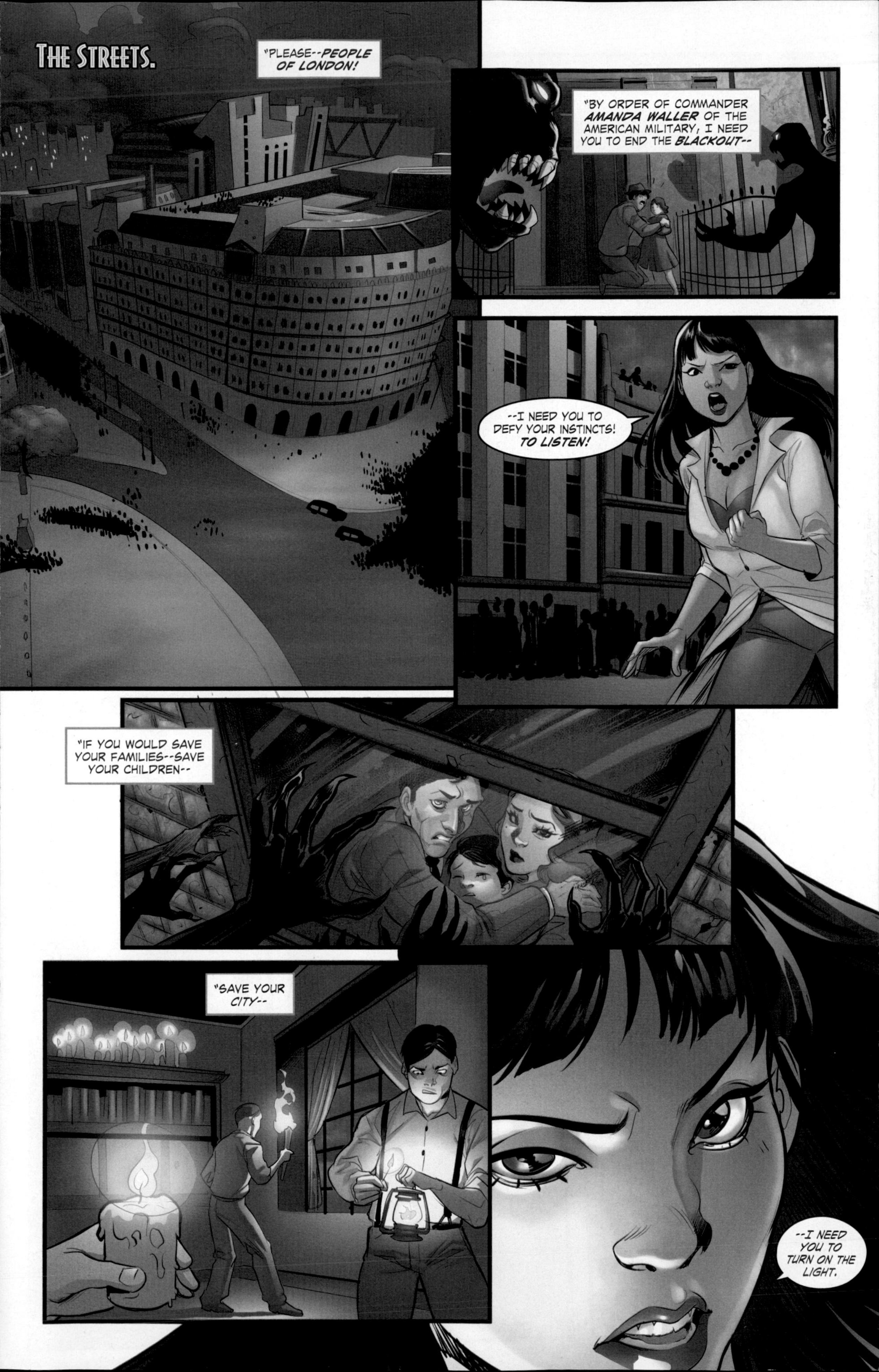
THE STREETS.
"PLEASE--PEOPLE OF LONDON!
"BY ORDER OF COMMANDER AMANDA WALLER OF THE AMERICAN MILITARY, I NEED YOU TO END THE BLACKOUT--
--I NEED YOU TO DEFY YOUR INSTINCTS! TO LISTEN!
"IF YOU WOULD SAVE YOUR FAMILIES--SAVE YOUR CHILDREN--
"SAVE YOUR CITY--
--I NEED YOU TO TURN ON THE LIGHT.

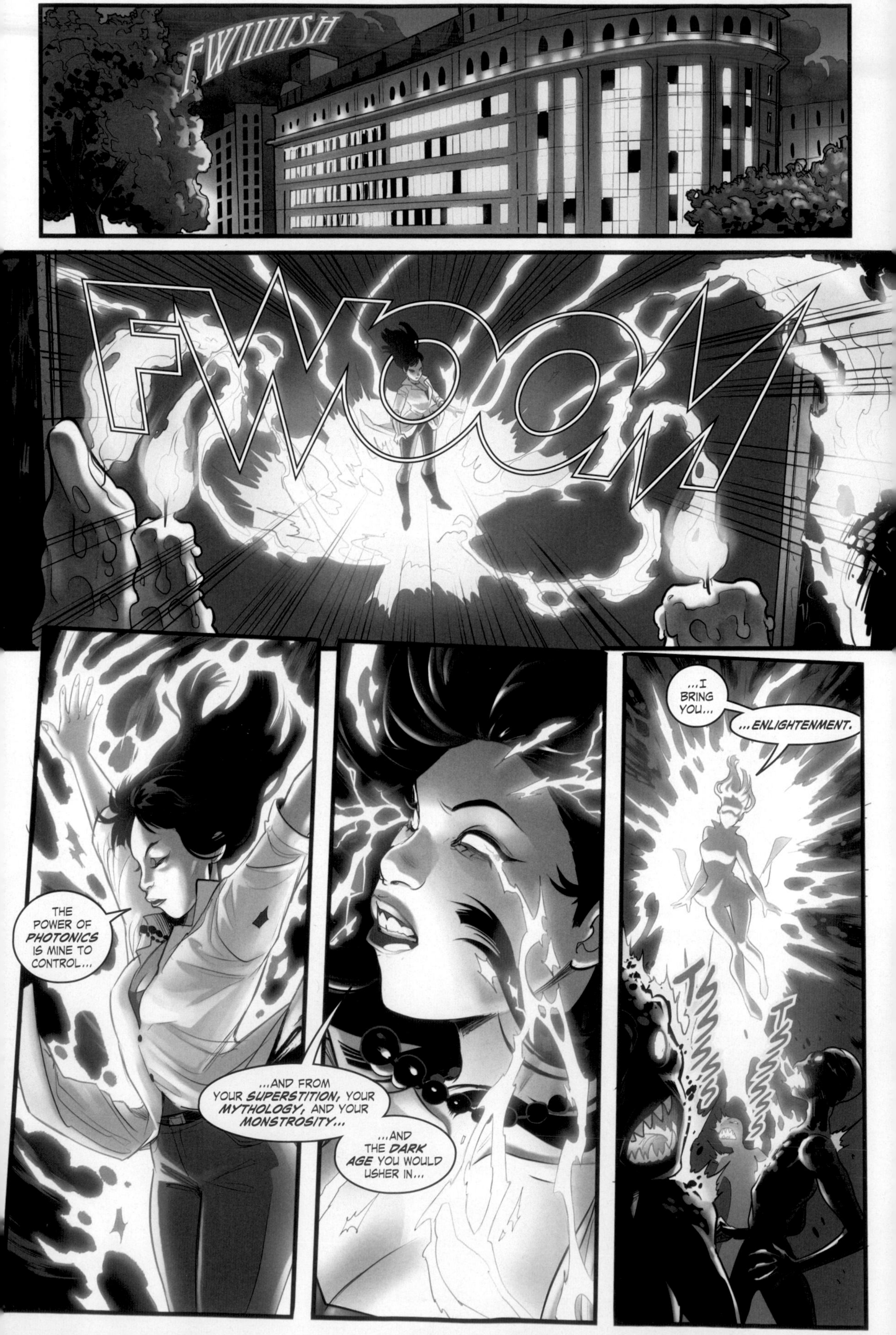
FWIIIIISH
FWOOM
THE POWER OF PHOTONICS IS MINE TO CONTROL...
...AND FROM YOUR SUPERSTITION, YOUR MYTHOLOGY, AND YOUR MONSTROSITY...
...AND THE DARK AGE YOU WOULD USHER IN...
...I BRING YOU...
...ENLIGHTENMENT.
TSSSSSS
TSSSSSS

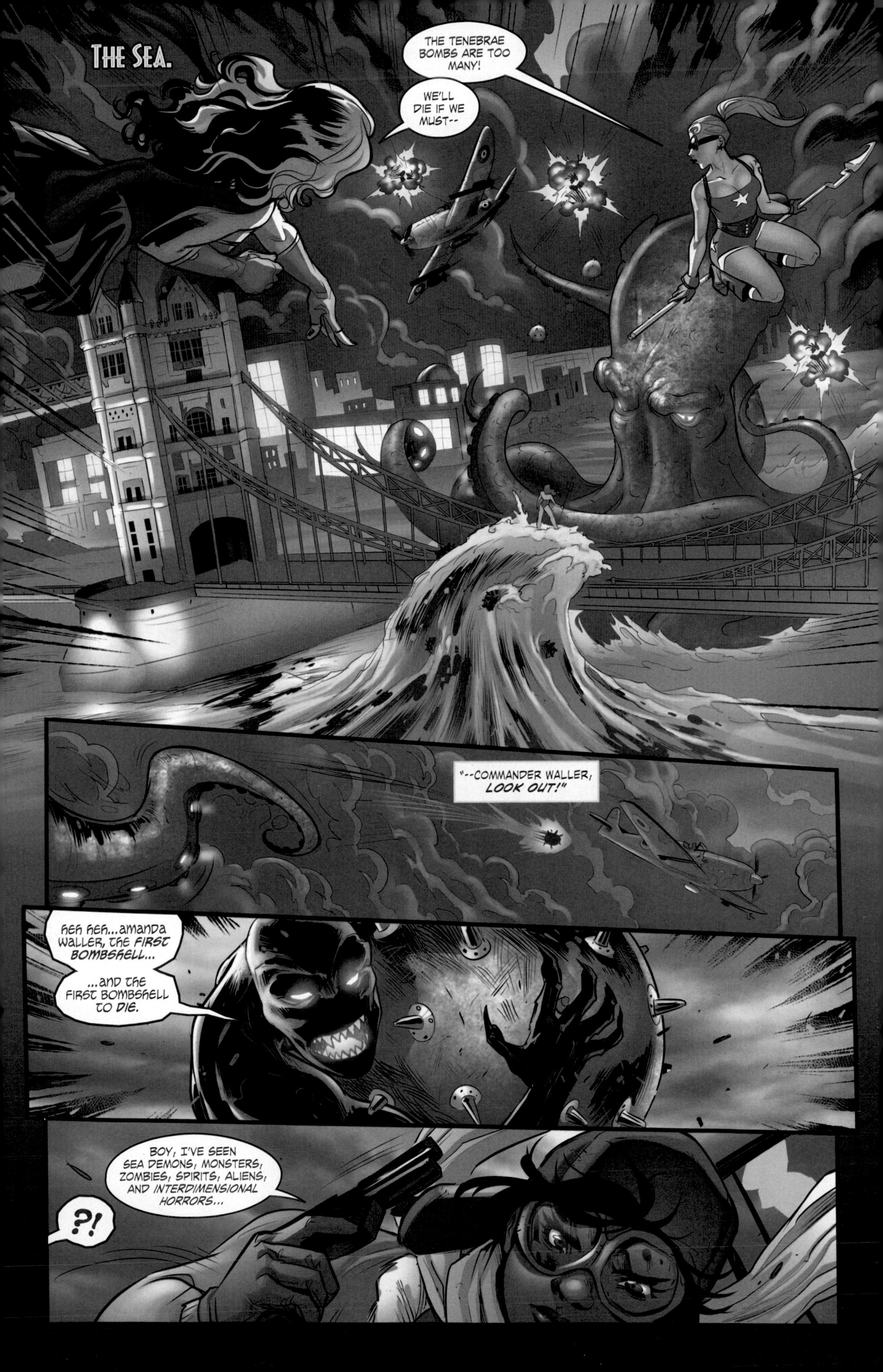
THE SEA.
THE TENEBRAE BOMBS ARE TOO MANY!
WE'LL DIE IF WE MUST--
"--COMMANDER WALLER, LOOK OUT!"
HEH HEH...AMANDA WALLER, THE FIRST BOMBSHELL...
...AND THE FIRST BOMBSHELL TO DIE.
BOY, I'VE SEEN SEA DEMONS, MONSTERS, ZOMBIES, SPIRITS, ALIENS, AND INTERDIMENSIONAL HORRORS...
?!

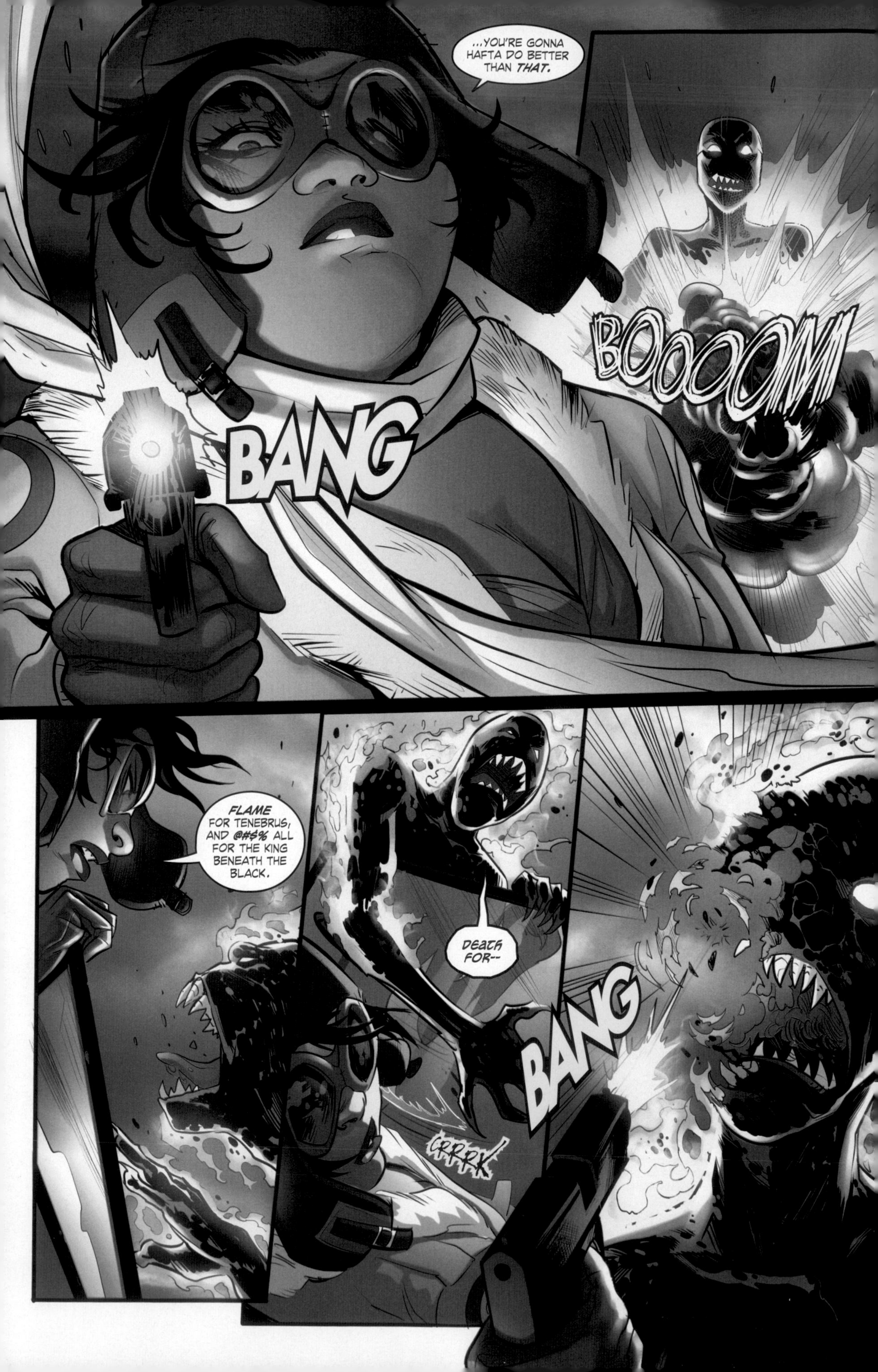
...YOU'RE GONNA HAFTA DO BETTER THAN *THAT*.
BOOOOOM!
BANG
FLAME FOR TENEBRUS, AND @#$% ALL FOR THE KING BENEATH THE BLACK.
Death for--
BANG
CRRRK

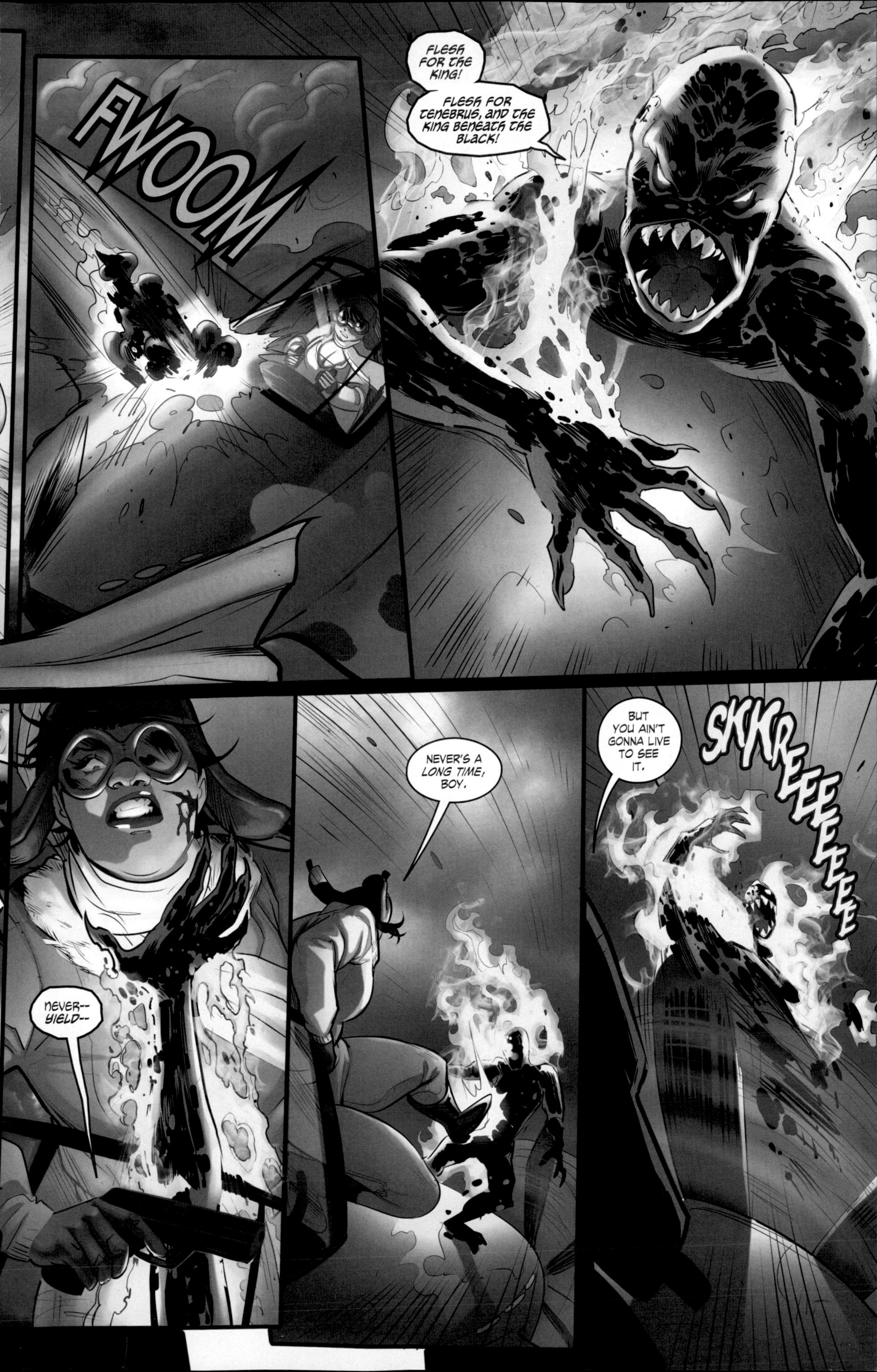
FWOOM
FLESH FOR THE KING!
FLESH FOR TENEBRUS, AND THE KING BENEATH THE BLACK!
NEVER--
YIELD--
NEVER'S A LONG TIME, BOY.
BUT YOU AIN'T GONNA LIVE TO SEE IT.
SKKREEEEEEEE

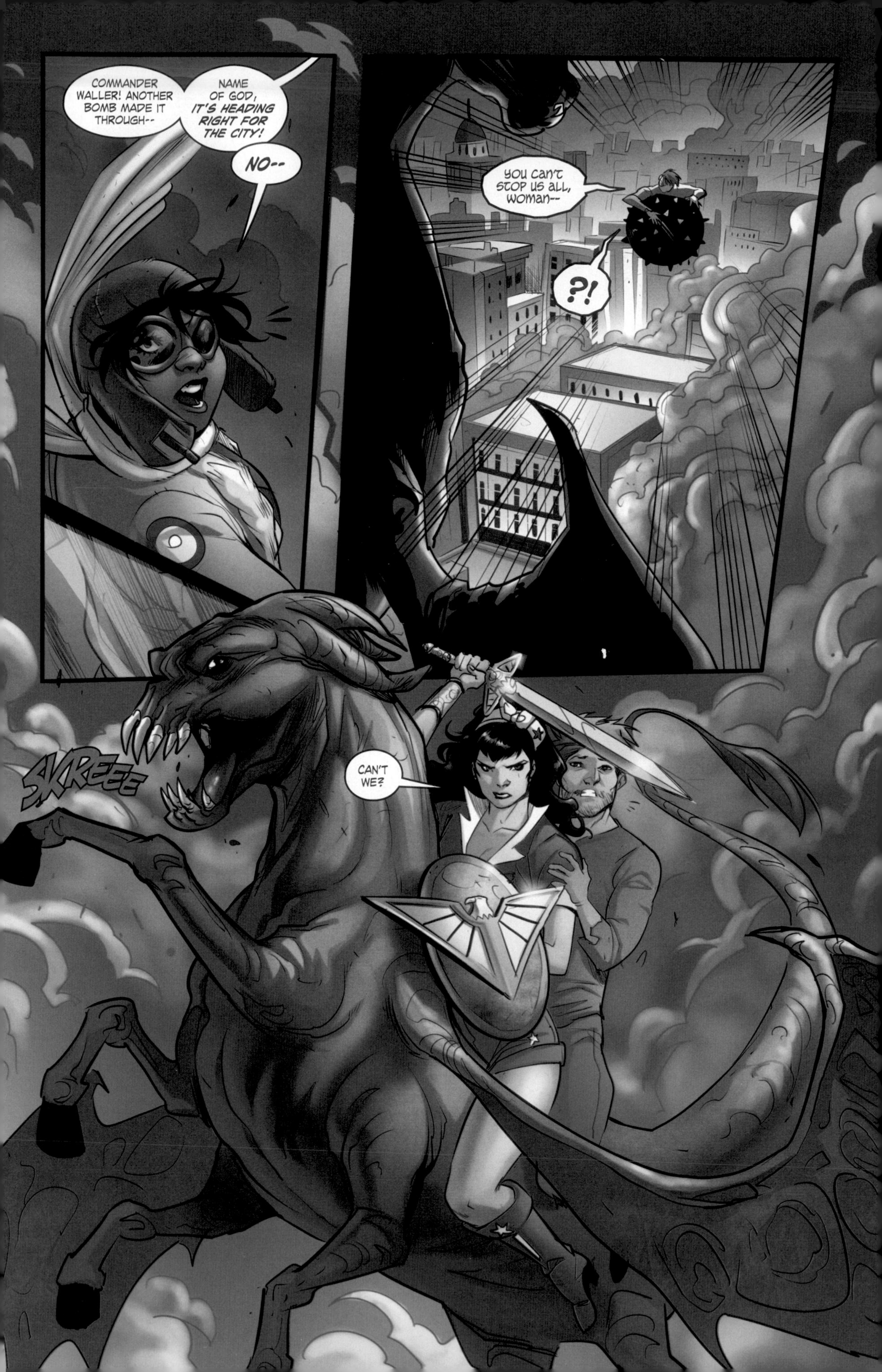
COMMANDER WALLER! ANOTHER BOMB MADE IT THROUGH--
NAME OF GOD, *IT'S HEADING RIGHT FOR THE CITY!*
NO--
YOU CAN'T STOP US ALL, WOMAN--
?!
SKREEE
CAN'T WE?

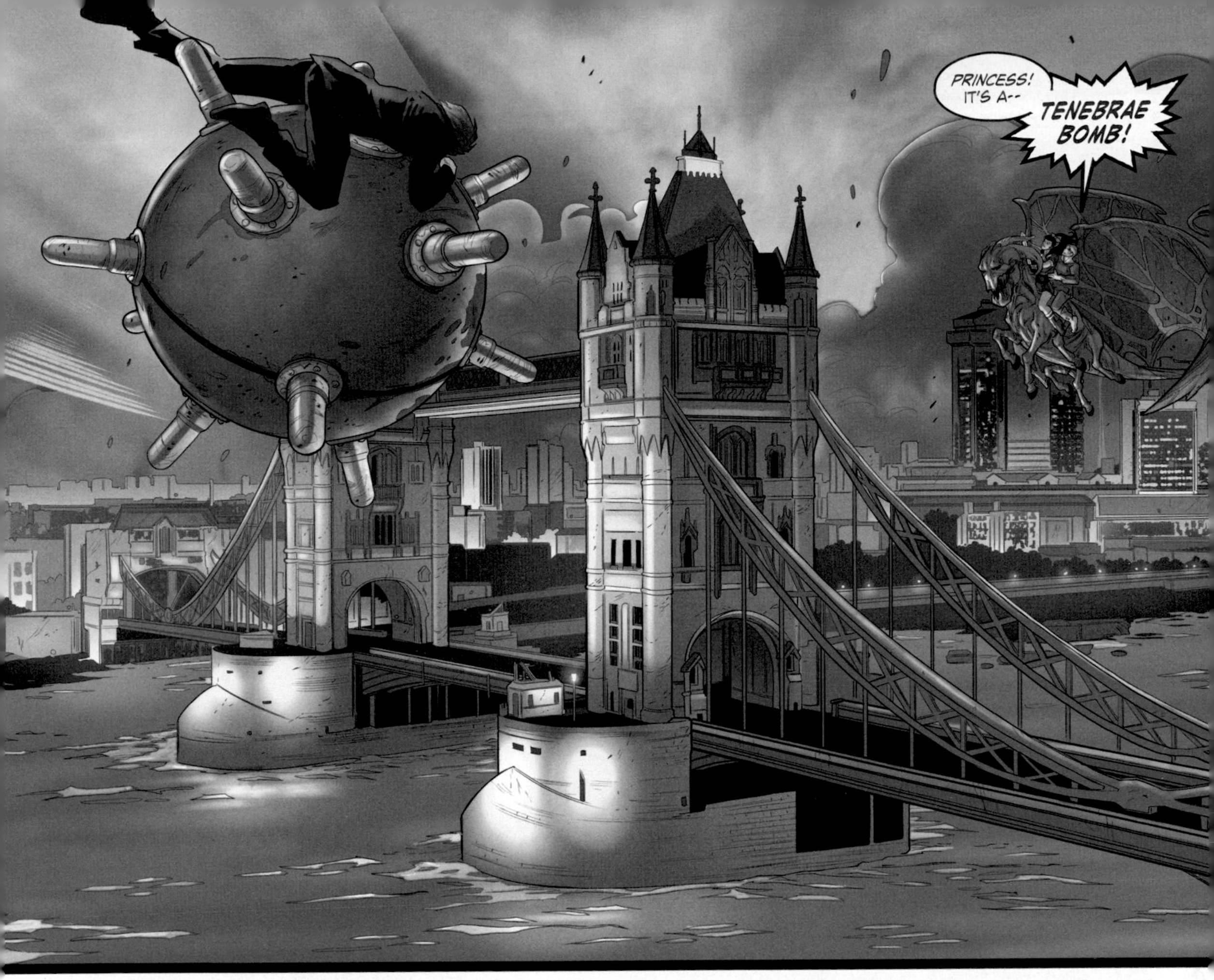
PRINCESS! IT'S A--
TENEBRAE BOMB!

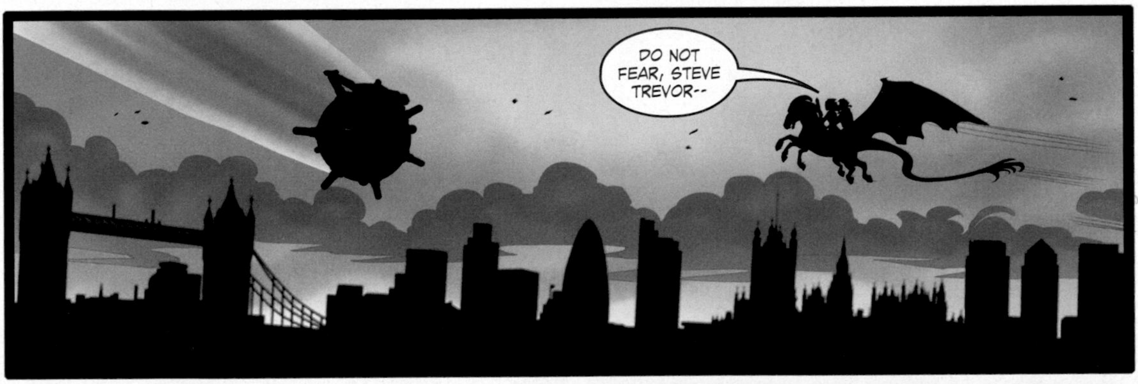
DO NOT FEAR, STEVE TREVOR--

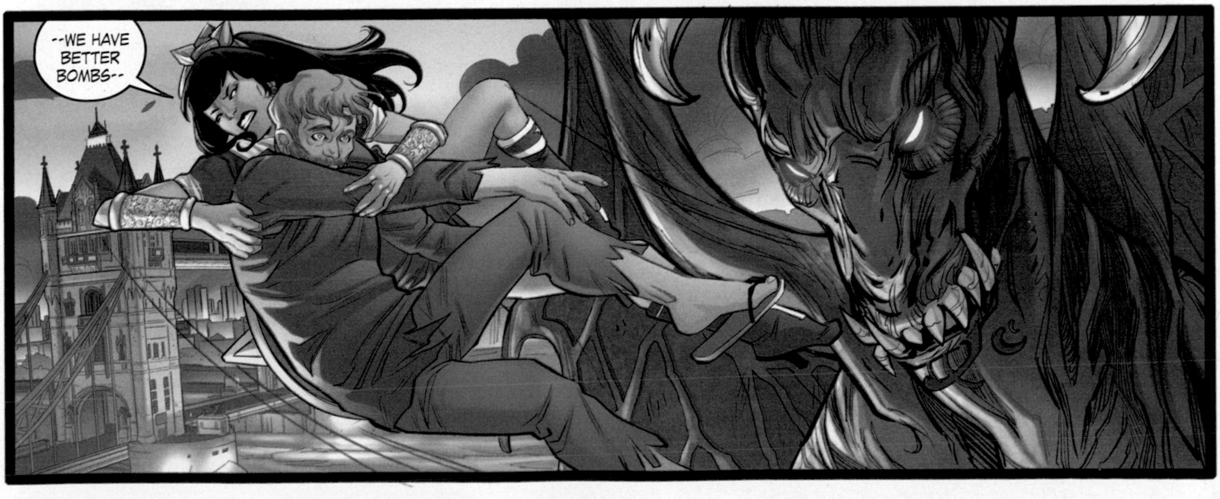
--WE HAVE BETTER BOMBS--

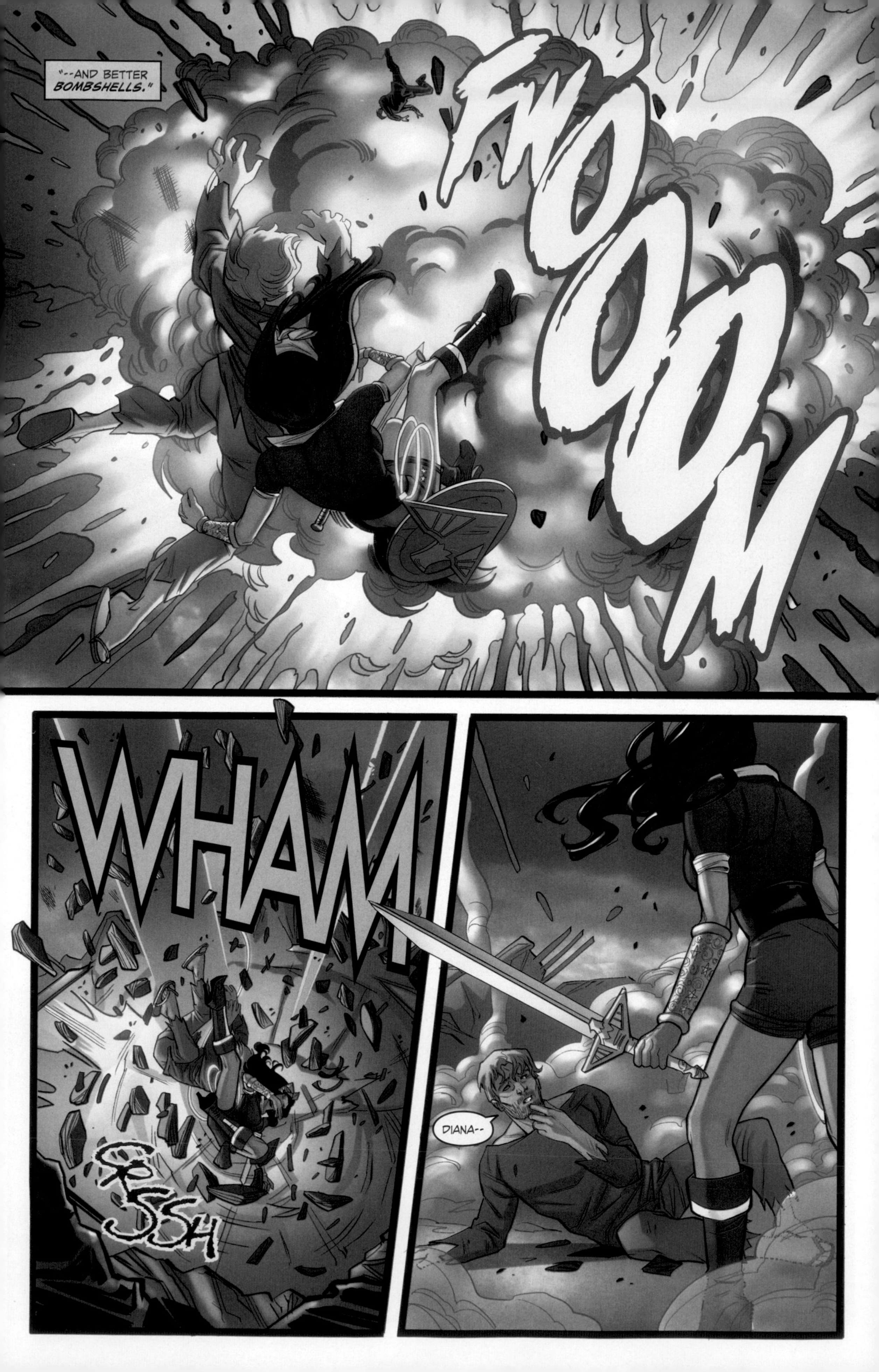
"--AND BETTER BOMBSHELLS."
FWOOOM
WHAM
CRSSH
DIANA--

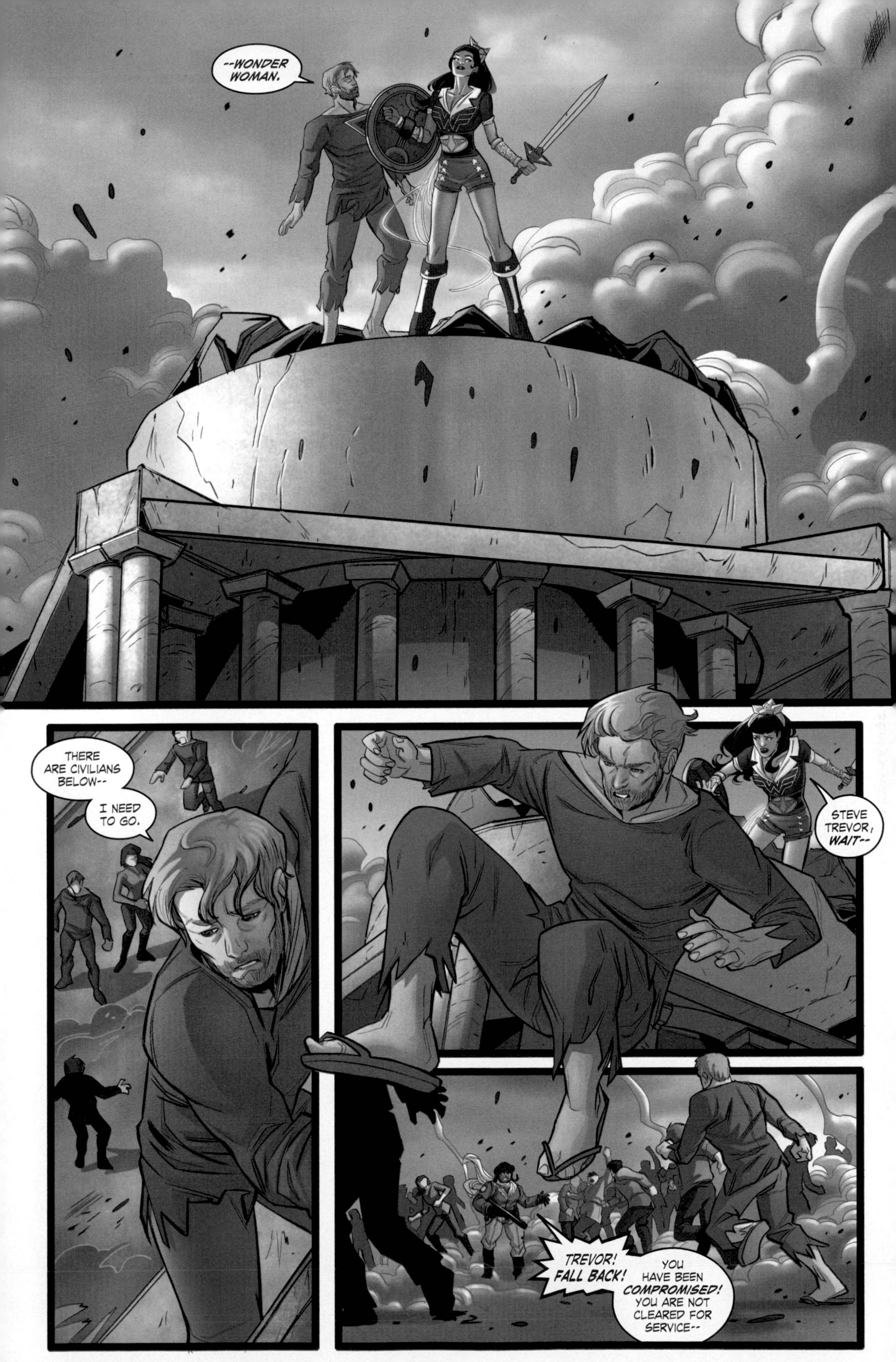
--WONDER WOMAN.
THERE ARE CIVILIANS BELOW--
I NEED TO GO.
STEVE TREVOR, WAIT--
TREVOR! FALL BACK!
YOU HAVE BEEN COMPROMISED! YOU ARE NOT CLEARED FOR SERVICE--

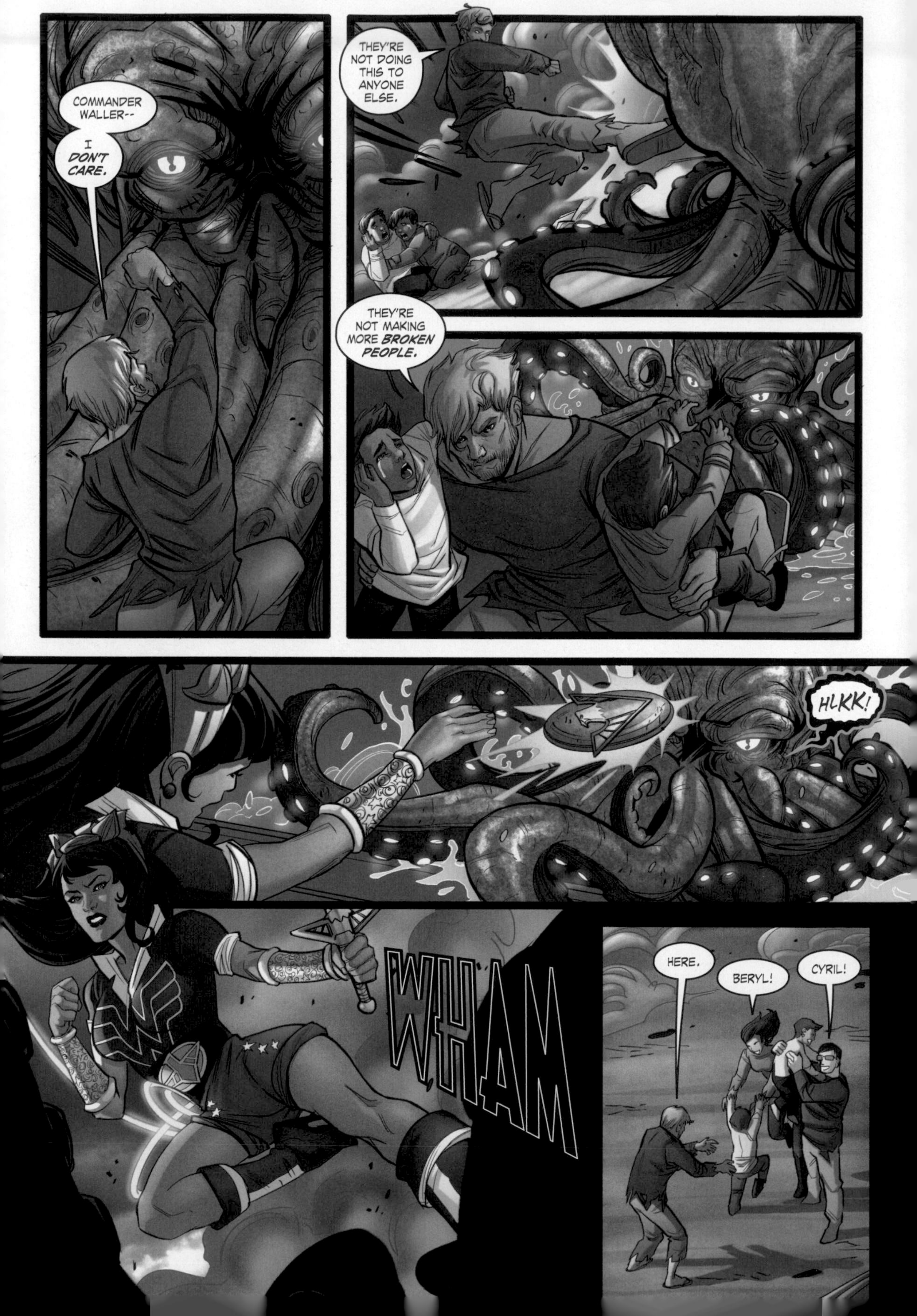

COMMANDER WALLER--
I DON'T CARE.
THEY'RE NOT DOING THIS TO ANYONE ELSE.
THEY'RE NOT MAKING MORE BROKEN PEOPLE.
HLKK!
WHAM
HERE.
BERYL!
CYRIL!

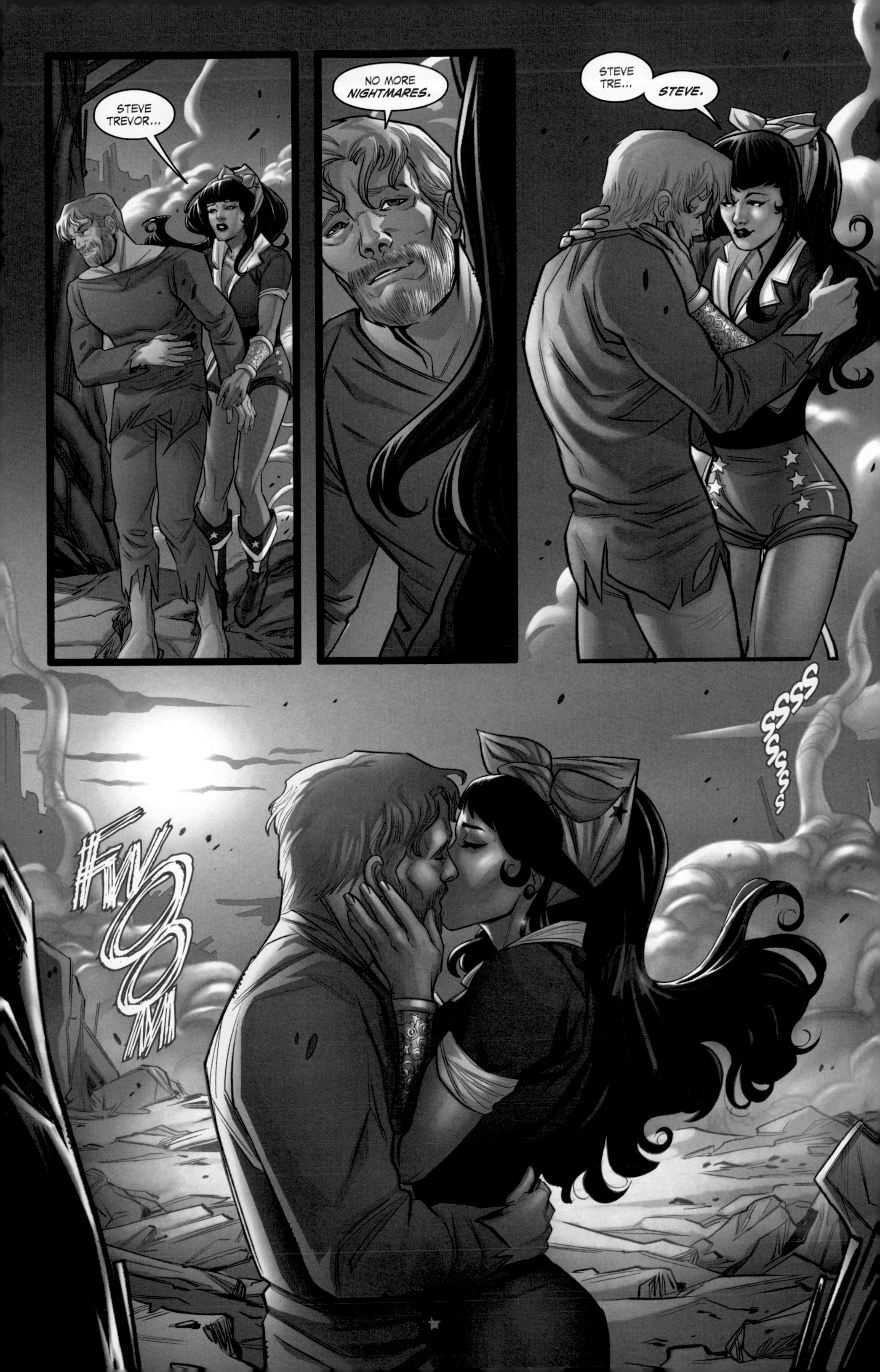
STEVE TREVOR...
NO MORE NIGHTMARES.
STEVE TRE...
STEVE.
SSSS
FWOOM

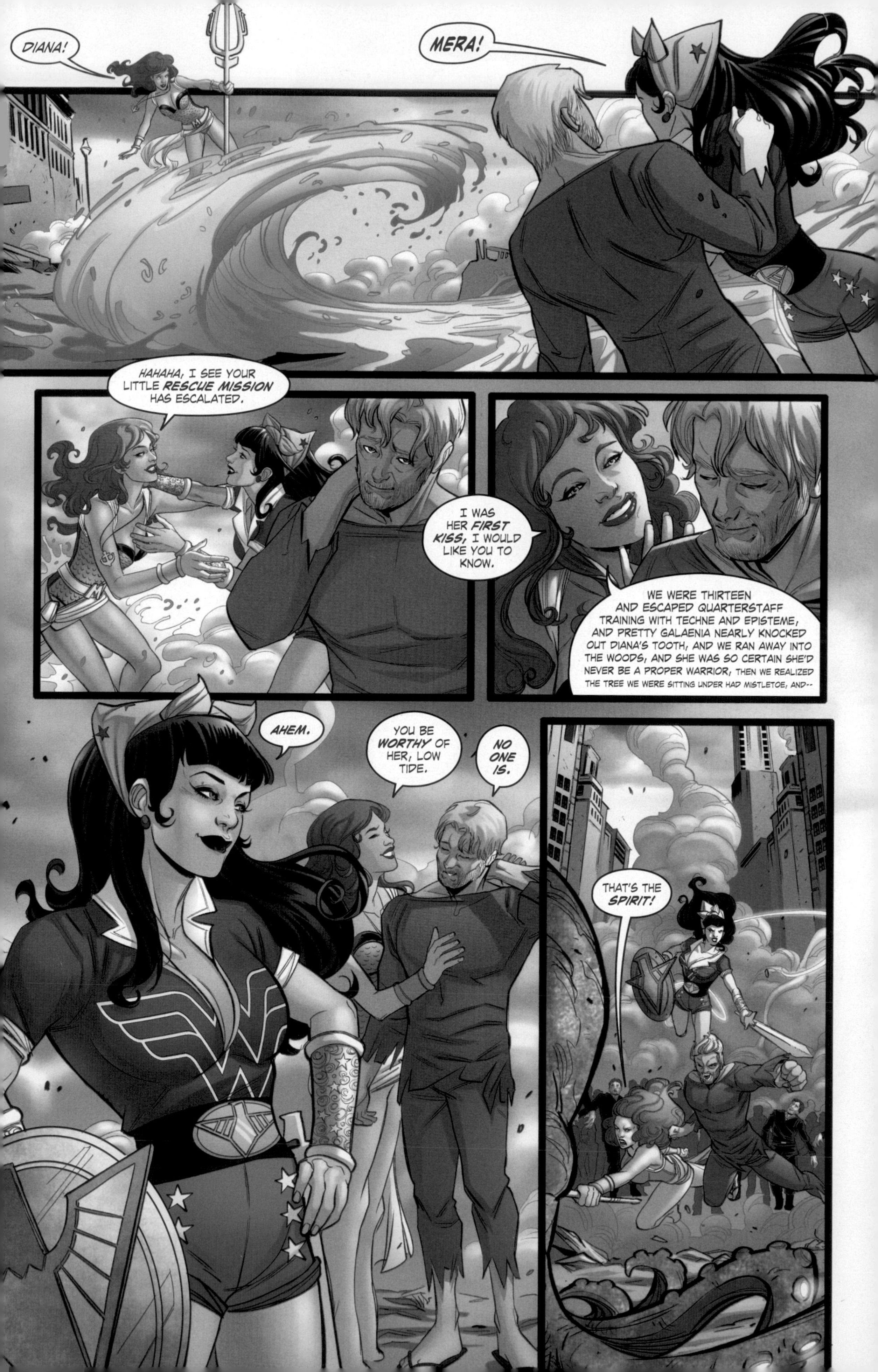
DIANA!
MERA!
HAHAHA, I SEE YOUR LITTLE RESCUE MISSION HAS ESCALATED.
I WAS HER FIRST KISS, I WOULD LIKE YOU TO KNOW.
WE WERE THIRTEEN AND ESCAPED QUARTERSTAFF TRAINING WITH TECHNE AND EPISTEME, AND PRETTY GALAENIA NEARLY KNOCKED OUT DIANA'S TOOTH, AND WE RAN AWAY INTO THE WOODS, AND SHE WAS SO CERTAIN SHE'D NEVER BE A PROPER WARRIOR, THEN WE REALIZED THE TREE WE WERE SITTING UNDER HAD MISTLETOE, AND--
AHEM.
YOU BE WORTHY OF HER, LOW TIDE.
NO ONE IS.
THAT'S THE SPIRIT!

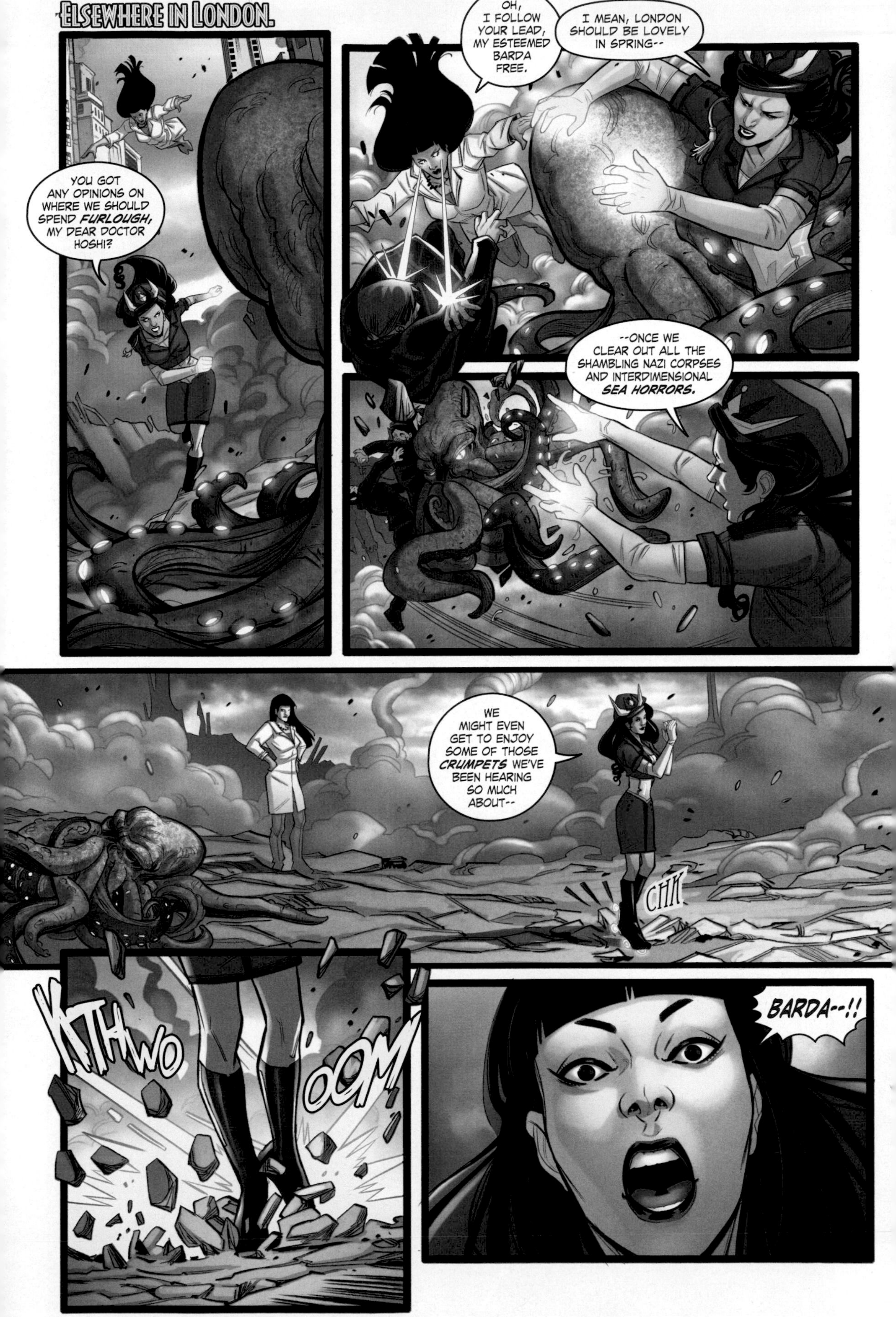
ELSEWHERE IN LONDON.
YOU GOT ANY OPINIONS ON WHERE WE SHOULD SPEND FURLOUGH, MY DEAR DOCTOR HOSHI?
OH, I FOLLOW YOUR LEAD, MY ESTEEMED BARDA FREE.
I MEAN, LONDON SHOULD BE LOVELY IN SPRING--
--ONCE WE CLEAR OUT ALL THE SHAMBLING NAZI CORPSES AND INTERDIMENSIONAL SEA HORRORS.
WE MIGHT EVEN GET TO ENJOY SOME OF THOSE CRUMPETS WE'VE BEEN HEARING SO MUCH ABOUT--
CHK
KTHWOOOM
BARDA--!!

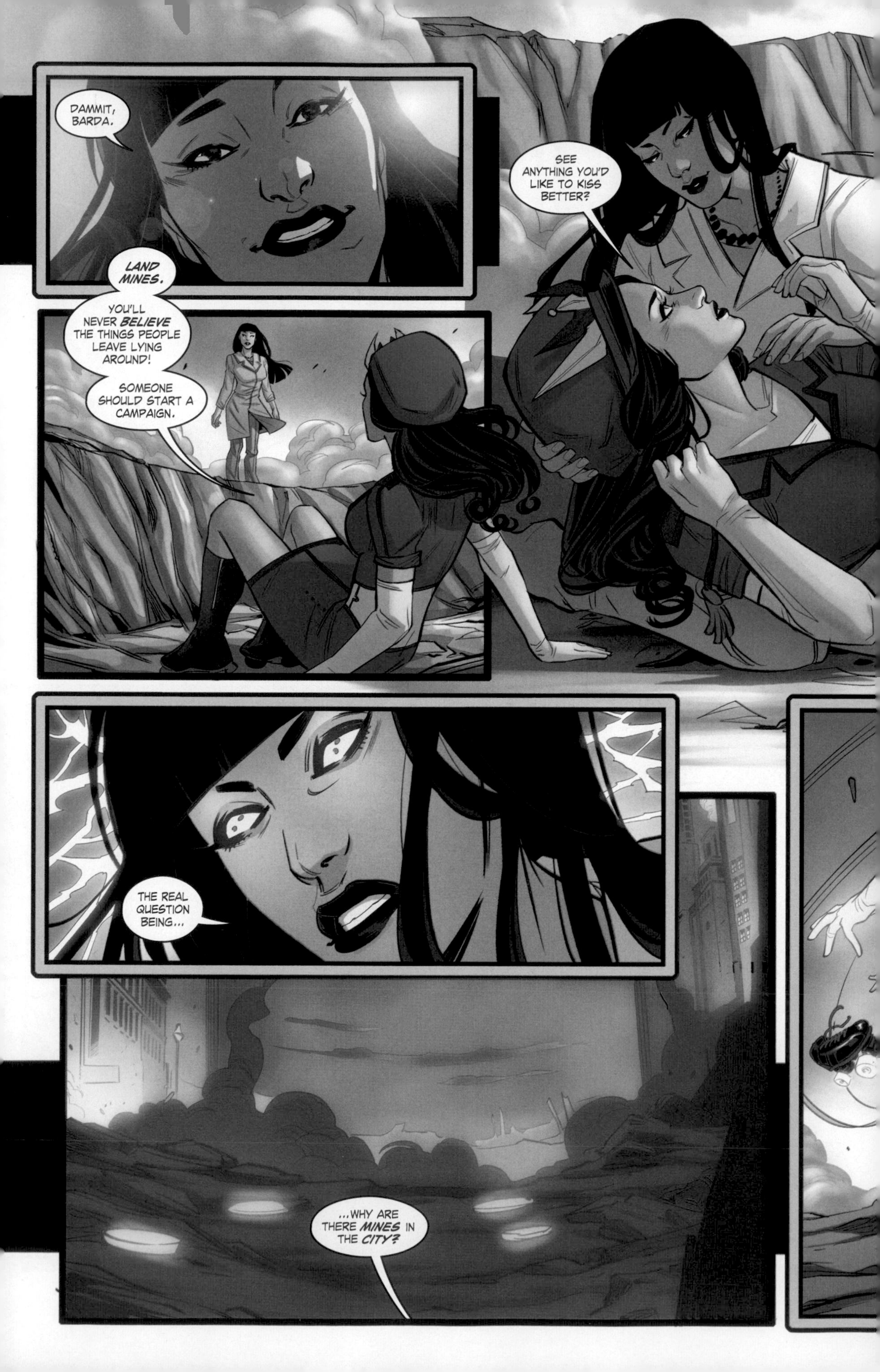
DAMMIT, BARDA.
SEE ANYTHING YOU'D LIKE TO KISS BETTER?
LAND MINES.
YOU'LL NEVER BELIEVE THE THINGS PEOPLE LEAVE LYING AROUND!
SOMEONE SHOULD START A CAMPAIGN.
THE REAL QUESTION BEING...
...WHY ARE THERE MINES IN THE CITY?

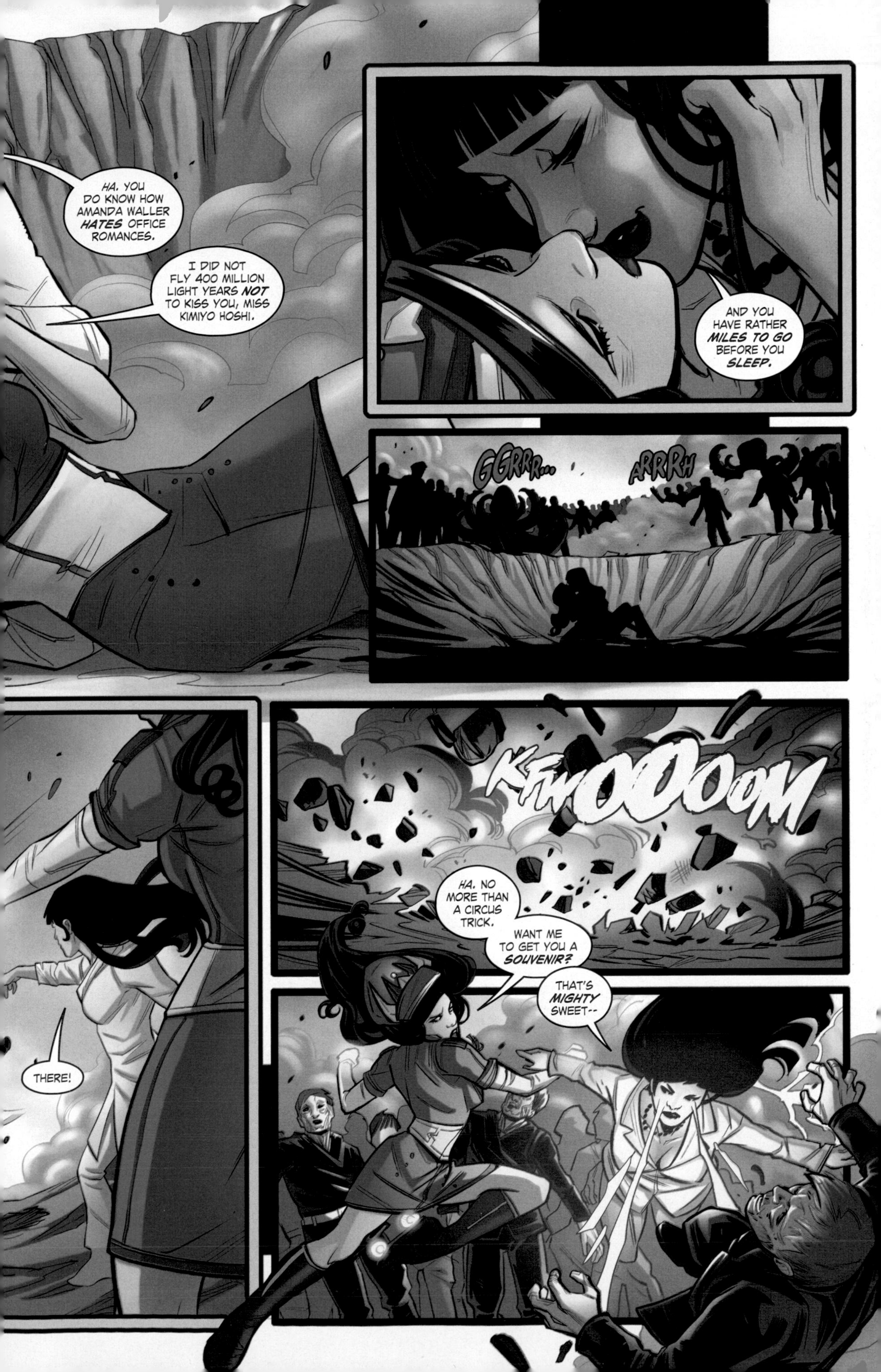

HA. YOU DO KNOW HOW AMANDA WALLER HATES OFFICE ROMANCES.
I DID NOT FLY 400 MILLION LIGHT YEARS NOT TO KISS YOU, MISS KIMIYO HOSHI.
AND YOU HAVE RATHER MILES TO GO BEFORE YOU SLEEP.
GGRRR...
ARRRH
THERE!
KFWOOOOOM
HA. NO MORE THAN A CIRCUS TRICK.
WANT ME TO GET YOU A SOUVENIR?
THAT'S MIGHTY SWEET--

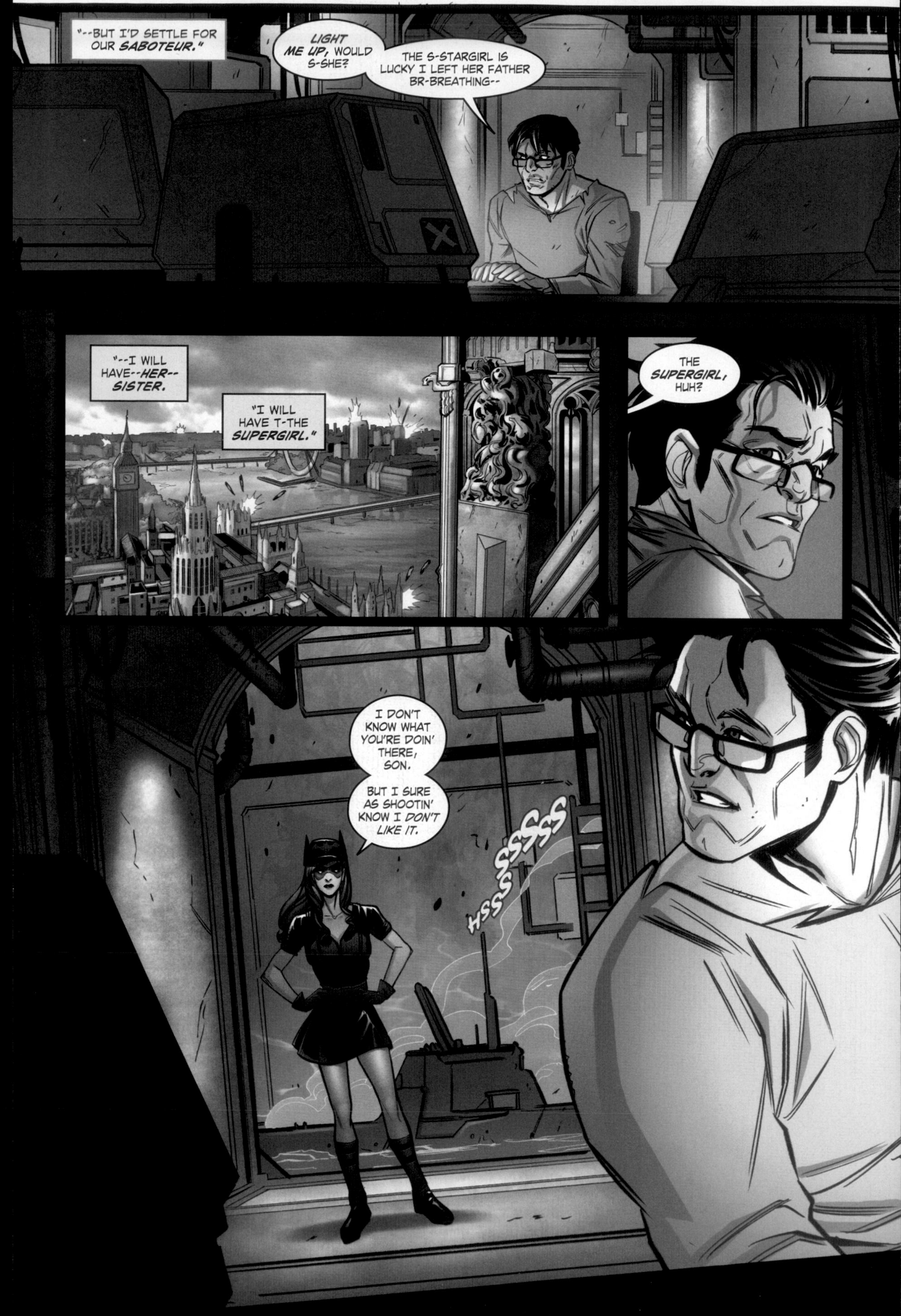
"--BUT I'D SETTLE FOR OUR SABOTEUR."
LIGHT ME UP, WOULD S-SHE?
THE S-STARGIRL IS LUCKY I LEFT HER FATHER BR-BREATHING--
"--I WILL HAVE--HER--SISTER.
"I WILL HAVE T-THE SUPERGIRL."
THE SUPERGIRL, HUH?
I DON'T KNOW WHAT YOU'RE DOIN' THERE, SON.
BUT I SURE AS SHOOTIN' KNOW I DON'T LIKE IT.
HSSSSSSSS

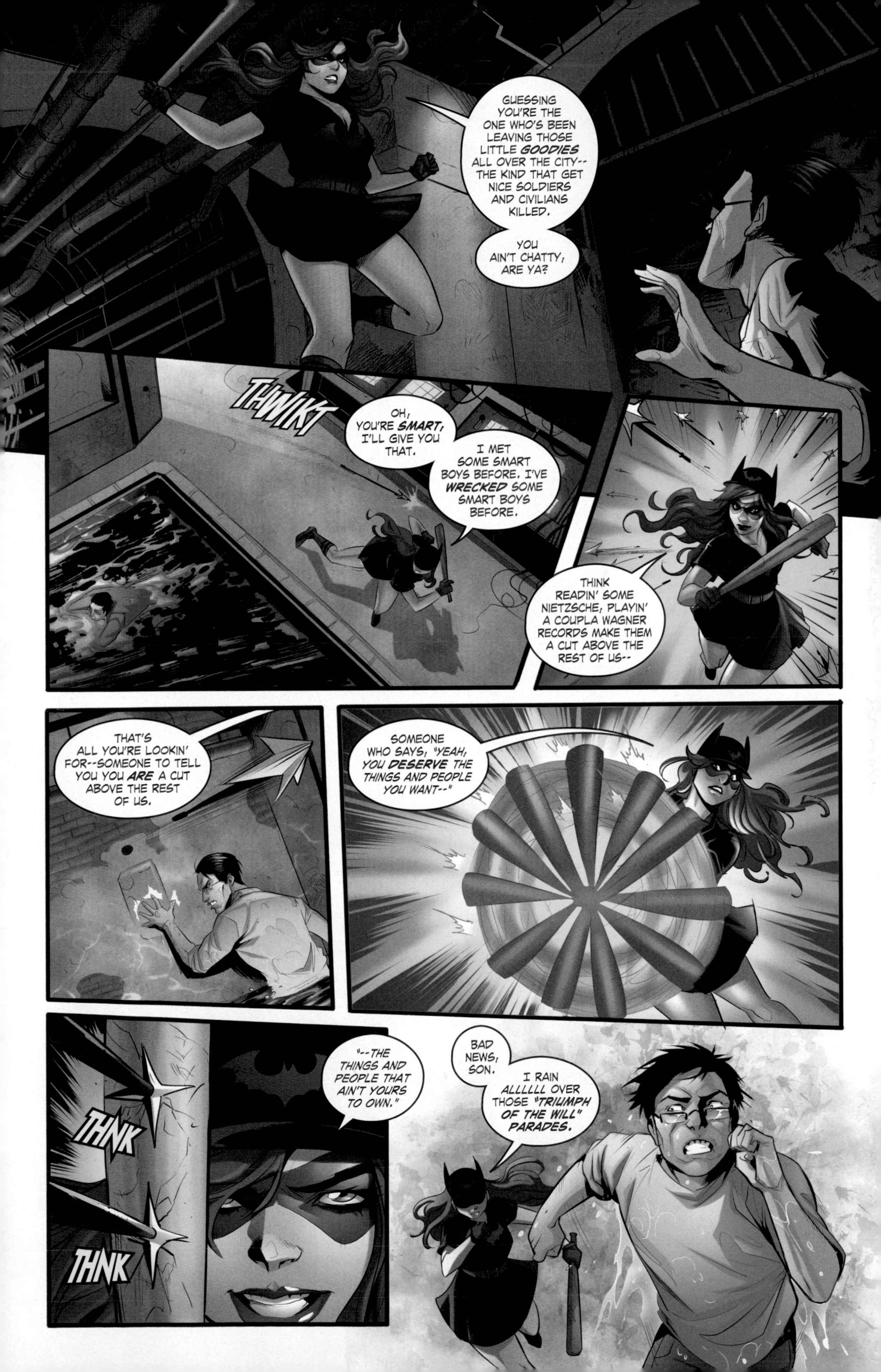
GUESSING YOU'RE THE ONE WHO'S BEEN LEAVING THOSE LITTLE GOODIES ALL OVER THE CITY-- THE KIND THAT GET NICE SOLDIERS AND CIVILIANS KILLED.
YOU AIN'T CHATTY, ARE YA?
THWIKT
OH, YOU'RE SMART, I'LL GIVE YOU THAT.
I MET SOME SMART BOYS BEFORE. I'VE WRECKED SOME SMART BOYS BEFORE.
THINK READIN' SOME NIETZSCHE, PLAYIN' A COUPLA WAGNER RECORDS MAKE THEM A CUT ABOVE THE REST OF US--
THAT'S ALL YOU'RE LOOKIN' FOR--SOMEONE TO TELL YOU YOU ARE A CUT ABOVE THE REST OF US.
SOMEONE WHO SAYS, "YEAH, YOU DESERVE THE THINGS AND PEOPLE YOU WANT--"
"--THE THINGS AND PEOPLE THAT AIN'T YOURS TO OWN."
THNK
THNK
BAD NEWS, SON.
I RAIN ALLLLLL OVER THOSE "TRIUMPH OF THE WILL" PARADES.

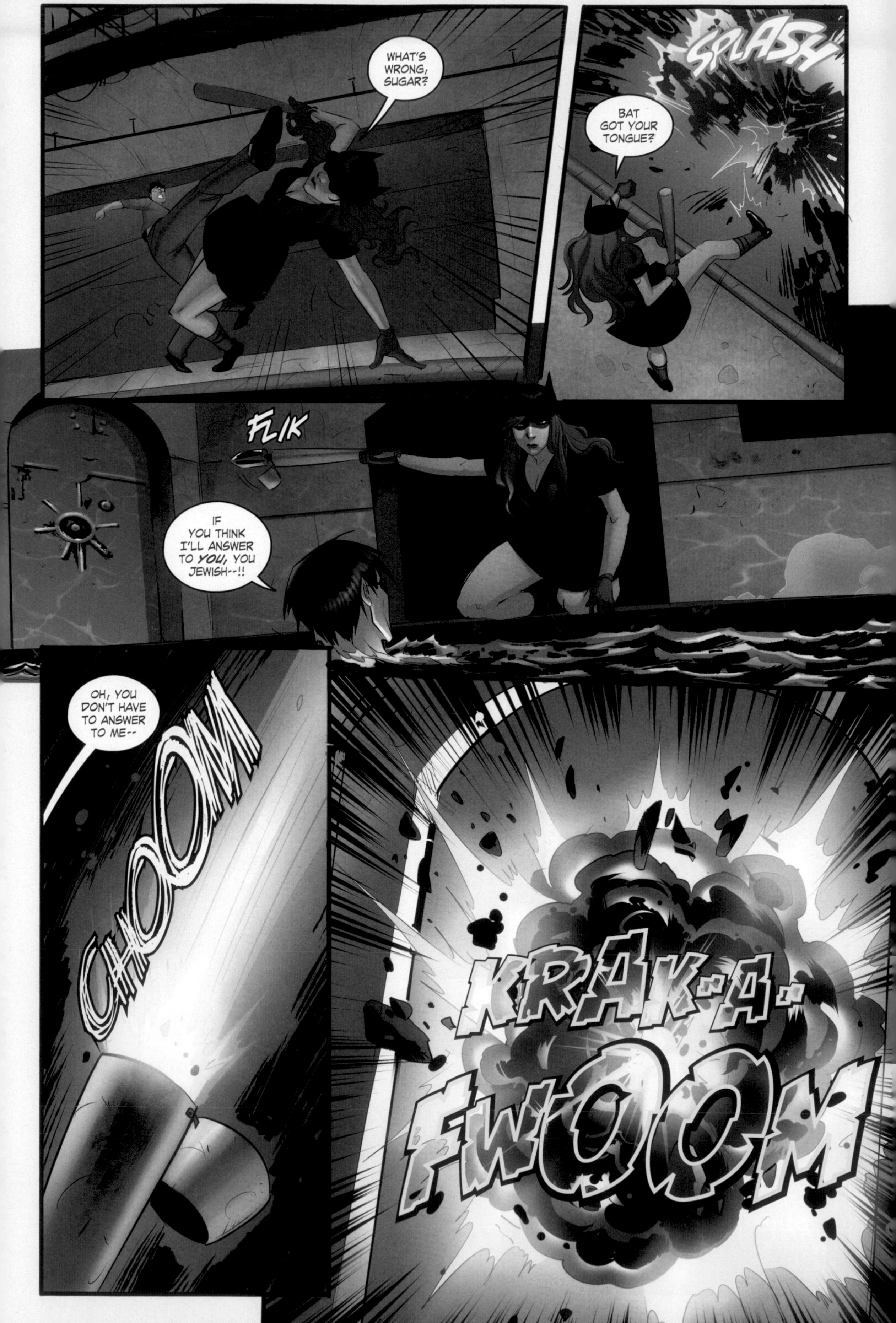
WHAT'S WRONG, SUGAR?
SPLASH
BAT GOT YOUR TONGUE?
FLIK
IF YOU THINK I'LL ANSWER TO *YOU*, YOU JEWISH--!!
OH, YOU DON'T HAVE TO ANSWER TO ME--
CHOOOM
KRAK-A-FWOOOM

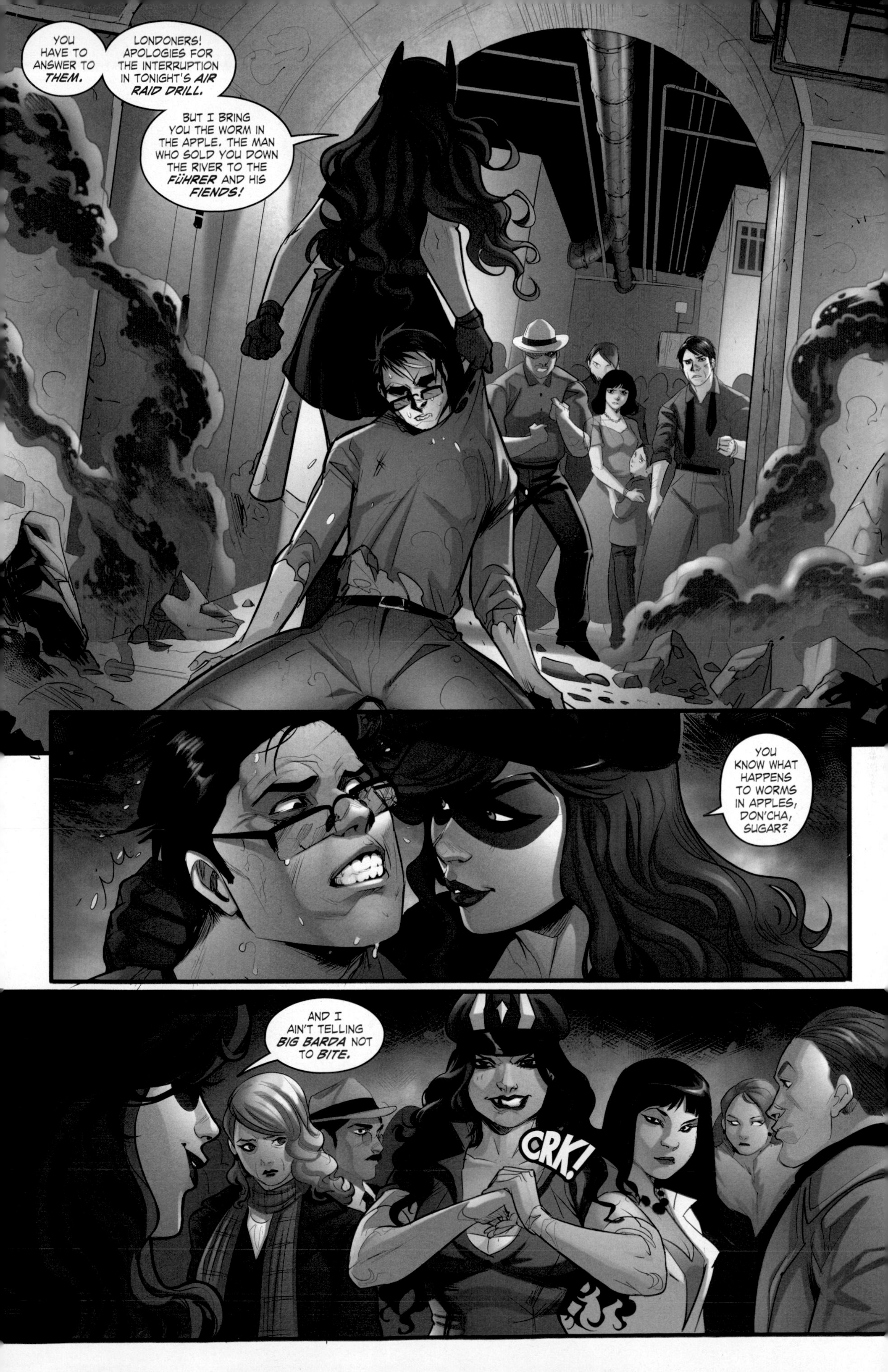
YOU HAVE TO ANSWER TO *THEM.*
LONDONERS! APOLOGIES FOR THE INTERRUPTION IN TONIGHT'S *AIR RAID DRILL.*
BUT I BRING YOU THE WORM IN THE APPLE. THE MAN WHO SOLD YOU DOWN THE RIVER TO THE *FÜHRER* AND HIS *FIENDS!*
YOU KNOW WHAT HAPPENS TO WORMS IN APPLES, DON'CHA, SUGAR?
AND I AIN'T TELLING *BIG BARDA* NOT TO *BITE.*
CRK!

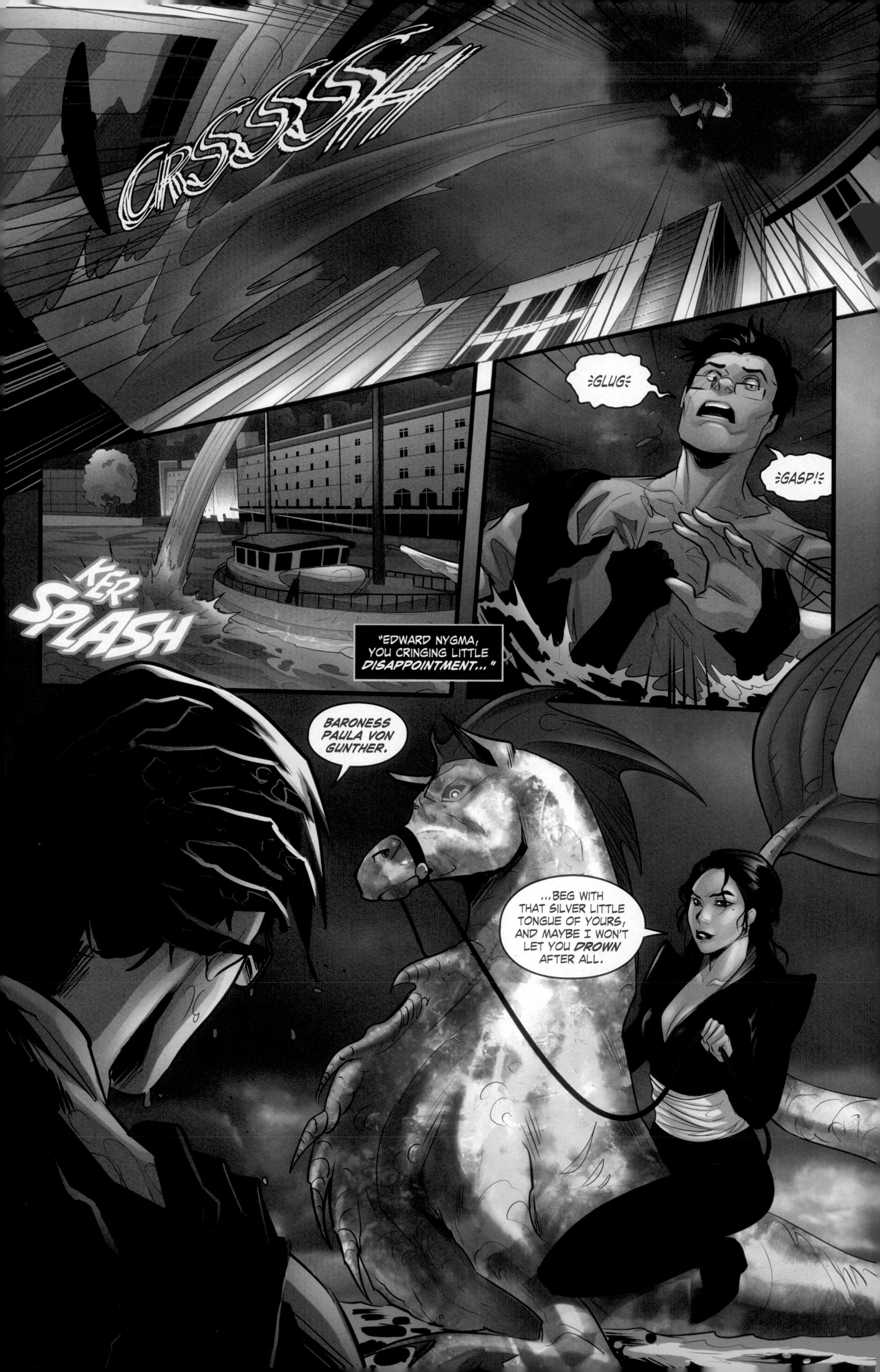

CRSSSSH
KER-SPLASH
GLUG
GASP!
"EDWARD NYGMA, YOU CRINGING LITTLE DISAPPOINTMENT..."
BARONESS PAULA VON GUNTHER.
...BEG WITH THAT SILVER LITTLE TONGUE OF YOURS, AND MAYBE I WON'T LET YOU DROWN AFTER ALL.

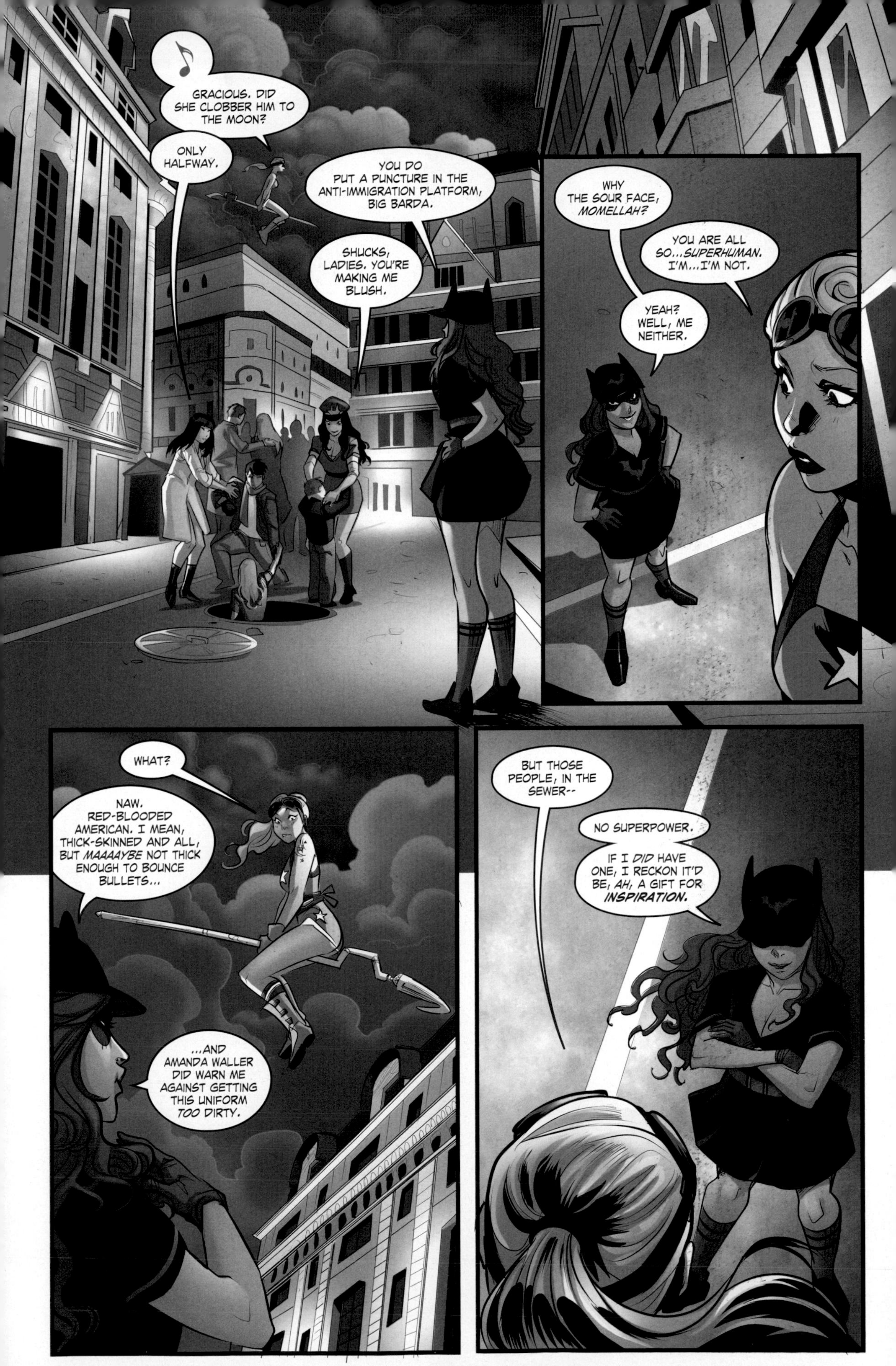
♪
GRACIOUS. DID SHE CLOBBER HIM TO THE MOON?
ONLY HALFWAY.
YOU DO PUT A PUNCTURE IN THE ANTI-IMMIGRATION PLATFORM, BIG BARDA.
SHUCKS, LADIES. YOU'RE MAKING ME BLUSH.
WHY THE SOUR FACE, *MOMELLAH?*
YOU ARE ALL SO...*SUPERHUMAN.* I'M...I'M NOT.
YEAH? WELL, ME NEITHER.
WHAT?
NAW. RED-BLOODED AMERICAN. I MEAN, THICK-SKINNED AND ALL, BUT *MAAAAYBE* NOT THICK ENOUGH TO BOUNCE BULLETS...
...AND AMANDA WALLER DID WARN ME AGAINST GETTING THIS UNIFORM *TOO* DIRTY.
BUT THOSE PEOPLE, IN THE SEWER--
NO SUPERPOWER.
IF I *DID* HAVE ONE, I RECKON IT'D BE, *AH,* A GIFT FOR ***INSPIRATION.***

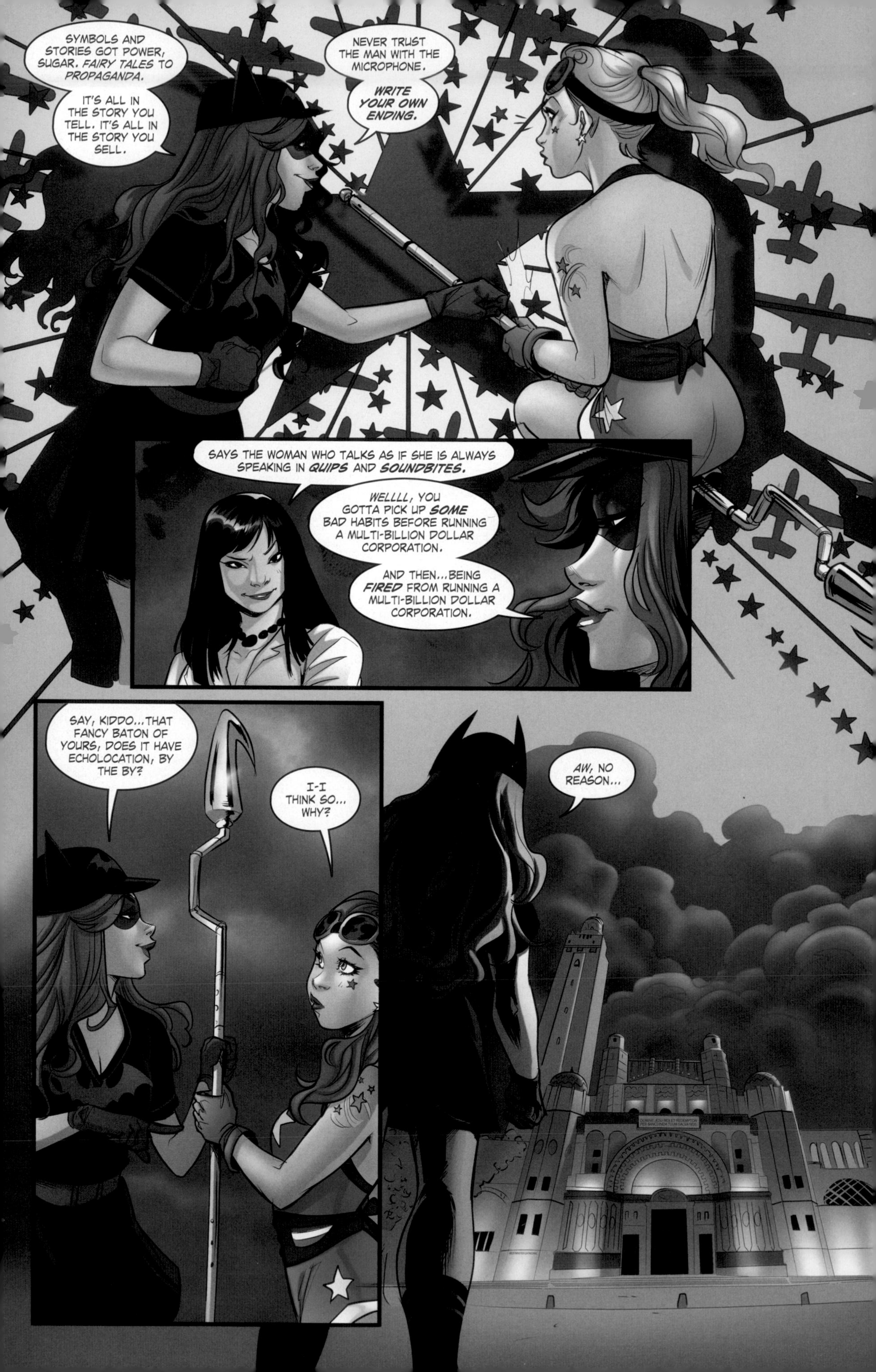
SYMBOLS AND STORIES GOT POWER, SUGAR. *FAIRY TALES* TO *PROPAGANDA*.
IT'S ALL IN THE STORY YOU TELL. IT'S ALL IN THE STORY YOU SELL.
NEVER TRUST THE MAN WITH THE MICROPHONE.
WRITE YOUR OWN ENDING.
SAYS THE WOMAN WHO TALKS AS IF SHE IS ALWAYS SPEAKING IN ***QUIPS*** AND ***SOUNDBITES.***
WELLLL, YOU GOTTA PICK UP ***SOME*** BAD HABITS BEFORE RUNNING A MULTI-BILLION DOLLAR CORPORATION.
AND THEN...BEING ***FIRED*** FROM RUNNING A MULTI-BILLION DOLLAR CORPORATION.
SAY, KIDDO...THAT FANCY BATON OF YOURS, DOES IT HAVE ECHOLOCATION, BY THE BY?
I-I THINK SO... WHY?
AW, NO REASON...

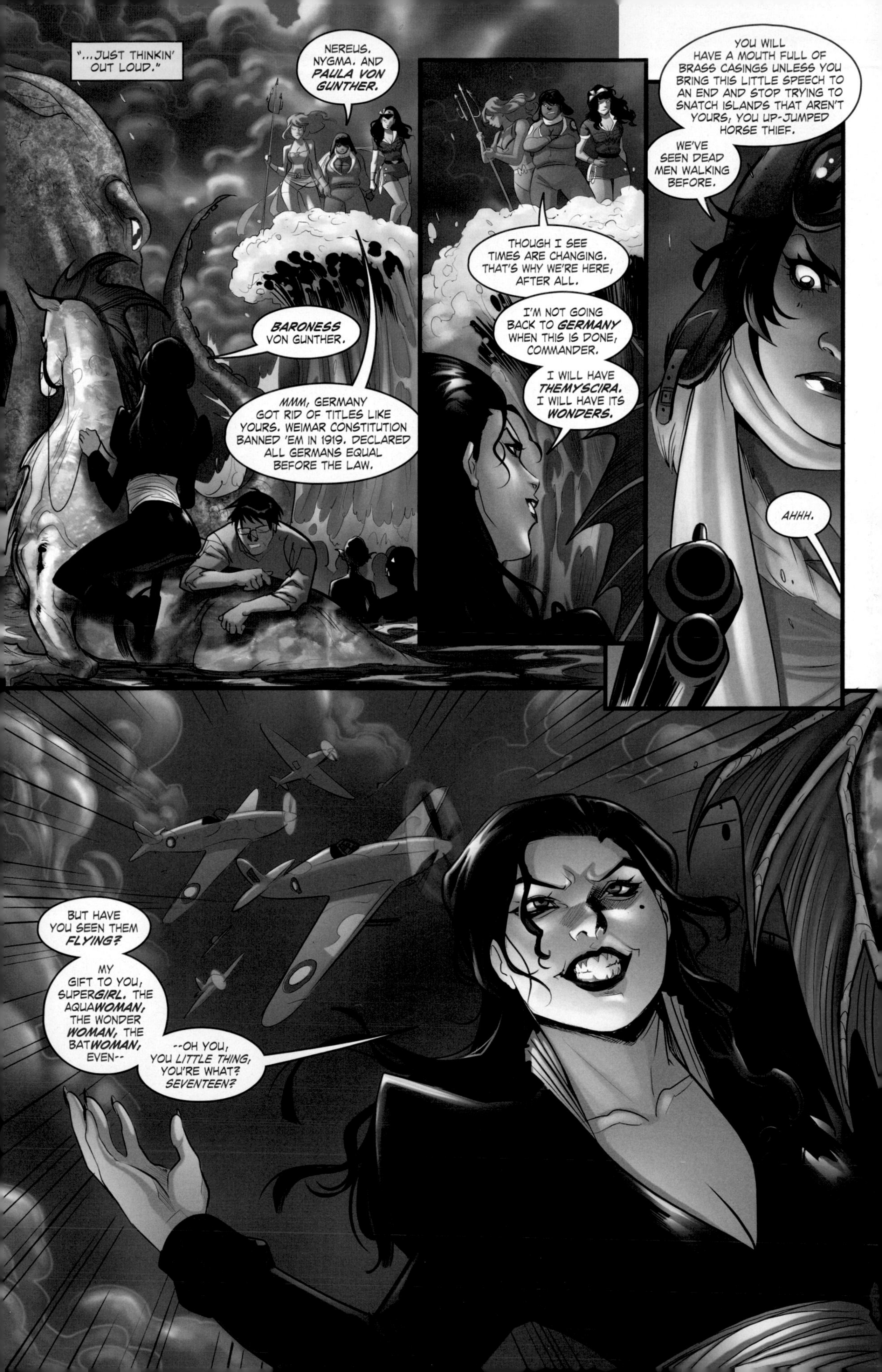
"...JUST THINKIN' OUT LOUD."
NEREUS. NYGMA. AND *PAULA VON GUNTHER.*
THOUGH I SEE TIMES ARE CHANGING. THAT'S WHY WE'RE HERE, AFTER ALL.
YOU WILL HAVE A MOUTH FULL OF BRASS CASINGS UNLESS YOU BRING THIS LITTLE SPEECH TO AN END AND STOP TRYING TO SNATCH ISLANDS THAT AREN'T YOURS, YOU UP-JUMPED HORSE THIEF.
WE'VE SEEN DEAD MEN WALKING BEFORE.
BARONESS VON GUNTHER.
MMM, GERMANY GOT RID OF TITLES LIKE YOURS. WEIMAR CONSTITUTION BANNED 'EM IN 1919. DECLARED ALL GERMANS EQUAL BEFORE THE LAW.
I'M NOT GOING BACK TO *GERMANY* WHEN THIS IS DONE, COMMANDER.
I WILL HAVE *THEMYSCIRA.* I WILL HAVE ITS *WONDERS.*
AHHH.
BUT HAVE YOU SEEN THEM *FLYING?*
MY GIFT TO YOU, SUPER*GIRL.* THE AQUA*WOMAN,* THE WONDER *WOMAN,* THE BAT*WOMAN,* EVEN--
--OH YOU, YOU *LITTLE THING,* YOU'RE WHAT? *SEVENTEEN?*

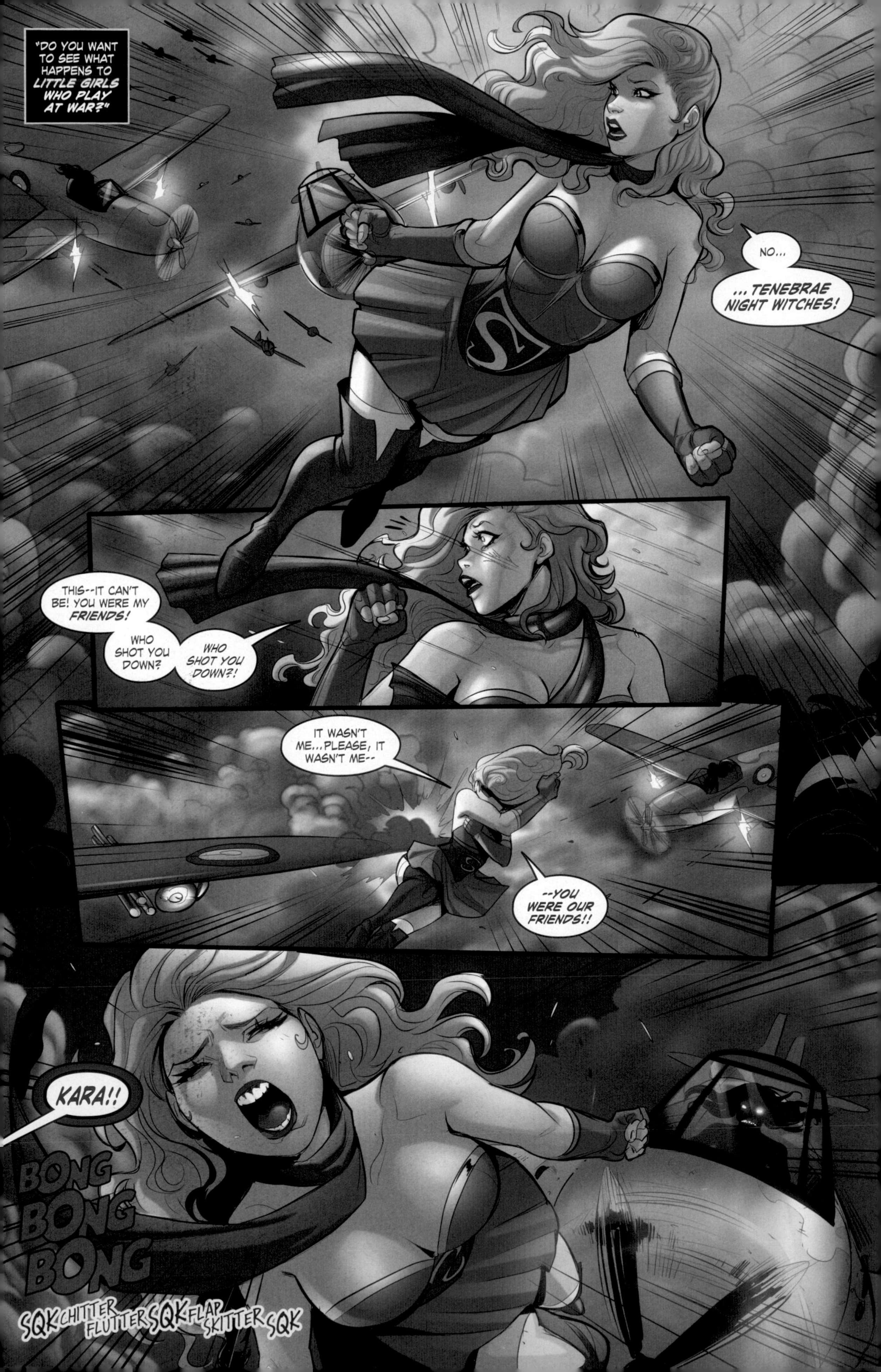
"DO YOU WANT TO SEE WHAT HAPPENS TO LITTLE GIRLS WHO PLAY AT WAR?"
NO...
...TENEBRAE NIGHT WITCHES!
THIS--IT CAN'T BE! YOU WERE MY FRIENDS!
WHO SHOT YOU DOWN?
WHO SHOT YOU DOWN?!
IT WASN'T ME...PLEASE, IT WASN'T ME--
--YOU WERE OUR FRIENDS!!
KARA!!
BONG BONG BONG
SQK CHITTER FLUTTER SQK FLAP SKITTER SQK

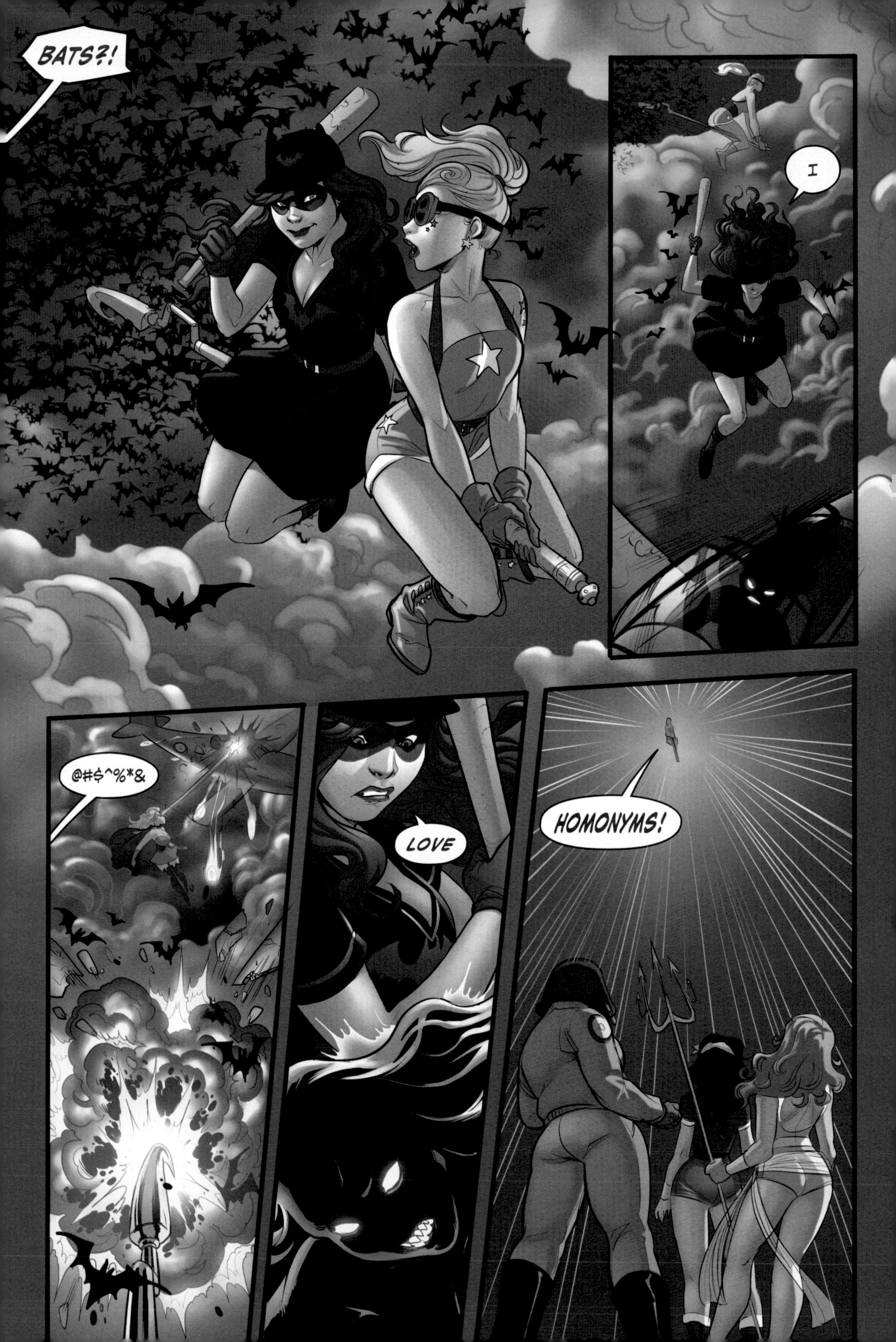
BATS?!
I
@#$^%*&
LOVE
HOMONYMS!

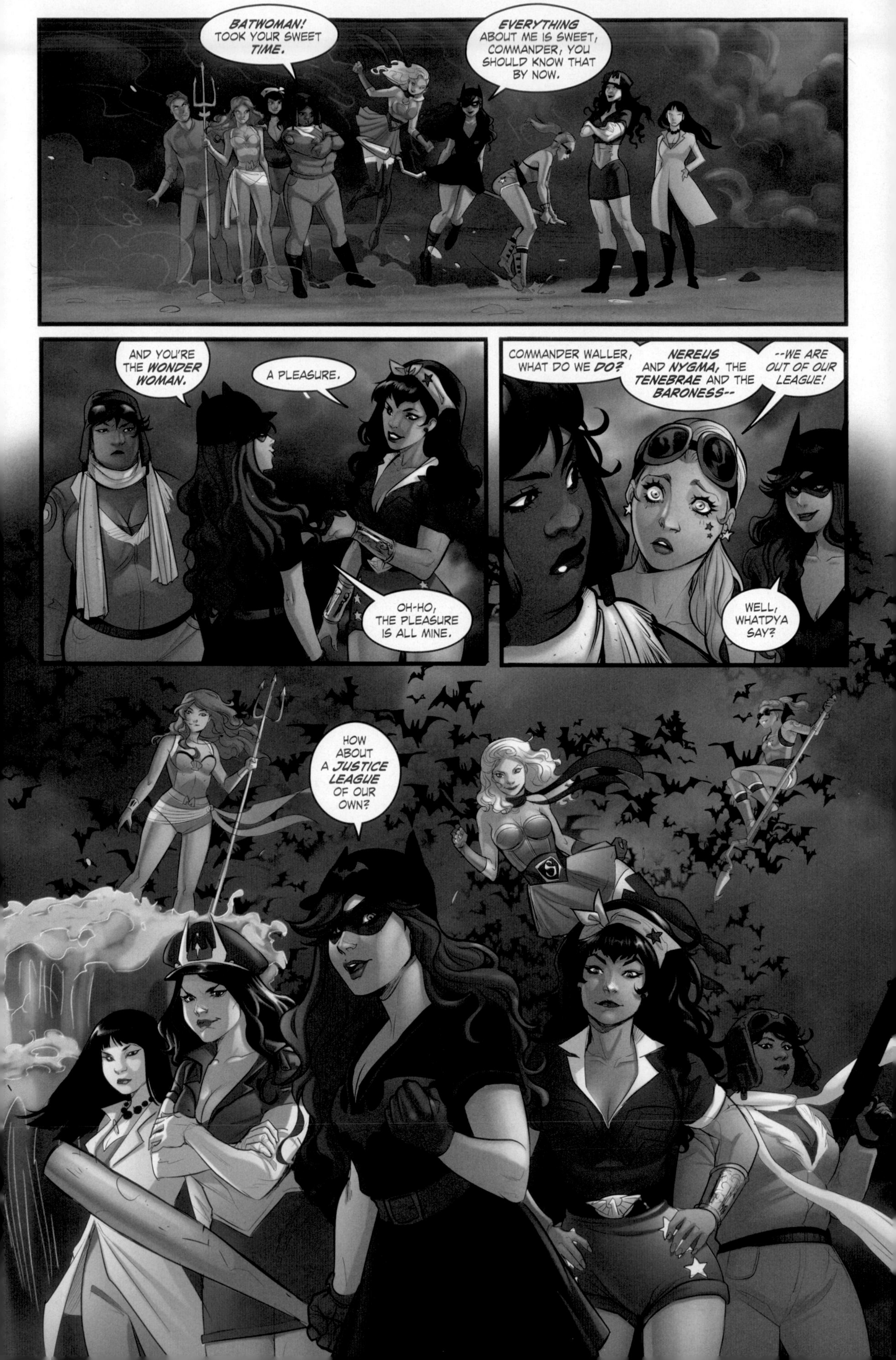
BATWOMAN! TOOK YOUR SWEET TIME.
EVERYTHING ABOUT ME IS SWEET, COMMANDER, YOU SHOULD KNOW THAT BY NOW.
AND YOU'RE THE WONDER WOMAN.
A PLEASURE.
OH-HO, THE PLEASURE IS ALL MINE.
COMMANDER WALLER, WHAT DO WE DO?
NEREUS AND NYGMA, THE TENEBRAE AND THE BARONESS--
--WE ARE OUT OF OUR LEAGUE!
WELL, WHATDYA SAY?
HOW ABOUT A JUSTICE LEAGUE OF OUR OWN?

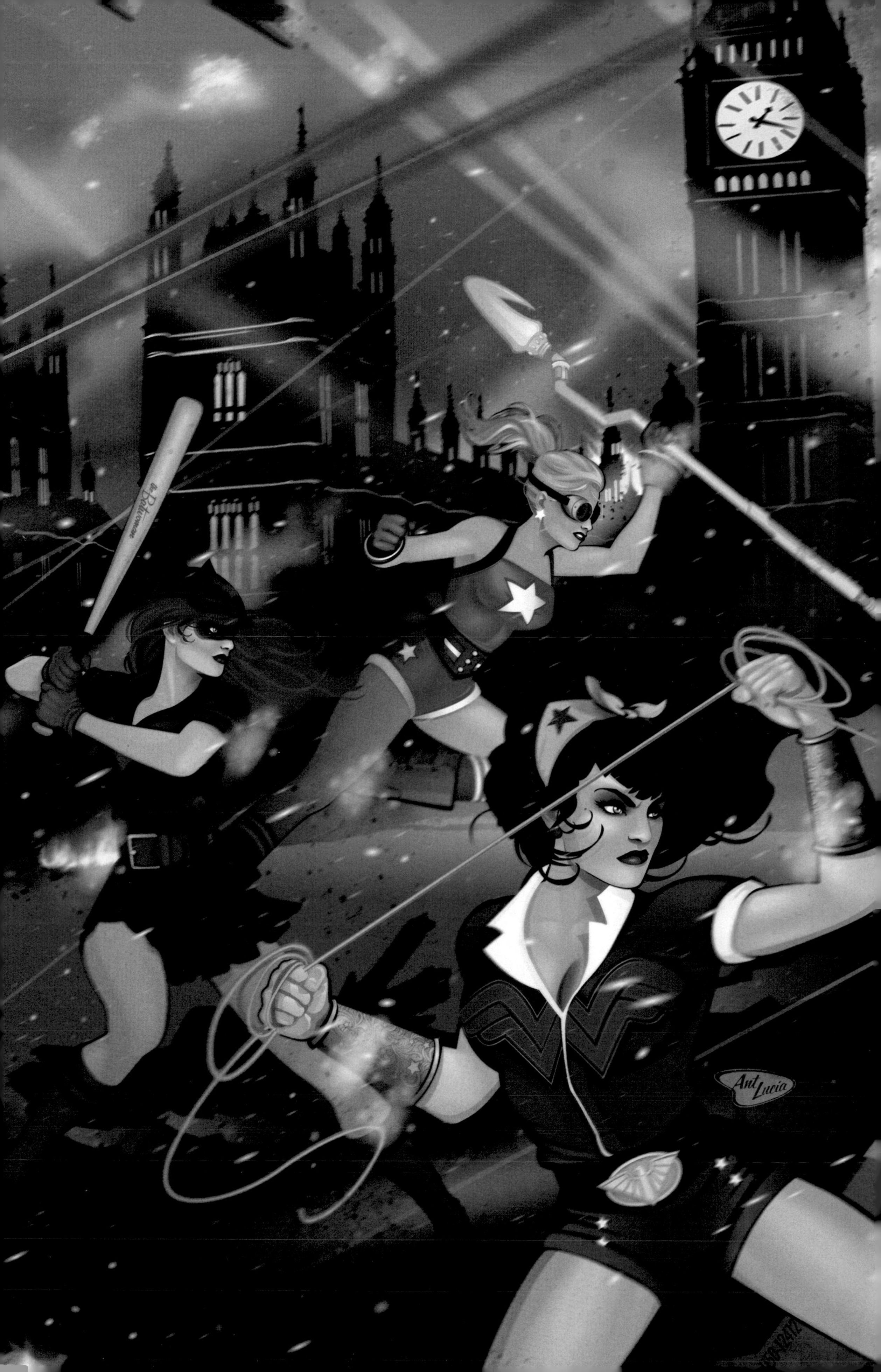
the Batwoman
Ant Lucia

THE BATTLE OF BRITAIN
PART TWO

MARGUERITE BENNETT
Writer

LAURA BRAGA
MIRKA ANDOLFO
Artists

WENDY BROOME
Colorist

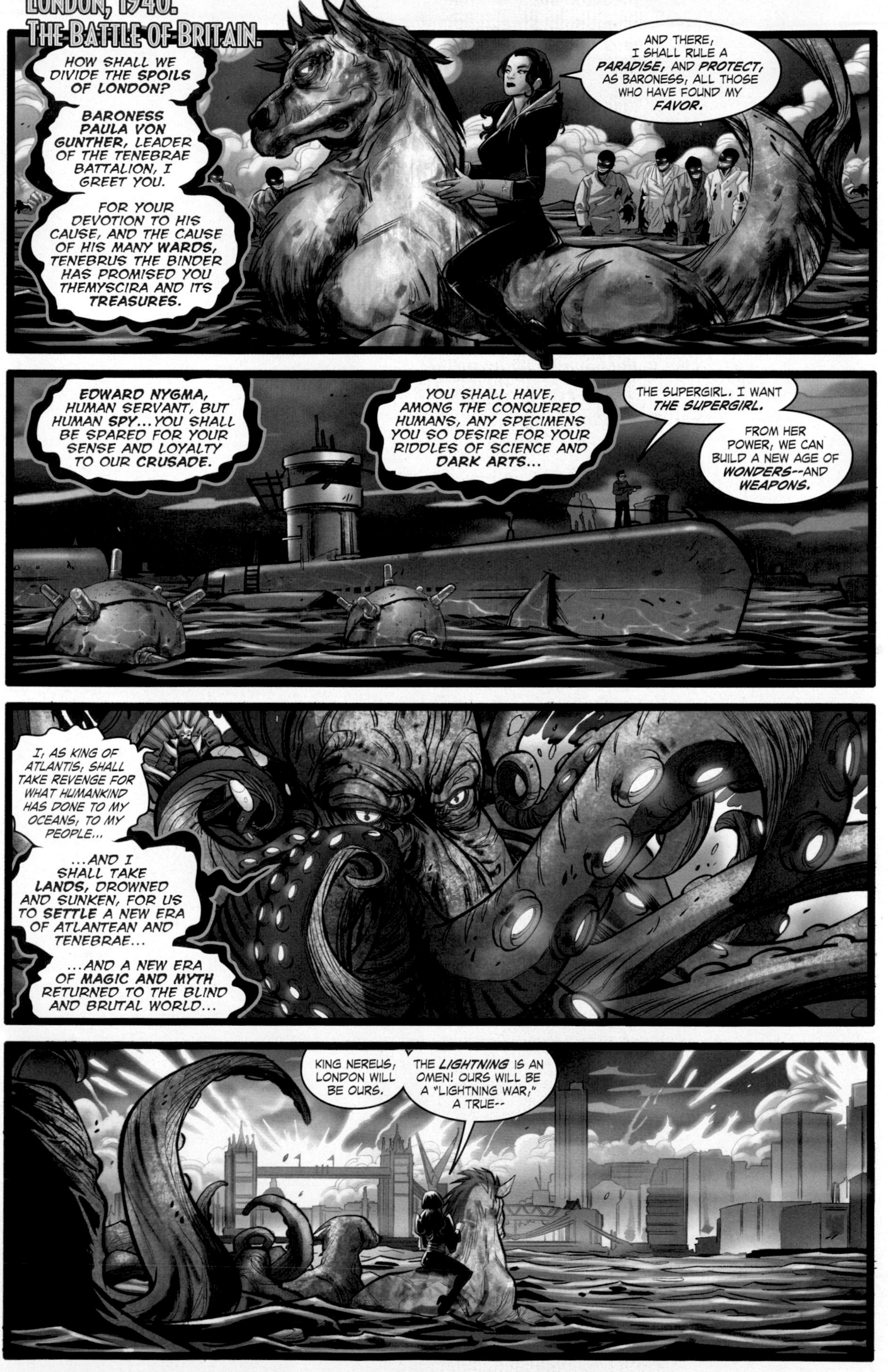

LONDON, 1940.
THE BATTLE OF BRITAIN.
HOW SHALL WE DIVIDE THE SPOILS OF LONDON?
BARONESS PAULA VON GUNTHER, LEADER OF THE TENEBRAE BATTALION, I GREET YOU.
FOR YOUR DEVOTION TO HIS CAUSE, AND THE CAUSE OF HIS MANY WARDS, TENEBRUS THE BINDER HAS PROMISED YOU THEMYSCIRA AND ITS TREASURES.
AND THERE, I SHALL RULE A PARADISE, AND PROTECT, AS BARONESS, ALL THOSE WHO HAVE FOUND MY FAVOR.
EDWARD NYGMA, HUMAN SERVANT, BUT HUMAN SPY...YOU SHALL BE SPARED FOR YOUR SENSE AND LOYALTY TO OUR CRUSADE.
YOU SHALL HAVE, AMONG THE CONQUERED HUMANS, ANY SPECIMENS YOU SO DESIRE FOR YOUR RIDDLES OF SCIENCE AND DARK ARTS...
THE SUPERGIRL. I WANT THE SUPERGIRL.
FROM HER POWER, WE CAN BUILD A NEW AGE OF WONDERS--AND WEAPONS.
I, AS KING OF ATLANTIS, SHALL TAKE REVENGE FOR WHAT HUMANKIND HAS DONE TO MY OCEANS, TO MY PEOPLE...
...AND I SHALL TAKE LANDS, DROWNED AND SUNKEN, FOR US TO SETTLE A NEW ERA OF ATLANTEAN AND TENEBRAE...
...AND A NEW ERA OF MAGIC AND MYTH RETURNED TO THE BLIND AND BRUTAL WORLD...
KING NEREUS, LONDON WILL BE OURS.
THE LIGHTNING IS AN OMEN! OURS WILL BE A "LIGHTNING WAR," A TRUE--

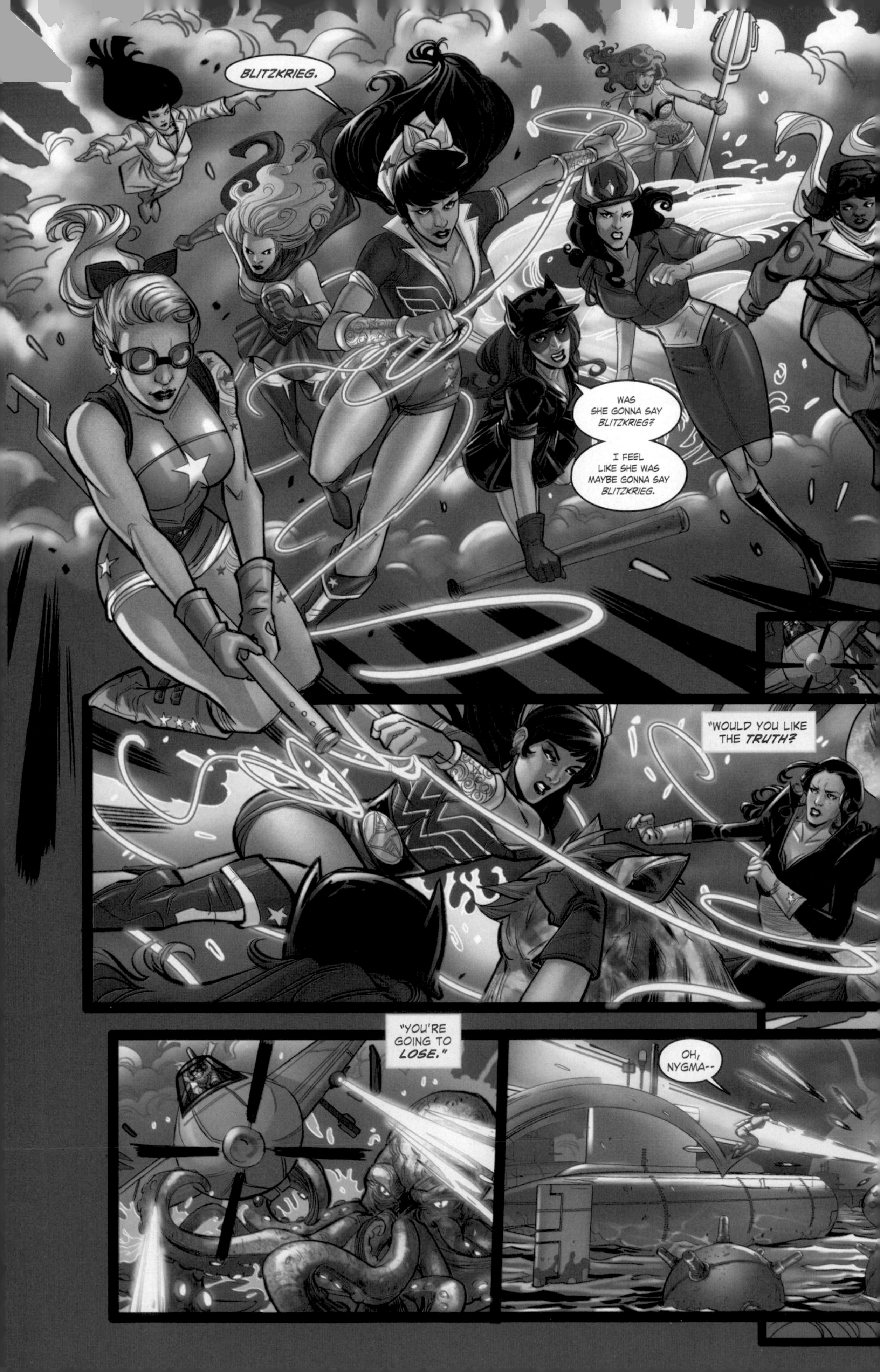
BLITZKRIEG.
WAS SHE GONNA SAY BLITZKRIEG?
I FEEL LIKE SHE WAS MAYBE GONNA SAY BLITZKRIEG.
"WOULD YOU LIKE THE TRUTH?
"YOU'RE GOING TO LOSE."
OH, NYGMA--

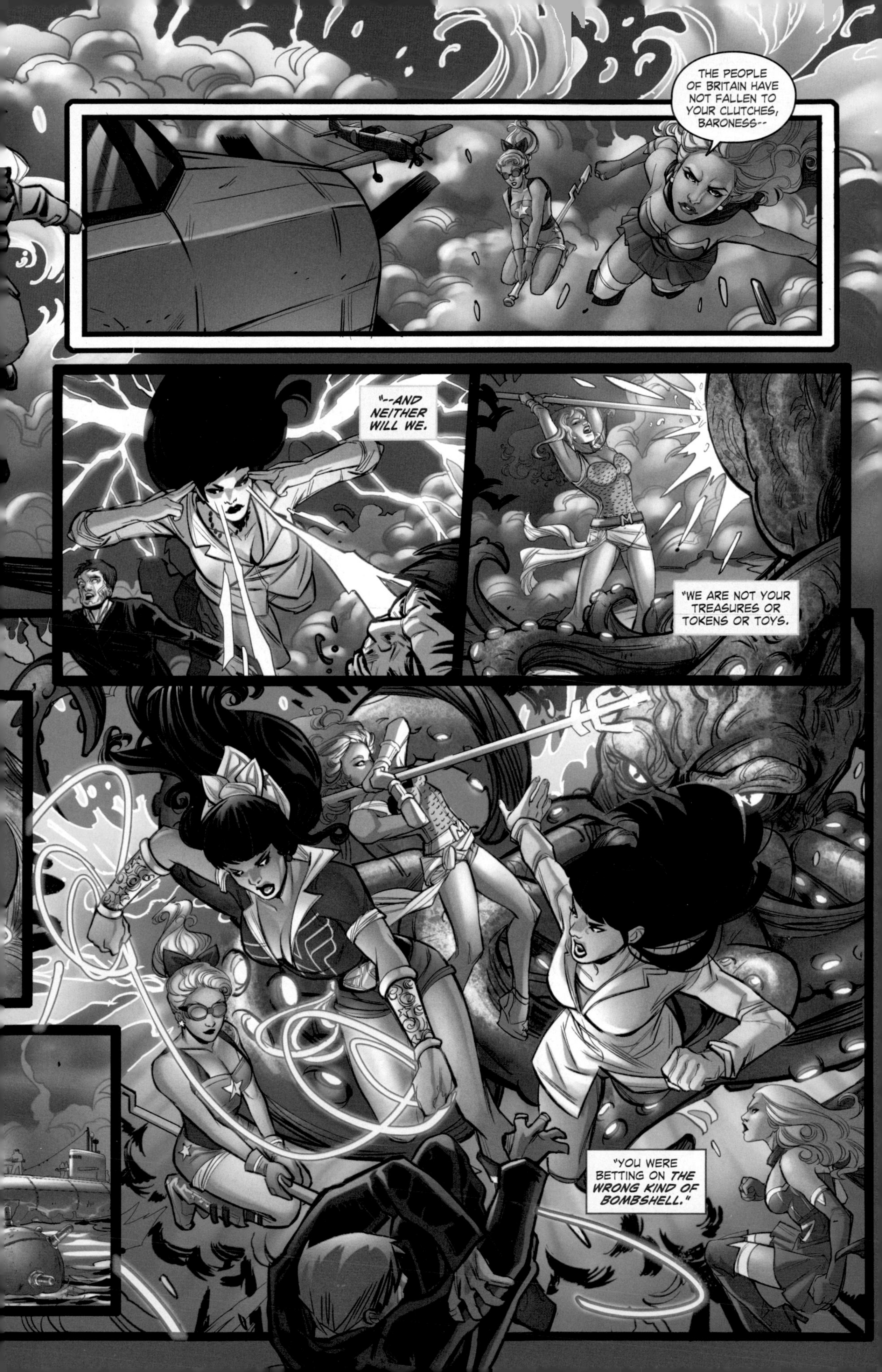

THE PEOPLE OF BRITAIN HAVE NOT FALLEN TO YOUR CLUTCHES, BARONESS--
"--AND NEITHER WILL WE.
"WE ARE NOT YOUR TREASURES OR TOKENS OR TOYS.
"YOU WERE BETTING ON *THE WRONG KIND OF BOMBSHELL.*"

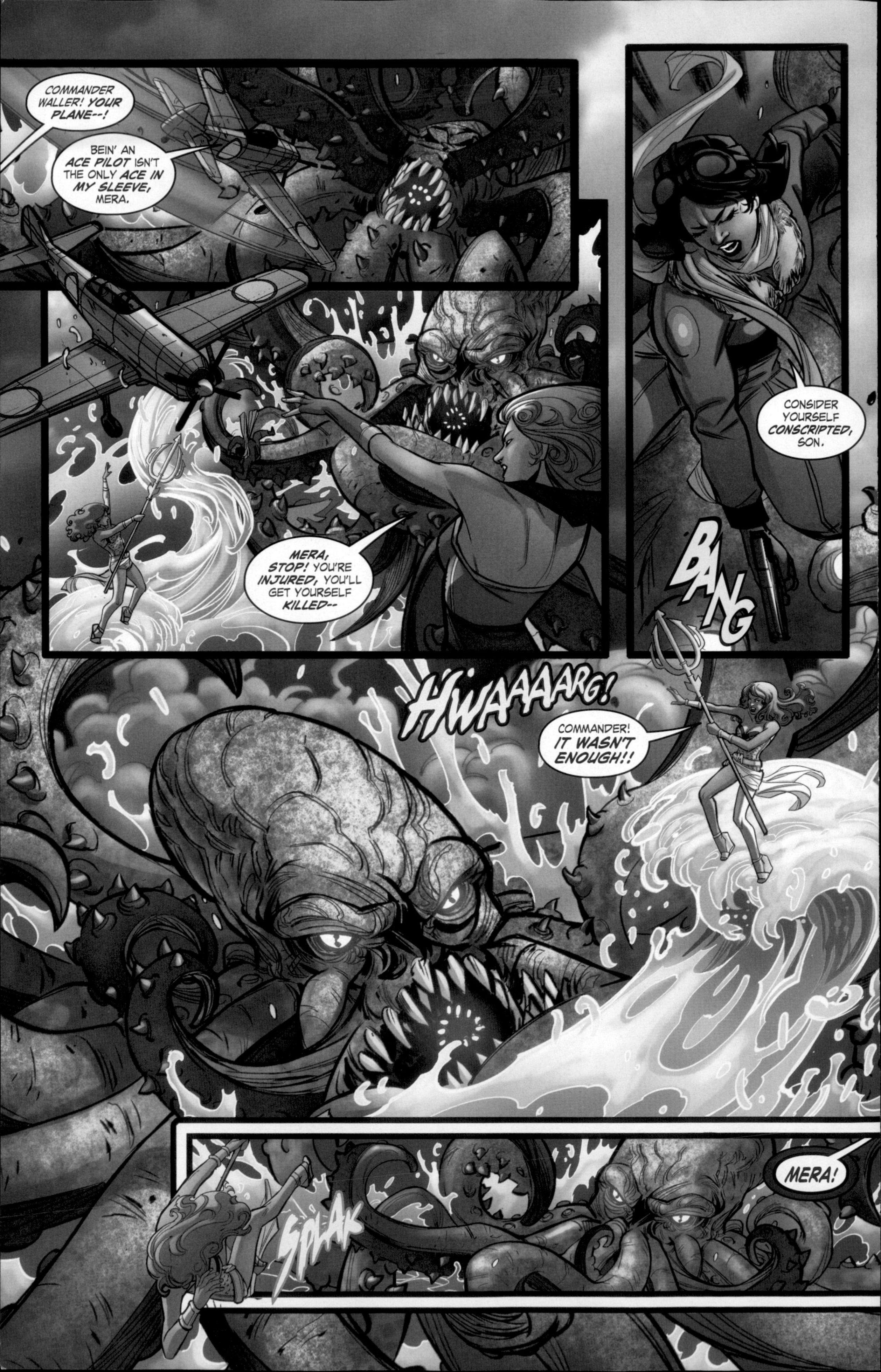
COMMANDER WALLER! YOUR PLANE--!
BEIN' AN ACE PILOT ISN'T THE ONLY ACE IN MY SLEEVE, MERA.
MERA, STOP! YOU'RE INJURED, YOU'LL GET YOURSELF KILLED--
CONSIDER YOURSELF CONSCRIPTED, SON.
BANG
HWAAAARG!
COMMANDER! IT WASN'T ENOUGH!!
SPLAK
MERA!

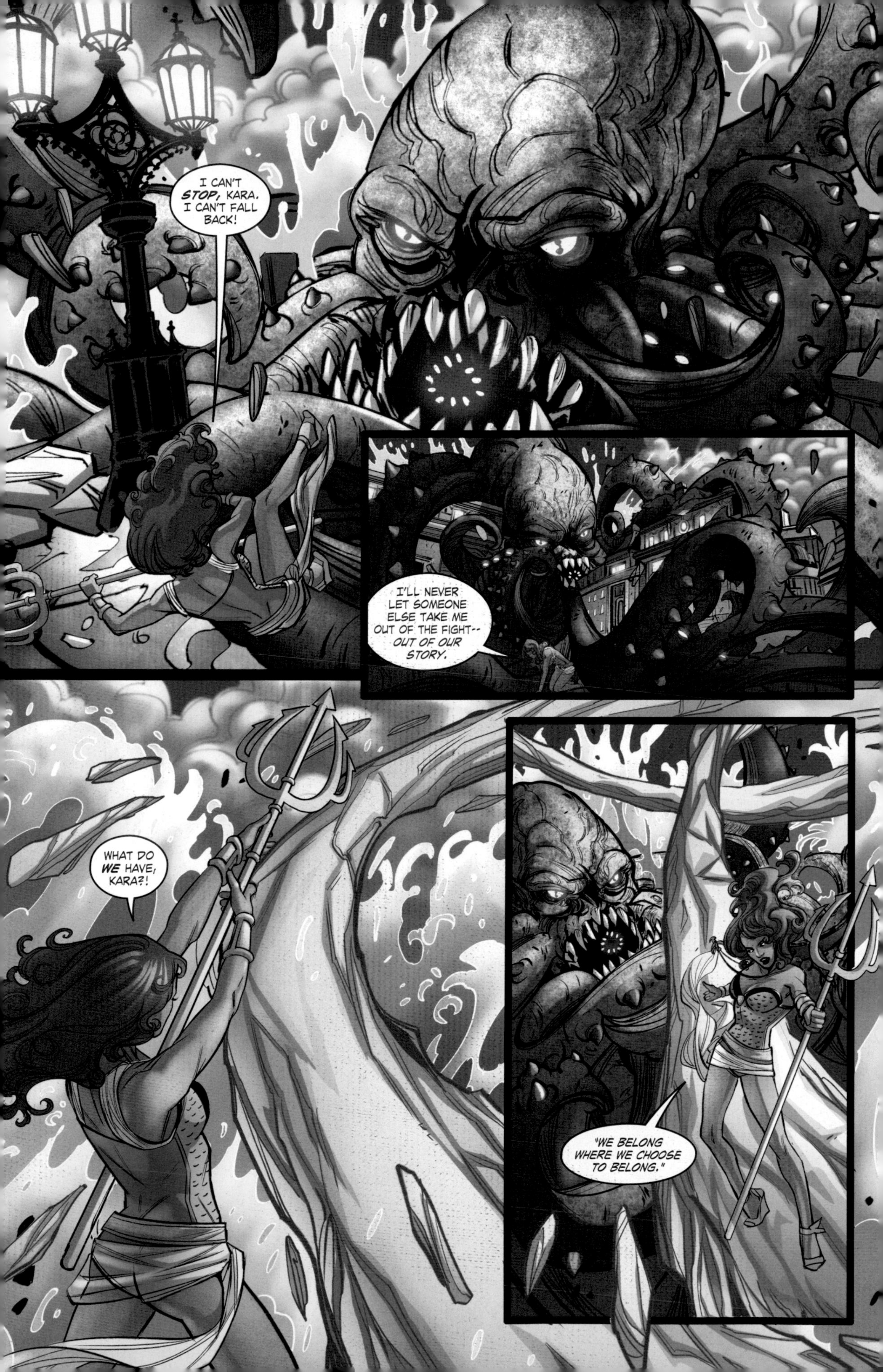
I CAN'T STOP, KARA. I CAN'T FALL BACK!
I'LL NEVER LET SOMEONE ELSE TAKE ME OUT OF THE FIGHT-- OUT OF OUR STORY.
WHAT DO WE HAVE, KARA?!
"WE BELONG WHERE WE CHOOSE TO BELONG."

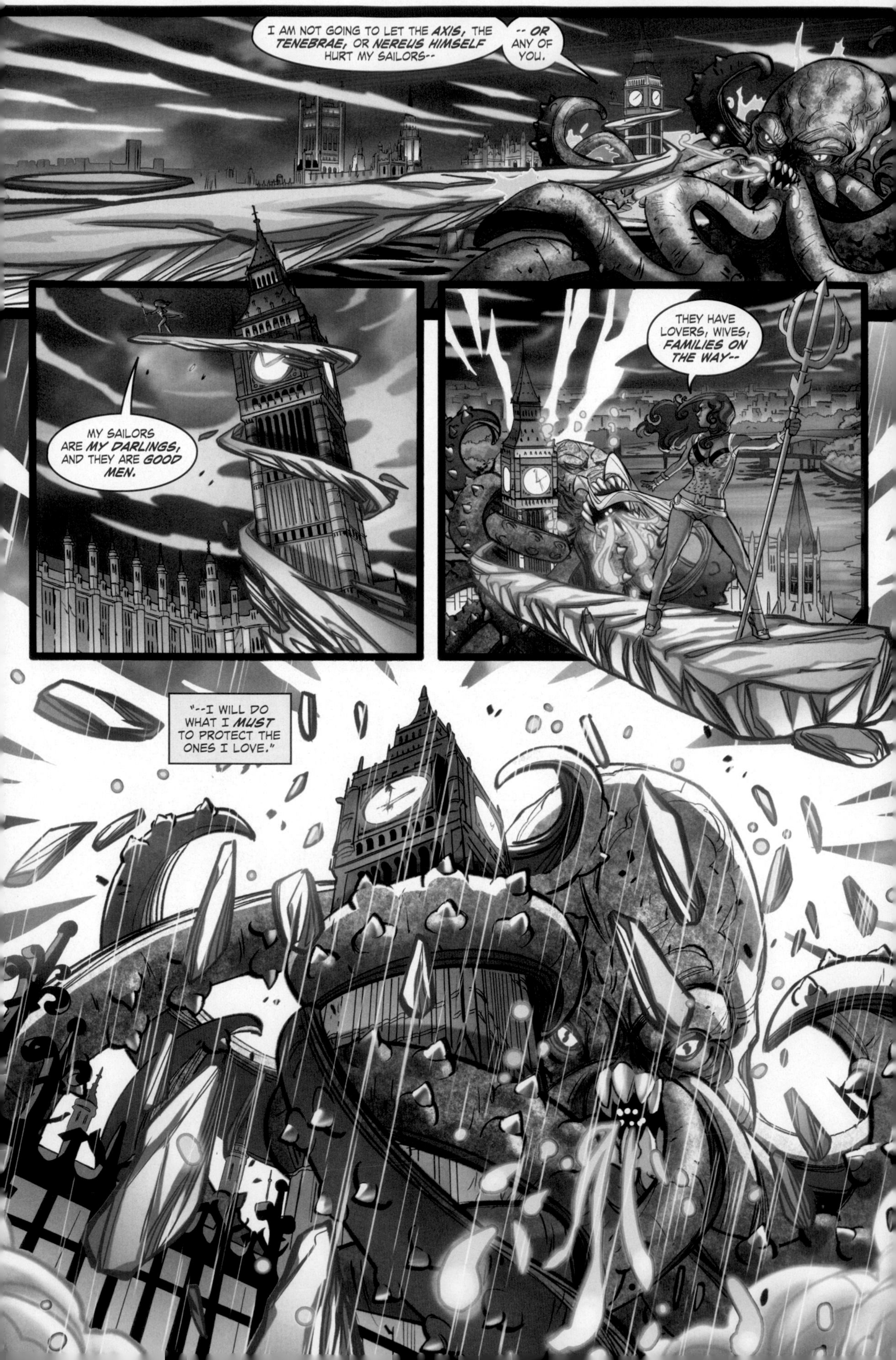
I AM NOT GOING TO LET THE AXIS, THE TENEBRAE, OR NEREUS HIMSELF HURT MY SAILORS--
-- OR ANY OF YOU.
MY SAILORS ARE MY DARLINGS, AND THEY ARE GOOD MEN.
THEY HAVE LOVERS, WIVES, FAMILIES ON THE WAY--
"--I WILL DO WHAT I MUST TO PROTECT THE ONES I LOVE."

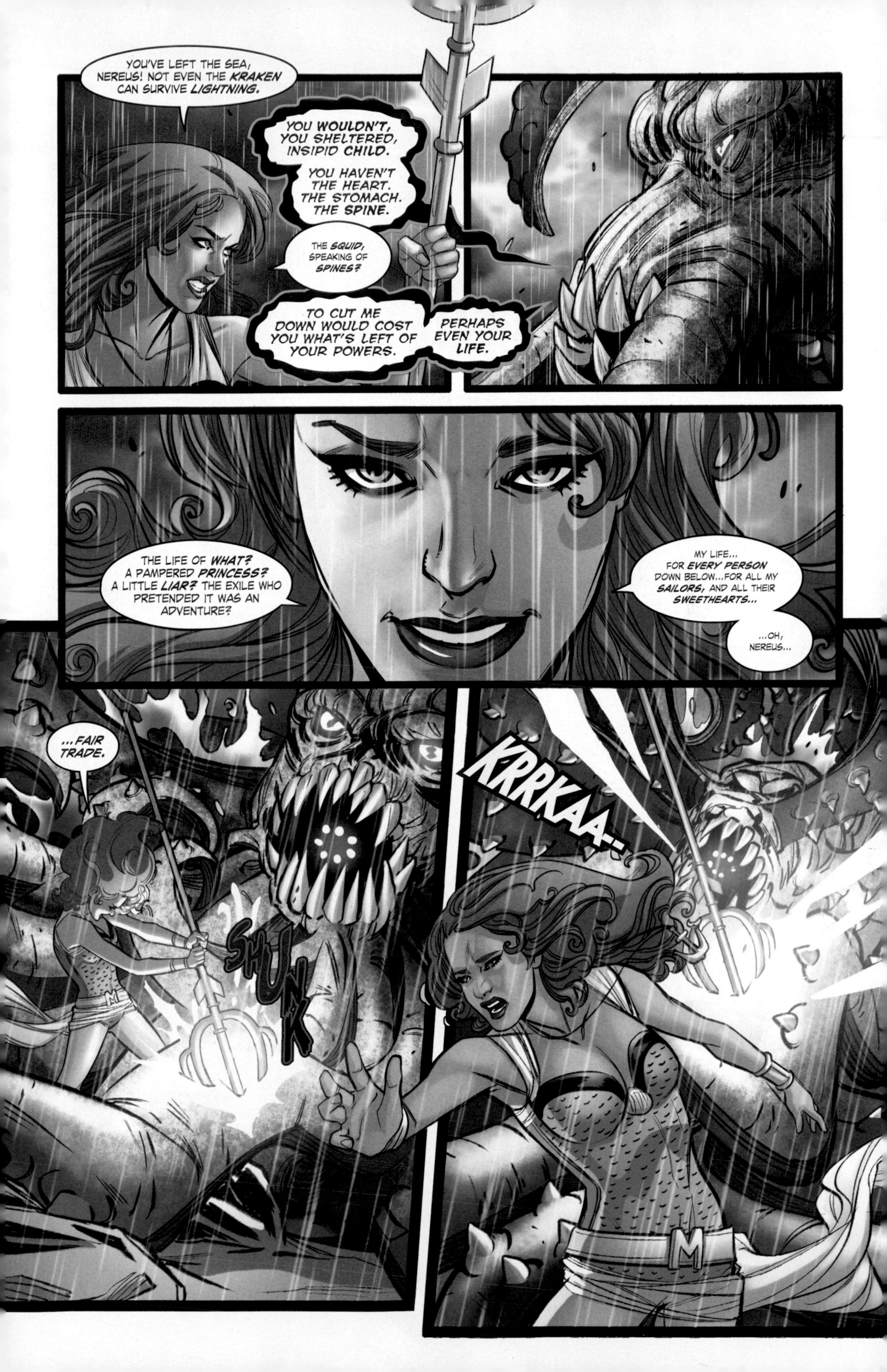
YOU'VE LEFT THE SEA, NEREUS! NOT EVEN THE KRAKEN CAN SURVIVE LIGHTNING.
YOU WOULDN'T, YOU SHELTERED, INSIPID CHILD.
YOU HAVEN'T THE HEART. THE STOMACH. THE SPINE.
THE SQUID, SPEAKING OF SPINES?
TO CUT ME DOWN WOULD COST YOU WHAT'S LEFT OF YOUR POWERS.
PERHAPS EVEN YOUR LIFE.
THE LIFE OF WHAT? A PAMPERED PRINCESS? A LITTLE LIAR? THE EXILE WHO PRETENDED IT WAS AN ADVENTURE?
MY LIFE... FOR EVERY PERSON DOWN BELOW...FOR ALL MY SAILORS, AND ALL THEIR SWEETHEARTS...
...OH, NEREUS...
...FAIR TRADE.
SHUNK
KRRKAA--

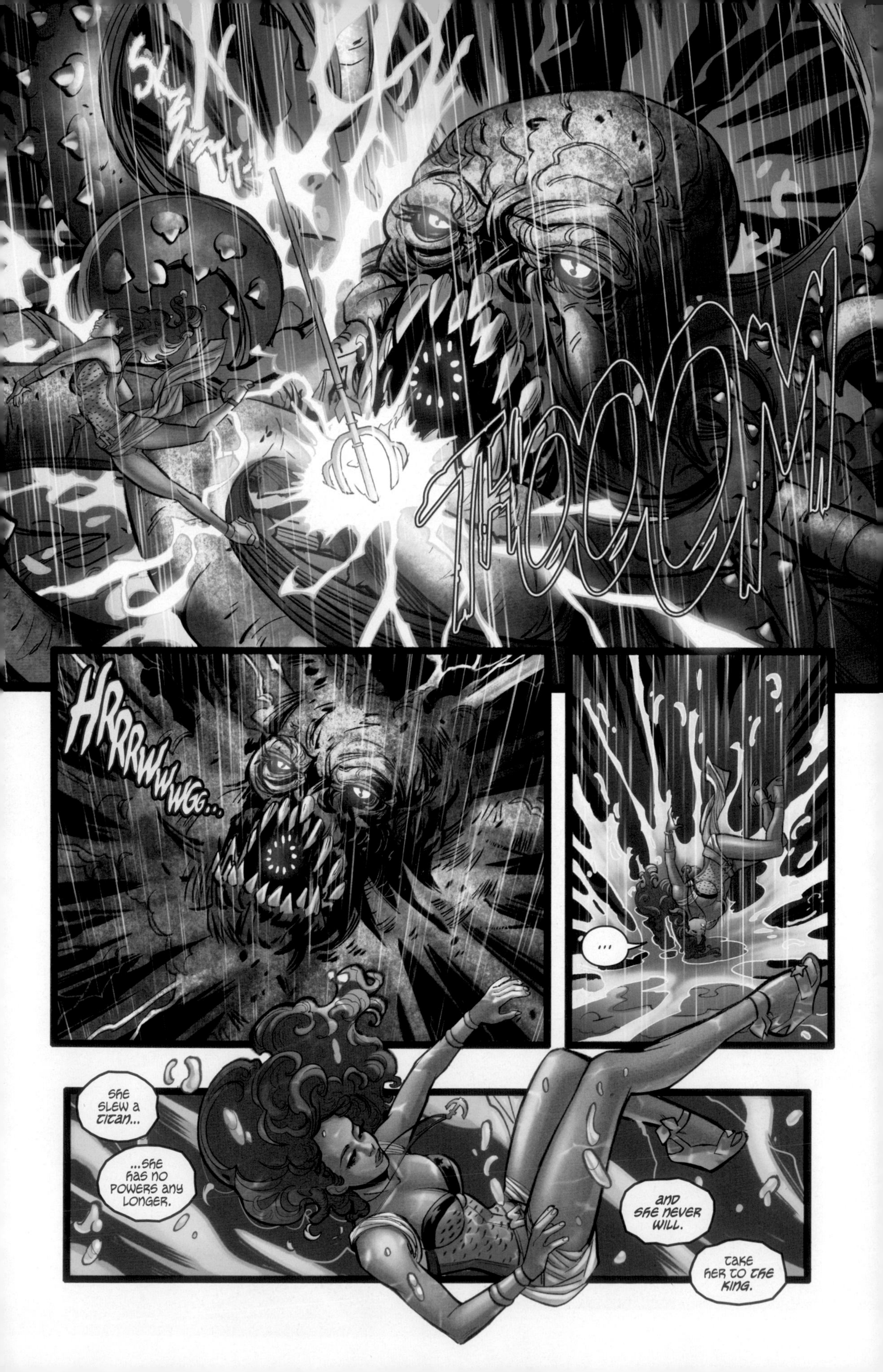
SKZZZTT-!
THOOOM
HRRRWWWGG...
...
SHE SLEW A TITAN...
...SHE HAS NO POWERS ANY LONGER.
AND SHE NEVER WILL.
TAKE HER TO THE KING.

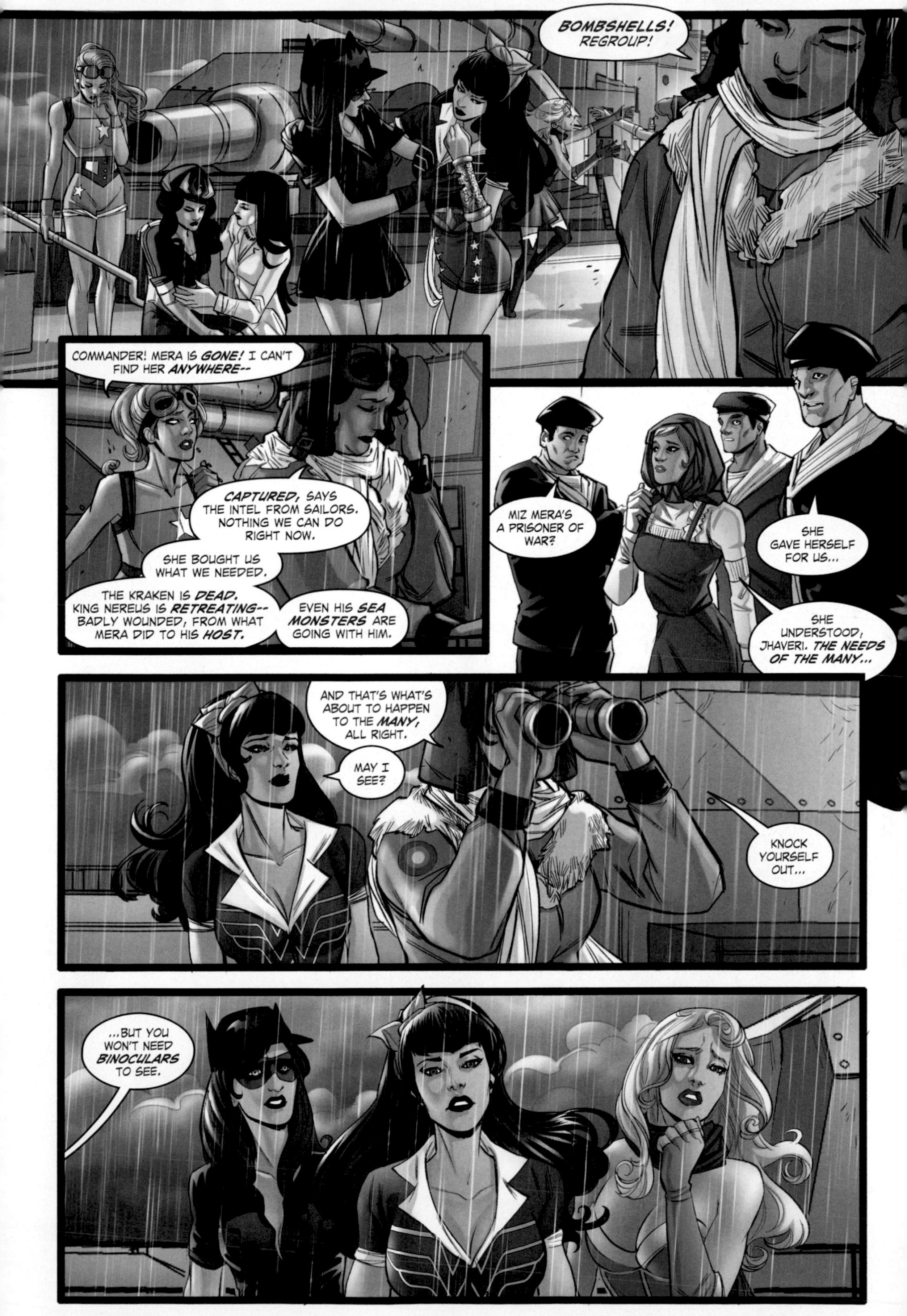
BOMBSHELLS! REGROUP!
COMMANDER! MERA IS GONE! I CAN'T FIND HER ANYWHERE--
CAPTURED, SAYS THE INTEL FROM SAILORS. NOTHING WE CAN DO RIGHT NOW.
SHE BOUGHT US WHAT WE NEEDED.
THE KRAKEN IS DEAD. KING NEREUS IS RETREATING-- BADLY WOUNDED, FROM WHAT MERA DID TO HIS HOST.
EVEN HIS SEA MONSTERS ARE GOING WITH HIM.
MIZ MERA'S A PRISONER OF WAR?
SHE GAVE HERSELF FOR US...
SHE UNDERSTOOD, JHAVERI. THE NEEDS OF THE MANY...
AND THAT'S WHAT'S ABOUT TO HAPPEN TO THE MANY, ALL RIGHT.
MAY I SEE?
KNOCK YOURSELF OUT...
...BUT YOU WON'T NEED BINOCULARS TO SEE.

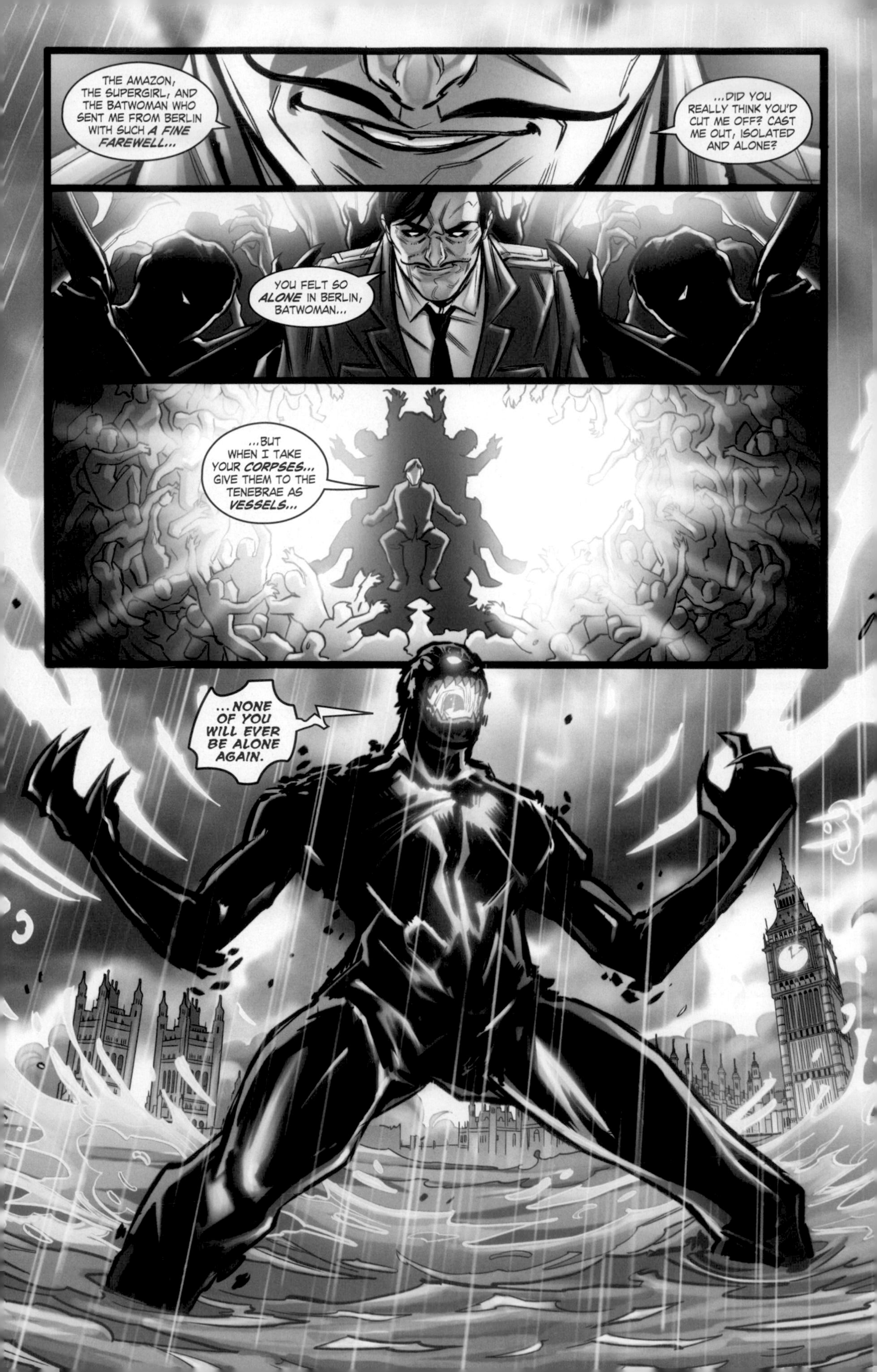
THE AMAZON, THE SUPERGIRL, AND THE BATWOMAN WHO SENT ME FROM BERLIN WITH SUCH A FINE FAREWELL...
...DID YOU REALLY THINK YOU'D CUT ME OFF? CAST ME OUT, ISOLATED AND ALONE?
YOU FELT SO ALONE IN BERLIN, BATWOMAN...
...BUT WHEN I TAKE YOUR CORPSES... GIVE THEM TO THE TENEBRAE AS VESSELS...
...NONE OF YOU WILL EVER BE ALONE AGAIN.

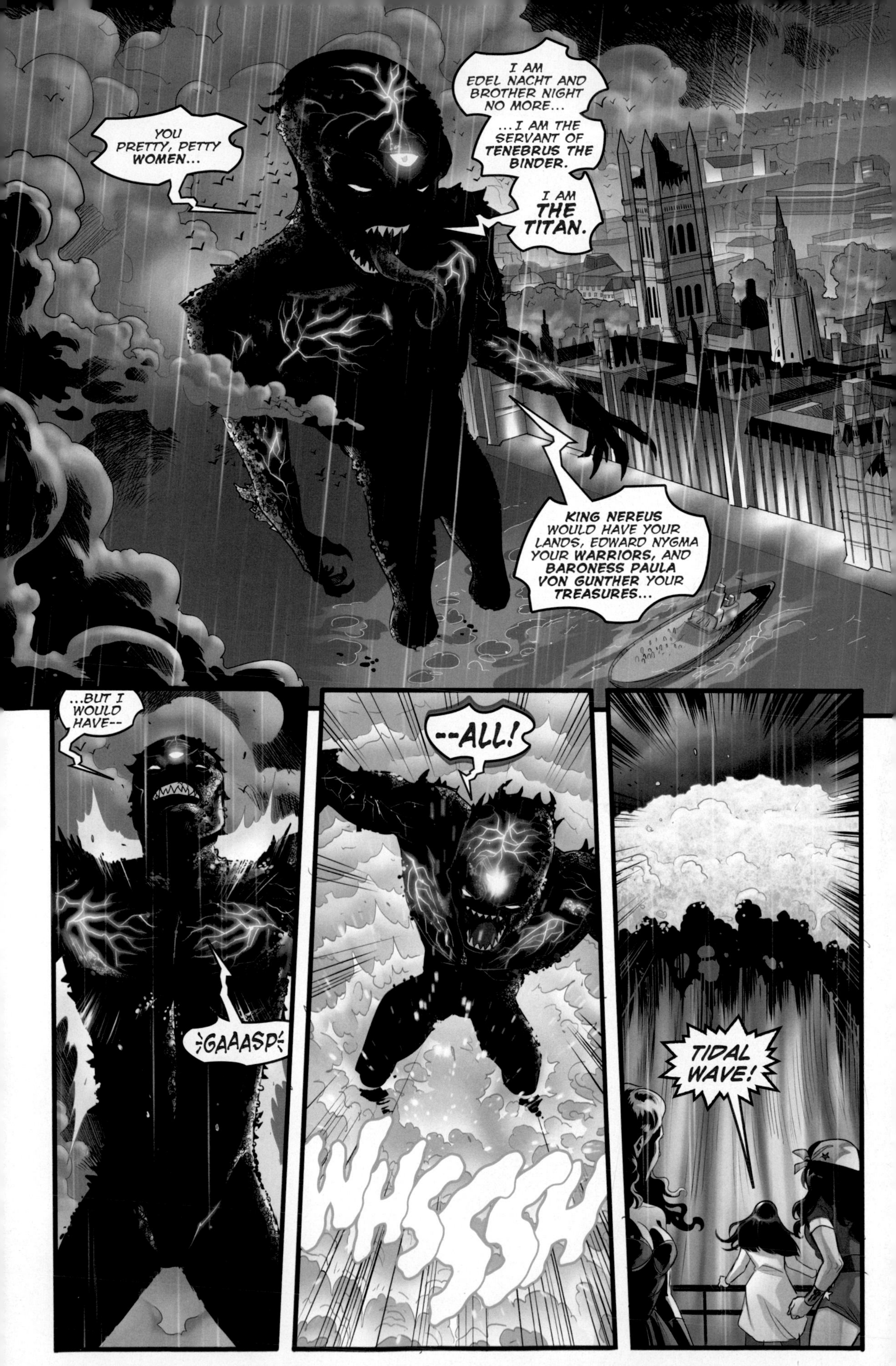
YOU PRETTY, PETTY WOMEN...
I AM EDEL NACHT AND BROTHER NIGHT NO MORE...
...I AM THE SERVANT OF TENEBRUS THE BINDER.
I AM THE TITAN.
KING NEREUS WOULD HAVE YOUR LANDS, EDWARD NYGMA YOUR WARRIORS, AND BARONESS PAULA VON GUNTHER YOUR TREASURES...
...BUT I WOULD HAVE--
GAAASP
--ALL!
WHSSSH
TIDAL WAVE!

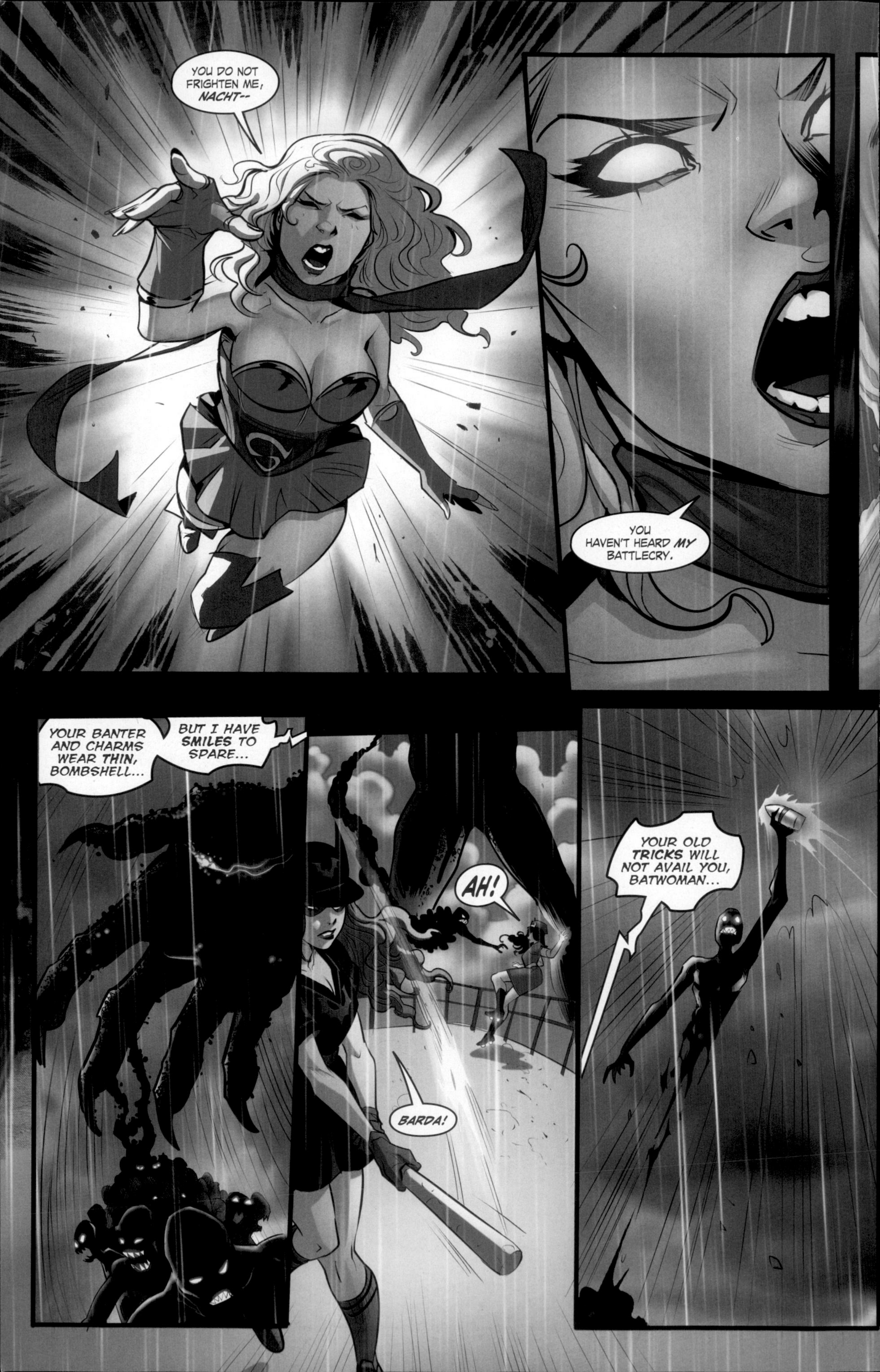
YOU DO NOT FRIGHTEN ME, NACHT--
YOU HAVEN'T HEARD MY BATTLECRY.
YOUR BANTER AND CHARMS WEAR THIN, BOMBSHELL...
BUT I HAVE SMILES TO SPARE...
AH!
BARDA!
YOUR OLD TRICKS WILL NOT AVAIL YOU, BATWOMAN...

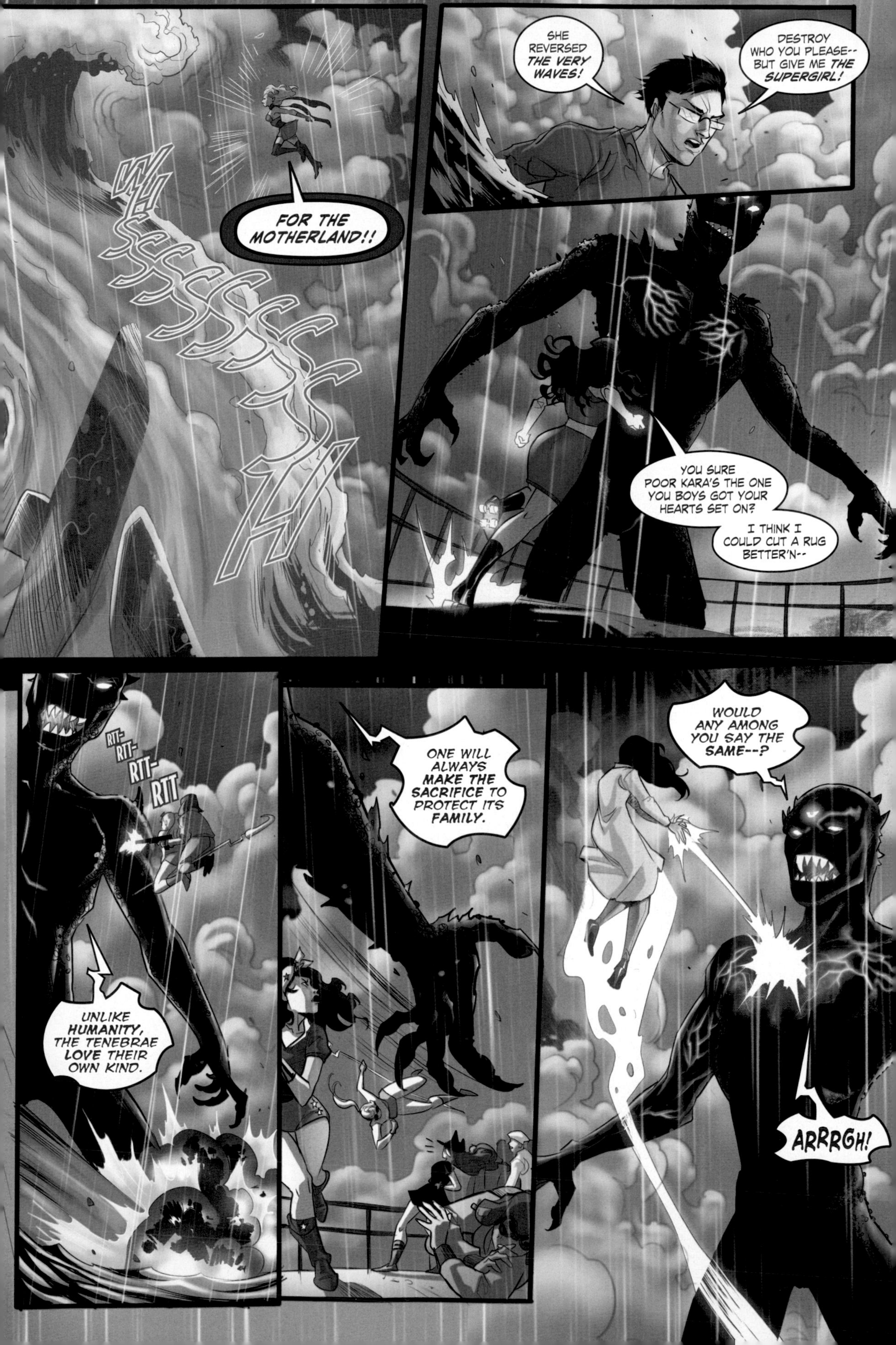
WHSSSSSSSSH
FOR THE MOTHERLAND!!
SHE REVERSED THE VERY WAVES!
DESTROY WHO YOU PLEASE-- BUT GIVE ME THE SUPERGIRL!
YOU SURE POOR KARA'S THE ONE YOU BOYS GOT YOUR HEARTS SET ON?
I THINK I COULD CUT A RUG BETTER'N--
RTT-RTT-RTT-RTT
UNLIKE HUMANITY, THE TENEBRAE LOVE THEIR OWN KIND.
ONE WILL ALWAYS MAKE THE SACRIFICE TO PROTECT ITS FAMILY.
WOULD ANY AMONG YOU SAY THE SAME--?
ARRRGH!

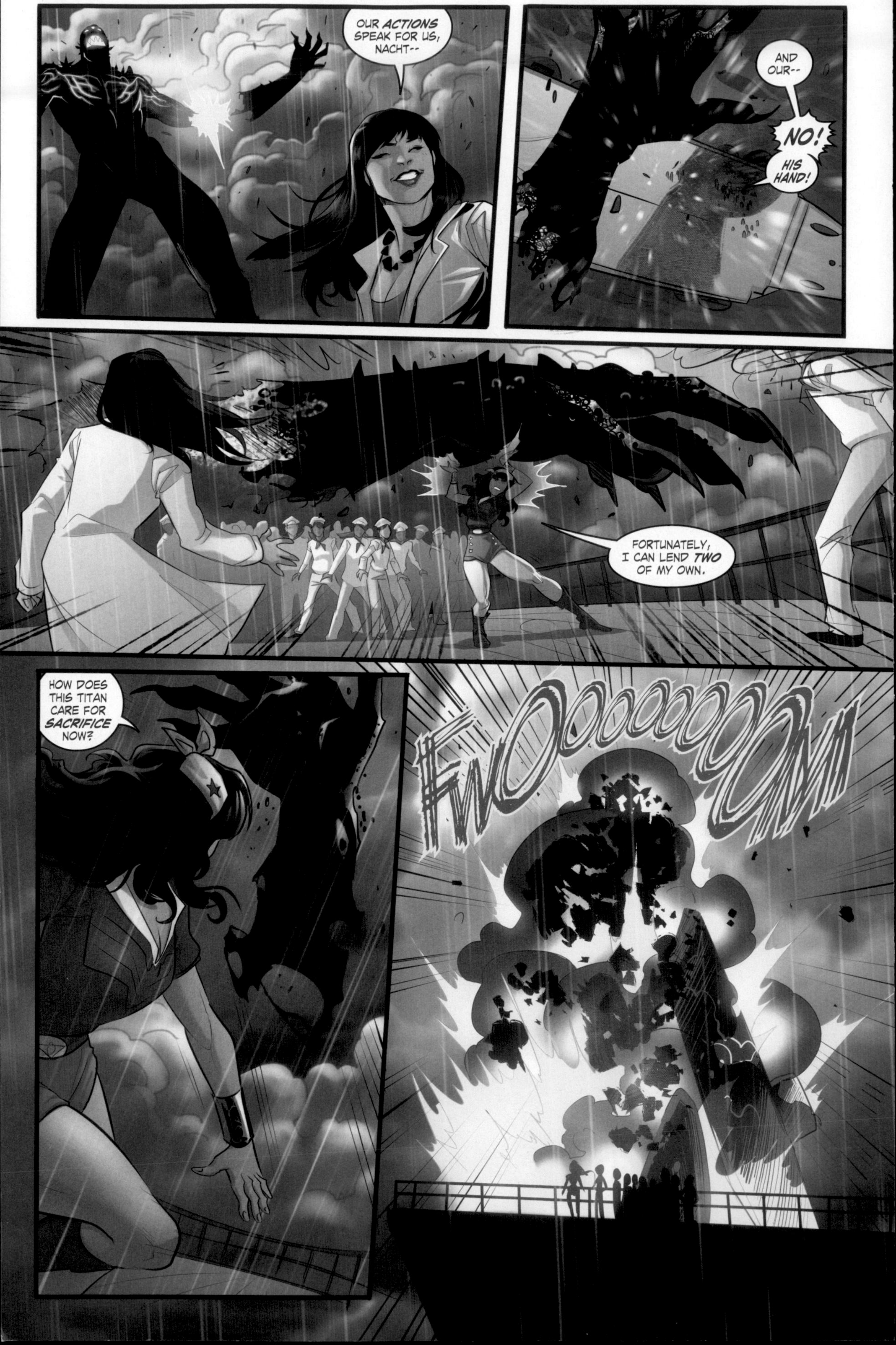
OUR *ACTIONS* SPEAK FOR US, NACHT--
AND OUR--
NO!
HIS HAND!
FORTUNATELY, I CAN LEND *TWO* OF MY OWN.
HOW DOES THIS TITAN CARE FOR *SACRIFICE* NOW?
FWOOOOOOOOOM!!

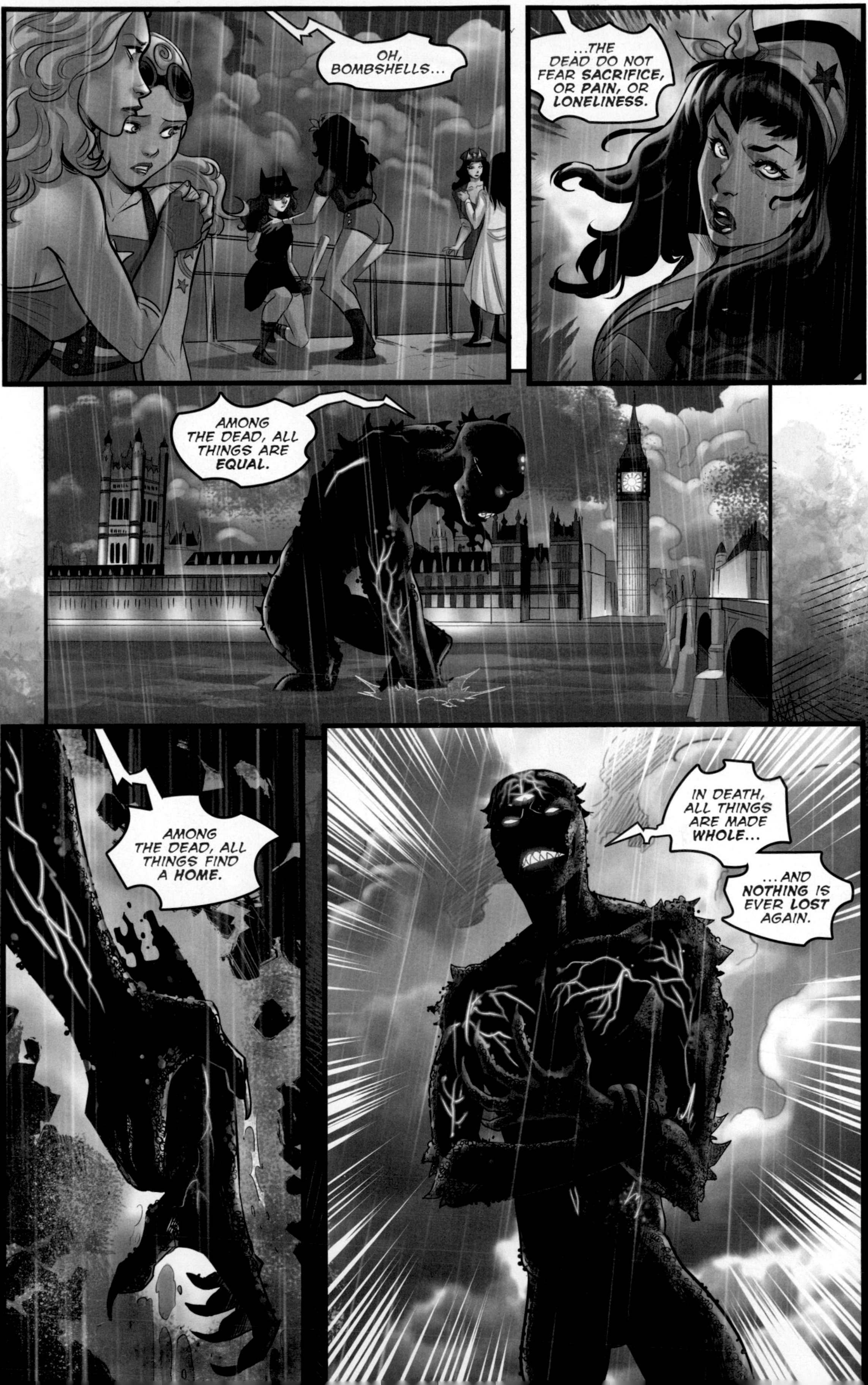
OH, BOMBSHELLS...
...THE DEAD DO NOT FEAR SACRIFICE, OR PAIN, OR LONELINESS.
AMONG THE DEAD, ALL THINGS ARE EQUAL.
AMONG THE DEAD, ALL THINGS FIND A HOME.
IN DEATH, ALL THINGS ARE MADE WHOLE...
...AND NOTHING IS EVER LOST AGAIN.

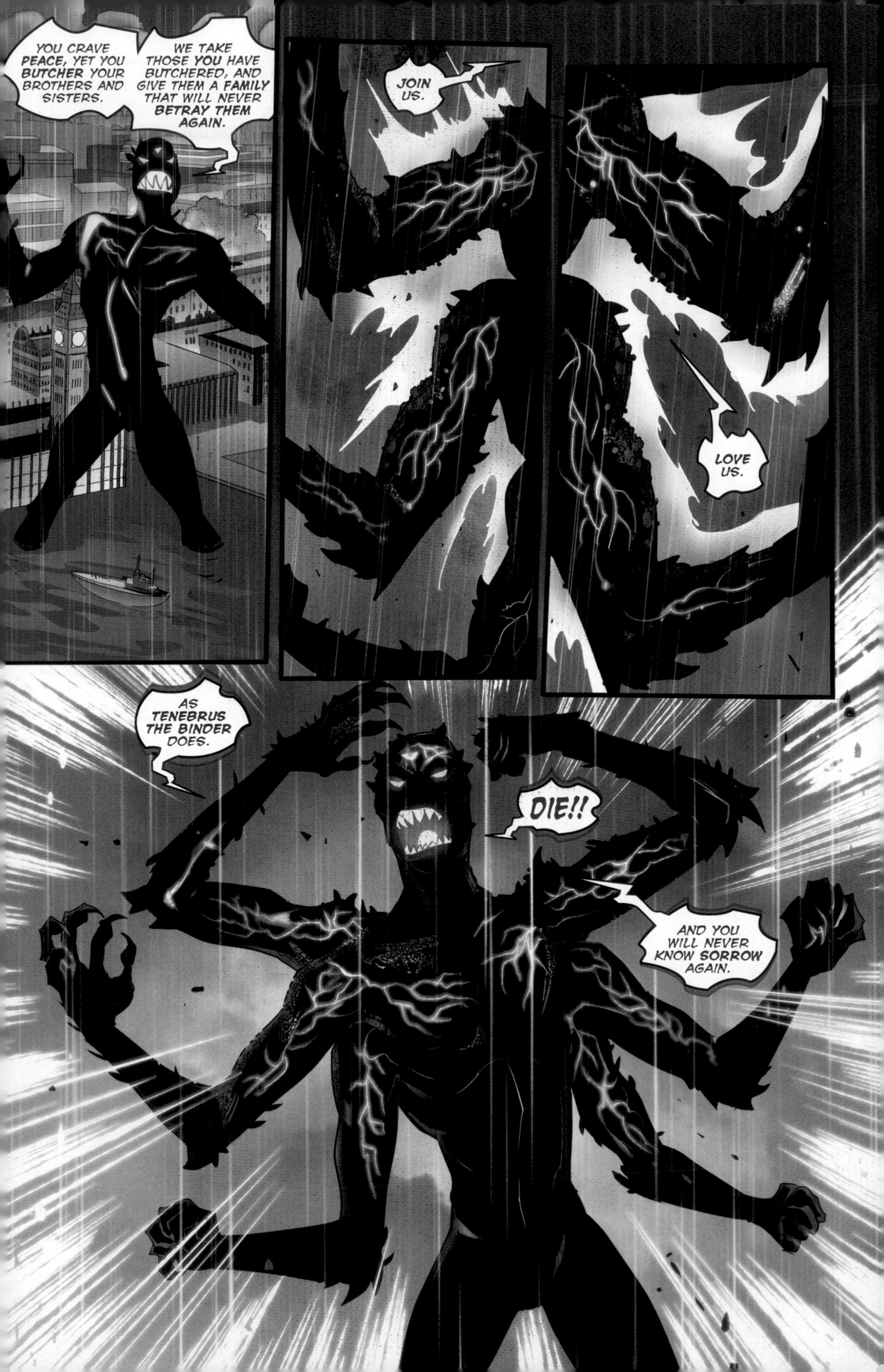
YOU CRAVE PEACE, YET YOU BUTCHER YOUR BROTHERS AND SISTERS.
WE TAKE THOSE YOU HAVE BUTCHERED, AND GIVE THEM A FAMILY THAT WILL NEVER BETRAY THEM AGAIN.
JOIN US.
LOVE US.
AS TENEBRUS THE BINDER DOES.
DIE!!
AND YOU WILL NEVER KNOW SORROW AGAIN.

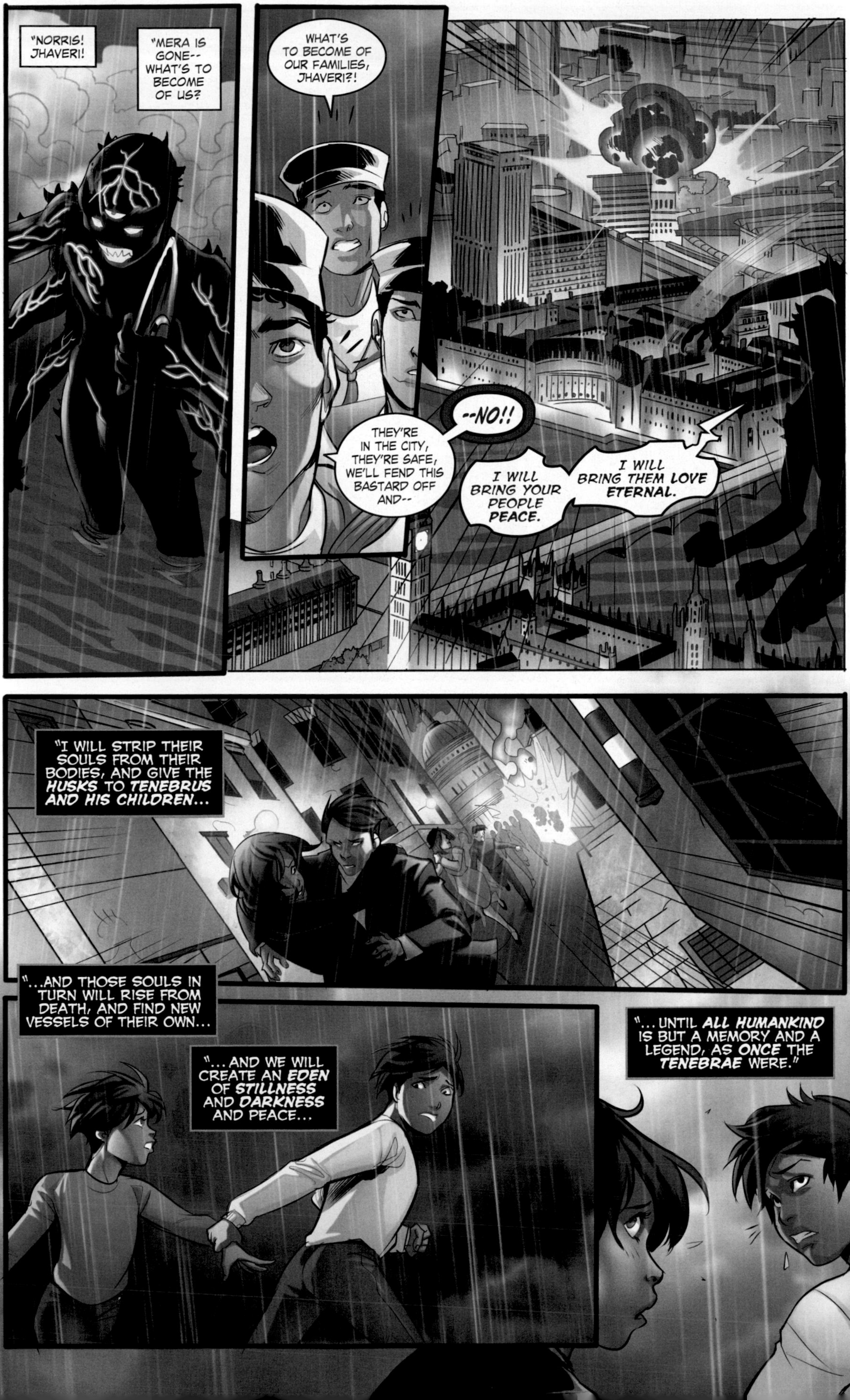

"NORRIS! JHAVERI!
"MERA IS GONE-- WHAT'S TO BECOME OF US?
WHAT'S TO BECOME OF OUR FAMILIES, JHAVERI?!
THEY'RE IN THE CITY, THEY'RE SAFE, WE'LL FEND THIS BASTARD OFF AND--
--NO!!
I WILL BRING YOUR PEOPLE PEACE.
I WILL BRING THEM LOVE ETERNAL.
"I WILL STRIP THEIR SOULS FROM THEIR BODIES, AND GIVE THE HUSKS TO TENEBRUS AND HIS CHILDREN...
"...AND THOSE SOULS IN TURN WILL RISE FROM DEATH, AND FIND NEW VESSELS OF THEIR OWN...
"...AND WE WILL CREATE AN EDEN OF STILLNESS AND DARKNESS AND PEACE...
"...UNTIL ALL HUMANKIND IS BUT A MEMORY AND A LEGEND, AS ONCE THE TENEBRAE WERE."

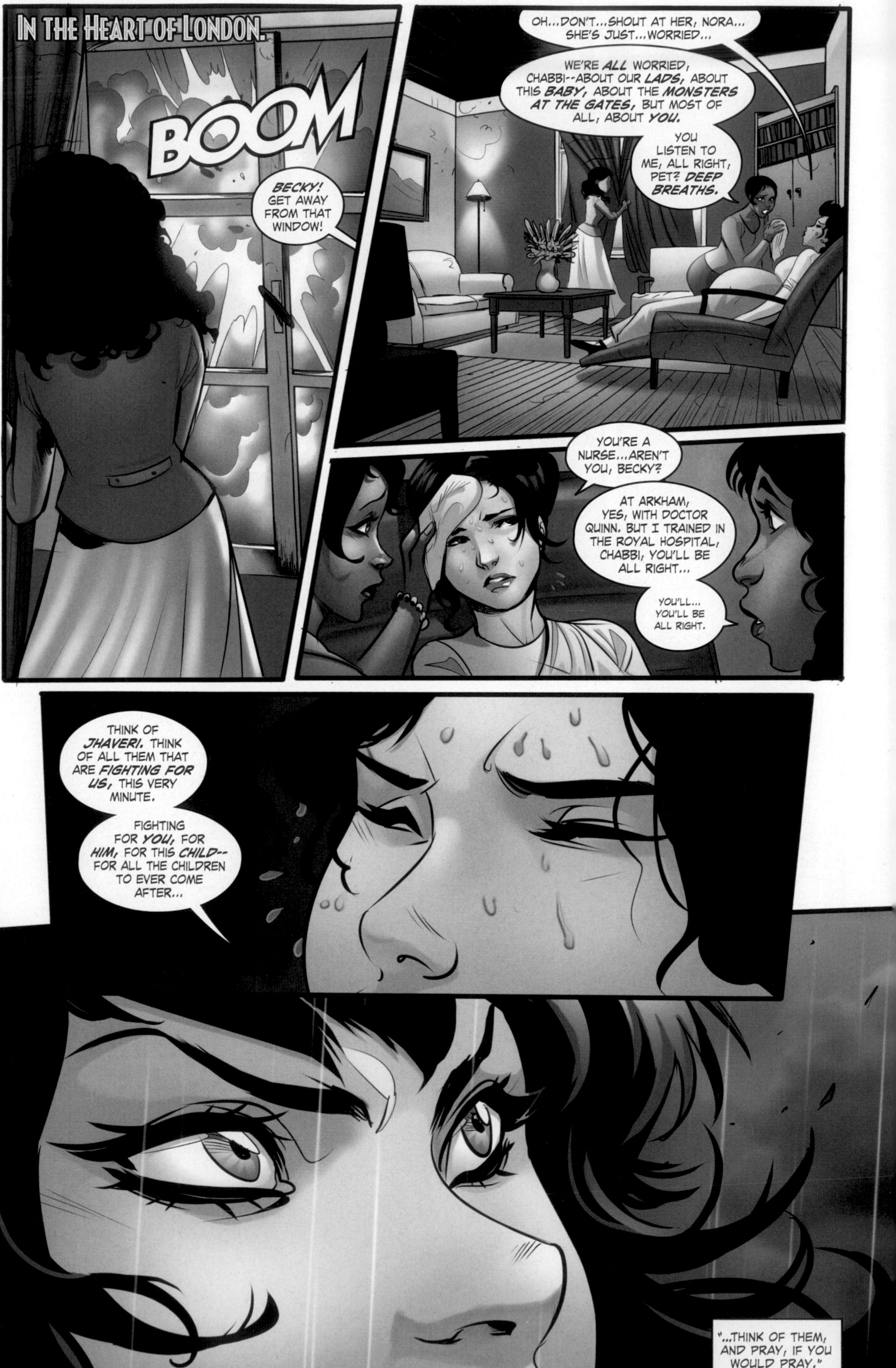
IN THE HEART OF LONDON.
BOOM
BECKY! GET AWAY FROM THAT WINDOW!
OH...DON'T...SHOUT AT HER, NORA... SHE'S JUST...WORRIED...
WE'RE ALL WORRIED, CHABBI--ABOUT OUR LADS, ABOUT THIS BABY, ABOUT THE MONSTERS AT THE GATES, BUT MOST OF ALL, ABOUT YOU.
YOU LISTEN TO ME, ALL RIGHT, PET? DEEP BREATHS.
YOU'RE A NURSE...AREN'T YOU, BECKY?
AT ARKHAM, YES, WITH DOCTOR QUINN. BUT I TRAINED IN THE ROYAL HOSPITAL, CHABBI, YOU'LL BE ALL RIGHT...
YOU'LL... YOU'LL BE ALL RIGHT.
THINK OF JHAVERI. THINK OF ALL THEM THAT ARE FIGHTING FOR US, THIS VERY MINUTE.
FIGHTING FOR YOU, FOR HIM, FOR THIS CHILD-- FOR ALL THE CHILDREN TO EVER COME AFTER...
"...THINK OF THEM, AND PRAY, IF YOU WOULD PRAY."

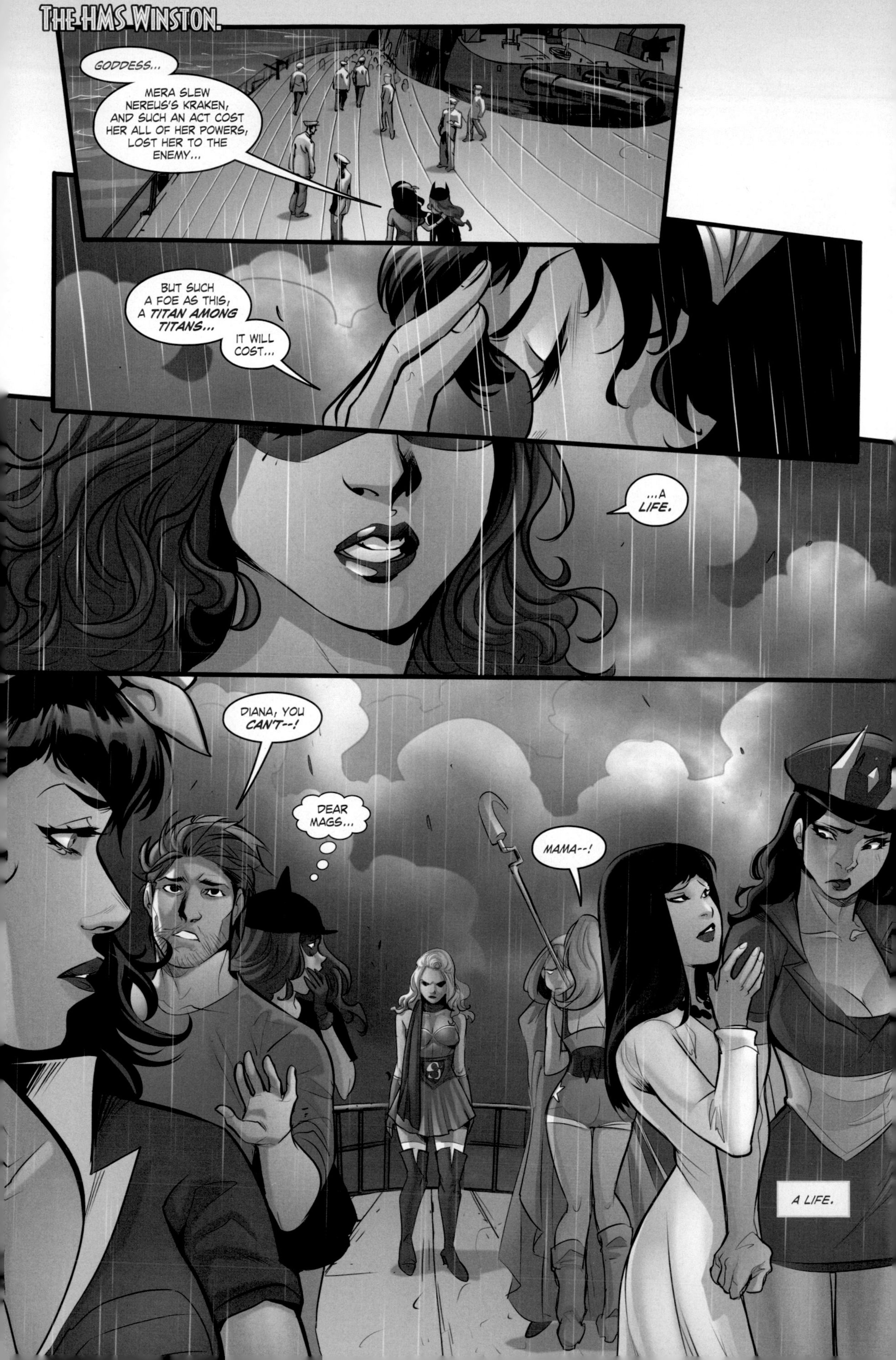
THE HMS WINSTON.
GODDESS...
MERA SLEW NEREUS'S KRAKEN, AND SUCH AN ACT COST HER ALL OF HER POWERS, LOST HER TO THE ENEMY...
BUT SUCH A FOE AS THIS, A TITAN AMONG TITANS...
IT WILL COST...
...A LIFE.
DIANA, YOU CAN'T--!
DEAR MAGS...
MAMA--!
A LIFE.

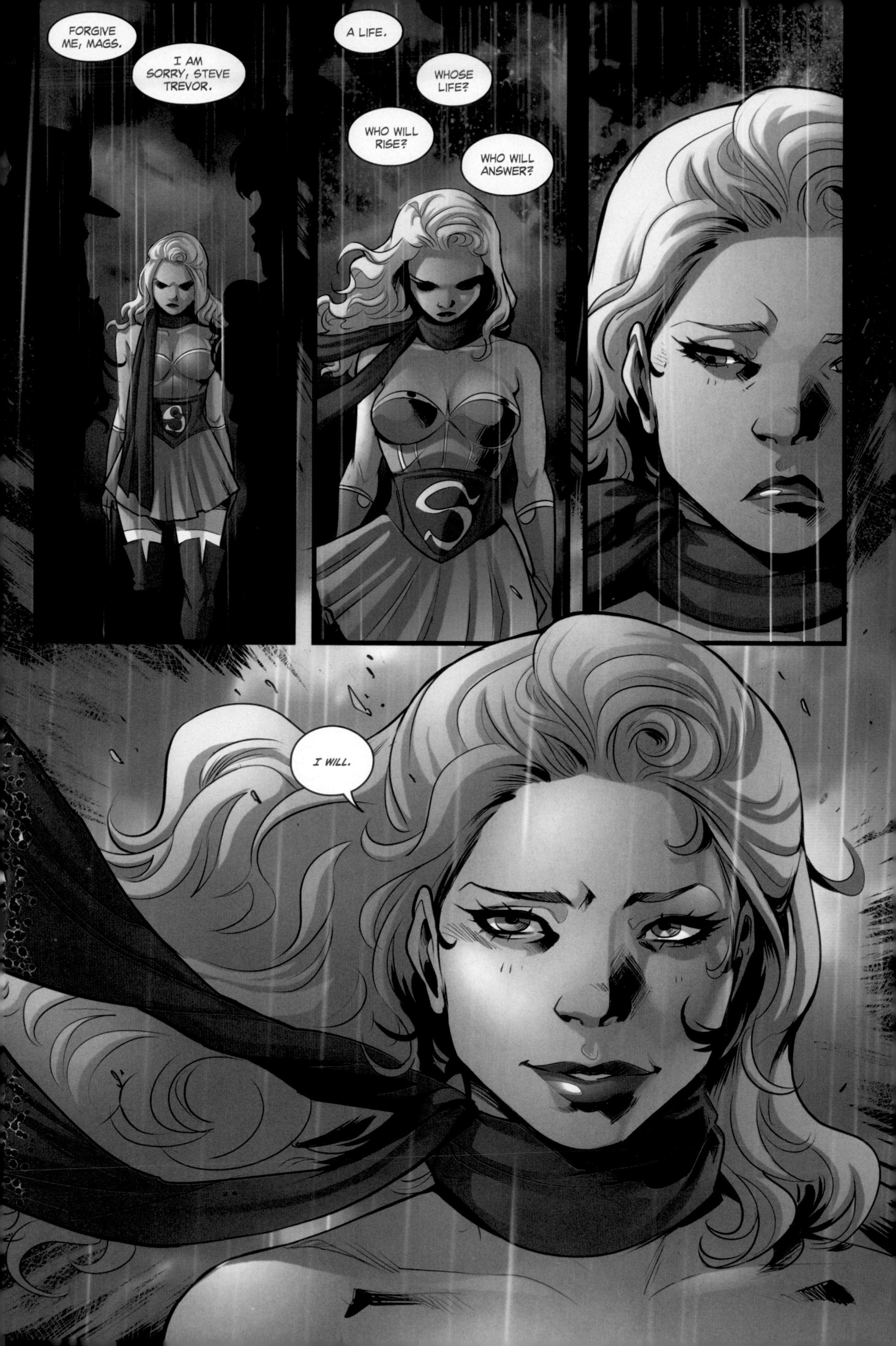
FORGIVE ME, MAGS.
I AM SORRY, STEVE TREVOR.
A LIFE.
WHOSE LIFE?
WHO WILL RISE?
WHO WILL ANSWER?
I WILL.

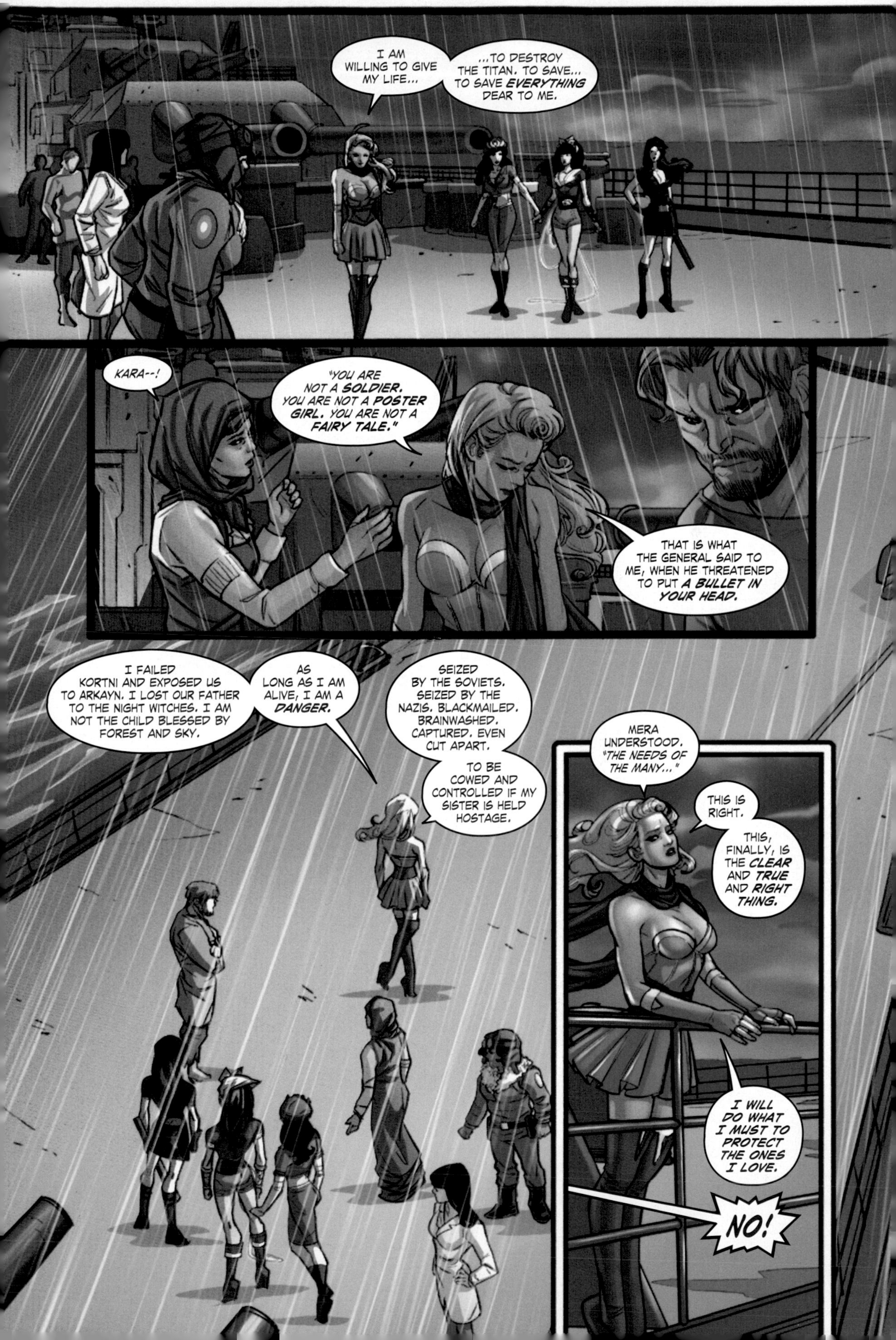
I AM WILLING TO GIVE MY LIFE...
...TO DESTROY THE TITAN. TO SAVE... TO SAVE EVERYTHING DEAR TO ME.
KARA--!
"YOU ARE NOT A SOLDIER. YOU ARE NOT A POSTER GIRL. YOU ARE NOT A FAIRY TALE."
THAT IS WHAT THE GENERAL SAID TO ME, WHEN HE THREATENED TO PUT A BULLET IN YOUR HEAD.
I FAILED KORTNI AND EXPOSED US TO ARKAYN. I LOST OUR FATHER TO THE NIGHT WITCHES. I AM NOT THE CHILD BLESSED BY FOREST AND SKY.
AS LONG AS I AM ALIVE, I AM A DANGER.
SEIZED BY THE SOVIETS. SEIZED BY THE NAZIS. BLACKMAILED. BRAINWASHED. CAPTURED. EVEN CUT APART.
TO BE COWED AND CONTROLLED IF MY SISTER IS HELD HOSTAGE.
MERA UNDERSTOOD. "THE NEEDS OF THE MANY..."
THIS IS RIGHT.
THIS, FINALLY, IS THE CLEAR AND TRUE AND RIGHT THING.
I WILL DO WHAT I MUST TO PROTECT THE ONES I LOVE.
NO!

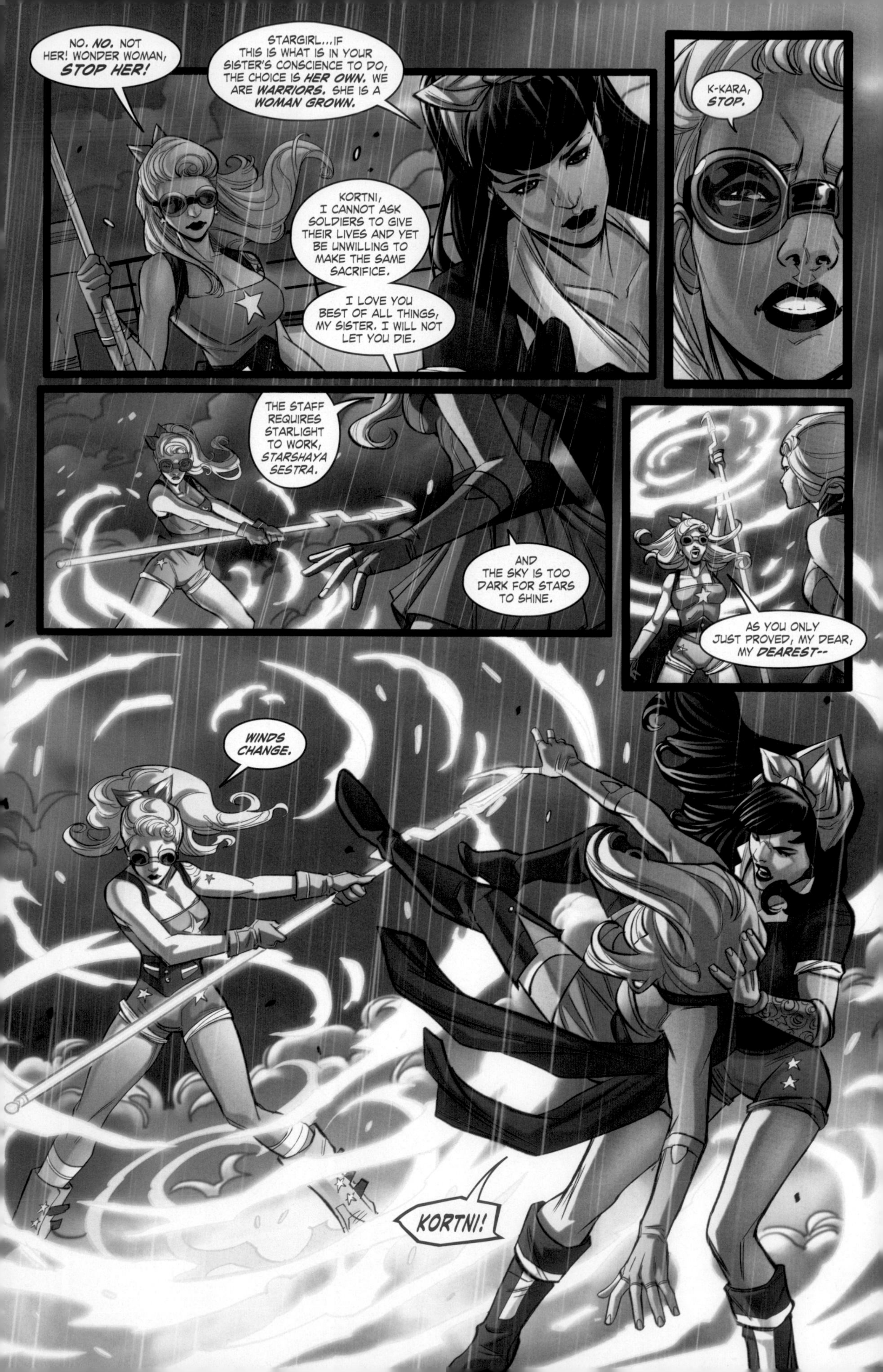
NO. NO. NOT HER! WONDER WOMAN, STOP HER!
STARGIRL...IF THIS IS WHAT IS IN YOUR SISTER'S CONSCIENCE TO DO, THE CHOICE IS HER OWN. WE ARE WARRIORS. SHE IS A WOMAN GROWN.
KORTNI, I CANNOT ASK SOLDIERS TO GIVE THEIR LIVES AND YET BE UNWILLING TO MAKE THE SAME SACRIFICE.
I LOVE YOU BEST OF ALL THINGS, MY SISTER. I WILL NOT LET YOU DIE.
K-KARA, STOP.
THE STAFF REQUIRES STARLIGHT TO WORK, STARSHAYA SESTRA.
AND THE SKY IS TOO DARK FOR STARS TO SHINE.
AS YOU ONLY JUST PROVED, MY DEAR, MY DEAREST--
WINDS CHANGE.
KORTNI!

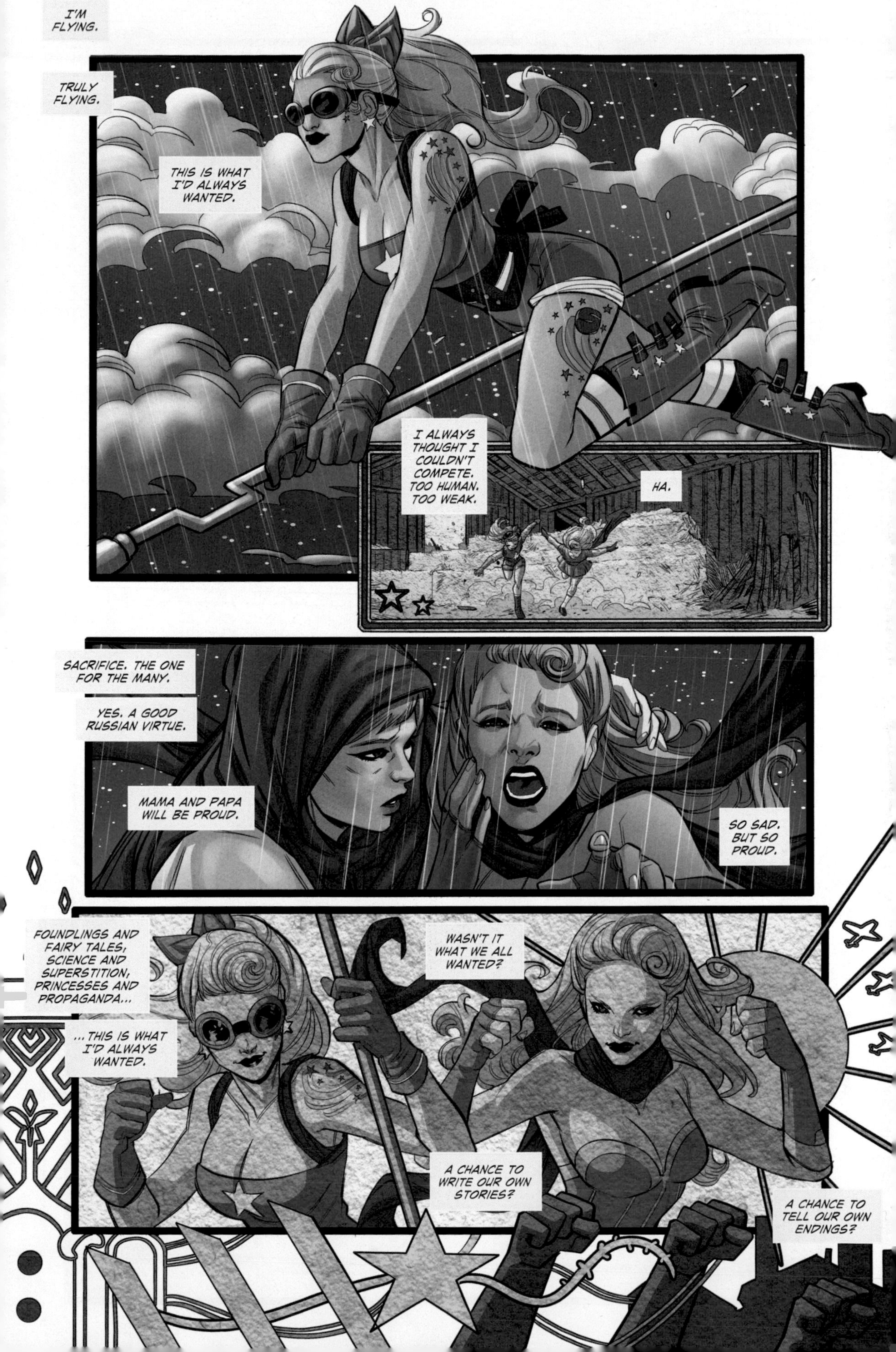
I'M FLYING.
TRULY FLYING.
THIS IS WHAT I'D ALWAYS WANTED.
I ALWAYS THOUGHT I COULDN'T COMPETE. TOO HUMAN. TOO WEAK.
HA.
SACRIFICE. THE ONE FOR THE MANY.
YES. A GOOD RUSSIAN VIRTUE.
MAMA AND PAPA WILL BE PROUD.
SO SAD. BUT SO PROUD.
FOUNDLINGS AND FAIRY TALES, SCIENCE AND SUPERSTITION, PRINCESSES AND PROPAGANDA...
...THIS IS WHAT I'D ALWAYS WANTED.
WASN'T IT WHAT WE ALL WANTED?
A CHANCE TO WRITE OUR OWN STORIES?
A CHANCE TO TELL OUR OWN ENDINGS?

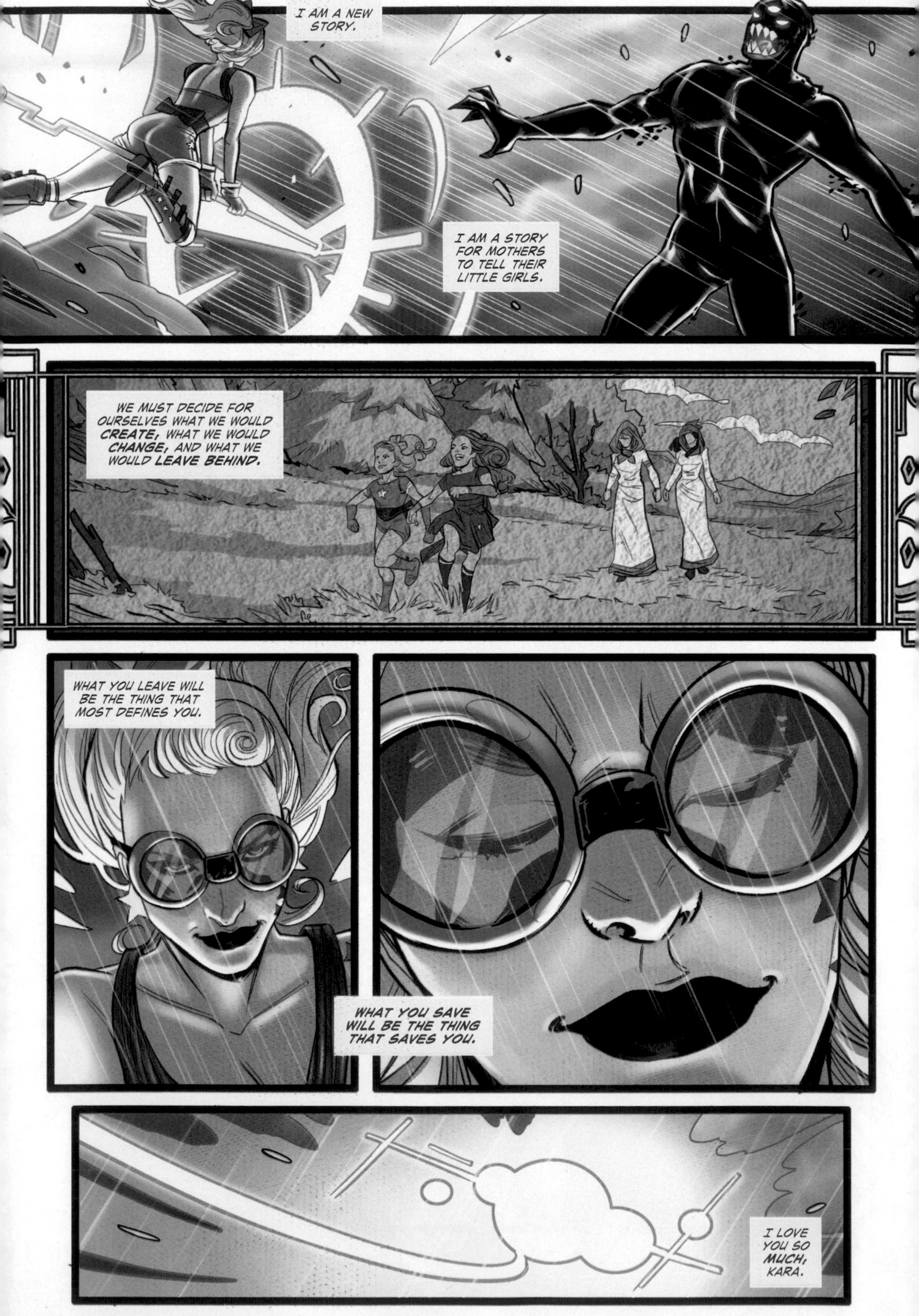
I AM A NEW STORY.
I AM A STORY FOR MOTHERS TO TELL THEIR LITTLE GIRLS.
WE MUST DECIDE FOR OURSELVES WHAT WE WOULD CREATE, WHAT WE WOULD CHANGE, AND WHAT WE WOULD LEAVE BEHIND.
WHAT YOU LEAVE WILL BE THE THING THAT MOST DEFINES YOU.
WHAT YOU SAVE WILL BE THE THING THAT SAVES YOU.
I LOVE YOU SO MUCH, KARA.

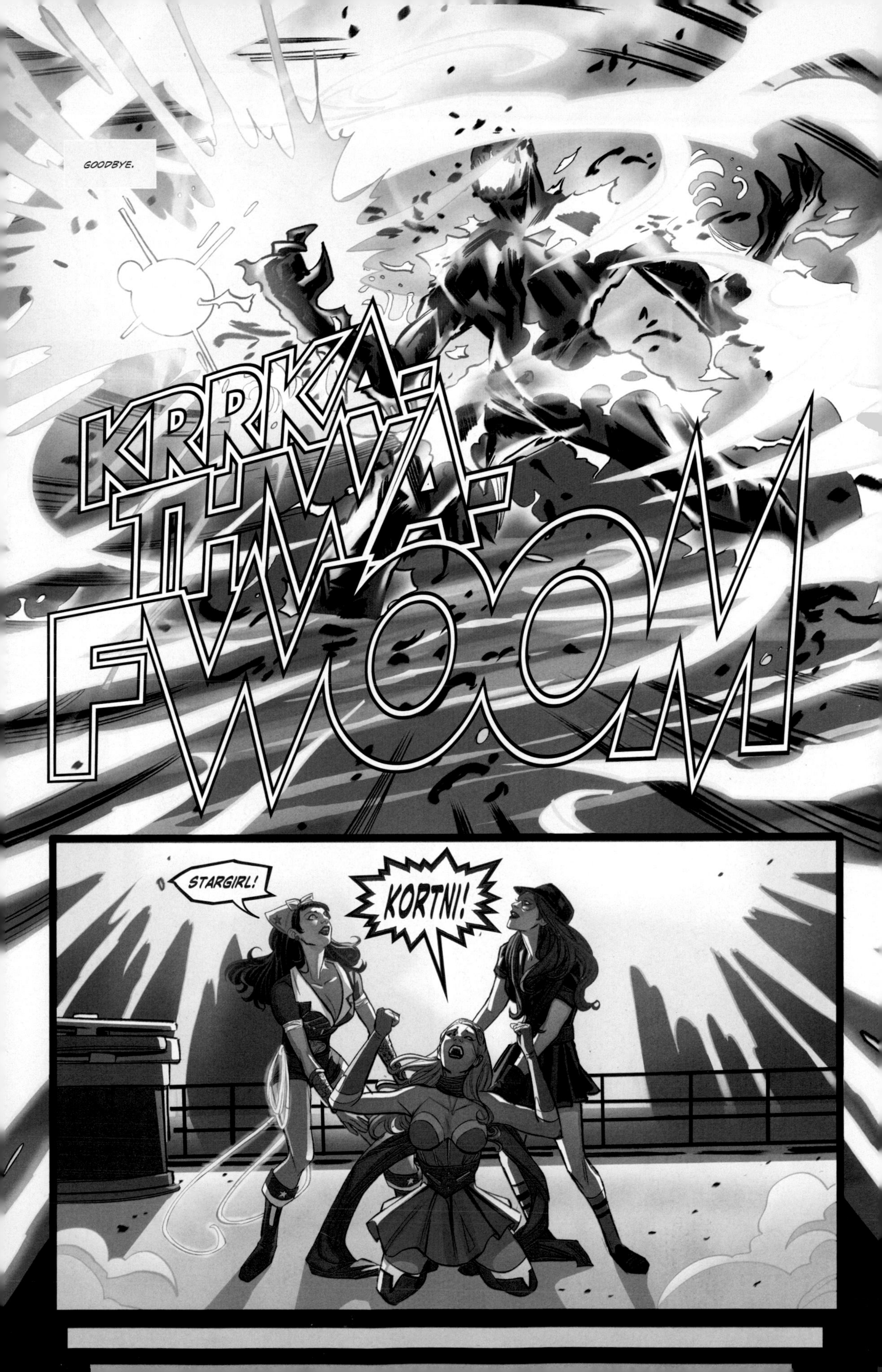
GOODBYE.
KRRKA-THWA-FWOOM
STARGIRL!
KORTNI!

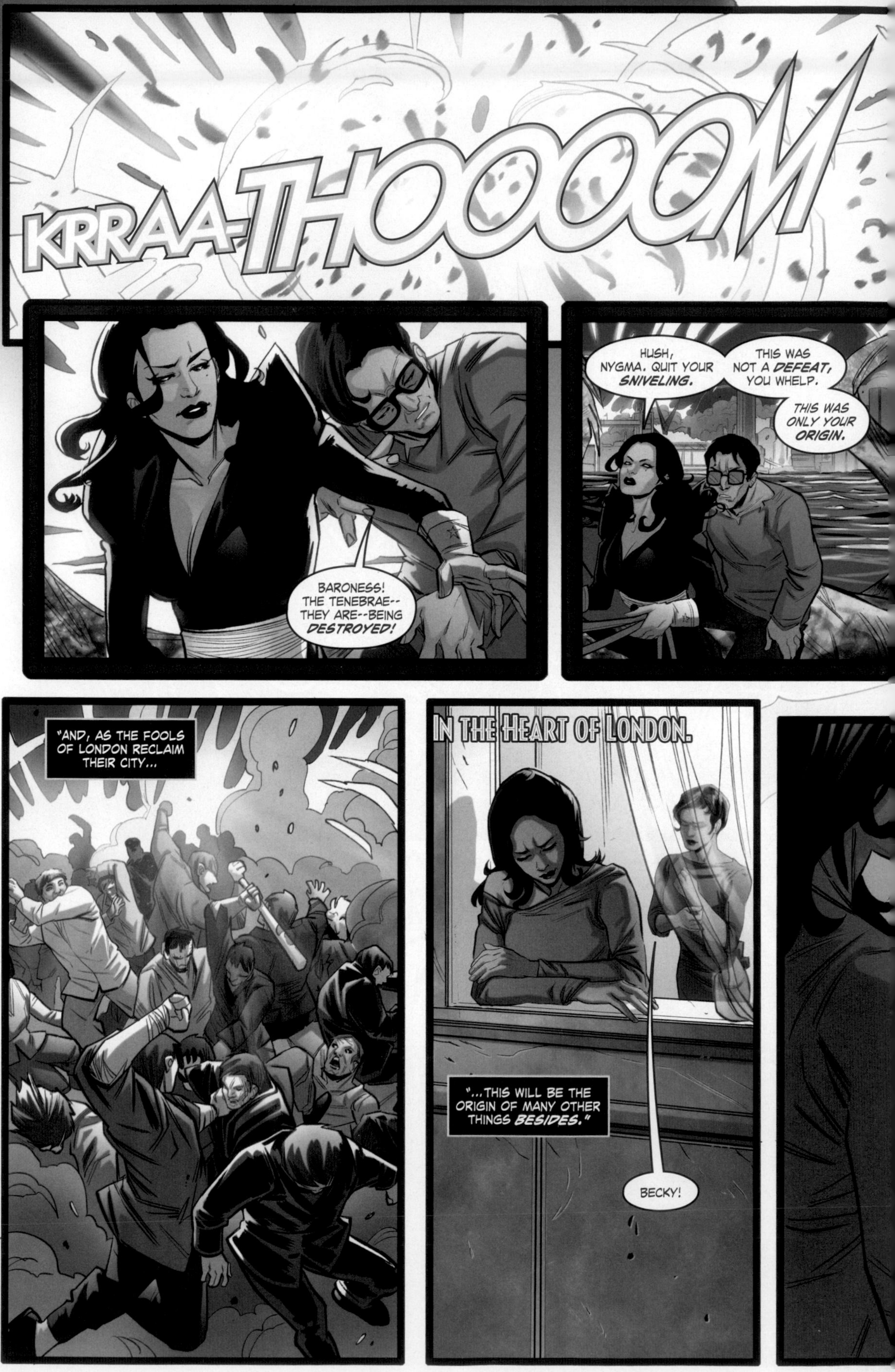
KRRAA-THOOOOM
BARONESS! THE TENEBRAE-- THEY ARE--BEING DESTROYED!
HUSH, NYGMA. QUIT YOUR SNIVELING.
THIS WAS NOT A DEFEAT, YOU WHELP.
THIS WAS ONLY YOUR ORIGIN.
"AND, AS THE FOOLS OF LONDON RECLAIM THEIR CITY...
IN THE HEART OF LONDON.
"...THIS WILL BE THE ORIGIN OF MANY OTHER THINGS BESIDES."
BECKY!

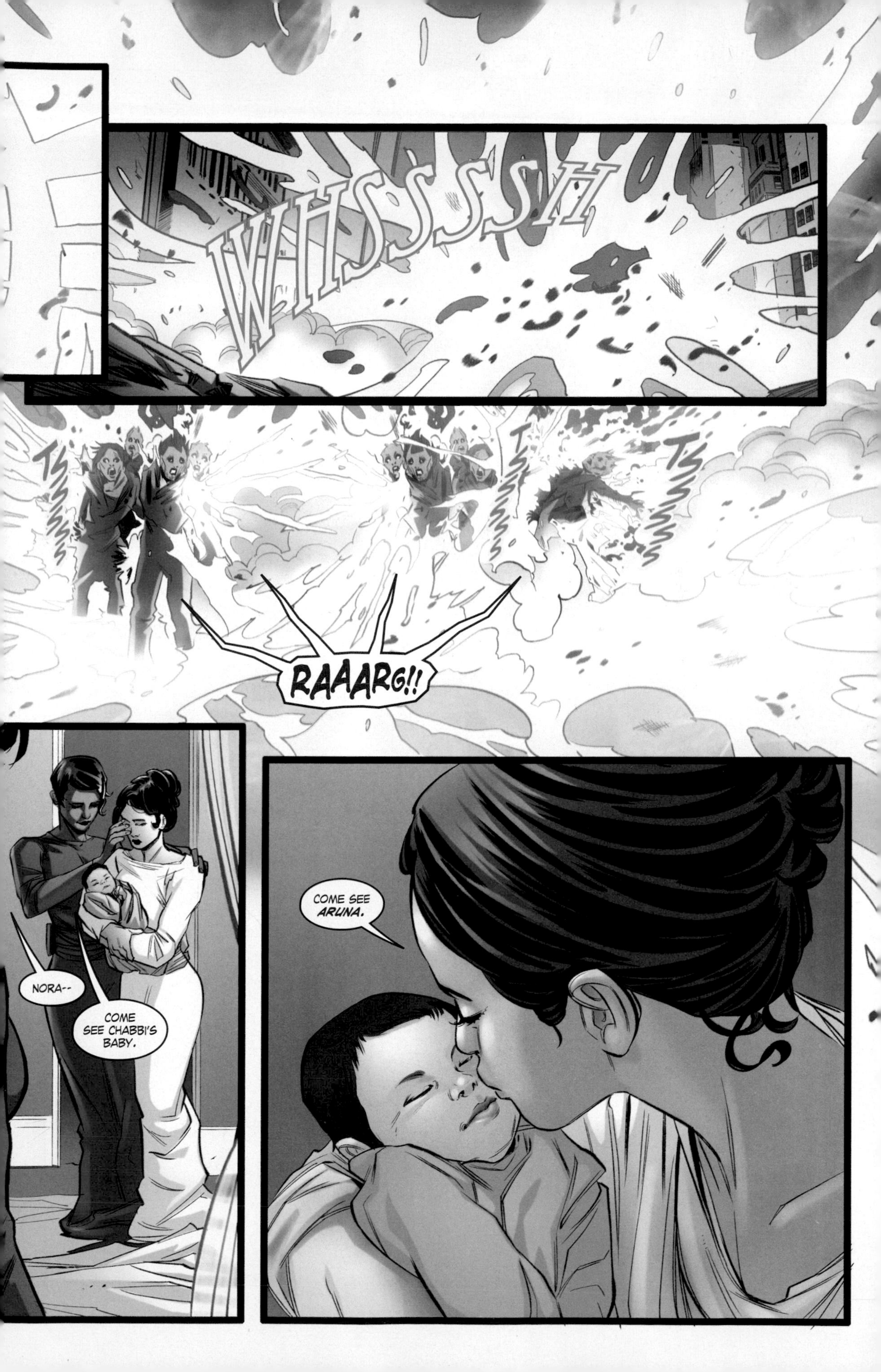
WHSSSSH
TSSSSSS
TSSSSSS
TSSSSSS
RAAARG!!
NORA--
COME SEE CHABBI'S BABY.
COME SEE ARUNA.

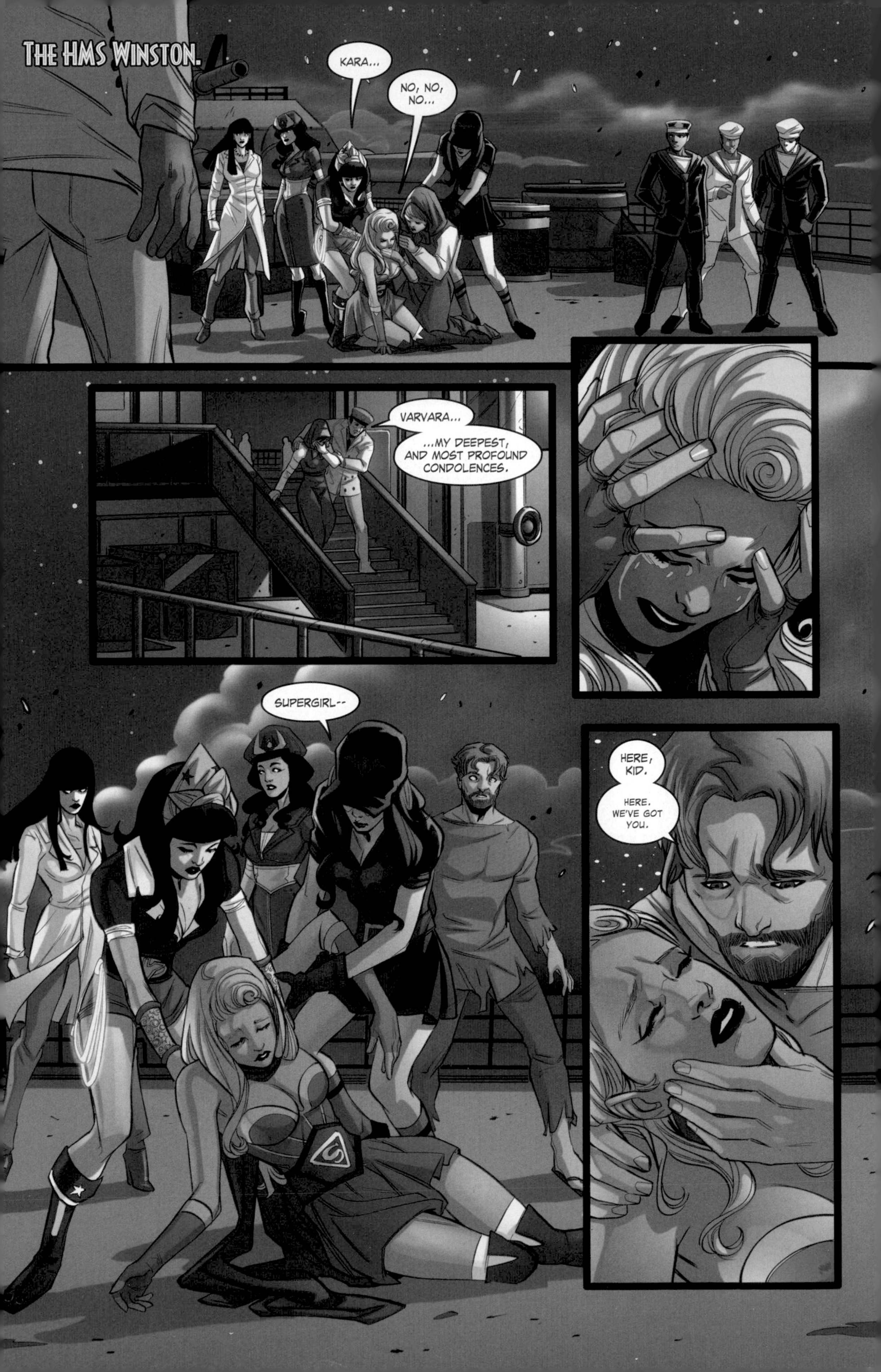
THE HMS WINSTON.
KARA...
NO, NO, NO...
VARVARA...
...MY DEEPEST, AND MOST PROFOUND CONDOLENCES.
SUPERGIRL--
HERE, KID.
HERE. WE'VE GOT YOU.

"Clear storytelling at its best. It's an intriguing concept and easy to grasp."—THE NEW YORK TIMES

"Azzarello is rebuilding the mythology of Wonder Woman."
—CRAVE ONLINE

START AT THE BEGINNING!

WONDER WOMAN VOLUME 1: BLOOD

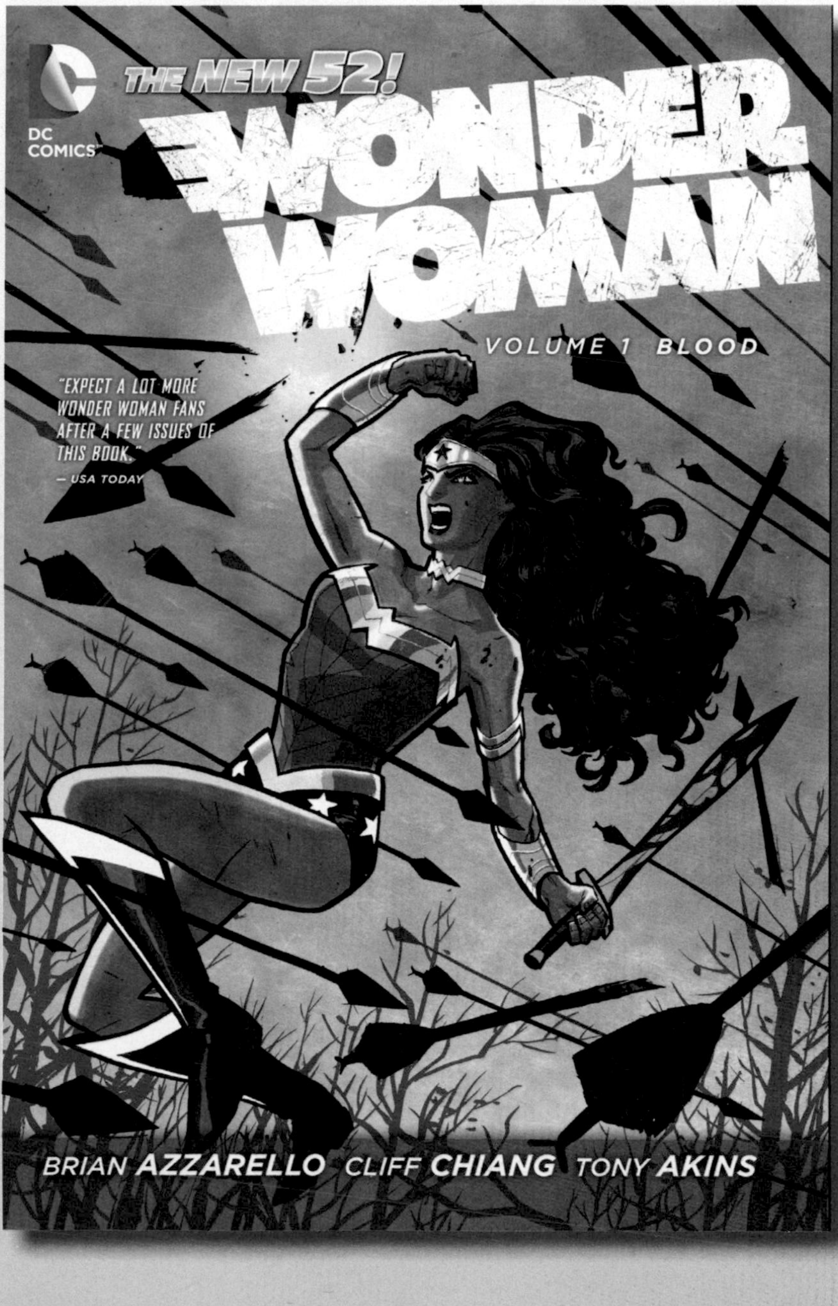

WONDER WOMAN
VOL. 2: GUTS

by BRIAN
AZZARELLO and
CLIFF CHIANG

WONDER WOMAN
VOL. 3: IRON

by BRIAN
AZZARELLO and
CLIFF CHIANG

SUPERGIRL VOL. 1:
LAST DAUGHTER OF
KRYPTON

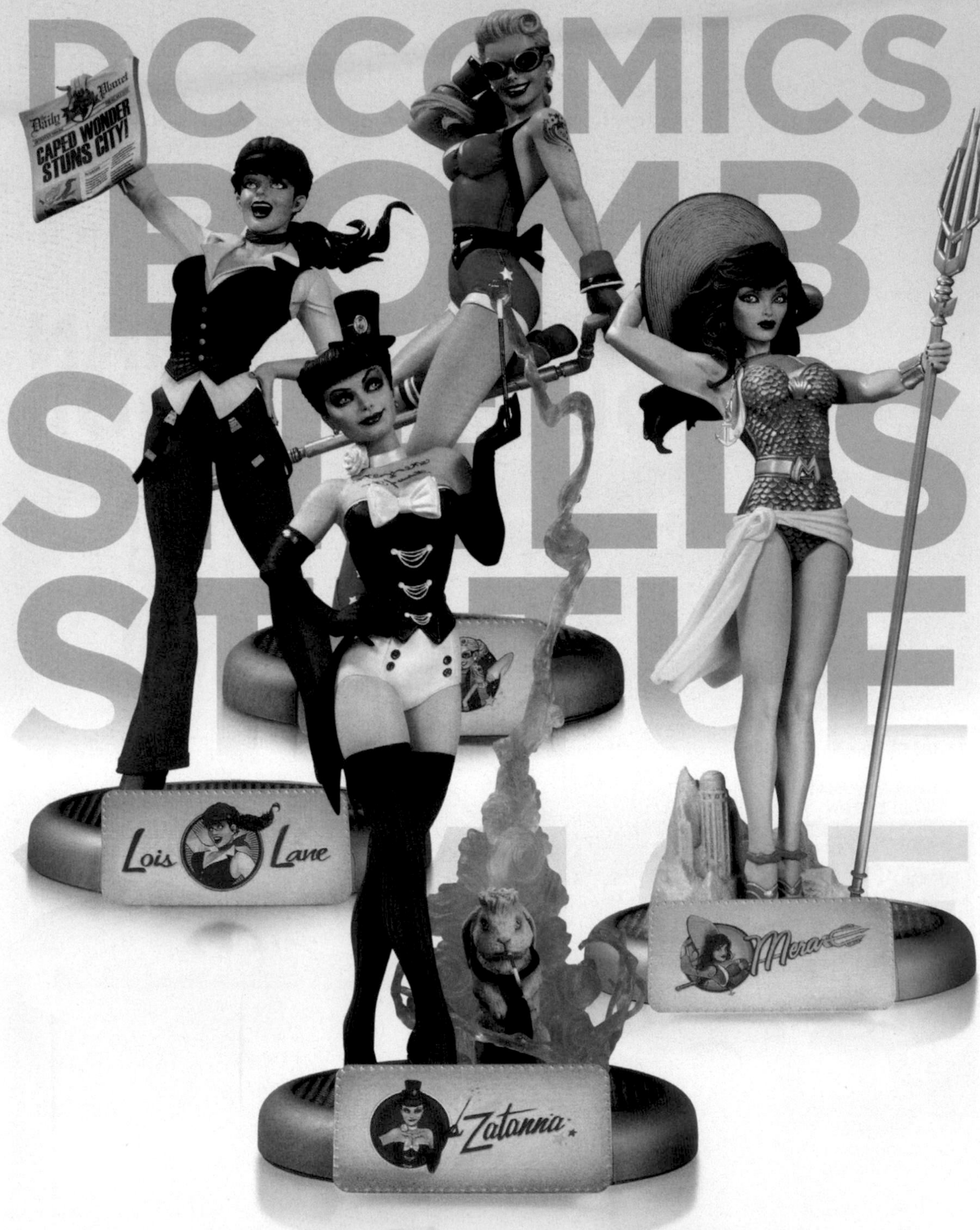
DC COMICS
CAPED WONDER STUNS CITY!
Lois Lane
Mera
Zatanna

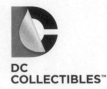

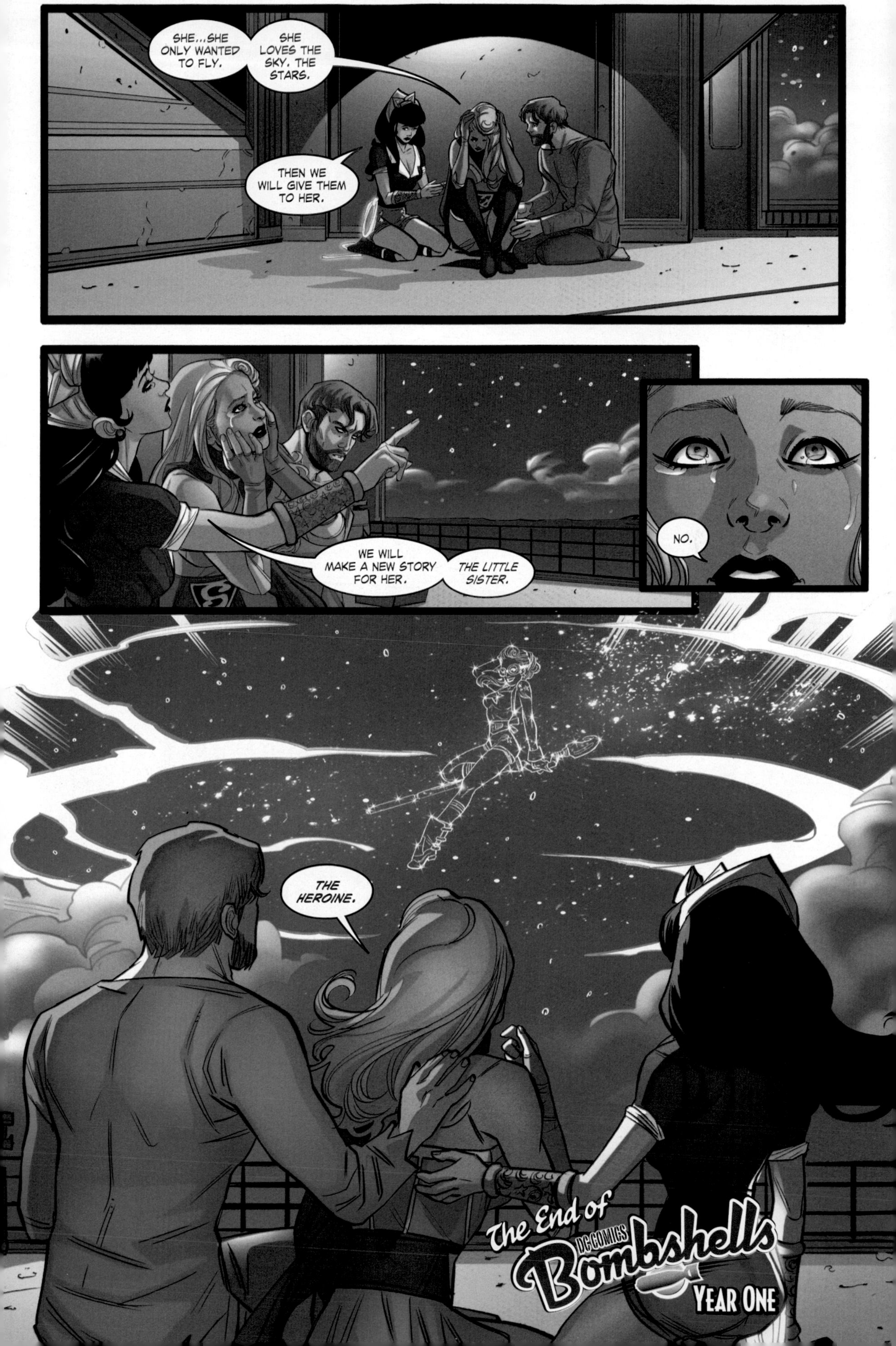
SHE...SHE ONLY WANTED TO FLY.
SHE LOVES THE SKY. THE STARS.
THEN WE WILL GIVE THEM TO HER.
WE WILL MAKE A NEW STORY FOR HER.
THE LITTLE SISTER.
NO.
THE HEROINE.
The End of DC COMICS Bombshells YEAR ONE

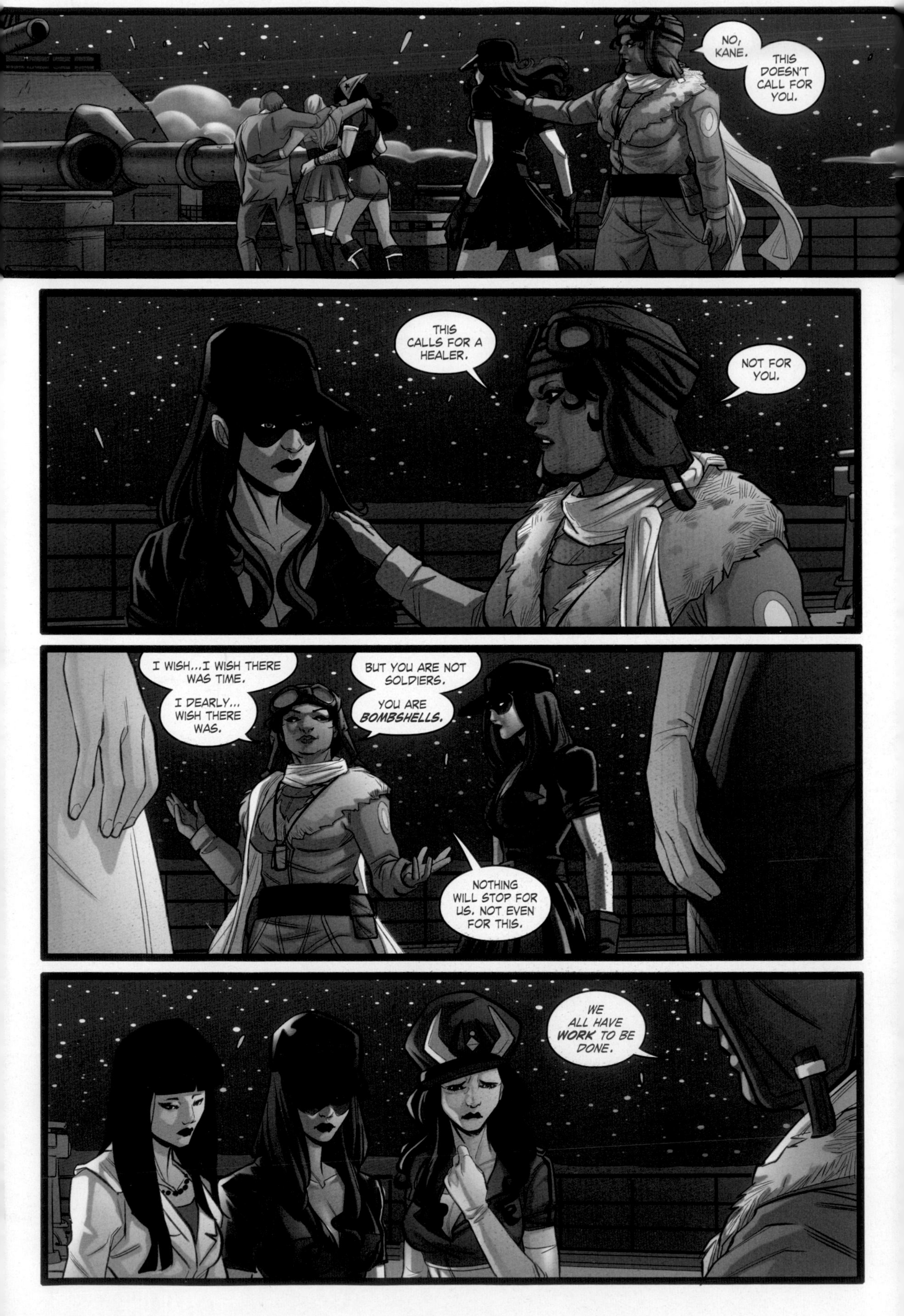
NO, KANE.
THIS DOESN'T CALL FOR YOU.
THIS CALLS FOR A HEALER.
NOT FOR YOU.
I WISH...I WISH THERE WAS TIME.
I DEARLY... WISH THERE WAS.
BUT YOU ARE NOT SOLDIERS.
YOU ARE BOMBSHELLS.
NOTHING WILL STOP FOR US. NOT EVEN FOR THIS.
WE ALL HAVE WORK TO BE DONE.